Writing & Technology:
Ideas That WORK!

The Best of The Writing Notebook, Volume 2

Edited by Sharon Franklin

A publication of
The Writing Notebook

Published by The Writing Notebook
PO Box 1268, Eugene, OR 97440-1268

ISBN 1-881395-01-4

Graphic design by Percy Franklin

Printed in Eugene, Oregon, USA

*With humble thanks to all contributors to this anthology,
and to all the spectacular teachers out there who are
doing the real work of educating our children.*

Special thanks also to the young writers whose feelings, words and visions fill these pages.

**The Writing Notebook wishes to thank Scholastic Software for their wise
understanding of what teachers need in order to use technology effectively
. . . and for translating that vision into their major support of this anthology.**

CONTENTS

Introduction

Sharon Franklin, Editor, The Writing Notebook

Acquiring hardware and software is not in itself a difficult task. All you need is money and a little space. But, as many schools have discovered from experience, there is much more to designing a successful, exciting writing program than collecting the raw materials.

Even when teacher training is included in the overall plan, all too often it fails to prepare teachers for the most challenging (and most neglected) step of all: how to weave the use of technology wisely into their teaching of writing.

This has been the mission of *The Writing Notebook* journal for almost ten years. The journal provides ongoing support and ideas to help K-12 teachers bridge this chasm between theory and practice. As a teacher, you are encouraged to form a writing community within your classroom and to write along with your students. Real-world writing, writing within all subject areas, cooperative learning, literature-based writing, writing as a process, creating a writing program within a classroom or lab, encouraging your students to view their writing as a form of communication and a way of thinking about a subject—these topics and more are a part of each issue of the journal.

Making the Literature, Writing, Word Processing Connection (The Best of The Writing Notebook, Volume 1) compiled the best articles from The Writing Notebook up to 1989. After the continuing success of this first anthology, we are proud to present **Writing & Technology: Ideas That WORK!**, which continues where Volume 1 left off. Within these pages you'll find discussion—and answers—to questions like these:

- How can I best encourage my students to revise their writing?

- My school is restructuring, and we want writing in all subject areas to be a strong component. How have other schools accomplished this goal?

- Writing in language arts is easy. How can I make writing an equally strong part of social studies, math, and science?

- How can I use multimedia to enhance the teaching of literature?

- Telecommunications is one way of building in a real audience and purpose for my students' writing. How can I create a meaningful program within my classroom?

- What can I learn from the research available on writing and technology?

This book is meant for you to *use*. Dog-ear the pages, copy freely for your personal use, change ideas to suit your style and curriculum, and share articles with your colleagues. Let this anthology be a trusted friend—one that will lead you back to the things you do best in your classroom with your students, only now with the added advantages—and maybe the completely new vision!—that technology may present to you.

A special note for readers who are just beginning to use technology to support and enhance their writing program:

Whenever I do technology and writing workshops with teachers, I leave them with these reminders. As you will see, most of them are not specific to using technology; they are important in learning *anything* brand new. I encourage you to pay attention to them as you embark upon your journey.

1. Start with what you love.

2. Take small steps.

3. Think out loud. Give your students the gift of hearing you work through issues and dilemmas that arise.

4. Practice using the computer as a personal tool.

5. Find a friend to accompany you on your journey.

6. Trust the process.

CHAPTER 1
RESTRUCTURING AND WRITING

*It's not so much that we're afraid of change, or so in love
with the old ways, but it's that place in between . . .
it's like being in between trapezes. It's Linus when his blanket is
in the dryer. There's nothing to hold on to.*

—Marilyn Ferguson

Restructuring from the Inside Out: Starring Roles for Classrooms

Gary A. Carnow

School people all over the country are involved in many discussions these days. The new 3Rs seem to be reform, renewal, and restructuring. Once we get beyond the "they'll never let us" syndrome, restructuring is exciting. It offers a window of opportunity. We have the chance to get in touch with our own personal visions and do what we want to do to improve education. We have the opportunity to hear what other educators are saying and have a chance to reveal our own visions to others.

The articles I've read and the people I've heard lecture all seem to think that change will not come about incrementally. They argue that our school systems must be given a huge shock and that small pushes are simply tinkering. Although there are many "break the mold" ideas out there, I believe that the real work will happen—and is happening now—from within the four walls of the classroom. Change from within.

For the last five years I've been involved in restructuring classrooms, although we didn't call it that when we began. As Director of a California Model Technology School Project, I've been part of a team of dedicated people who have rethought classroom practice. Alhambra School District, in partnership with Pepperdine University, was funded 2½ million dollars from the State of California to implement a technology-rich school complex. Now in its fifth year, the Alhambra Model Technology Schools Project (AMTS) evolved from a student-centered philosophy, negotiating their way through classroom technologies to create a school culture that is vital and exciting.

Although there are many stories to tell and ample research data to share, it is in these classrooms at Alhambra High School and Emery Park School (K-8) that the real look and feel of restructuring is taking place. All of these classrooms use "projects" to create synergy. They all use technology and feature thematic teaching. The students in these classroom are active participants, decision-makers, and technology users.

 High School English Multimedia Literature Projects

In Jim McClure's English classroom you'll find nine Macintosh computers, a scanner, a CD-ROM drive, two laserdisc players, a VCR, and a monitor. In fact, you will find four Macs in almost every English classroom on campus. In Jim's class students are reading *Around the World in 80 Days*. His students use HyperCard and the movie on laserdisc to create interactive reports—a kind of "electronic term paper." They use new tools like sound recorders, buttons, cards, and fields. They create and manipulate visual images. They discuss and negotiate. They work in small groups and, as he puts it, they are "all in this together."

Across the way, Barbara Ontiveros uses *To Kill a Mockingbird* on laserdisc, along with a barcode reader, to illustrate class discussions. But it's more than teacher-driven technology in a presentation mode. Barbara puts the technology tools in the hands of the students and the students make it their own. They create the presentations. They design and teach. Using *Bar n Coder* software they create bar codes that are printed on the classroom printer and used as navigational tools in their literature study.

Multimedia Research in High School Social Science

Ed Riegler, in the social science department, also uses multimedia and technology-based student projects. Along with Char Carden, the school's technology coordinator, Ed's students research and create presentations using IBM's LinkWay; their projects are highlighted with video footage from the 40 volumes of CEL's *Video Encyclopedia of the 20th Century*. Ed challenges his students to do multimedia research projects on 20th Century topics because he feels this area is not adequately covered in the textbook. One group recently completed a LinkWay folder entitled ''The Traditional American Family: Does It Still Exist?''

All of these classrooms use "projects" to create synergy. They all use technology and feature thematic teaching. The students in these classroom are active participants, decision-makers, and technology users.

The project focused on babies, daycare, ethics, economics, and single parenting. The folder combined text, student-created graphs, scanned images, digitized still images from a laserdisc, and full motion video sequences. The completed project was presented to the whole class, followed by a question-and-answer session. After this initial success, Ed and his students now plan future projects on topics that include the Renaissance, the Civil War, and the American Revolution.

Notebook Computers and High School At-Risk Students

Barbara Sedano currently uses a class set of Tandy 102s with a group of at-risk students. Her students have all checked out a 102 for their use during this school year. This notebook computer has some remarkably powerful features, including a built-in

modem. Each night, students log-on to a district-wide bulletin board system and ''chat'' on one of ten telephone lines. They ''talk'' in real time and upload and download messages, programs, and documents. They plan cooperative projects and check up on the progress of their classmates. A recent essay contest awarded a winning at-risk student with a 102 donated by a local businessperson. Every student in Barbara's class participated and every student turned in a completed essay. The magic and synergy of technology is at work in this classroom.

LogoWriter, Math, and Writing for Grades 7 and 8

At Emery Park School, Marilyn Lim's seventh and eighth grade math students integrate geometry, computers, and writing with LogoWriter. Students use problem-solving skills in the seventh grade to learn LogoWriter fundamentals, plot their own initials, and create structures that incorporate the use of circles and arcs in several colors. Eighth graders create their own ''storefront business'' in cooperative groups and plot their floor plan and store exteriors using LogoWriter. They develop a monthly profit statement using Apple-Works, build an actual model of their store based on the floor plan and exterior plan, and use a word processing program to write letters of introduction and advertisements to the community.

The California Gold Rush: Video & Interact, 4th Grade Style

In Lynn Nevin's and Gloria Ramiriz's fourth grade classrooms, the California Gold Rush really comes alive with student-created newscasts from the past. Expanding from traditional teacher-directed, text-based lessons, these students ''lived'' the Gold Rush era. The fourth graders in this multicultural school studied many facets of the period, including how Chinese people were exploited, which led to discussions on prejudice and the sharing of personal experiences.

Then classes began the *Interact Gold Rush* simulation, with student-made gold-painted beans used as rewards. As part of the simulation, students drew ''fate'' cards. For example, ''Rats got into your tent and ate your food, costing you 50 nuggets.'' At the end of the unit, students with the most nuggets were honored.

After this "basic knowledge" phase, students met in their job groups and completed research in order to produce their newscasts from the past. In Gloria's class, the Wardrobe group completed research to see if people wore T-shirts, cowboy hats, and tennis shoes during the California Gold Rush. The Props group studied books for ideas to use for set backgrounds and locations. The Camera group experimented with camera shots and practiced operating the equipment. The Writers and Reporters wrote the script for the newscast—the reporters were responsible for the questions to ask the actors and the writers wrote the anchorperson's narration. Meanwhile, Lynn's class compiled research that would help them to answer the reporter's questions during the interview.

Gloria showed her class a newscast recorded from a local television station for them to analyze. They discussed the various segments: weather, world news, commercials, local news, commentary, and live action field reports. They listed these segments on the board and decided on the parts they wanted to include. They examined the commentary segment and wanted theirs to focus on the treatment of the Chinese laborers. They interviewed the notorious "Black Bart" in jail, along with the mother of slain outlaw Joaquin Murietta. James Marshall described how he discovered gold at Sutter's Mill, and John Sutter spoke about how his discovery had changed his life.

It took students three weeks to get ready. The script took the longest; once it was completed, the other pieces fell into place. After the final project had its premier, students took home copies of their collaborative work.

Where Do We Go From Here?

These are just a few of many classroom stories that could be told. In the next few months we will be finishing two books, "The Look and Feel of Empowerment" and the "Joy of Tech-ing." Both books try to record accurately some of our adoptable and adaptable practices. We also will have video examples completed to show what classroom change with technology looks like. If you visit the Los Angeles area during the school year, drop us a line. We hold tours through our sites one Wednesday each month. As we continue to grow and change, as we continue to tinker and restructure, we invite you to join with us on the journey.

Dr. Gary Carnow serves as the Coordinator of Instructional Technology Education, K-12 for the Alhambra School District and is also the Director of the California Model Technology Schools Project at Alhambra. He frequently lectures about technology classroom issues and grantwriting around the country. To get on the MTS mailing list, you may write to him at Alhambra School District, 15 W. Alhambra Road, Alhambra, CA 91801.

Kindred Waters

Deep pools hemorrhage
Pulsating through veins—
Warming bodies with ancient prosperity.
Pure blood splattered upon a battered continent—
Descending into recessive gene pools.

Luxurious plasma from African royalty
Flows like the Nile—
Seeping into raging rivers
That stir ebony bonded entities—
Layered with brown sienna dreams.

I am the speckled drops
That moisten the dry earth—
Whose trees bare the epiphany of fruit—
Ebony seeds that prosper and grow.

Miesha Price

Stereotypes

I am black even though my skin is brown.
I am a peasant even though my ancestors once
  wore crowns.
I am ignorant even though I have a degree.
I am blind even though I can see.
I am Black, and despite all the things they say,
I would rather say "hello" than "hey."

Shazzar Kallie

*These poems are reprinted with permission from Jordan High School's literary art magazine, **Stylus**. Special thanks to Marie Tollstrup and these students in her creative writing classes. Jordan High School, 6500 Atlantic Ave., Long Beach, CA 90805.*

A New Look at an Old Issue— Planning for Educational Change

Joanne Koltnow

You know what planning is like. It's a time-consuming, seemingly never-ending process filled with meetings, reports, and experts of one sort or another. It's usually done at the district level. And it results in a new curriculum, a new building, a new staff development program, or a new computer lab.

When the planning goes well, the outcome is worth the effort. But many times, plans—or purchases—just sit on the shelf.

Recently, however, changes have occurred in the climate for educational planning, and it's worth taking another look.

What's different now?

The concept of educational planning is changing—and at the same time we're seeing changes in the perception of teaching and learning, increasing uses of technology in education, and more interest in education from the business community.

Educational planning is in transition. Traditional planning involved district-level experts and often had a single-issue focus. Now more decisions are being pushed down to the building level, either as a result of a mandate for site-based management or simply to put planning closer to those responsible for its implementation. At the same time, more emphasis is being placed on comprehensive planning—developing long-term objectives that address changes in the entire school, and making plans to meet them.

The perception of teaching and learning is changing. As educational researcher Karen Sheingold points out, "Educators and policymakers nationwide now recognize the critical need for students to learn how to think, to understand concepts and ideas, to apply what they learn, and to be able to pose questions and solve problems." This means that students must construct their own knowledge and understanding and that teachers facilitate and coach, rather than simply dispensing information. Sheingold refers to this approach as "active learning/adventurous teaching." (See the box for more information about Sheingold's ideas.)

Technology is becoming more available for education— and more appropriate. Computers and other technologies are moving into the schools, both because they're seen as a part of modern life that students should know about and because educators are finding ways to use them to enhance learning. Now teachers are learning how to integrate computer use with classroom learning, rather than simply teaching about computers.

Businesses are getting involved. Companies realize that they need an educated work force— workers with skills that include being able to solve problems, work cooperatively, and accept change. No longer content to retrain graduates after they're hired, businesses are becoming involved with the educational institutions that send them prospective employees.

What are the implications?

These differences raise some issues to consider.

You'll probably have to develop new expertise at the school level. District-level experts will still be available for planning, but more likely as consultants than as team

---

Restructuring for Learning with Technology: The Potential for Synergy, by Karen Sheingold, in *Restructuring for Learning with Technology,* a joint project of the Center for Technology in Education and the National Center on Education and the Economy.

 Sheingold suggests that if student learning is to be transformed, the three agendas of active learning, well-integrated uses of technology, and school restructuring must be brought together. The paper includes examples of schools where this is taking place.

 Copies of the report, which also includes four other papers on related topics, can be obtained by sending a check for $10 made payable to Bank Street College. Mail to L. A. Bryant, Center for Technology in Education, Bank Street College of Education, 610 West 112th St., New York, NY 10025.

Strategic Planning for a New Generation of American Schools: Or How to Turn a Very Large Supertanker in a Very Small Harbor, by Daniel E. Kinnaman in *Technology & Learning*, September 1991.

 In this article, the first of a three-part series on planning, funding, and evaluation, Kinnaman provides guidelines for creating and implementing an effective plan. Like Sheingold, he emphasizes the need for integrating technology planning with other plans for school improvement. Although the article takes a district-level approach, it's a useful resource for anyone interested in educational planning.

leaders. So although a school-based committee might not have ''experts in planning,'' it can include more people who are actually responsible for implementing the

suggestions—teachers, parents, and students. And this will improve the chances of success.

You'll want to think strategically. This means considering some long-range views of your educational environment and building short- and long-range goals to get you there. Although many strategic plans start with a needs analysis, you may find that starting with a vision is a better way to keep planners on track and enthusiastic. A vision-based approach is used in *Teaching, Learning and Technology—A Planning Guide*. (See the sidebar for more information.)

There is an opportunity to combine educational, technology, and restructuring agendas. Too many times, technology planning is isolated from other plans for improving the educational climate. And too often this isolation results in acquiring technology that is underutilized or poorly integrated. In her paper, Sheingold suggests that a useful synergy can be achieved by advancing educational, technology, and school-restructuring agendas in combination.

A larger community wants to be involved. The thousands of business/education partnerships and community/education foundations are abundant evidence that community and business leaders want to play a role in K-12 education. It's appropriate to consider as planning resources the parent groups, civic organizations, and businesses in your community.

What's next?

The first step doesn't have to be difficult. Begin by doing some informal research to determine how much of this applies to your situation. Start reading; the materials suggested in the boxes offer additional ideas. Talk with your colleagues. And look for appropriate sessions at professional conferences. What better time than now to take a fresh look at where you're going—and how you're getting there.

Joanne Koltnow writes about computers in education. She is based in Palo Alto, CA.

Teaching, Learning, and Technology—A Planning Guide, produced by Apple Computer, Inc.

This guide differs from traditional technology planning guides in two notable ways: it emphasizes the integration of technology with teaching and learning, and suggests that planners begin with a vision instead of with a needs analysis. (It emphasizes five key educational elements: active learning, cooperative learning, interdisciplinary learning, individualized learning, and teacher professionalism. A needs analysis is suggested after the vision is developed, along with an examination of what is needed to make the vision a reality.) Figure 1 shows the six-step model the guide proposes.

Figure 1. A vision is central for this six-step—and continuing—planning process.

The planning guide comes in two forms: a print-based Basic Kit and a multimedia-based Interactive Kit. The Basic Kit consists primarily of a strategic planning workbook. The Interactive Kit includes the same workbook, as well as a videodisc with an hour of video clips and a CD-ROM with nearly two hours of audio interviews. The guide gives planners access to advice and comments from other educators and examples from scores of classrooms where technology is currently being used to enhance teaching and learning. And, they can use the technology to create and present their own plan.

The Basic Kit includes a:
- Workbook: A step-by-step planning guide with templates
- Video: Shows what successful technology integration looks like

The Interactive Kit includes a:
- Workbook with planning templates
- CD-ROM disc: Two hours of audio success stories as well as HyperCard stacks containing both an interactive planning process and a presentation maker
- Videodisc: An hour of video success stories and tips, plus everything on the video

The Basic Kit ($49) and the Interactive Kit ($149) can be ordered from Intellimation. (Prices do not include shipping or applicable taxes.) Call 1-800-3INTELL or write Intellimation, 130 Cremona Drive, Santa Barbara, CA 93116.

In Between Trapezes:
Living Between OLD and NEW

Bernajean Porter

**One doesn't discover new lands without consenting to
lose sight of the shore for a very long time.**

—Andre' Gide, French novelist

This article is dedicated to the Glenbrook Faculty from whom I am continually learning—ready or not!

Change is the decision to create a writing lab; the transition is the psychological process the faculty must go through as they make meaning of the new situation. Without a successful transition, you are left with the technology but few of the envisioned benefits and, in the end when the fluff settles, very little is different.

This year I have the pleasure and challenge of working as a resource consultant to support Glenbrook district faculty. The goal is to establish school-wide writing labs while evolving new curriculum and new ways of learning and teaching throughout the content areas. I am excited to be part of the team.

Faculty envision the writing lab as a place for innovation, experimentation, and practice in writing to communicate and writing to learn. The technology-based lab will expand beyond text to include mediums such as sound and visuals. Spelling and grammar checkers, collaborative groupware, presentation software, electronic references from CD ROMs, and multimedia add further to the teaching and learning strategies available to all Glenbrook faculty.

An "Information Highway" is being created within the entire building. The present writing lab, although housed and supported within the English department, is networked to four other computer labs in a building of 2,000 students. This fall we expect to add a workstation to 15 English classrooms. Future plans include obtaining class sets of portables that would allow a writing lab to go to the classroom rather than the classroom coming to the lab. Plans are also being made for off-campus remote access—anytime, anywhere. By every standard I have ever used, this project is designed for success!

The Writing Lab

The Glenbrook Writing Lab is state of the art. There are 36 networked Macintosh LCs, laserdisc players, CD

ROMs, LCDs, a Canon Xapshot for still video graphics, scanners, a network modem, and a wide range of dynamic software. The writing lab is staffed by a lab technician who takes care of the technical needs, maintenance of the file server, and daily management tasks; three English faculty members who team teach with other faculty during the school day are also part of the lab staff. The resource consultant coordinates the project, including staff development.

The Glenbrook English faculty are Macintosh users with access to Macintosh workstations in their offices. The faculty is positive; they looked forward to the writing lab and certainly welcomed the support of a resource consultant.

The administration, including the instructional supervisor, principal, assistant principals, and superintendent, are all positive, enthusiastic, and supportive. School board members have leading edge attitudes and visions of moving their schools even beyond current standards of excellence. (Glenbrook schools have a national reputation for high writing scores and quality performance in writing modes such as essays, reports, and research papers.)

AND STILL, bringing new, undefined possibilities to a school system that values their current success is a complex, challenging, messy, and frequently befuddling process. To quote William Bridges, ''It isn't the changes that do you in, it's the transitions.'' Change is the decision to create a writing lab; the transition is the psychological process the faculty must go through as they make meaning of the new situation. Without a successful transition, you are left with the technology but few of the envisioned benefits and, in the end when the fluff settles, very little is different.

This year, much effort is focused on the management of our ''neutral zone.'' This is the space between the OLD and the NEW—the limbo that exists between the old sense of identity and the new. As Marilyn Ferguson stated, ''It's not so much that we're afraid of change, or so in love with the old ways, but it's that place in between . . . it's like being in between trapezes. It's Linus when his blanket is in the dryer. There's nothing to hold on to.''

It's easy to ignore this transition time. Transitions are uncomfortable, and there is a distinct tendency to rush through them—or escape from them altogether. Often, people conclude that the confusion that accompanies a transition is a sure sign that something is wrong; to remedy the situation they then try to prematurely add structure (usually from the OLD ways, since a NEW structure hasn't had time to evolve yet) in order to create comfort and order again.

But the neutral zone isn't simply meaningless waiting and confusion—it is a time of reorientation and redefinition. Although it is a stressful time, it is also a creative time; it is during this window of time between old and new that the system's immune system is weak enough to let truly creative solutions emerge. Once the culture is developed

and attached to the change, it takes much more effort. This makes the neutral zone a time of great opportunity.

The Neutral Zone

We have attempted to optimize this time in several ways:

- For the first year or two, writing lab decisions will be made around ''What's best for our faculty?'' We know students will benefit more in the long run if the faculty can make curriculum decisions on using the lab from their own knowledge and experience. Thus, the faculty's learning curve has primary support.

- We started with our worst fears and best hopes for the writing lab and developed strategies to make our preferred vision happen.

- Experiences and feelings of the neutral zone are considered ''normal.'' Confusion, being uncomfortable, feeling lost or fearful, making mistakes, not knowing exactly where we're going, etc. are all part of this time. These feelings need to be expected and honored.

- All participation is voluntary. A small core of 13 teachers volunteered last spring to experiment with their classes, curriculum, and personal time during this school year. However, the rest of the staff are encouraged and supported to participate at any time. We have been wonderfully surprised at the early and extensive interest and involvement of faculty who in the summer were thought to be lukewarm or even negative about technology.

- The tone and atmosphere in the lab is friendly and playful with a dash of adventure. An ''adventure'' metaphor is used to describe the area, the events, and people's experiences. Positive metaphors influence attitudes and perceptions; for example, we have a traveling foam rubber ''byte bat'' trophy to celebrate ''amazing adventures'' like printer crashes, lost files, flubs, misunderstandings, etc.

- We balanced the harshness of the equipment by naming the machines, putting ''story T-shirts'' created by students in the art department on the walls, hanging plants, bringing in flowers, using lots of color, and posting polaroid pictures of activities on a bulletin board.

- We purposely avoided as much structure and as many premature assumptions as we could while still allowing the lab to function. We have established a tone and expectation that this is an important time to step back and question the ''usual.'' Staying curious and confused is a resourceful state. We try not to make too many rules too fast!

- We established the idea that the writing lab belongs to the community of teachers rather than an individual or a small group of individuals. Our key goals include establishing broad ownership, responsibility, and a spirit of entrepreneurship. No one but the lab technician has a desk in the lab, so territory is not established. Decisions and documents are reviewed by a variety of people, and reflection sheets are collected from everyone using the lab to refine our services. We expect the lab to fit the teacher and students rather than asking them to fit the lab. Teachers make decisions on their own assignments, their own lab usage, and details such as seating charts.

- New roles and relationships are evolving. The lab staff has done an excellent job in supporting teachers' preferences in how they want to use the lab. Teachers can elect to do the teaching themselves or team with the lab staff. Some teachers choose to become part of the class and learn new things along with the students. The structure and tone established has allowed a cross-pollination of ideas and a strengthening of relationships.

- We make every effort to support people where they are. Teachers decide what they want to learn or know. We have established a special training area outside the lab. We have large group all day workshops, small group training, and individual learning days. Substitutes are available for any of these learning plans. There are planning conferences with faculty before coming into the lab, reflection conferences after their experiences, and follow-ups on what's next for them personally. We make sure concerns voiced by the staff don't disappear. Individual support of all kinds is critical in order to help people through this transition time.

- In order to monitor our progress, we established a management team for this year, consisting of the Instructional Supervisor, the Lab Staff, the Resource Consultant, and the Lab Technician. I am fortunate to work this year with Tom Valentin, our English instructional supervisor, who is very savvy, supportive, and collaborative about process management. We meet weekly, using reflection sheets completed by teachers, our daily log book kept by the staff, and personal experiences to answer: Where are we? What's working? What needs to work better?

A Neverending Story

There are, of course, many phases to any restructuring effort. But letting go of the old, managing the neutral zone, and beginning the new is where most envisioned opportunities for technology sink or swim. It is even more difficult for people to let go of the old when the new is not clearly defined, but in fact is evolving. Helping people understand the process, honoring where everyone is in the moment, living with the paradox of old and new at the same time, and challenging ourselves to be creatively involved in this adventure is making this a successful period of time at Glenbrook. We consider it an ongoing process that should be a neverending story.

Bernajean Porter, Senior Partner, The Confluence International Group, a national team of educators. She is presently on contract as a resource consultant with Glenbrook School District #225, Glenbrook, IL.

The author gratefully acknowledges content collaboration and editing by Tom Valentin, English Instructional Supervisor, Glenbrook School District.

VISIONS FOR THE WRITING LAB: A Work In Progress from the Glenbrook Staff

- Use color to create dialectic journals on *Moby Dick*.
- Use page layout programs to create visual essays from students' text essays of "The Nature of Mankind."
- Use page layout programs to create newspapers reflecting various points of view in *To Kill a Mockingbird*.
- Create processes to evaluate visual essays with students.
- Design computer screens for special writing needs; for example, two windows opened and sized to collect both sides of a debate issue.
- Use databases and spreadsheets for story summaries, character analyses, and book reports.
- Put assignments, study guides, and templates on the file server, rather than in paper form.
- Graphically plot story elements in order to look at identifiable patterns.
- Use a still video camera with video tapes, electronic slide shows, and laserdiscs to reflect poetry created in words.
- Use an electronic "drop box" for students to turn in papers.
- Have students do peer review with color, pop-up memo boxes, and voice message inserts.
- Use analysis software printouts for revision conferences.
- Use one computer in the classroom with an LCD for group revision.
- Use groupware software for collaborative assignments.
- Use a laserdisc along with a printed essay so students can illustrate their supporting quotes on the topic "Why did Hamlet delay his revenge?" with full motion video.

A "Restructured" School in Action—
O'Farrell Community School:
Center for Advanced Academic Studies

Sharon Franklin

Dream with me if you will. . . . Can you see a school that children want to go to, that teachers want to go to, that parents want to go to, where teachers work closely together to provide the best education possible for all kids, where students succeed academically, where adults and children work closely together, where people smile, where the feeling is warm and the environment is safe, where decisions made about children are shared decisions, where responsibility is shared, where creativity is high, where gender and race are just part of your uniqueness and not a barrier to your learning, where there is an extended family of teacher/family/community/agency, where classrooms are exciting places to be, where teachers are turned on to teaching, where students are the number one concern? . . .

> Robert Stein, Team O'Farrell CEO
> and "Keeper of the Dream," 1990

This is the dream of O'Farrell Community School: Center for Advanced Academic Studies, the first middle school magnet school in San Diego City Schools. O'Farrell opened in September 1990 with 430 seventh graders and a staff of 26. This year the number of students tripled to 1300 in grades six through eight with over 40 new faculty members hired. More than 50% of O'Farrell students are African-American or Latino and, unlike many magnet schools, most come primarily from the surrounding area, a poor, gang-ridden neighborhood in southeast San Diego.

O'Farrell's bold goal: to teach the same advanced curriculum to all its students and specifically to prepare all students for advanced level high school courses.

The O'Farrell team, made up of teachers, administrators, and community members, began their planning process in the summer of 1989. In subsequent retreats and meetings the team planned every aspect of this student-centered, activity-oriented adventure in learning. For the school district, O'Farrell represents an important testing ground in the areas of governance, instruction, and assessment.

Educational Program

Instruction in language arts, math, computers, physical education, science, and social studies is thematic, taught by interdisciplinary teams of six teachers known as educational "families." Students stay in their family groups all day long. All students are mainstreamed.

Art, foreign language, industrial arts, and music teachers make up "discovery" teams; these teachers support thematic units and expose all students to their content areas. Teaching teams meet daily to plan strategy and share information.

All academic decisions rest with the teachers by consensus. Other decisions are made by the Community Council, composed of teacher, support staff, student, parent, and community agency representatives.

A Home Base program, with 20-25 kids in mixed grades, begins and ends each school day. It is here that teachers take primary responsibility for the social and emotional needs of students. When student or family problems prove too challenging, they take advantage of the on-campus social services wing. O'Farrell and the county Department of Social Services each fund one-half of a full-time social worker.

Stein maintains that a lot of money is not needed to restructure a school. "The major restructuring we did," Stein says, "was to work with the same money and put it in different places." Team O'Farrell eliminated several administrator positions, including principal, vice principal, and counselor, and spent the money on more teachers in order to ensure an average class size of 28. Federal magnet and Chapter One funds bought additional teachers and technology.

Technology at O'Farrell

O'Farrell added three more Macintosh computer centers in September 1991, bringing the number of centers to six, each supported by a computer teacher.

New sixth and seventh graders learn the basics of using a Mac, including use of a mouse, finder, windows, and network. They learn the rudiments of word processing by writing name poems, bio-poems, and their personal goals for success. Returning eighth graders continue where they left off, applying their skills in graphics, word processing, and Hypercard to create their own projects. All O'Farrell students will use the Mac to produce their first portfolio and unit project of the year.

Thematic Units

The school year is divided into four nine-week thematic units. All grade levels and "families" work with the same four themes, with a project focus chosen from among several options. In addition, students' interdisciplinary projects all must involve components relating to community service, career planning, and future educational opportunities. Community service hours are documented with each progress report.

To see how a project overlaps several subject areas, one group of about eight students worked together on a proj-

---

THEMATIC UNITS

Quarter 1: PRIDE
- *What are my strengths? How do I learn best?*
- *What are my goals?*
- *What is the "O'Farrell Way?"*

Project: "Presenting Myself" (see Figure 1 for a detailed look at the components and criteria for this project). Time will be spent on orientation to the O'Farrell way, including habits, standards, expectations, conflict management skills, culture, school tours, big brother-sister, and personal goals.

Quarter 2: CHOICES
- *How do my choices affect myself and others?*
- *How can I best go about solving a problem?*

Project: "Problem-Solving Convention," which combines Invent America with solving school and community problems. Group projects optional.

Quarter 3: RELATIONSHIPS
- *How can I help make a team work?*
- *What are the advantages and disadvantages of working with others?*

Project: Group project to create simulations such as space travel, disasters, historical events, and current issues using computer microworlds, role playing, video, or drama.

Quarter 4: MOTION: RITES OF PASSAGE
- *How have I grown this year?*
- *How can I demonstrate I am ready to move on?*

Project: Olympics and portfolio presentation, including assessment of goals.

---

ect called "microworlds," part of the third quarter Relationships unit. They decided to use the outbreak of the Black Death in 1348 as their theme. In science class they studied and researched the symptoms, causes, and results of the outbreak of the disease, along with the attempted cures. During language arts they created a storyboard for

---

Unit 1: PRIDE
Essential questions:
- What are my strengths? How do I learn best?
- What are my goals? What do I do well?
- What is the "O'Farrell Way?"

The Essential Questions are a component of the unit but are incorporated within the curriculum on an individual basis. They are addressed in the student's portfolio.

Project: Presenting Myself

A. Criteria for Presenting Myself project
1. Demonstrates knowledge of own physical makeup and dimensions (e.g., contents of body, nutrition, elements and compounds, blood components).
2. Demonstrates knowledge of cultural contributions and geographic origins (e.g., family tree, culture of neighborhood/family, customs, personal timeline).
3. Demonstrates ability to describe qualities of self (e.g., personality, interests, strengths, future goals, learning style, personal journals).
4. Demonstrates pride in work through:
   - Neatness
   - Organization of materials (resources), presentation
   - Completeness
   - Attention to detail
   - Timeliness in accordance with due dates
   - Creativity

B. Presentation Modes: Final projects can include a written, oral, and visual component.
1. Video: Project for 8th graders (alternatives may include a Hypercard stack or photography)
2. Package: Project for 6th/7th graders (box, book, collage, mural, slide show, or display board)

C. All students required to introduce themselves on video. Students must address at least one of the options listed below:
1. State one of your long-term goals
2. What do I do well?
3. Describe yourself, including personality and interests

D. Understanding of the O'Farrell Way will be demonstrated in a written project and incorporated as a component of the portfolio. This activity will be completed in Home Base class. Teachers will be provided with a writing prompt from the curriculum committee. Home Base teachers will grade this assignment.

Figure 1. Components and criteria for
Unit 1: PRIDE project, "Presenting Myself."

a computer game. Then, in computer class, they used their research and story board and the Macintosh to create a complex, factual computer game around this disease and the city of Florence.

Students are rightfully proud of the level of responsibility they carry—and the results. As 12-year-old Shaunte said, "We created the game, we did the assignments, we did the research, we did *everything*!"

Assessment

Assessment of student learning is accomplished through a variety of activities that include portfolios and exhibitions as well as progress reports. No letter grades are given and students are not "tracked."

Eighth Grade Project

Eighth graders have a major thesis project that becomes part of their eighth grade portfolio. Under the thematic unit CHOICES, two students chose thesis projects on "Depletion of the Rain Forests" and "Racial Strife in America." In a thesis project, students identify a problem for which they *must come up with a solution*. They also are asked to contact at least one "expert" in the field.

The research for the thesis project is carried out during social studies. In language arts they work on taking notes and the format for their project, and during math they focus on data collection. A Thesis Project Checklist (see Figure 2) guides students as they complete their project.

Looking Ahead

O'Farrell is not "finished." Restructuring is an ongoing, fluid process. It is a journey with few roadmaps. As such, it asks a lot of everyone involved. Even so, teachers readily identify the plusses of teaching at such a school. "The team is wonderful support—I've never, ever felt isolated here," says Lenora Smith, one of the original seven teachers.

"You really touch base; you really get to know these kids," said art teacher Jo Ann Berman. "I would never want to go back [to my old school], and I was at an excellent school."

But the challenges cannot be understated. District Superintendent Tom Payzant says the true test for the school remains three or four years down the road. "The issue is, can they sustain the energy level necessary to keep them going year after year? How will they find ways to replenish their energy and their commitment?"

This is where the ever-optimistic Stein comes in. Called Keeper of the Dream for good reason, he helps the staff keep focused and centered on their common vision.

"Do it for the children," he told the staff at a retreat last year. "Through O'Farrell we are going to change the world."

Special thanks to Computer Teacher Roland Garcia for allowing me to spend time at O'Farrell and for his help with background material for this article. For more information, write O'Farrell Community School, 6130 Skyline Drive, San Diego, CA 92114-5699.

THESIS PROJECT CHECKLIST
O'FARRELL STANDARD

HB TEACHER_____ FAMILY_____ HOUSE_____

PROJECT TITLE _____

_____ **Title Page**
_____ **Abstract/Summary**
_____ **Acknowledgments**
_____ **Table of Contents**
_____ **Introduction**
    _____ Statement of problem/issue
    _____ Hypothesis/thesis statement
    _____ Significance of problem/issue
_____ **Background Research**
    _____ Information applies to issue/project topic
    _____ Demonstrates adequate knowledge of topic area other viewpoints
    _____ Ideas and information not originated by student are footnoted or otherwise indicated
    _____ Written in student's own words—not a string of quotes
_____ **Procedures**
    _____ Clear, step-by-step explanation of how project carried out or issue investigated, including explanation of how tests and surveys used were developed, how observations were made, how models were built and modified, etc.
    _____ Describe/discuss factors that might affect the outcome of the problem or issue
    _____ Description included of resources, materials, and/or equipment used
_____ **Findings/Results**
    _____ Summaries of data recorded (tallies, tables, graphs) included
    _____ Data thoroughly analyzed
    _____ Statistical measurement of significance of data may be included
    _____ Actual data such as measurements, surveys, observations, interviews included
_____ **Conclusions**
    _____ Results of experiment/research interpreted
    _____ Conclusion supported by arguments or data from the body of the work
    _____ Results related to problem/issue and to hypothesis/thesis
_____ **Recommendations**
    _____ Recommends additional investigations or changes that should be made in procedure if project repeated
    _____ Recommends any real-life applications of results/findings
_____ **Bibliography**
    _____ Proper bibliographic format
    _____ 12 or more sources
    _____ 10 sources that are not encyclopedias
    _____ At least one expert contacted (and qualifications listed)
    _____ (15 or more sources)
    _____ (Two or more experts contacted)
_____ **Appendices**
    _____ Supplementary information not included in body of paper (graphs, photos, statistical work, correspondence, etc.)
    _____ Project log
_____ **OVERALL PERFORMANCE LEVEL**
Comments:

Figure 2. Thesis Project Checklist.

Reading, Writing, and Restructuring: A Case for Renewal

Henry F. Olds, Jr.

Roots of Restructuring

The motivation for restructuring schools started with a need to move decision making in schools closer to those whose lives are most affected—students and the teachers who teach them. In this way, schools perhaps would be more responsive to their immediate constituents and use resources more effectively to help teachers teach and students learn. Not only that, they might also be more responsive to the needs of parents and other concerned citizens in the immediate community.

The need for extensive curriculum reform has added fuel to the restructuring fires. There is a growing awareness by curriculum reformers that the structure of schooling has multiple interlocking constraints that resist innovation. Mathematician and curriculum reformer Jack Easely once pointed out to me that schools have incredibly effective immune systems that successfully defend against any intrusion perceived as threatening their well-being.

If past experience is any indication, the success of whole language will likely be short lived without more fundamental restructuring of the schools in which whole language instruction occurs.

Many reformers agree that you can't substantially improve what goes on in schools simply by injecting independent changes into the system; you must be willing to change the entire system. Thus, as the awareness of the poor performance of schools grows and the press for curriculum reform increases, the pressure for restructuring builds. It has become clear that the effort and money invested in improving what is taught in schools and in training teachers to teach better will be wasted if schools are not fundamentally restructured.

Enter Whole Language

The recent move toward a whole language approach to teaching reading and writing has generated much enthusiasm for changing the language arts and English curriculum, fueled by a growing recognition that traditional language arts instruction is not helping students become fully fluent, literate citizens. The problem is aptly portrayed in the following monologue:

> *"Good morning, class!*
> *Today I will prepare you for the future.*
> *Listen carefully,*
> *and don't interrupt!*
> *Are there any questions? . . .*
> *None?*
> *Good!"*[1]

So far, the whole language approach, like many earlier curriculum reforms, is having some short-term success. But if past experience is any indication, its success will likely be short lived without more fundamental restructuring of the schools in which whole language instruction occurs. Let's look at a few reasons why.

Stumbling Blocks

Testing poses the most obvious stumbling block. A whole language approach proposes that children's growing abilities in reading, writing, speaking, and listening can best be evaluated in the context of performing some real language-mediated tasks. The school, on the other hand, evaluates students' abilities in terms of standardized test scores—tests which at best may evaluate only a small portion of a child's emerging abilities. In order to prove that their approach works, whole language advocates must argue for changing the tests. Some alternative methods such as portfolio evaluation show promise, but this movement is in its infancy. And even if they succeed, changes in the mode of evaluation in one subject area will struggle in the face of the school's larger commitment to other forms of evaluation.

Use of instructional time poses another major obstacle that has bedeviled all curriculum reformers. For example, in a whole language approach, one can choose to spend an extended amount of time helping a student develop a single written composition on a topic of interest to him or her. From the teacher's perspective the time may be well spent because the student has had the opportunity to practice several skills in developing that single piece of writing. From the hyper time-conscious perspective of the school, however, the student has spent too much time on one assignment, neglecting other activities/lessons, including the predetermined syllabus. By insisting on superficial coverage of many topics over real understanding of a few, a school puts considerable pressure on the teacher to yield to its dictates.

The **lack of teacher support** is evident also in the level of ongoing help given teachers seeking to change their teaching methods. While the school district may support a teacher's attendance at a summer workshop, for example, when she returns to school in the fall, full of enthusiasm and ready to put into practice what she has learned, she finds minimal support in working through the many challenges she encounters. On the simplest level, there is no time during the school day to do the complex planning it takes to implement her new ideas. She must do it on her own time or not at all. Then, when problems arise, there is no one to turn to for help and support. She feels lonely and isolated in her efforts and all too often begins to wonder if the changes that once seemed so attractive are worth the effort.

The Challenge

Many more examples could be given of the defense mechanisms marshalled by schools to resist reform. Without significant restructuring, schools will continue to do an excellent job of defending against and ultimately assimilating any significant efforts to improve them; the result is preservation of the status quo—a mediocre education for some and a poor education for most.

With a commitment to restructuring, the door is open for changes. Schools might actually do what children and parents (and our society) need. They might actually teach in a way that honors what teachers know and what research has proven to be effective. They might actually prepare students to effectively face the challenges of a fast-changing workplace and an increasingly interdependent world.

With a commitment to restructuring, we might have schools where we would no longer hear this kind of lament from our students:

> *I was good at everything—*
> *honest, everything!—*
> *until I started being here with you.*
> *I was good at laughing,*
> *playing dead,*
> *being king!*
> *Yeah, I was good at everything!*
> *But now I'm only good at everything*
> *on Saturdays and Sundays. . . .*[1]

Henry Olds, Senior Scientist, Bolt Beranek and Newman, Cambridge, MA.

[1]Cullum, Albert. *The Geranium on the Window Sill Just Died But Teacher You Went Right On.* Harlin Quist, 1971.

OBITUARIES

Cratchet and **John**, two of the king's private guards, were executed by Macbeth after they had been accused of assassinating the King. At the time, Duncan was paying a royal visit to his cousin Macbeth at the Inverness Castle. The guards were executed without any type of public trial. Macbeth has expressed his regret over not investigating the matter further.

Cratchet leaves behind a wife and five children. The youngest, named Tiny Tim, is crippled. John is survived by his mother and an elderly aunt. Both are widows residing in Doe, a province of Skoal. Both men died in disgrace and will therefore be buried in the Poor Souls mass grave. No funeral services are planned.
by Giuseppe S.

Hamlet, 60, of Denmark, died Saturday in his garden. Born in Denmark, Hamlet was the King of Denmark for 50 years. He was a member of the Royal Church and was a former member of the Royal Church, serving as prince. Husband of the late Gertrude, he is survived by one brother, Claudius of Denmark, and one son, Hamlet of Denmark. Relatives and friends are invited to attend mass at the Royal Church of Denmark at 10:00 a.m. Sunday. Buriel will be in the Danish Royal Cemetery.
by Tina R.

from Bristol High School Writing Center, Bristol, PA.

CHAPTER 2
WRITING ACROSS THE CURRICULUM

*Writing is not a special language that belongs to English teachers
and a few other sensitive souls who have "a gift for words."
Writing is the logical arrangement of thought. It enables us to find out what
we know—and what we don't know—about whatever we're trying to learn.*
                                                                    —William Zinsser

Computer Writing Labs:
A New Vision for Elementary Writing

Jeannine Herron

The work of the primary years is to develop "habits of mind," to lay down vast networks of neuronal associations that become so familiar that they begin to function at an automatic and unconscious level. This is the importance of writing, writing, and more writing, and why writing must have as honored a place in the curriculum as reading.

Today is a writing day. The first graders hurry into the computer room and find their places on the rug. There are more and more writing days, now that the class has almost learned to keyboard. Jonathan is bursting to tell everyone about the overhead projector he made with his sister. He's thinking about how he might write about it.

Developing the Vision—What Do We Need?

• **Computers in writing labs.** Research has shown that when the computer is used for composing, editing, and revising, student work goes faster—the writing becomes longer and more elaborate, it is revised more, and it gets read more. But in most elementary schools there are still not enough computers for students to use them every day, and they're not dedicated to writing.

• **Keyboarding and word processing in first grade.** Computers make writing easier, especially when students have keyboarding skills. But in most schools keyboarding is taught as a separate skill, usually after fifth grade. For the first four years (one-third of their school experience), students cannot efficiently benefit from the advantages of word processing because they don't know the keyboard. Keyboarding *can* be taught in first grade. It can be taught as an integral part of learning to write. Instead of being learned as a separate skill, keyboarding itself can facilitate the whole process of learning how to encode.

Jonathan is learning how to keyboard in a new way. He thinks about the sounds in the words he wants to write and associates each sound with a finger stroke on the keyboard. He has actually learned a difficult cognitive task—the whole process of encoding— as part of learning to keyboard and word process. He is not at all daunted by putting words like "overhead projector" into the story he wants to write.

• **Excellent software for writing.** If computers are going to be used primarily for writing throughout school, the tools should be the best. Sometimes teachers underestimate the value of a good dictionary, thesaurus, or spell checker as a teaching device. There are many ways to use these software applications to find patterns in language or discover a new rule.

- **Cooperative, project-oriented learning.** We know that younger students benefit from periodic help by capable "big kids," especially when they work together cooperatively on specific projects. But in most schools, students stay within their own classrooms, working mostly alone or with their own classmates.

- **Excellent staff development.** Some teachers still are reluctant to teach with computers and have not personally experienced the benefits of writing with a word processor. But when teachers have adequate training in teaching writing with computers, they can become powerful advocates at their school, making writing labs happen even if it means lining the computers up in the hallway.

- **Holistic projects and assessment.** There is ample evidence that children benefit more from holistic projects and assessments than from filling out worksheets or multiple choice tests. But there are still many schools where real writing happens once a week and the rest of "writing time" involves practicing penmanship, listing spelling words, or filling in the blanks.

Teachers need support and time to develop projects together and learn holistic assessment procedures. Student writing puts language processing down on paper and makes it visible. The hard copy becomes a window through which the teacher can view a child's progress, development, evolution of critical thinking skills, and creativity. Assistance in learning how to "see" this evolution makes the teacher a more effective guide. And the computer can store a portfolio documenting this development all the way through a child's school career.

Miss Rechif hands students their portfolios. Jonathan glances down at the familiar drawing of the keyboard houses on the paper cover. His favorite keyboard character is Jik, a boy who likes to write secret things in his journal. Miss Rechif starts the warm-up game and they spend a few minutes practicing some new words. The children all chant the sounds together while they rhythmically practice the strokes on the paper keyboard houses.

What is the Vision?

In this vision of elementary computer writing labs, there are enough computers so that everyone can write at least half an hour each day. Everyone learns keyboarding and word processing in first grade; once the whole student body knows how to keyboard, only the first graders and other new students need keyboarding each year. Students are always involved in making books and reading to each other. There are lots of interesting writing projects that span age groups and subjects. Editing and revising are fun because they don't require laborious recopying.

There is good software available for keyboarding, word processing, and encoding; for composing (dictionary, thesaurus, encyclopedia) and editing (spell checker, grammar checker); and for graphics, layout, and presentation purposes, which children learn to use when the need arises.

Teachers create their own lessons. They have time to meet together and plan cooperative projects. There is also staff development time to learn how to teach elementary writing with computers, to develop holistic projects and assessments, and to maintain and evaluate portfolios that grow each year and show the development and progress of each child.

Is This Vision Possible?

Yes! It's already happening in Los Altos, California. Last year teachers at Springer Elementary School decided to pilot some new early writing software called *Talking Fingers*— designed, developed, and tested by California Neuropsychology Services, an educational research institute at the Media Learning Center in San Rafael, California. The teachers pooled 15 computers into one writing lab and developed a schedule that cycled 400 students through the lab. One year later the entire student body knew how to keyboard and word process. These students can now sit down and write on a computer anywhere—in the back of the classroom, in the library, or at home.

When the warm-ups are over, Jonathan goes to his computer, "TYRANNOSAURUS," and spends ten minutes doing Typing Challenges with Talking Fingers, practicing sentences using the sound "mmm." He likes making Mom walk across the screen as he types. She dances a little jig when she gets to the other side of the screen. When he finishes the lesson, he inserts his Trophy Disk. He has already won six trophies, but it is still exciting to see the Incredible Trophy Machine jiggle and whirr, and it's always a surprise to see what it will produce!

Teachers from other Los Altos schools have visited Springer Elementary School, and researchers from the Media Learning Center have given several staff development workshops for teachers throughout the whole district. In one Writing with Computers workshop, teachers spent two days working at the computers, learning how to teach different kinds of writing, including autobiographies, report writing, and poetry. In addition to *Talking Fingers*, they used *Print Shop* (Broderbund), *The Writing Center* (The Learning Company), and *Write Now* (T/Maker). In the process they discovered how to use a word processor effectively and came away with lots of ideas for their own writing programs.

This year there are computer writing labs at all six elementary schools in the Los Altos School District. Of the 300 other teachers who have attended the Writing with Computers workshops, many have taken the ideas back to their schools, and there are now at least 20 schools in other California districts implementing this vision.

Jonathan is eager to start his story. He tries to remember each step he and his sister took as they built their overhead projector. He switches to Write Now, his word processing program. "I made a," he writes. He whispers "overhead" slowly and then repeats each sound, typing the letters one by one as he says the sounds in the word—ovrhedpjektr.

Jonathan's brain is considering first the whole (the meaning of the word) and then the parts (the sequence of sounds, the finger strokes he needs to type those sounds, and the letters that stand for those sounds). Back to the whole and again to the parts. In the process, pathways are forming in Jonathan's mind, a criss-crossing of neuronal trails and highways connecting everything known and experienced about the word "overhead." He re-reads what he has typed, checking to see if the sequence makes sense.

Jonathan is excited. This emotion deep in his brain sends arousing signals upward to every part of his cortex, including his frontal lobes, which help him focus his attention on his work in spite of distractions in the room. He is processing on many levels simultaneously. His brain is monitoring the "big picture"—his story, the meaning of this sentence, and even the projection of the next sentence. At the same time it is also producing a multitude of individual segments—the auditory, visual, and sensory-motor details that include the sounds in the word, the sight of each letter, the feel of each finger stroke.

It takes more than one period to finish, and Jonathan works hard at his story whenever he can during the week. He is proud of his finished product as he reads it to the class and prints out a copy for his parents.

I made a ovrhedpjektr

Me and My sistr made a ovrhedpjektr. Imade it with a big box and a litl box, and a mere and a magnafire and a flashlite. When the flashlite shines thruwe the magnafire and then it shines on the mere and it bountsis off the mere and it shines on the wall. And we made a play.

jonathan giffard (1st grade, Springer School)

Why is This Vision Exciting?

The work of the primary years is to develop "habits of mind," to lay down these vast networks of neuronal associations that become so familiar that they begin to function at an automatic and unconscious level. This is the importance of writing, writing, and more writing, and why writing must have as honored a place in the curriculum as reading. Specifically,

1. Writing engages the writer's mind in language at all levels, including the most fundamental link to the body, the sensory-motor system (an indispensable ally when it comes to the work of sequencing things together).

2. Writing demands both "top-down" and "bottom-up" processing; the writer must monitor "the whole" while producing "the parts."

3. The writer's mind is driven by two powerful forces— the emotion and the ideas to be conveyed, both of which must be nurtured as young children develop their own voices and learn how to become thoughtful, informed citizens.

Jeannine Herron is the Director of the Media Learning Center at Dominican College in San Rafael, CA.

Talking Fingers is available for the Apple family (Apple II, Apple GS, and Macintosh with an Apple emulator card). ($149; 5-pack, $399; 8-pack, $499.) A DOS version will be available Fall 1992. Write California Neuropsychology Services, 50 Acacia Ave., San Rafael, CA 94901-8008.

In a new approach to keyboarding, children imagine two houses in the keyboard, one for the left hand, one for the right. The houses are inhabited by interesting story characters whose names start with the sound of the letter where they live. Students learn to type whatever they can say by associating each speech sound with a finger stroke on the keyboard.

A Thinking Block for Literature

Stephen Marcus

By correlating alternative itineraries, literary theory should help critics both to reach specific destinations and to plan further trips within the charted critical landscape. [Any] "map" of literature . . . must stay ready to be redrawn in the light of texts, interpretations, and evaluations to which it turns out not to have done justice. [1]

We must reintroduce the element of play into criticism. [2]

The Problem

Your students have a problem. They are faced with the task of trying to figure out what to say about a work of literature they are studying in class. This entails figuring out what to think about it. If they are typical students, many of them have begun to develop thinking blocks at about the same time you have finished giving the assignment.

A Solution

A device for helping students deal with their thinking blocks is described below.[3] Used by teachers and students around the country, it involves transforming a Rubik's Cube-type puzzle[4] into a tool for thinking and writing about literature and demonstrates the transition from thinking block to Thinking Block. The method encourages a certain kind of intellectual dexterity, zest, and fluidity of form—in other words, a kind of mental break-dancing. The point is to give yourself a "whack on the side of the head"[5] (or, if these metaphors are too percussive, a whispering kiss from the mists of imagination).

The Method

A Rubik's-type cube has six sides—or faces, or perspectives. On each side there is a small center square (or "tile" in the Rubik's Cube world), surrounded by eight additional tiles. I picked one of those sides and defined it as the THEME perspective. I then selected eight common themes that are likely to occur in any novel or short story.[6] Using adhesive paper, I labeled the center tile "THEME" and put a different theme on each surrounding tile on the THEME side of the cube (see Figure 1).

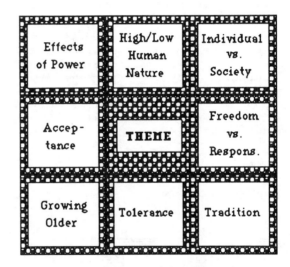

Figure 1. The THEME Perspective.

To what extent is the work of literature "about" any of the following, and what does the work have to say about any given theme?

The effects of gaining, losing, and exercising power. The higher versus lower aspects of human nature. The individual versus society-at-large. Being accepted. Exercising freedom versus taking on responsibilities and obligations. Growing older. Being tolerant. The role of tradition in human affairs.

I had previously noticed that most works of fiction deal with people, so I defined another side of the cube as the CHARACTER perspective and thought of eight questions you might ask of any character in a work of fiction. The CHARACTER side of the Thinking Block is shown in Figure 2.

The other four faces of the block were defined in terms of the author's METHOD in creating the work of fiction, the kind of WORLD that exists in the story,

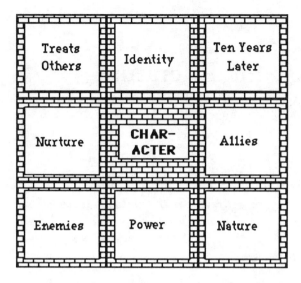

Figure 2. The CHARACTER Perspective.

What can you say about a particular character in the story?

How does this character treat others? How would you describe this character's identity? What do you imagine this person will be like ten years after the story ends? To what extent was this person's character formed by upbringing or nurture? Who are this person's allies? Who are this person's enemies? What powers does this person have and to what extent are they exercised? To what extent is the person's character determined by heredity or "human nature"?

the role of CHANGE in the plot, and the relationship between the READER and the work of fiction being studied. These perspectives are shown in Figures 3-6.

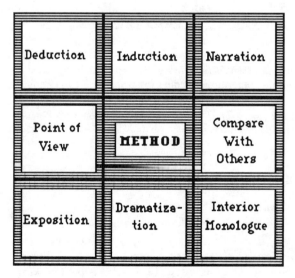

Figure 3. The METHOD Perspective.

What can you say about the way this work is constructed, about the author's method or technique?

How does the author lead you from the general to the particular

(deduction)? —from the particular to the general (induction)? What special role does narration play in accomplishing the author's ends? From what point of view is the story told and how does that serve the work? How does this work fit in with others like it and does it draw on or make fun of any literary traditions? What special role does exposition play in accomplishing the author's ends? What special role does dramatization play? What special role does interior monologue play?

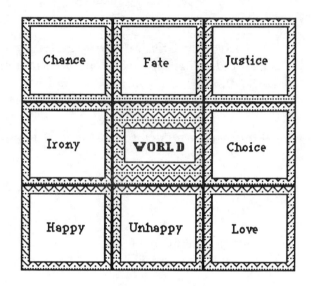

Figure 4. The WORLD Perspective.

What kind of world is it in the story?

To what extent are things determined by chance (even if this seems a contradiction in terms)? To what extent by fate? Is it a world in which justice exists (even if it doesn't prevail)? To what extent is the world an ironic one? To what extent are events determined by real choices people have? Is the world in general one in which happiness is the norm? Is unhappiness the norm? What part does love play in this world?

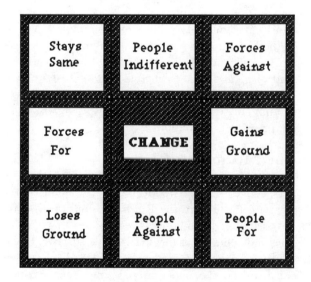

Figure 5. The CHANGE Perspective.

How is what happens in the story affected by changes in people and things?

Who stays the same? Who's indifferent to change? What are the forces (not people) acting to inhibit change? What are the forces (not people) acting for change? Who gains some ground? Who loses ground? Who's against change? Who's for change?

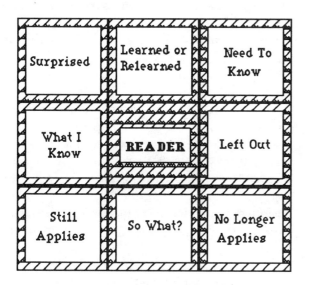

Figure 6. The READER Perspective.

What special reactions did you as the reader have relative to the work?

What elements in the work surprised you? What are some things you learned or relearned from reading the work? What are some things you need to know in order to understand, appreciate, or "get" this work? What are some things you already know that will help you understand, appreciate, or "get" this work? What about this work still applies to you, to people you know, or to the world at large? So what? That is, what is the significance or importance of this work for you personally? What about this work no longer applies to you, to people you know, or to the world at large?

The Practice

Here's how the Thinking Block works. Suppose you want to think and write about *The Red Badge of Courage*. First, you pick a perspective on which to focus—the theme of the novel, for example. You take hold of your Thinking Block and give its rows of tiles several twists—five to ten are usually sufficient. You then locate the center tile that contains the word THEME and note the random collection of tiles that now surrounds it, tiles that represent questions drawn from the other five perspectives. Your task now is to ask yourself each of those questions and to relate them to each other and to your central concern: the book's theme.

In one case, the eight tiles that turned up around the THEME center tile dealt with Fate, Exposition, Stays Same, For Change, Tolerance, Ten Years Later,

Choice, and Need to Know. Here is one set of questions that can be generated from this collection of tiles:

- In *The Red Badge of Courage*, to what extent is the world of the novel controlled by fate and to what extent by free choice?

- Who and what stays the same, and what's the relation between lack of change and the kind of world it is in the terms just considered?

- Who is personally trying to change, or to change others or situations?

- What's the relationship between these attempts and the kind of world it is?

- How is tolerance a factor in all this?

- Speculate on what all this may mean for one of the characters ten years after the story ends.

- To what extent do you find answers to these questions from what the author *tells* you (as opposed to *shows* you)?

- And, which of your answers to these questions can you weave into a statement about what *The Red Badge of Courage* is "about"?

If some of these questions don't seem to be working out, give the cube a few more twists. Depending on your personality, it may be comforting or disconcerting to know that there are some 42,000,000,000,000,000,000 (42 quintillion) arrangements of your cube[7]—and you have only been examining *one* side of *one* of those arrangements.

Never again can your students bemoan, "But I don't have anything to write about!"

What the Thinking Block does is allow you to do industrial strength clustering,[8] or power sentence-combining.[9] It may not be possible to interrelate *all* the questions that turn up around the selected central perspective. The goal is to *try* to relate them—and in the course of doing so to try to develop new ideas and insights.

The Theory

The Thinking Block method is embedded in the following deeply superficial model of the thinking process.[10] Start with the notion of a "thinking process" analogous to the composing process; that is, prethinking, thinking, and rethinking. (It's hardly necessary to point out that these represent recursive stages.)

Prethinking includes making the implicit explicit. On a given topic, we can generate, record, and note the prejudices, facts, feelings, values, speculations, etc. that we're already in possession of. We might also engage in some research to acquire more of such material. The *Thinking* stage consists of the application of heuristic procedures that provide us with a "whack on the side of the head." It is in the Thinking stage that we try new perspectives, new angles. It is here that we engage in creative thinking—making the familiar strange and the strange familiar.[11] The *Rethinking* stage derives from attaching the prefix "re-" to almost any apposite word: reformulate, reconsider, reaffirm, review—rethink. It's in this stage that we can feel free to change our minds—if we think we should—and to articulate those changes.

As in the case of the composing process, some people confuse earlier stages with later ones. They attempt to do their rethinking before their prethinking. They mistake confirming their prejudices and assumptions with examining them. Others indulge in compulsive rethinking. This often leads to thinker's block and is especially troublesome when approaching the deadline for a paper or book manuscript.

It's also the case that these stages don't even begin to capture the complexities of the process under consideration. On the other hand, by suggesting a focus on the process of thinking, the stages encourage the development of teaching strategies appropriate to each stage.

This discussion only begins to explore the utility, and limitations, of this model for the thinking process. Suffice it to say that its main virtue is perhaps that it helps us think about thinking—and, if not more importantly at least more practically, such a framework helps us generate and structure our efforts to focus on process, not solely on product.

The Thinking Block is most useful during the Thinking stage of the thinking process. While a traditional Rubik's Cube-type puzzle has a drive toward order (i.e., getting all the tiles of one color back to the same side), the Thinking Block has a drive toward randomness. The point is to create an unexpected grouping of elements and to use our own abilities for constructing meaning to bring order out of "chaos." The Thinking Block also illustrates in a concrete way that, even though we are considering the elements of one perspective, there are all those other elements just waiting to be brought into the picture.

Thinking Blocks Across the Curriculum

The particular questions (and tile labels) provided above are obviously arbitrary. Different central perspectives could have been chosen, and other questions could be substituted. The important feature is the mechanism. Realizing this, it is clear that Thinking Blocks can be created by teachers and students for other English and language arts areas, other grade levels,[12] and other disciplines.

As usual, however, the implementation of a bright idea is never as easy as expected. Experience in training workshops designed to develop other kinds of Thinking Blocks suggests that participants can use guidance. Center-tile topics must be at the right level of abstraction. Surrounding-tile questions should be sufficiently open-ended in nature to encourage the kind of cross-pollination that is at the heart of the whole approach.

The very *enterprise* of developing a Thinking Block is, however, an enriching and rewarding experience. This was certainly the case for two social studies teachers who decided to develop their own Thinking Block for History.[13] They first had to consider common dimensions of historical events, deciding tentatively on the following: PEOPLE, IDEAS, HABITAT, PLACE, and ECONOMICS. Their continuing efforts to refine their topics and accompanying questions have provided them, their students, and their colleagues with quite a valuable "new look" at how their discipline is organized and thought about. The stages of developing a Thinking Block have themselves provided occasions for thinking and writing about history.

Brief Conclusions

Even though the Thinking Block "breaks down" ideas about literature into bits and pieces, the Block itself is an integrative and synthesizing device. It's a concrete metaphor and reminder of the richness and complexity of literature. The work under consideration is clearly both all that is on the Block and much more that is absent from it.

The Thinking Block, in fact, allows and encourages students to constantly "redraw" their mental map of a work of literature. It evokes "alternative itineraries" through the landscape of the text. And it does this with a cultural icon that connotes both problem solving and "play." The Thinking Block is also an antidote for those people (like the author) who could never solve a Rubik's Cube in the first place. "Solving" the

Thinking Block is the *last* thing you want to do.

The Thinking Block for Literature is on one level merely a three-dimensional version of "take one from column A, one from column B," etc. In practice, however, it has proven at a variety of grade levels to be an engaging and intriguing challenge for teachers and students who like to play with ideas and who enjoy having a concrete and colorful way to represent them.

A Note for Computer Enthusiasts

The Thinking Block is a method for organizing, storing, and retrieving information. As such, it is a "data base" (as is any dictionary or novel), and was, in fact, developed in the course of creating more traditional data base files for thinking and writing about literature.[14] It should be clear from the discussion above that the Thinking Block is thus both a data base and thought processor. It has 42 trillion megabytes of RAM and a high resolution, interactive digital-kinetic interface. Its neural-wetware[15] operating system is compatible with all known brands of commercial hardware. There is already a large installed base of uninitialized Thinking Block hardware in the United States, and thus the Thinking Block system is readily available as a very low-cost peripheral device for English classes. It is advised, however, that third-party developers exercise care in keeping the sticky paper from slipping into the drive system.

Stephen Marcus, Ph.D., Associate Director, South Coast Writing Project, University of California, Santa Barbara, CA 93106.

Notes

1. Paul Hernadi in *What is Criticism?* (Bloomington, IN: Indiana University Press, 1981).
2. Paul Hernadi, in an address to the Literature Institute for Teachers, South Coast Writing Project, Graduate School of Education, University of California, Santa Barbara, July 1985.
3. I was introduced to this use of the Rubik's Cube in 1982 by Hugh Burns, who had applied the technique to help his debate students at the U. S. Air Force Academy.
4. The name Rubik's Cube is a trademark, although it has popularly, if not legally, become a generic term. Similar cubes are marketed under names like "Wonderful Puzzler."
5. The "whack" formulation is taken from Roger Von Oechs' book on creative training, *A Whack on the Side of the Head* (New York: Warner Books, 1985).
6. The themes I selected were culled from the *Model Curriculum Standards: English/Language Arts, Grades 9-12* (Sacramento, CA: State Department of Education, 1985).
7. People are regularly surprised at the number of possibilities that the Rubik's Cube provides. Its namesake was perhaps referring to its unexpectedly interactive nature when he noted that "We turn the Cube and it twists us." See John Tierney's, "The Perplexing Life of Erno Rubik," *Discover*, March 1986, pp. 81-88.
8. The most extensive treatment of clustering as a prewriting technique is Gabrielle Rico's *Writing the Natural Way* (New York: J. P. Tarcher, Inc., Houghton Mifflin, 1983).
9. See William Strong, *Sentence Combining and Paragraph Building* (New York: Random House, 1981).
10. This discussion of the thinking process is taken from the author's "Computers in Thinking, Writing, and Literature," in *Writing at Century's End*, Lisa Gerrard, ed. (New York: Random House, 1987).
11. The familiar/strange approach is a standard one in creativity training based on the work of William J. J. Gordon, *Introduction to Synectics Problem-Solving* (Cambridge, MA: Porpoise Books, 1972).
12. The author has been pleasantly surprised at the enthusiasm expressed by elementary and junior high school teachers at the possibilities of the Thinking Block for their students.
13. Developers of the History Thinking Block, Morrie Aborne and Doug Sterling, were participants in the History/Social Studies Summer Technology Institute, Graduate School of Education, UC Santa Barbara, July 1986.
14. Stephen Marcus and Beverly Hunter, *Literature and Composition Activities for PFS: File* (New York: Scholastic, Inc., 1986).
15. Neural wetware refers, of course, to your brain. I am indebted for this formulation to neurophysiologist Karl Pribram, *Languages of the Brain* (Englewood Cliffs, NJ: Prentice-Hall, 1971).

Poe and Prolixity

John Powers

Prolixity? I had to look it up, too. It refers to wordiness; the word ironically appears in "The Fall of the House Of Usher" in reference to an imagined work that Poe admonishes for "its uncouth and unimaginative prolixity." Poe's work could never be called unimaginative, but at times it certainly is wordy.

The works of Edgar Allen Poe are part of the cultural literacy of almost all high school students in the U.S. However, when questioned about the Poe works they have read, students usually can name only *The Telltale Heart*. Most of their experience with Poe's literature comes from films, stories read to them earlier in their schooling, or from conversations with those who have read Poe. Students' curiously high interest in the *content* of Poe's work is often overwhelmed by the difficulty of his prose.

In teaching *The Fall of the House of Usher,* I have tried different strategies to help students through the prose with varying degrees of success. By far the best results come from using writing not only as a tool to decipher the story but also to teach a valuable lesson in creative writing and style. I recently found a method that combines both of these goals and also shows students how a text changes when it is either abridged or adapted.

Adaptation and Abridgement: A Visual Demonstration

I start the lesson by visually demonstrating to my class what *adaptation* and *abridgement* are. To do this I show the students two versions of a reproduction of a painting I have chosen. I use Winslow Homer's "Gulfstream," the compelling painting of a black man floating on a demasted sailboat, surrounded by a stormy sea complete with menacing sharks and waterspouts. This painting works extremely well because it is so dramatic.

The first version I show them is simply a line tracing I have done of the major elements in the painting's composition. I ask them to pick out what they can. Most can see the major details, which they list on their papers.

I then show students the painting itself, but with a mat hiding the outer one-fourth of each side of this long, horizontal piece. I ask students to write about how this version differs from the first. Their answers usually speak of color, fleshing out, depth, more realism, and intensity.

Finally, I show them the uncropped painting. When they write about the differences now, they see a ship on the horizon and a possible rescue vessel, as well as the vastness of the ocean. When asked, they of course prefer this version.

I then explain that the line drawing is an adaptation, the cropped version is an abridgement, and the unmatted version the original. They brainstorm other media that have been likewise altered and the reasons for the alterations, which include movies shown on television, news footage, interviews, and some sporting events. They question the reasons for the alterations. Some they accept as practical, but generally they would prefer to view the original.

I then add literature to the list and promise them that they will likewise prefer the original to either an adaptation or an abridgement. The looks I get might charitably be called skeptical.

We begin with a cold reading of "The Fall of the House of Usher." I read aloud, asking them to follow along and to try to understand as much of the story as possible. The frustration is evident on their faces as I read.

After the reading I ask them to write as much of the detail of the story as they can—a good assignment to complete using the computer. This assignment is done without sharing and is collected as soon as it is finished. Most students have a general idea of the plot but see few of the subtleties.

We then discuss what makes the story difficult to read. Answers include difficult vocabulary, strange syntax, and general verbosity. At this point they are asked to "improve" the text: They are going to abridge and adapt it to make it easy for a typical high school student to read it.

Writing to Understand: Abridging/Adapting Poe

I divide the class into groups of four and give each group a dictionary, a thesaurus, and one page from the story. Their task is to (a) replace difficult words with simpler ones, (b) rearrange syntax, and (c) eliminate anything that seems unnecessary or confusing. I also ask them, as a goal, to shorten the total content of the page by approximately one-half and, as a final instruction, to make a list of any words or sentence structures they replace.

These adaptation/abridgements can be written out or typed directly into a computer. The entire process takes one to two class periods to complete due to the meticulous reading the students attempt.

Here is the opening passage as written by Poe:

During the whole of a dull, dark, and soundless day in autumn of the year, when the clouds hung oppressively low in the heavens, I had been passing alone, on horseback, through a singularly dreary tract of country; and at length found myself, as shades of evening drew on, within view of the melancholy House of Usher. I know not how it was—but, with the first glimpse of the building, a sense of insufferable gloom pervaded my spirit. I say insufferable; for the feeling was unrelieved by any of that half-pleasurable, because poetic, sentiment with which the mind usually receives even the sternest natural images of the desolate or terrible.

One student's abridged/adapted version read like this:

For the most part of a dull, dark day in autumn, I rode on horseback through a bad stretch of country, when I found myself at the House of Usher. I don't know why but when I first saw the building, a chill went through my spine. I say a chill because it was a feeling one gets when one sees something desolate or terrible.

—Heather M.

I made no judgments on how they rewrote the passages. With their tasks finished, it was time to print out the combined files (or separate pages) with a copy for each group. One person read the abridged/adapted version aloud, while others followed along in the original text.

Invariably each group felt that it had done a better job of maintaining the integrity of the original, while other groups had destroyed or mutilated it. They were quick to point out examples of passages or words that they had understood, which other groups had changed needlessly.

When they had finished reading, I had them again write out what they knew about the story. I gave them back their original responses after the cold reading and had them write about the differences between the two. Everyone agreed that that their second versions were more complete and detailed, but when pressed did not necessarily feel that the abridged/annotated version had helped their understanding that much. Instead, they felt that the work they had done on their individual pages and the close reading of the original as the annotated/abridged version was read was far more useful.

When asked which text they preferred, they universally chose the original—with some reservations. They felt that they needed to proceed more slowly, needed to read the text twice, possibly consult a dictionary or thesaurus, and talk in groups about the problems they encountered. I explained that this would take extra time and work, but they felt if the book was "important" we should take the time and read fewer texts.

I now asked them to apply this method. Each group was given a short story by Poe to read in their small groups and then summarize to the large group. This went far more quickly than I had expected. Each group summarized their story and we brainstormed a list on the board of the elements of the "typical" Poe story.

A Final Assignment: Writing a New Poe Fragment

As a final assignment, I retrieved the lists of words and passages they had eliminated from "The Fall of the House of Usher." (The lists can either be printed out from the computer or transferred to butcher paper for the whole group to see.) I asked students to create a fragment from a "lost" Poe manuscript. The fragment was to be at least one paragraph long, contain some elements typical to Poe stories, and include vocabulary and syntax removed from "The Fall of the House of Usher." Students eagerly took to this task, rereading Poe stories and pouring over the passages and vocabulary lists.

In this sinister castle I rest, as thoughts of betrayal linger in my head. As the day became enshrouded in the grip of night, I recuperated in a high-backed, black velvet chair. I had of late been obsessed with all things phantasmic and dark. The black, mystical, gruesome, eerie side of reality had played such a cruel role in my battered life. I sit enshrouded in black, adorned with ancient symbols of druids, contemplating an end to my tortured life. The latter of this, says I, due to the loss of my beloved wife, taken from me by wretched demons in the form of the plague. Now I sit, alone and afraid, but soon I will return to the earth, as will everyone.

—Mike L.

Most of the fragments were extraordinarily close to the Poe texts in both mood and style. In fact, as an extra activity, I printed out student samples at random and then added a few excerpts from Poe stories we had not read. The students, working in groups, tried to find the real "Poes," but actually had a great deal of difficulty identifying them.

I have done rewrites and parodies before, but I felt my students learned valuable lessons from these sequenced activities than they had when just doing these activities at random.

1. They learned that they could read and understand difficult texts through careful study, without teacher intervention.

2. They learned that an abridgement/adaptation can destroy the integrity of the original text and may not necessarily help the audience to which it was targeted.

3. Through their written fragments, my students found out how much they had internalized one author's style.

With this type of learning you wonder whether the learning will carry over. I had my answer the next week when we began Hawthorne's "Rappicini's Daughter," another difficult work. The reading seemed to go rapidly and easily. Afterward, one of my students asked me, "Are you sure this wasn't adapted? It was so easy!"

John Powers, Magonia High School, 2450 West Ball Road, Anaheim, CA 92804-5298.

The Tea Party
INTO, THROUGH, & BEYOND
a Piece of Literature

Susan Perona

The Tea Party is an activity designed to help students in grades 2-12 interpret and celebrate a piece of writing both *before* and *after* reading it. Although it is a language arts activity, it can be used successfully in social studies or science.

Instead of holding a traditional teacup and tiny crumpet, students hold individual file cards, each containing one line or quote from a novel, play, or poem. Before reading the piece of literature, students share their lines with each other and respond individually in writing. Both the reading and writing lead to an inductive brainstorming about the plot, characters, and setting of the material they are about to read.

At the conclusion of the reading of the novel, play, or poem, students choose one line from the text that is meaningful to them. They share that line with members of the class and finally move to the computer to respond in writing.

INTO: Before Reading

1. Prepare approximately 30 quotes on file cards (enough for each student in your class) from one novel, poem, or play, and hand them out to students. Here, for example, are three quotes, two for older students and one for younger children:

> We are the hollow men
> We are the stuffed men
> Leaning together
> Headpiece filled with straw. Alas!
> *(from **The Hollow Men** by T.S. Eliot)*

> On the breast of her gown, in red cloth, surrounded with an elaborate embroidery and fantastic flourishes of gold thread, appeared the letter A.
> *(from **The Scarlet Letter** by Nathanial Hawthorne)*

> They roared their terrible roars and gnashed their terrible teeth.
> *(from **Where the Wild Things Are** by Maurice Sendak)*

2. Have students rehearse their lines for vocabulary, clarity, and expression.

3. After rehearsing, give students about 10 minutes to walk around the room, reciting their lines in a variety of ways to as many other students as possible.
   Variation: A signal may be used to indicate a time for students to exchange cards so they will have the opportunity to become familiar with more than one line.

4. Instruct students to write the title of the novel, play, poem, etc. on a sheet of paper and then rewrite or tape their file card quote below it. Have them respond to the quote, letting their imaginations suggest the meaning.

5. Give students an opportunity to share their writing in small groups.

6. Before looking at the text, brainstorm with the class their ideas and possibilities about the plot, setting, characters etc.
   Variation: If the Tea Party lines are numbered, students can read them once again in sequence to further hypothesize the piece of literature about to be read. Or, in another variation, students can see how writers appeal to our senses. Make a chart on the board with the five senses as headings. Have students read their lines, decide to which sense(s) the line appeals, and place a tally in the appropriate column(s).

THROUGH: Read the Story, Poem, Play, or Novel

You may read the story or poem to young children; older students may read the story individually. A long novel may take several weeks.

BEYOND: After Reading

1. Ask students to look through the novel, play, text, etc. and select their favorite line or quote. Have them copy that line on a file card for a post-Tea Party activity. (If you read younger students the story, you might put the book in a corner of the room after reading and give students several days to look through the book and copy the line they like best —one that impresses them in some way.)

2. Have students meet in small groups to discuss their favorite lines.

3. Ask students to write about the significance of the lines they chose. This writing, done on a computer, can lead to a final class project—perhaps an anthology of some kind—on what the novel or story means to them. (David Bleich from the University of Rochester has found this to be a powerful and engaging activity with his college-level students as well. At the end of the reading of a piece of literature, Bleich asks his students to choose one or two lines that have special meaning to them and to write a paper connecting their lives to that piece of literature.)

4. Create a bulletin board of "Notable Quotes" generated by students' Tea Party lines.

Whether you call this activity a Tea Party (for young children) or Pizza Party (for teens), whether your students are second graders or high school seniors, this activity gives students a chance to experiment with language. It gets them out of their seats, it's open to interpretation, and . . . it's fun! For teenagers, especially, it's an opportunity to leave behind the rigidity that characterizes so many assignments, giving them a chance to interpret lines and interact with each other in a playful way—and with a piece of literature on a very personal level.

_____

Susan Perona, 929 Cheltenham Rd., Santa Barbara, CA 93105

Cooperative Integrated Reading and Composition:
A Success Story

Mary Male

Are you one of the many elementary teachers struggling to incorporate the best teaching techniques and materials into your reading and language arts program? If so, perhaps some of these reactions may sound familiar to you:

"I'd love to use cooperative learning in my reading/language arts program, but I don't have time to prepare all those materials!"

"I know it makes sense for students to use a word processor for their compositions, but they can never think of anything to write about."

"I'm having a hard enough time teaching reading with basals and workbooks—how will I ever have time to learn to incorporate literature and whole language approaches?"

Bracher School in Santa Clara (CA) Unified School District, faced with the challenges mentioned above, was one of a number of schools across the country to try out a program developed by The Johns Hopkins Center for Research on Elementary and Middle Schools. Titled CIRC (Cooperative Integrated Reading and Composition), the program was developed to solve a number of identified problems encountered by teachers (and students) in reading/language arts classes:

- Reading groups did not provide enough practice for students to become fluent;
- Independent seatwork did not keep students sufficiently engaged while other students worked with the teacher;

- Workbook activities were not well planned or sequenced and tended to fragment reading/language arts into meaningless subskills;
- Wide ranges of reading skills among students made grouping difficult and tended to keep students in homogeneous groupings rather than encouraging heterogeneous cooperative learning groups.

Putting these three powerful components—cooperative learning, research-based teaching practices in reading and writing, and word processing—together offers teachers new hope for super-charging their students' achievement and motivation.

Bracher's staff, led by principal Sherry Garvey and assisted by Staff Development Director Delberta Meyer, Johns Hopkins trainer Anna Marie Farnish, and the author, have been using the CIRC process with some modifications for three years. In addition to gains on scores of reading comprehension, students in the Bracher program showed a marked increase in their attitude toward reading as well as confidence in their reading ability.

Basic elements of the CIRC process are outlined

below. For all of the written language activities, word processing adds an additional powerful dimension to the CIRC process.

COOPERATIVE READING

Teams: Students are assigned to 4-5 member teams composed of pairs from two different reading groups.

Reading Groups: Students are assigned to homogeneous reading groups where the teacher introduces vocabulary and sets the stage for the new story.

Team Practice: While the teacher meets with each reading group, the other students are engaged in highly structured and sequenced activities, listed on the ''Assignment Record Form'' which must be initialed by a teammate (see Table 1).

Silent Reading: Students read to a designated point in a story and stop (designed to encourage students to make predictions about what might happen).

Partner Reading: Students read orally with the partner on their team who is in the same reading group/reader the same section they have just completed reading silently.

Treasure Hunt Worksheets: The worksheets emphasize the main points of the story and ask students to predict what will happen next. (Section 1 of the worksheets are completed after students have read half the story and ask them to make predictions about the second half; Section 2 is completed when the story is finished.) Students discuss their answers before writing them down.

Word Meaning Practice: Students learn to write ''meaningful'' sentences with specified vocabulary words from the story.

"Words Out Loud" Practice: Students practice reading the list of vocabulary words out loud with their partner.

Reading Comprehension Direct Instruction: Exercises designed to introduce and reinforce a spiral of reading comprehension skills that can transfer from story to story.

Story-Related Writing: Ideal for word processing, these activities ask students to write a brief composition which ties in with the story (e.g., ''Have you ever hurt someone's feelings, like the character did in this story? Write a paragraph or two explaining what you said and how you tried to make up for it.''). Students are instructed to talk about their ideas before they write them down and then read their paragraph to their partner and edit the work, including any suggestions from the partner.

Story Retell: Students take turns answering questions about the story they have just read and check each other.

Testing: Students are tested individually in three ways:

The Story Test, in which they answer questions about the story; Words Out Loud Test, in which they read the word list to the teacher; and the Word Meaning Test, in which they write meaningful sentences for the selected vocabulary words in the story. Students also take a test on the targeted Reading Comprehension skill. Students earn points toward a team score for each of the testing activities. They can also earn points by demonstrating targeted social skills that help the group work together effectively. Each team works toward a criterion score, rather than competing with other teams. All teams that reach their criterion earn recognition or small rewards such as special activities or certificates. Figure 1 presents a sample Team Score Sheet.

Table 1
ASSIGNMENT RECORD FORM

Name:_____   Date:_____

Story Name: _____

Team Practice and Mastery

	Initials	
Silent Reading Section I	____	
Partner Reading Section I	____	DAY 1
Treasure Hunt Section I	____	
Spelling Pretest	____	
Other _____	____	
Silent Reading Completed	____	
Partner Reading Completed	____	
Treasure Hunt Completed	____	
Word Meaning Pretest	____	DAY 2
Words Out Loud Pretest	____	
Story Retell Pretest	____	
Other _____	____	
Spelling Mastery	____	
COMPLETE TESTS		
—Story Test		
—Word Meaning Test		DAY 3
—Words Out Loud Test		
Other _____	____	
Reading Comprehension Practice	____	
READING COMPREHENSION TEST		
Story Related Writing Completed	____	DAY 4
Other _____	____	
SPELLING TEST		
Other _____	____	DAY 5

COOPERATIVE WRITING

Although "story-related writing" is included in the reading process described above, CIRC also includes a similar sequenced and structured program for the writing process. In a reading/language arts block, students can remain in the same heterogeneous teams. The process approach to writing is followed.

- The teacher provides a stimulus for writing such as a piece of literature (e.g., *Wilfrid Gordon McDonald Partridge* by Mem Fox).

- Large group discussion, culminating in the specific writing assignment (write about a favorite memory).

- Students brainstorm and "mind map" (cluster) their responses to the writing assignment in a large group and in teams.

- Students do individual mind maps and share them with a teammate.

- Students begin their first draft, using a word processor if possible, and print out their draft double-spaced to make it easy to mark revisions.

- Students read their first draft aloud to a different teammate and get structured feedback (What did you hear? What did you like? What could the writer do to make this an even better story?).

- Students return to the word processor to make revisions. When their second draft is complete, they print it out.

- Students take turns sitting in the "Author's Chair" in front of their whole team (or class). The team gives feedback as outlined above, and the author notes three things to change or improve.

- Students also receive direct instruction on language mechanics in exercises similar to the reading comprehension activities described above. These exercises may focus on skills such as sentence combining or using descriptive words, which tie in with current writing assignments.

- Students earn points for their team with their compositions as seen in Figure 1.

- Students process how well each team member helped each other with writing.

- Publication.

Initial field studies of CIRC have provided encouraging data on its effects on reading comprehension, writing skills, and oral reading proficiency. Results are particularly impressive for low-achieving students (Stevens, Madden, Slavin, & Farnish, 1987). Efforts are currently underway to develop literature-based materials for the reading portion of CIRC, as well as to continue to evaluate its effectiveness in different school settings.

Putting these three powerful components—cooperative learning, research-based teaching practices in reading and writing, and word processing—together offers teachers new hope for super-charging their students' achievement and motivation.

References

Stevens, R., Madden, N., Slavin, R., & Farnish, A. (1987). Cooperative integrated reading and composition: Two field experiments. *Reading Research Quarterly, XXII*(4), 433-454.

Mary Male, PhD, Division of Special Education, Department of Education, San Jose State University, San Jose, CA 95193.

For more information, contact Dr. Robert Slavin, CREMS, 3505 N. Charles, Baltimore, MD 21218.

TEAM SCORE SHEET

Team_____   Week of _____

Team Members	Story Test	Word Meaning	Words Out Loud	Spelling	Reading Comp.	Lang. Skills	Writing Assign.	Teamwork Points	Book Report 1	Book Report 2	Signature	AVERAGE

Super Team: 95+ points
Great Team: 90-94 points
Good Team: 80-89 points

Team Total _____

TEAM SCORE _____

Figure 1. Team Score Sheet

Poetry: Reinventing the Past, Rehearsing the Future

Linda M. Christensen

Poetry needs to dust its knees and hurry to the nearest basketball court to shoot a little hoop, grab one of its rusty medals and use it for a hopscotch marker, jump rope on a crowded asphalt playground, scrawl graffiti on bathroom walls, get off the shelf and into the lives of kids.

Poetry is held too sacred, revered a bit too much to be useful. Someone lied to us a long time ago when they whispered, ''Kids hate poetry.'' Kids might hate the poetry that rustles in old pages and asks them to bow and be quiet when they come into the room. They might hate reading poetry unlocked only by the teacher's key and writing poetry that's delivered up like the *New York Times* crossword puzzle, but give them poetry that presses its ear against the heartbeat of humanity and they're in love.

Poetry allows students to crawl inside their own lives as well as the lives of literary and historical characters where they can empathize with the Arawaks' anger and despair when Columbus ''discovered'' America, the determination of the striking miners in Pittston, or the triumph of Celie at the dinner scene in Alice Walker's *The Color Purple*. Through poetry kids can give voices to people, including themselves, who usually don't find their way into their classrooms or textbooks.

Poetry and Literature: Personalizing the Connections

Literature does more than provide an account of the lives of its characters—it offers students a chance to peer into the society of a given time period. Earlier in my teaching career, I bypassed opportunities to read this social history and concentrated instead on the elements of fiction. I did this in good faith because I wanted to develop my students' skills and their love of literature, so they would be lifelong readers. But I didn't prepare them to ''read'' the real world, to decipher the texts that bombard them daily. Now, I see reading as a chance not only to rediscover the past, but to teach students to ''read'' the untold stories in the daily news as well. In literature, as in history, many voices have been silenced—women's, African Americans', Hispanic Americans', Native Americans', Asian Americans'. Poetry and other kinds of writing that let students respond on an emotional level to society can be a vehicle to excavate these untold lives.

History is the tale of the winners. Poetry helps students hear the rest of the story.

Because poetry melts students' understanding into a ''raw core of feeling'' as Sonia, a senior in my Contemporary Literature and Society class, says, it also develops children's ability to empathize with others. In Portland, Oregon, the city where I live and teach, violent, racially motivated crimes have become part of the social landscape. I attribute this, in part, to the view of people of color as ''other,'' to the inability of too many folks to ''walk in another's shoes.'' This is, of course, a very partial explanation for a complex problem, but when the literature that we read—*Huckleberry Finn, Gone With the Wind,* and other ''classics''—ignores or stereotypes women and people of color, our students begin to develop one-dimensional portraits of ''others'' in our society. The poetry students write from the point of view of literary characters can be an entry into the concerns of people who come from different cultural or socioeconomic backgrounds.

After reading *The Color Purple,* for example, students in Literature and American History, a class I co-teach with social studies teacher Bill Bigelow, choose one of the characters and write a poem from that character's point of view. (We use Anne Sexton's ''Love Song'' (1981) as a prompt; it begins, ''I was/ the girl of the chain letter,/ the girl full of talk of coffins and keyholes. . . .'') Don writes from Celie's voice:

I am Celie.
I am the cold hard black floor
everyone walked on.

People have stained me and laughed
but I stayed solid under them
and did not squeak.

I am the floor now
but once you go downstairs
I become the ceiling.

After he reads his poem, the class discusses it. *His* poem opens the analysis of Celie. Instead of simply imposing our questions on the class, Bill and I raise our concerns in the context of the students' insights. How is Celie like the floor? Why is she stained? What does that mean? What events caused that? In what ways did she stay solid? How does Don's vision change at the end? Why? What brought about the change? The ending is hopeful—not only about Celie, but about life. It suggests that people can change. What circumstances are necessary for change to occur? Don's metaphor gives us a shorthand to discuss Celie.

Many of the young men in class choose to write with women's voices. Through these writings they begin to explore the lack of power these women, especially Celie and Squeak, feel in the beginning of the novel. They can hook into their own feelings of fear and helplessness and, we hope, develop a greater understanding of contemporary women's issues.

Many female students explore Celie's character through a list of details either from her life or from language "stolen" from Alice Walker. Stephanie remembers Celie as the "'sure is ugly' child/ who was given away/ with a cow" and "put under a man." Ednie says she was "Sold to marriage/ Sold to life/ Sold to love/ Sold like agates to children/ Sold to a man." Gina writes that she was "unsightly trash/ tossed to the side of the room. . . . The girl whose life held no worth."

The language these young women use is threaded with the words of commerce—"given," "sold," "worth"—which provides an opening for Bill and me to lead the class in a discussion of women as commodities. In this transaction women without beauty are "trash" who must be "given away." The poems become a lens through which we can focus on how women are valued, not only in the *Color Purple* but in our society. Sometimes the poems are masks for the students' questions about their own worth or value as women.

While most students write from Celie's, Harpo's, Sofia's, or Shug's lives, a few, like Omar, take on the Olinka people.

Olinka

The Olinka people were a West African tribe in Alice Walker's novel, *The Color Purple*. The Olinka, like indigenous tribes throughout the world, were pushed off their land for the sake of profit.

I was the roofleaf plant you killed, replaced with rubber.

I was the village you plowed over, replaced with asphalt.
I was the quiet you destroyed, replaced with bulldozers.
I was the children playing in the sun, chased away, replaced with apathetic workers.
I was the land stolen, for which you gave nothing, replaced with nothing.
I was the Olinka people.

Omar makes links with our Native American unit earlier in the year. When we ask students to write these poems, we say, "Find your passion. Twist and manipulate the assignment until you can find something you care about." Assignments written only for the teacher are bland and uninspiring. Omar takes us at our word. He is less interested in the dynamics between the men and women in the novel than he is in the fate of the Olinka. During class discussion, a poem like Omar's allows us to recall the Cherokee Trail of Tears and to link the colonial justifications of the British in Africa with Andrew Jackson's similarly racist attitudes toward Native Americans. But it also offers an opportunity to think whose story is untold when we read about new developments. Whose land was taken?

The discussions that follow student poetry are simply more engaging than those in which Bill and I provide all the questions and answers. What struck them, what moved them in the novel is focused and concentrated into a poem—the heart of their interaction with the book. Class discussion looks into this heart and reads it. Students are more involved because they had a hand in shaping the content of the discussion.

Not every aspect of the novel will be revealed in the poetry, perhaps not every character will be written about. But Bill and I can weave in important points that escape the students' lines and discuss missing characters in the context of those who are present. Mr. _____, for example, is rarely if ever written about. This omission alone gives us an opportunity to raise a number of questions.

The poem can serve as a rough draft, or an outline, for an essay. Once they've found their "passion," students can translate it into another form. They must learn to extend their metaphors, to articulate the flash of insights they found in their poems. Don can use his floor/ceiling metaphor as a framework to describe Celie's change. Ednie and Stephanie can write about the objectification of women. Omar can use his poem as a trajectory to pursue a comparison of the treatment of the Olinka and Native American tribes. "The essay grows out of the poem," Sonia says.

Getting students to write poetry is obviously not enough, nor is it the only strategy we use to discuss the novels, stories, and autobiographies read in class. But it is a valuable method that can help students develop empathy for the "others" in our society whose stories don't find their way into the novels stored in our textbook rooms, and in the process, students discover poetry as a tool of communication.

Poetry in History: Blowing Life into the Dry Skeleton of Facts

History is the tale of the winners. Poetry helps students hear the rest of the story. What's untold? Students reinvent history by writing through a real or imagined character from the past. They live, at least momentarily, the lives of the people they create and, by doing so, come to a greater understanding of the struggles those people were engaged in. Instead of viewing history as a dry skeleton of facts to be memorized, students become aware that those "facts" were the choices made by or imposed on people at the time. Those "facts" were the results of struggles won or lost by those whose lives were affected by the outcomes. This is important. When we, students or teachers, see history as inevitable, we become passive and accept the status quo. By giving voice to historical characters, students not only see the possibility of the past being different, but they also learn to see the future as unwritten, a field of possibilities, the outcome dependent, in part, on *their* actions.

When I talked with students about why poetry should be used in history, Mira, a student in the Literature and American History class, said, "Poetry made history come to life. When we wrote after *Hearts and Minds,* I was there. I was a soldier. I identified with what was going on. I felt their feelings. I got more involved. This wasn't just history. This was life. Poetry helped me examine why the war happened because I got inside the people who witnessed it."

Rachel "witnesses" the war from the point of view of a pilot from the documentary film *Hearts and Minds* (1985) during a unit on Vietnam. Rachel uses the poem to solve a puzzle. How can men produce the bloodshed she's witnessed in the film? How can they talk about people as targets? How can they become immune to the suffering their planes leave behind? In her poem "I Flew the Plane," she tries to understand the emotional distance the pilot creates between himself and his victims: People become machines—"metal heads" and "machine arms." If the pilot denies their humanity, then he can't feel the pain of the deaths he delivers. He is the "technician" who "only flew the plane." War becomes a video game, and he's a champion player.

Flying high over
the patchquilt
of an unknown country
leaving exploding shells
behind me,

I never saw their blood.
I never heard their screams.
I never felt their pain.

Flying low over
burning huts
torched by green men
with metal heads
and machine arms,
leaving corpses
in bomb craters
that I,
the technician,
created.

I never saw their blood.
I never heard their screams.
I never felt their pain.

I only flew the plane.

Instead of becoming the pilot, Keely writes to the pilot—telling him what he missed after he dropped the bombs.

. . . You didn't smell the flesh,
Caught in a barbed wire,
Torn like an old rag,
Soft brown skin heated to black . . .
You didn't taste the blood,
Mixed with dirt and rice,
Staining the walls of the huts
Splashed on the faces of young
  girls. . . .

By giving voice to historical characters, students not only see the possibility of the past being different, but they also learn to see the future as unwritten, a field of possibilities, the outcome dependent, in part, on *their* actions.

Keely sees the devastation the soldier left behind, but she wants to forgive him. She feels the enormity of his guilt and understands how hard these deaths would be to live with. She ends her poem

You must have missed those things.
If you hadn't you would have turned
  back,
Picking up every shell you dropped,
And putting a bandage on every
  scrape you caused.

Margo's confusion over the war pours into the present as she tries to understand a co-worker who is a veteran.

If I touched what was left
of your fingers
would they split open
and gush images to me?

Would I see the dead
of Vietnam—
thanks to you?

Would I see the heroin and
alcohol you found
your comfort in?

If I watched long enough
would I see what I
didn't know before—
A gentle man
always kind,
instead of this rough exterior
always pushing me away?

Louie, I don't want you
to be a murderer
because I haven't known
you long enough to
let that slide.

Margo uses her poem to explore questions she has about Louie. Before the war, was he a "gentle man/ always kind,/ instead of this rough exterior/ always pushing me away"? Was the heroin and alcohol an escape from the deeds he committed in Vietnam? She wants to know more, but she's afraid to learn too much because she's not sure she could "let [murder] slide."

The poems are not a substitute for information. Students need to investigate why the war happened. The emotional intensity students invest in these poems would be impossible without that knowledge. In addition to reading numerous first person accounts and historical documents chronicling the involvement of France and the United States, they participate in a role play Bigelow (1988) created, taking the parts of Viet Minh cadre and French government officials. They study timelines and compare different interpretations of French and U.S. involvement in Vietnam; they read Bobbie Ann Mason's *In Country* (1985), selected poems from Yusef Komunyakaa's *Dien Cai Dau* (1988) and Vietnamese poetry from the anthology *Of Quiet Courage* (Chagnon & Luce, 1974). Perhaps the most difficult and ultimately the most powerful assignment asks them to interview veterans. Students' anger and angst are fueled with knowledge.

After Rachel, Keely, Margo, and classmates read their poems, we discuss reasons for the anger, the guilt, the withdrawal, the "rough exterior" of the soldiers. The poems become prompts to explore the lives we invent. Why did soldiers consistently dehumanize the enemy? What happened to the veterans after they returned home? Margo is reluctant to let Louie "slide." Was this a common reaction when soldiers came back from the war? How did these men and women learn to live normal lives again, after their experiences?

Still, poetry is not social analysis. Students' poems won't help them figure out why Truman and Eisenhower sided with the French against the Viet Minh or why the United States created South Vietnam after the 1954 Geneva Accords and then backed one petty tyrant after another. However, the poetry will draw students into the pathos of Vietnam by depicting the human consequences of those decisions. And by humanizing the war, students may care enough to join our investigation into its causes.

Or they may not. What makes this experience intense and good also raises problems. Through their poems students live with their characters. They are emotionally attached to the soldiers or the peasants they create. They can be reluctant to leave the arena of feelings and move into the world of analysis. That's the seduction of poetry. When Bill and I begin edging towards the kinds of questions I've listed above, students may groan, "Can't we just write? Do we have to talk about it?" The poetry works. Sometimes too well.

Personal Poetry: Wrestling with Your Life
Just as poetry helps students imagine the pain and struggles of the Vietnamese and the characters in *The Color Purple,* it can also provide an opening for us, students and teachers, to investigate our own lives. Through the writing and sharing of poetry, we can probe our wounds and try to discover their roots, we can share our joy and

learn, like the characters in history and literature, that we don't have to suffer or struggle or laugh alone. With luck, we can develop an interest in analyzing our own lives: What gives us fulfillment? What are our common problems—divorce, loneliness, gangs, loss, drug and alcohol abuse, shame—and how can we confront them? How can we help each other confront them?

Mira says, "Poetry helped me get rid of pain. It got things out—helped me deal with my problems. My poem, 'Her Wedding Day,' where I talk about my mother getting remarried, I've been dealing with since I was five. I worked through that pain when I

Through the writing and sharing of their lives, students practice for the future. Students' histories are the texts we study. These "texts" together with the methodology all help rehearse students to become more active and critical participants in their world.

---

wrote the piece. Learning to write poetry is not about technique, it's about wrestling with your life." In class, we wrestle together—and try to build a collective text from the stories of our lives that both heals and illuminates.

Read-arounds are filled with students coming to terms with their parents' divorces. In the poem, "Saying Goodbye," Katy addresses her father:

My mama washed
your clothes for twenty-one
years and now you want
me

to show you how to operate
that washing machine hidden behind
the basement stairs   show you
as if her hands weren't good
enough   her elbow grease
not greasy enough   her sweat
not clean enough   show you
as if forty-eight isn't too old
to start

My mama washed your clothes
for twenty-one years
and now you fold your own or bribe
your good son Matt with a trip
to Powell's or flowers for his Rachel
as if a gray beard signaled you
to learn to take care
of yourself as if you would do
   without
her   as if you meant to say goodbye
with a spin cycle and a box full
of powdered detergent

Katy's voice crackles with anger. Her father learning to operate the washing machine, a duty her mother performed for twenty-one years, provokes Katy's wrath. This is not about unlearning sex roles; this is about leaving. When Katy shares, others will add their stories. "Yeah, when my dad left . . ." or "Catch this, the dude. . . ." The pain students nurture privately is shared. They learn they are not alone. The characters differ. The leaving differs. The pain remains common ground.

The dance of acceptance and rejection is repeated throughout school. Students practice feeling okay about themselves without buying designer jeans. They discover how it feels to fit under someone's shoulder, to get a part in a school play and to lose a best friend on the same day. Too often students learn to numb themselves with food, drugs, alcohol, new tennis shoes, or success. Too often schools don't teach them how to handle the explosive feelings that come with adolescence. By writing and sharing the "raw core of feelings" that are creating havoc in their lives, they can practice a more effective way of handling their emotions. They discover the comfort of finding an accepting group who listens sympathetically and often identifies with their troubles. They learn they are not alone. While I don't believe that writing poetry will stop drug and alcohol abuse, I do think that we need to teach students effective ways of dealing with their volcanic emotions. Poetry is an effective beginning.

Poetry also provides an opportunity to explore the social origins of some of the problems students face individually. In the following poem, "I Need to Belong," Bobby adopts the persona of a gang member.

Yeah, I sell drugs
and I know it's wrong.
Yeah, I'm a gang member,
but I need to belong.
I had little of mother
and of father I had none,
so my only family
is my gang and my gun.
Why work at Burger King
or Sea Galley
when selling drugs,
I can make five times that salary?
See, I want what you got
money, clothes, a fancy car
even if that means
I have to go behind bars.
My life is harsh
and my heart is cold,
but to survive this game I've got to
   be bold.
I know
I could die any day.
But I ain't afraid of death anyway.
'Cause the way I see it
I died a long time ago.

Through Bobby's poem, we can discuss why young people turn to the Crips or Bloods. Instead of wringing our hands, we begin to build a social analysis of the conditions that push kids into gangs. Bobby's poem provides evidence for our talk: Why work at Sea Galley? What other options do students have? Who is working in their neighborhood? Who has money? Who drives fancy cars and wears the latest brand of tennis shoes? Who doesn't? How is a person's value measured in our society?

When students begin to take measure of the part society plays in their problems, they can use that knowledge to explore their problems more thoroughly instead of immediately blaming themselves. For example, young women who feel the necessity of dieting, binging and purging, or not eating can be exposed to the role that advertising plays in their self-esteem.

School life is often alienating. Students sit in rows, and they're told not to talk to the people around them. In the five minutes between classes, they don't have time to be "real" or to find out much about each other. When the bell rings, students are usually asked to put their lives aside and get to work. Writing and sharing their own lives begins to confront this alienation. Their interactions with each other are part of the content of this course, their feelings legitimated. Nicole, a senior, says, "When I hear Mira or Rachel read, I think, 'Hey, they have the same feelings I do. Even though they were brought up differently, even though they're Asian and White and I'm Black, we've experienced some of the same things. They teach me about humanity.'"

And through the writing and sharing of their lives, students practice for the future. Students' histories are the texts we study. These "texts," together with the methodology—sitting in a circle; student *and* teachers sharing; students calling on and questioning each other; kids discovering they can learn from each other, from their own histories as well as from the teacher; teenagers calling sacred social cows into question, asking 'So what can we do about it?'—all help rehearse students to become more active and critical participants in their world. They learn to expect more—a voice in shaping a discussion and the curriculum, a dialogue about their grades, an opportunity to read and study about people like themselves, purposeful work in a community of learners.

They begin to sense that they don't have to accept life as it presents itself. Some learn to object to the inequities they find in school—and in the world. Katy, for example, attended a well-known and distinguished private college after she graduated from Jefferson. She continually challenged her professors: Where were the women writers? Where were the African American writers? The Asian American writers? Where were the assignments linking their lives to the course, to contemporary world problems? Finally, disgusted with the school's lack of responsiveness, she left that college. Last I heard, she was organizing a student boycott of multiple-choice exams in a literature class on her new campus.

Of course, it oversimplifies the complex weaving of literature, history, social analysis, writing, and classroom discourse to state that poetry alone allows Katy and her peers to resist the society they find themselves in. But poetry is one of the strands in the weaving—an effective one.

Linda M. Christensen, Jefferson High School, Portland, OR.

References

Bigelow, W. (1988). Role-playing the origins of US involvement. *Social Education,* 52(1), 55-57.

Chagnon, J., & Luce, D. (Eds.). (1974). *Of Quiet Courage.* Washington, DC: Indochina Mobile Education Project.

Hearts and Minds. (1985). Dir. Peter Davis. Embassy.

Komunyakaa, Y. (1988). *Dien Cai Dau.* Hanover, NH: Wesleyan University Press.

Mason, B.A. (1985). *In Country.* New York: Harper.

Sexton, A. (1981). Love song. *The complete poems.* Boston: Houghton, pp. 115-116.

Reprinted with permission from *English Journal,* April 1991.

Fairy Tales—A Reading/Writing Workshop

Harriet Bender

After attending the Literature Institute at The University of California at Santa Barbara during the summer of 1988, I began to rethink the reading and writing curriculum in my fifth/sixth grade classroom. Donald Graves, Nancie Atwell, Lucy Calkins, and Jane Hansen provided initial inspiration. Now all I needed was a curriculum topic that would allow me to totally integrate reading and writing. I selected the literature genre of fairy tales.

Introduction

I brought into my classroom many different fairy tales, both anthologies and single book stories, written at varying degrees of difficulty. I selected ten well-known ones as core stories and placed them around the classroom. I selected three characters from each story and wrote each character's name on a card. As students entered the room, a card was pinned on the back of each student. The students were not to tell each other the names that were on their backs; instead, they circulated around the classroom asking yes/no questions until all characters were identified. At this point, they removed their cards, pinned them on the front, and began acting out in mime an action that their character might do in the fairy tale.

When all characters had been identified, students found the desk containing their fairy tale. They sat down in groups of three and read the story orally, taking turns as readers. Each group then generated three questions not answered in the story. They came up with questions such as: *How does it feel to dance in a glass slipper? Why did you always wear a red cape with a hood?* These questions were shared with the whole class, after which the groups returned to their group desk and wrote answers to their own questions, an activity that encouraged students to use higher level thinking skills in response to their reading.

Reading Workshop

I read a traditional fairy tale or "fractured " fairy tale to the class each day. We discussed settings, characters, and themes. We took fairy tales to the kindergarten class and read aloud to them.

Students were assigned to select and read 15 fairy tales during the following week, recording in their Fairy Tale Profile Log the title, author, setting, lead (a quote of the beginning line), theme, props (objects important to the story), and two main characters with a list of personality traits.

During the second week students met in groups designated "Setting," "Leads," "Characters," "Themes," and "Props," referring to their individual reading logs to record similarities and repetitions. For example: *How often was "Once upon a time" used as a lead? How often was the main character a princess? How often did the number "3" occur? What kinds of animals were the villains? How often did they encounter the "good triumphs over evil" theme? How many stories expressed morals?* Following this, the whole class discussed what makes a story a fairy tale. Then, students wrote in their individual reading logs an entry demonstrating their understanding of the genre of fairy tales.

Writing Workshop

Writing activities centered around three projects:

1. I read the book *The Jolly Postman* by Janet and Allan Ahlberg to the class. Students immediately asked if they could do a class book of their own fairy tale letters. During the next several days, students created letters to Cinderella, the Three Little Pigs, and many more of their favorite characters. Each was put into a specially created envelope.

2. Many students began writing "fractured" fairy tales of their own. They reversed and exchanged personality traits of the characters, used contemporary settings for old themes, and combined several different plots. These stories were written, illustrated, and often acted out in front of the class, and many were published as individual books.

3. For the final unit project, the class created a Fairy Tale Newspaper, *The Character Chronicle*. Students were divided into five "page" committees: Front page; Local News; Art, Travel, and Entertainment; People Today; and Sports page. In addition, all students could contribute to the Classified Ads page. Students looked at our local newspaper for ideas for their page, created interesting headings, and typed their articles onto the computer.

One student served as editor for each page. The editors met with their committees to brainstorm ideas and plan the page, acted as consultants when needed, and pasted up the finished word-processed articles onto large, poster board "pages." These finished newspaper pages are now displayed in the classroom.

This unit ended many weeks ago, but students continue to read fairy tales, and many continue to write "fractured" fairy tales. Fairy tale characters have appeared in improvised class skits, and an article on Hans Christian Anderson was included in a social studies report on Denmark.

Fairy tales quickly activate a child's imagination. The characters, settings, and themes are readily understood. The students can easily translate and adapt them for their own writing pieces. Fairy tales provide an excellent genre for teaching the elements of literature, as well as a wide variety of examples to explore writers' craft. Too often students are given isolated assignments in language arts. When students are given the opportunity to make connections between what they read and what they write, real learning takes place.

The author thanks Sydney James, Santa Maria School District, for the "ask a question not answered" activity.

Harriet Bender, Monte Vista School, Hope School District, 730 N. Hope Ave., Santa Barbara, CA 93110.

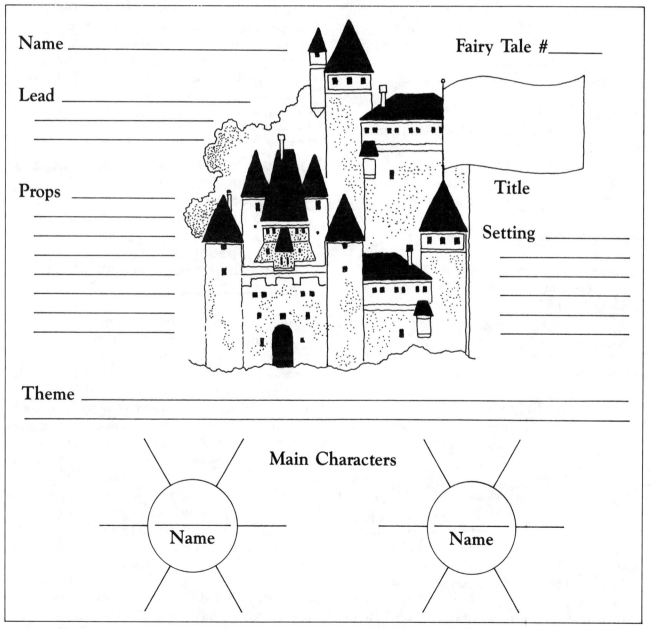

Name _____   Fairy Tale # _____

Lead _____
   _____
   _____

Props _____   Title
   _____
   _____   Setting _____
   _____   _____
   _____   _____
   _____   _____

Theme _____

Main Characters

Name   Name

Creating a Writing Studio

Hugh Platt

Freshman composition classes are unique in the college curriculum. Their primary aim is to teach writing and yet, as far as the development of writing ability is concerned, there is no body of knowledge to be mastered and no concepts to be studied and applied. In order to compensate for this lack of real "matter," we often augment the course content by teaching related subjects such as critical or literary analysis. Sometimes we teach the stylistic analysis of essays and/or short stories, novels, etc. in the hope that if we can bring some of the elements of stylistic grace into the open, students will emulate the likes of E.B. White or Annie Dillard.

We also spend a good deal of time teaching levels of abstraction, essay structure, grammar, and sentence fluency. Some would say that these topics are most directly related to the skill and art of writing, yet perhaps there is a fundamental illusion in believing that studying these topics directly impacts students' ability to write well. It's well documented, for example, that the study of grammar, with all the attendant exercises and tests, has scant effect on improvement in student writing (Hillocks, 1987, p.75). However, we continue to believe that grammar has a place in freshman composition courses, possibly because the topic adds a modicum of esoterica to the course.

With the help of computer technology, we can reorient the typical English 1A (first semester, freshman level) writing course so that more time and effort are focused on the students' own writing.

The Recursive Nature of Writing

Over the past 15 or 20 years, researchers such as Janet Emig (1971) and Linda Flowers (1989) have emphasized the complexity of the writing process. We English teachers now realize that a developmental model of the writing process is misleading—that the stages of writing can't be compartmentalized. Rather, writing is a recursive process (Flowers, 1989, pp. 282-319). When we write our minds go forward and backward, predicting text and reviewing it in the course of writing it. You may hover over the last sentence you wrote, rewrite it once to alter the sentence structure, and then rewrite it again to improve the sense of what you wanted to communicate. You are writing recursively if you make changes as you go or if your mind darts forward and locates a thought it wants to be sure to discuss when the time comes. Then, after the drafting stage (or what some researchers call the translating-into-sentences stage), you may change sentences, words, and paragraphs once again.

Thus, it turns out that there's not a clear point at which to say, "Now it's time to revise." There are implications for our students in this realization. We know how loathe students are to revise their writing. And they may be even more reluctant to alter their first drafts when the writing has been composed on a computer than when it has been written in cursive. There is something so final, so "official" about that good-

---

One way to make revising more focused and productive in a composition classroom with computers available is to use the model of a studio art class or newsroom. This implies a reorganization of our classroom and especially the way the space is used.

---

looking type that it creates a kind of halo effect. On the other hand, computers abet the recursive aspect of writing because they make it relatively easy to effect changes in one's text. And then, once one sees the changes wrought by the process of deleting, moving, or replacing a word, sentence, or paragraph, one can reflect on the text and make additional changes to it. Stephen Bernhardt's (1989) study at Southern Illinois University offers fairly conclusive proof that students do more revising and that their papers are ". . . substantially improved. . . ." (p. 108) when they do their composing and revising on a computer.

Of course, revising is time-consuming (too time-consuming, some might say, to warrant using class time), and one might wonder if writing and revising aren't best consigned to the realm of homework. It's true that a good deal of dead time is likely to be created while students struggle to find the right words or stare off into space, trying to hear a sentence in their heads before commiting it to text. How can we tolerate a class full of students who aren't being *noticeably* productive? At least when we give a lecture about Annie Dillard's ''Lenses,'' we can feel as though *we're* being productive.

Nevertheless, isn't the point of the class to help students write better? The voice in the student's head, rehearsing the sound of a sentence, may be a good deal more helpful than my voice in his or her ear talking *about* Annie Dillard's use of parallelism.

The Writing Class as Studio

One way to make revising more focused and productive in a composition classroom with computers available is to use the model of a studio art class or, as Boiarsky (1990, p. 49) suggests in her article, a newsroom. This implies a reorganization of our classroom and especially the way the space in our classroom is used. It involves positioning computer workstations so that there is ample space on either side of the computer for handwriting. This arrangement not only allows room for students to work on revising hard copies of their writing but also allows space for students to view each others' work on a monitor.

In a traditional classroom, which Barker and Kemp (1990) call the proscenium classroom, because the furniture and lighting are arranged so that students naturally concentrate their attention on the front area (pp. 9-10), the teacher accrues a good deal of authority. The kind of reorganization of space mentioned above necessarily shifts the focus of attention away from the front of the classroom.

The teacher's role in the computer studio/class can be compared with that of a coach. The teacher circulates among the students, reads their texts, listens in on their discussions, makes suggestions, etc. If the instructor comes across some felicitous writing, he or she can show it to the whole class using a liquid crystal display (LCD) or a networked display. An LCD, together with a standard overhead projector, projects text from a monitor screen onto a standard wall mounted screen for everyone to see. If the computers are interconnected with each other and with a file server, the model piece of writing can appear on each student's screen.

Critiquing

The teacher/coach can write along with the class and can take part in the pair or group discussions about on-screen text or about text in hard copy form. These critiques produce one of the most valuable results of redesigning the class, especially when the critiquers are students. If a student critic appraises another student's text while it's on the screen, several things happen: The writer will develop a strong sense of audience; he or she can immediately try out some of the critiquer's suggestions by inserting or deleting text; and the collaborators can, if the word processor has split screen capability, look at two versions of a sentence, for example, and discuss which is more effective. The students' own texts now become the ''matter'' of the course.

Peer Response

Because the students' writing is central to the course, it's important that students be taught how to respond to the writing of their peers. Each student needs to learn and practice asking questions as if he or she were a news editor helping a cub reporter. Cyganowski (1990, pp. 78-79) presents the following list of thoughtful questions designed to elicit substantial reactions from a critiquer:

1. What are you asking me to understand? —think? —do? —be? —buy?
2. Who? What? Where? When? Why? How?
3. Is this supposed to be good or bad? Do you think this is important? —most important? Is this the only reason? Is this the best reason? Can you tell me how this connects?
4. Specific responses such as: *How'd he do that?* [request for causality] *Not me.* [objection to overgeneralization] *Apples and apples.* [objection to the same level of specificity or to repetition] *This could be anything.* [objection to vagueness, lack of concrete detail]
5. Assuming personas: *Say it was a biology teacher reading this. Say it was my Aunt Helen reading this.*
6. *What I hear is. . . . What I see is. . . . Do you mean. . . ?*

Rather than asking peer critiquers if a paragraph is coherent or has an effective thesis statement, these questions ask peer readers to retell the writing in their own words or to tell how the text makes them feel or what the piece of writing is trying to say. As a way of making the writer conscious of the rhetorical requirements of different audiences, some questions prompt the writers/readers to experiment with different styles of writing given different audiences. In light of this latter exercise, the advantage of a computer is evident.

There are other advantages. One is that writers can make hard copies of their texts at the end of a class session and work on revising before the next session.

But we should keep a simple prerequisite in mind: All critiquing is likely to work best if the collaborators are grouped somehow. Learning style diagnostic tests, for example, could be used to determine which students would work well together.

The Teacher's Role in the Revision Process

Putting a bunch of computers in a room and providing direct instruction in peer response editing isn't enough to make effective revising happen. According to Bernhardt (1989, p. 112), one of the most important factors is teacher enthusiasm. A committed, interested teacher can challenge a class by providing both stimulus and motivation and by giving much of the responsibility for meaningful critiquing to the students. Such enthusiasm will enable the class to use the computers to optimum effect.

Some consequences of the program as described thus far should be noted. One is that students may have to work at their own pace, which means that not all students will be turning in all the assignments at the same time. But when a paper is finally finished, it will have gone through scrutiny that may well be more meaningful to the student than the teacher's comments. I'm not saying that a teacher's reading of, and commenting on, a student's rough draft is meaningless, but we know in our heart of hearts that students are likely either to make the recommended changes in a very perfunctory, literal way or disregard the recommendations altogether.

Part of the problem lies in our expectations. If I recommend that a student reorient his or her paper so that there is a closer connection between the thesis and the discussion of various points in the body of the essay, my picture of what the realigned essay will look like is totally different from the student's. Furthermore, if I continue to suggest how the rewrite might be approached and give examples for the sake of clarification, in many cases those examples will show up verbatim in the rewrite. My point is that teachers' comments don't have the desired effect. A peer's comments about the clarity and coherence of a piece of writing are much more likely to be constructive and to be taken to heart by the writer.

Because a small critiquing group can quickly become a "what did you do last weekend?" group, it's very important that students be given all the help and encouragement they can to become absorbed in their own writing. We can create ways to help students see their writing as something that they can be ana-

lytical about and that is part of them, part of their lives. As things stand now, students too often feel alienated from their writing. Making students' own writing the subject of the course is one way of honoring their ideas and engaging them with the efficacy of their own words. In this way one of the drawbacks of electronic writing—the lack of immediacy compared with handwritten text (Haas, 1989, p. 26)—may be counteracted.

The students' own texts now become the "matter" of the course. Because of this, it's important that students be taught how to respond to the writing of their peers.

The fewer barriers there are to students getting their writing into the computer and up on the monitor screen, the better. The simpler the word processing program, the better. Once the students learn how to use the word processor, they can do a practical writing assignment such as the one Boiarsky (1990, p. 63) suggests to help students learn the word processing program, get them started writing, and provide some ice-breaking experiences with small group work. The assignment goes like this: Each small group chooses a word processing function, such as the Delete function, to explain. Each group explains in a written composition how to enact the function. The directions may be compiled into a class handbook.

Drawbacks

Lest I paint too rosy a picture of technology in the service of learning and the teaching of writing, there are limitations of which you should be aware if you intend to put a writing studio idea to work in your classroom.

In recent articles, both Theismeyer (1989) and Gerard (1989) attest to the shortcomings of programs that analyze texts. They say, among other things, that text analyzers don't locate the important kinds of errors that occur in freshman writing. Not only that, the names of the categories of errors are drawn from the lexicon of traditional grammar; these categories are, as I'm sure you know, baffling to students. Such a program is likely to put a teacher back into the role of explaining a fine point of grammar such as parallelism, the knowledge of which has little to do with writing improvement. For the time being, then, text analyzers don't seem to have much value in the writing studio. However, the Search function, which most word processors have, can be used to ferret out cliches, unwanted redundancies, possible reference problems, and a host of other unclear uses of the language.

Some of us might wonder if a writer's inexperience with a keyboard might be an impediment to an effective writing studio. Many English teachers I've talked with testify that even one-finger typists can handle composing on a computer. For those students who feel at a disadvantage there are some easy keyboarding programs that can be put to use.

Aside from these minor obstacles, it's not difficult to transform a computer writing class into a writing studio. If you have the means and the desire to create the kind of writing studio described here, you'll find that computers offer a way to put the spotlight on student writing and help students stay focused on their own texts.

_____

Hugh Platt, Language Arts Department, Cuesta College, San Luis Obispo, CA.

References

Barker, T. T., & Kemp, F. O. (1990). Network theory: A postmodern pedagogy for the writing classroom. In C. Handa (Ed.), *Computers and community* (pp. 1-27). Portsmouth, NH: Boynton/Cook.

Bernhardt, S., et. al. (1989). Teaching college composition with computers. *Written Communication, 6,* 108-125.

Boiarsky, C. (1990). Computers in the classroom: The instruction, the mess, the noise, the writing. In C. Handa (Ed.), *Computers and community* (pp. 47-67). Portsmouth, NH: Boynton/Cook.

Cyganowski, C. K. (1990). The computer classroom and collaborative learning: The impact on student writers. In C. Handa (Ed.), *Computers and community* (pp. 68-99). Portsmouth, NH: Boynton/Cook.

Emig, J. (1971). *The composing processes of twelfth graders.* Urbana, IL: NCTE.

Flowers, L. (1989). Cognition, context, and theory building. *College Composition and Communication, 40,* 282-319.

Gerard, L. (1989). Computers and basic writers: A critical view. In G. Hawisher & C. Selfe (Eds.), *Critical perspectives on computers and composition instruction* (pp. 94-104). New York: Teachers College Press.

Haas, C. (1989). Seeing it on the screen isn't really seeing it: Computer writers' reading problems. In G. Hawisher & C. Selfe (Eds.), *Critical perspectives on computers and composition instruction* (pp. 16-29). New York: Teachers College Press.

Hillocks, G., Jr. (1987, May). Synthesis of research on teaching writing. *Educational Leadership,* 71-82.

Theismeyer, J. (1989). Should we do what we can? In G. Hawisher & C. Selfe (Eds.), *Critical perspectives on computers and composition instruction* (pp. 75-93). New York: Teachers College Press.

_____

Should We Teach Zone Typing
Before Touch Typing?

Jon Madian

The diversity of opinions about when and how to teach keyboarding indicates that no answer or method is fully accepted.

One question recurs: At what grade should students be introduced to touch typing? Current research indicates that grade 4 or higher is a good time, due to hand size and finger dexterity. However, many educators report success teaching touch typing at much earlier levels, even into kindergarten.

I suggest beginning as early as you have students using the keyboard for writing, but don't begin by teaching true touch typing (unless there will be lots of time for learning and practicing, and you feel your students are ready). Instead, use any good keyboarding program and teach "zone typing."

Simply use the first few lessons that teach the homerow. Once students are used to resting their fingers on the homerow, have them reach for other keys with the finger that is closest, or in the "zone." In about three sessions, students of any age begin "zone typing." It seems likely that "zone typing" will lay the proper groundwork for later touch typing.

Another tip: Remember when we taught students how to spell by writing their words B I G in the air to help them make necessary kinesthetic connections? Keyboarding is also largely a kinesthetic skill; since students don't have enough time to practice on the computer anyhow, use a few minutes each day to have them visualize a very large keyboard in the air. Have them exaggerate large motions to properly connect the correct finger with the correct key. This is also a great way to practice spelling words while learning to "zone type."

_____

Jon Madian, Humanities Software, P. O. Box 950, Hood River, OR 97031.

On a Need-to-Know Basis:
Keyboarding Instruction for Elementary Students

William J. Hunter, Gordon Benedict, and Bohdan Bilan

Although a rich variety of computer input devices are available, at present, most of the work that students do on computers requires the use of the keyboard. This is particularly true in the case of language arts applications, where word processing has become an important feature of much instruction in writing. Consequently, there is increasing interest in the question of how to help students become more adept in the use of the keyboard. This question draws forth strong opinions, yet, unfortunately, has attracted scant research attention. This article attempts to summarize the research findings that are available and makes suggestions that may be useful to teachers and administrative decision-makers.

Method of Learning

Current thinking about teaching methodologies in language arts, mathematics, science, and social studies emphasizes the role of the learner in actively *constructing* meaning and developing personal organizations of knowledge. The methods supported by this thinking require the teacher to serve as a guide and an enabler who helps students to explore new areas, gather and interpret information, and express ideas in oral and written form. Consequently, teachers who have been influenced by this thinking tend to doubt the value of traditional keyboarding instruction, which has emphasized precisely the kind of drill and practice that many teachers are seeking to minimize in

their own classrooms. In particular, elementary language arts teachers often argue that simply letting children use the keyboard should be sufficient instruction and that children will acquire speed and accuracy with time. Secondary typing teachers, on the other hand, argue that technique (proper fingering) is essential and must be taught and practiced. Furthermore, they claim (e.g., Britten, 1988; Rauch & Yanke, 1982; Stewart & Jones, 1983) that students who have learned "bad habits" pose particular difficulties when they later take typing courses: ". . . any typewriting instructor who has experienced the challenge of retraining a typist under such conditions will readily admit that the task is difficult if not impossible" (Stewart & Jones, 1983, p. 11). Although this concern has a long history, we were unable to find an empirical study that actually examined the keyboarding achievements of students who entered typing classes with or without "bad habits."

To resolve this dilemma, it is important to recognize that keyboarding is a psychomotor skill and to allow for the possibility that such skills may be learned in a manner different from that which we apply to the acquisition of cognitive information/organization. Specifically, the practice-with-feedback methods of behavioral training generally are acknowledged to be successful in helping individuals to develop more skilled motor performances. Granting this, it seems reasonable to suggest that young children be en-

couraged to explore and use keyboards freely until such time as they begin to learn to use word processors. At that time it is reasonable to expect them to learn such fundamentals as "home row" and proper fingering for the letters of the alphabet. Having acquired these skills, meaningful practice with their own compositions should enable them to continue to develop both speed and accuracy. Since children are unlikely to have a sense of what constitutes reasonable proficiency in the use of a keyboard, it would also be desirable if they were given frequent opportunities to observe adult typists of varying levels of proficiency. This experience should help to motivate the child to set higher personal standards for speed and accuracy.

Age for Starting Instruction

There is limited but fairly consistent research related to this question with respect to children in the upper elementary grades. Although Cowles and Robinson (1983) demonstrated that children as young as five years can learn to use a keyboard correctly, Warwood, Hartman, Hauwiller, and Taylor (1985) question whether children younger than grade 4 are ready to learn this skill. Still, Jackson and Berg (1986) indicate that third grade children can learn to keyboard. Thus, while there is some question about the readiness of children in grades K-3, there is general agreement that by grade 4, children are ready for keyboarding instruction.

This may be a moot point, however, since both Ball (1985) and Warwood et

48

al. (1985) point out that the software used in the early grades generally requires only single keystroke responses. (Teachers who use word processors, databases, and LOGO with young children might well want to take issue with this observation.) Perhaps the most reasonable approach to the question is that taken by Byfield and LaBarre (1985). They suggest that the time to teach keyboarding is just before the introduction of word processing. If we take that stance, then the more important questions become: At what age should we begin to teach word processing? If word processing begins early enough, can we postpone or omit instruction in cursive writing? Although the benefits of writing with a word processor are still open to question (e.g., Hunter et al., 1988), enthusiasts would argue that children should be introduced to word processing as soon as possible. Until better data are available, it might be best to take the position described by Lockard, Abrams, and Many (1987): Introduce word processing when it is appropriate to expect students to write at the length of at least a short paragraph (this will vary with the methods used to teach writing and the individual development of the children). It would then be reasonable to begin keyboarding instruction two or three weeks ahead of the introduction of word processing and to continue to teach keyboarding until established performance criteria have been met.

Performance Criteria

Since the rationale for teaching keyboarding to younger children is to enable them to achieve more in writing than they might otherwise, it would be sensible to develop keyboarding performance standards related to that objective. However, any set of standards also should be sensitive to the norms of children's keyboarding achievement at various ages. Unfortunately, such norms are not yet available. Reported figures range from the observation by Wetzel (1985) of third, fourth, and fifth graders typing at 2.5 words per minute

to Ray's observation (reported in Warwood et al., 1985) of fifth and sixth graders typing at 40 words per minute following one year of daily instruction (one hour per day). On the other hand, Wetzel (1985) reported that even when students were typing from copy as slowly as 7 words per minute, they did not scan the keyboard, did not become frustrated with use of the keyboard, and did not lose their place on either keyboard or paper. This indicates that, despite their speed, the students had begun to master keyboarding technique. In the long run, we can expect that speed (and accuracy) will improve with practice if appropriate technique is being used. To achieve the desired effects on writing, then, we should perhaps focus on individual children's comparative rates with pen and keyboard, rather than seeking normative guidelines. As long as a child is typing at a speed that equals or exceeds his or her own longhand speed, the potential for beneficial use of word processors exists. If, in addition, the child uses correct fingering, we may expect continued improvement over time.

Student Attitudes

To date, there have not been systematic studies of students' attitudes toward the use of keyboards or to instruction in keyboarding. However, researchers and writers in the area have reported informal observations. In general, it can be said that students who learned to use a keyboard for the purpose of word processing do not seem more positive about the process than students who use word processors without having had keyboarding instruction (e.g., Gerlach, 1987; Palmer, Dowd, & James, 1984). However, Wetzel (1985) noted that students who lack keyboarding skills become more frustrated as a result of looking back and forth from notes to keyboard to screen, frequently losing their place in the process. It is perhaps unrealistic to expect students to be immediately enthu-

siastic about instruction that requires disciplined practice and repetition. If we are to find positive attitudes toward keyboarding, it is likely to be among students whose instruction is well behind them and who are now reaping the benefits of easier, more fluid word processing. More evidence on this matter will likely be forthcoming as more and more schools confront the issue of keyboarding instruction for elementary school students.

Other Issues

Any change in educational practice tends to require many practical adjustments to the way things are ordinarily done. In the case of teaching keyboarding to elementary children, one significant practical problem is: Who will teach keyboarding at the elementary level? Naturally, business education teachers argue that they have special expertise in this area (e.g., Headley, 1983; Kisner, 1984), but Williams (1988) reported that elementary teachers who could type required only one day of instruction to be able to successfully teach keyboarding skills to their students. Those without typing skills required three weeks of instruction in order to teach keyboarding to their students. The use of computer-based keyboarding tutorials might serve to reduce this time even further. Given the age-appropriate training and experience of elementary teachers and the fact that they have chosen to work with young students, we believe it preferable to entrust elementary keyboarding instruction to elementary teachers willing to undertake the necessary additional instruction.

Another practical problem is the availability of keyboards with which to teach. Learning to use a keyboard requires a one-to-one person to machine ratio—it cannot be done vicariously. On the other hand, the instructional programs used in the research reported here generally involve 30 to 50 minutes per day for 40 to 60 days. Depending on the school's schedule and size of classes, this means a lab of

15 computers could serve from 7 to 45 keyboarding classes, with most elementary schools falling somewhere between these two extremes. It must be remembered, however, that the purpose of keyboarding instruction is to enable students to benefit from the use of word processors, so it is essential that sufficient hardware be available to also leave time for students' writing activities. Wetzel (1985) summed up the problem of hardware limitations by pointing out that if children's access to time on machines is limited by a shortage of hardware, ". . . there is no time—or need—to teach keyboarding" (p. 17).

Finally, we must also question the assumption behind our interest in teaching keyboarding; that is, that students will ultimately write better as a consequence of their more efficient use of the keyboard. There currently is no research to support this assumption. Gerlach (1987) assessed the quality of fourth graders' writing whether or not they used a keyboard properly. "Good" keyboarders did not write more words nor did they make more or different revisions than their classmates. However, Gerlach was looking for rather immediate effects (8-week keyboarding intervention, 3 months experience with a word processor) and we might more justifiably expect that any benefits of keyboarding instruction would not be seen in measures of the quality of students' writing until they had ample opportunity to apply their skill to many writing assignments. Furthermore, as Daiute (1986) and Macarthur (1988) point out, word processing simply makes revision easier, it does not help the writer to know what needs to be revised or how to go about making revisions. Increased efficiency in entering letters at the keyboard might result in students having more time available for revision, but it will not ensure either that they will, in fact, spend that time in revision or that they will be any more capable of productively revising their work.

Conclusion

It is far too soon to draw conclusions about the benefits of teaching children to use a keyboard, but it is not too soon to conclude that the increased use of word processors as part of writing instruction demands that we take keyboarding seriously. We should expect that today's elementary students will graduate into a world in which the ability to directly manipulate information will be an essential part of many occupations. It is certainly possible that advances in computing technology (voice recognition, handwriting analysis) will make other input options available, but it would be short-sighted of us to fail to provide students with the skills necessary to use keyboards as one way of working with information stored in computers. It would be equally short-sighted for us to pursue this course without gathering the information to address the many unanswered questions raised in this article.

William J. Hunter, Director, Education Technology Unit, 836 Education Tower, The University of Calgary, Calgary, Alberta, CANADA T2N 1N4.

References

Ball, S. (1985, September). *Valuable alternatives to keyboarding in grades K-3.* Austin, TX: Paper presented at the Fall conference on perspectives on the young child and the computer. (ERIC Document Reproduction Service No. ED 264 957)

Britten, R. M. (1988). The effects of instructional keyboarding skills in grade 2. *Educational Technology, 28*(4), 34-37.

Byfield, J. S., & LaBarre, J. (1985). Integrating information processing into keyboarding typewriting. *Business Education Forum, 39*(Apr/May), 53-56.

Cowles, M., & Robinson, M. (1983). *An analysis of young children and learning keyboarding skills.* Nashville: Tennessee State University, Center for Training and Technical Assistance. (ERIC Document Reproduction Service No. ED 275 394)

Daiute, C. (1986). Physical and cognitive factors in revision: Insights from studies with computers. *Research in the Teaching of English, 20*(2), 141-159.

Gerlach, G. J. (1987). *The effect of typing skill on using a word processor for composition.* Washington, DC: Paper presented at the Annual Meeting of the American Educational Research Association, April 20, 1987. (ERIC Document Reproduction Service No. ED 286 465)

Headley, P. L. (1983). Keyboarding instruction in elementary school. *Business Education Forum, 38*(3), 18-19.

Hunter, W. J., Begoray, J., Benedict, G., Bilan, B., Jardine, G., Rilstone, P., & Weisgerber, R. (1988). *Word processing and writing: A critical synthesis.* Alberta: University of Calgary, Education Technology Unit.

Jackson, T. H., & Berg, D. (1986). Elementary keyboarding—Is it important? *The Computing Teacher, 13*(6), 10-11.

Kisner, E. (1984). Keyboarding—a must in tomorrow's world. *The Computing Teacher, 11*(6), 21-22.

Lockard, J., Abrams, P., & Many, W. A. (1987). *Microcomputers for educators.* Boston: Little Brown and Company.

Macarthur, C. (1988). The impact of computers on the writing process. *Exceptional Children, 54*(6), 536-542.

Palmer, A., Dowd, T., & James, K. (1984). Changing teacher and student attitudes through word processing. *The Computing Teacher, 11*(9), 45-47.

Rauch, V. C., & Yanke, P. B. (1982). Keyboarding in kindergarten: Is it elementary? *Business Education Forum, 37*(3), 19-20.

Stewart, J., & Jones, B. W. (1983). Keyboarding instruction: Elementary school options. *Business Education Forum, 37*(7), 11-12.

Warwood, B., Hartman, V., Hauwiller, J., & Taylor, S. (1985). *A research study to determine the effects of early keyboard use upon student development in occupational keyboarding.* Bozeman: Montana State University. (ERIC Document Reproduction Service No. ED 265 367)

Wetzel, K. (1985). Keyboarding skills: Elementary my teacher? *The Computing Teacher, 12*(9), 15-19.

Williams, B. (1988). Preparing teachers to teach keyboarding to elementary students. *Business Education Forum, 42*(Mar), 27-29.

Time to Teach Keyboarding?

Sally Myers and Richard Spindler-Virgin

We must teach keyboarding . . . but when?

Administrators find themselves debating this question along with other curricular demands such as drug education, AIDS education, wellness education, problem solving, thinking skills, process writing, computer instruction—and more. When new topics are included, what will be removed? The East Lyme School District has found an alternative solution, choosing to integrate new objectives in a way that enhances the existing curriculum.

A search of the literature indicated that 10-year-olds have the requisite cognitive and fine motor skills to successfully learn keyboarding. Teaching keyboarding also was consistent with the fourth grade curriculum and process writing instruction emphasized in the East Lyme School District. We believed that students' writing would improve if they used a word processor,

---

"I've been teaching for 17 years and I've never had results like these."

---

a tool that would allow them to get their ideas down faster than they could writing by hand. We also believed that keyboarding would facilitate revision. On the basis of our research and underlying assumptions, we set out to create a keyboarding program that would meet our objectives and would meet with the approval of students, parents, teachers, and administrators.

Teachers chose to allocate 25 minutes of language arts instruction per day for keyboarding for the first six weeks of school. We looked for software programs that would be (a) motivational, (b) language-based, and (c) self-pacing, and selected *Type to Learn* (Sunburst), *Key Words* (Humanities Software), and *Keyboarding Primer* (MECC). Following the six

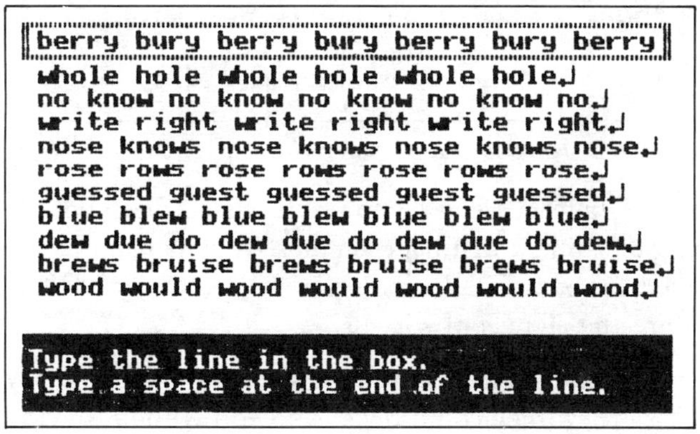

Figure 1. *Type to Learn,* Version 3, from Sunburst Communications.

weeks of instruction, teachers conducted their writing instruction in the computer center during three 40-minute periods weekly for the remaining 24 weeks of school.

Figure 2. *Key Words* from Humanities Software.

An evening presentation was planned for parents in order to explain the merits of the program, the allocation of keyboarding time from the language arts program, the incorporation of keyboarding into the process writing curriculum, and the anticipated effects on writing skills. We showed a videotape of their children in keyboarding classes and answered questions.

```
Now key this line.
Press [RETURN] when done.

  Key:
  Mary read a mystery yesterday.
  Mary read a mystery yesterday.

Your speed is 12 words per minute.

Press the [SPACE BAR] to go on.█
```

Figure 3. *Keyboarding Primer* from MECC.

When teachers began to see the effects of keyboarding on student writing, even those who had approached the project with hesitation became advocates. What were the signals of success?

1. **Students were enthusiastic about writing.** They knew they could revise and edit without having to rewrite the entire paper. Teachers commented that it was wonderful not to hear groans about revision. Parents noted that students were able to "let the juices flow" because they could get their ideas down and not worry about what it looked like while they wrote.

2. **Students spent more time on writing.** They chose to write when they were through with other assignments. They wrote during noon recesses and at home. Some joined the school newspaper staff.

3. **Students learned that a piece of writing is never finished.** Periodically they would retrieve a previously written piece and make revisions.

4. **Students were more fluent in their writing.** An evaluation at the end of eight months indicated that students who had been trained in keyboarding wrote longer narratives. The control group had a 53-word increase in length, while the keyboarding group had a 158-word increase.

5. **Students exhibited a new pride in writing.** Teachers were often greeted by enthusiastic students who had reworked papers, saying with a smile, "I think I'm ready to publish this."

6. **Students improved their holistic writing scores.** The evaluation of student writing when compared with a control group exhibited significant differences. At the end of eight months, the control group demonstrated an overall average gain of 0.4 (holistic scale of 1-8), while the keyboarding group had an increase of 1.3.

As with any curricular change, the proper groundwork must be laid with parents, teachers, and the school board. Administrators must be realistic in their expectations for a keyboarding program. Keyboarding does not by itself teach students to write. When faced with the question of when and how to teach keyboarding, administrators should realize that they have an unusual opportunity to integrate instruction into language arts and may find, as we did, that the return is significant for the time invested. As one fourth grade teacher commented, "I've been teaching fourth grade for 17 years and I've never had results like these."

Sally Myers is Computer Coordinator and Richard Spindler-Virgin is Principal at Niantic Center School, a K-5 elementary school in the East Lyme, CT, School District. Niantic Center School, 7 West Main St., Niantic, CT 06357.

Writing Projects Completed on Computer

- Pen pal letters.
  One class corresponded with another fourth grade class in the district. Another class corresponded with a third grade class in a neighboring city. The third graders from New London were invited to visit our computer center at the end of the year. Our students helped them word process one of their poems.

- Pictures and photographs as prompts for writing. Descriptive writing as well as narratives resulted from these prompts.

- Original story endings for read-aloud stories.

- Reflective writing.
  For example, a journal entry about a special day.

- Favorite pets.
  Students published this project on the hallway bulletin board.

- Sports themes.
  Favorite sports figures, playoff games, etc.

- Interviews and articles for the school newspaper.

- Reports for science and social studies classes.

- Personal experiences.

Teaching Don Murray to Write

Bonnie Sunstein

Follow the music of language where it takes you; allow words to reveal how much you know.
And then, having experienced the gift of reception, pass it on to your students by giving them the time, the environment, the response that will allow them to expect the unexpected.
If you are able to learn how to expect the unexpected on your own pages, you may be able to help your students discover what they have to say—and how to say it.

Donald Murray, *Expecting the Unexpected* (Heinemann, 1989)

When is an assignment honest?

When is it dishonest?

What price does a student pay in honesty with each assignment he or she writes?

What assumptions do we make about students when we design assignments for them?

Imagine 25 teachers sitting in a room at the University of New Hampshire, notebooks open and pens poised, waiting for a conference session called "Teach Don Murray to Write." The conference program promised that we would give him an assignment and watch as he worked on the blackboard. For this session, Don would be the professional writer that he is—a man with a long career that includes a regular column in the *Boston Globe* and a Pulitzer prize in journalism. For this hour he would not act as the teacher of writing teachers that most of us know, the author of writing texts that have guided us and our students for the last 20 years, but rather would give us insights into his own process as he talked about *what* he was doing, *why* he made the choices he made, and ultimately, *how* his process yielded the product he could create in an hour's time. As a colleague, teacher, and writing researcher, I would give a "play-by-play" narration of what was happening as he produced a response to our assignment, leading a dialogue with the other teachers in the room as we scrutinized together the strategies of this professional writer.

Most likely he wouldn't talk much. I'd seen him do these sessions before. He likes to write in public, to show us what he means about teaching writing by writing ourselves. He doesn't talk about writing: he just writes—honestly. When his writing goes well, we share his fluency. When it goes badly, we get stuck with him and watch him as he rethinks and re-drafts. Either way, for me, a session with Don Murray is always a little surprising.

The Writer and the Student

Six months earlier Don had suggested the title for this workshop. Pretty presumptuous, I had thought. What can **we** do to teach **him**? Furthermore, I didn't like the idea of not preparing and not rehearsing the session. In 23 years of teaching, rarely had I set out to "wing it" like this—certainly not at a conference of my peers in the company of my mentor without even a handout.

"Don't worry," he assured me. "If it's a bad assignment, that's even better. I'll write and you'll be the researcher. You explain what's happening pedagogically—look at my writing and describe what I'm doing. Let people observe, let them ask questions. Let it flow, and we'll all learn something. It'll be fun."

The old wooden seats filled with teachers. Don and I introduced each other and, as we had planned, he left the room for a few minutes. I asked for an assignment. "Write about your favorite spot in New England," began one teacher, ". . . and one activity you do there," added another, ". . . and use two layers of time," a third person suggested. Ah, a definite assignment, and a multilayered one at that.

I called him back. He heard the three parts of the assignment and asked us to repeat them. Later, he wrote to me that he was surprised by its complexity. "They probably felt that I was an advanced student and would need the challenge of a complex assignment. It had three parts, but I usually try to meld all the parts of what I am trying to write into a single 'line.'"

An obedient student would not allow him/herself to take the risk of turning rhetorical tricks like playing against the assignment or finding an "edge" the way a clever journalist would do. . . . Better play it safe and write something boring but acceptable.

Even before he began to write, Don's student-self and writer-self clashed. As a student he needed to respond to three parts: "favorite spot," "something he likes doing there," and "two layers of time." As a professional writer, he wanted to make the three parts into one: "My favorite spot in New England is . . . and I like to . . . when. . . ."

He started by writing the assignment on the board. The Writer Don was busy, purposeful, clever. I noticed that he tried, just by rewriting it, to get a sense of the meaning— of what "we" (the teacher) wanted. I wondered aloud how many students would have spent the time to write the assignment (blending its parts) and sense the teacher's meaning before beginning. The Writer Don looked for tension. He flipped the topic around for humor, he listed, he mapped, he mimicked, he slashed—all strategies most students would never try, but which all students could learn. He tried writing about his LEAST favorite spot in New England, Murkland Hall, the old brick building where we were sitting and where, as a college student, he had met with a tragedy of betrayed love. No good—no tension.

The teachers started to raise questions. What exactly were we doing and why did they have to give him an assignment anyway? What was our point? What did we intend to teach? What were they supposed to learn? Were we setting some kind of a trap? One woman said she had given

up assignments long ago, because since she teaches writing as a process, her students choose their own topics and this wasn't relevant at all. But then we talked about the kinds of assignments that *pretend* not to be assignments: statewide "prompts" given to thousands of students under pressure of time, story starters, placement essays, writing assessments. Infinite choices of topics with tight constraints on numbers of drafts. Portfolios with set numbers of pieces required. Writing only on certain days of the week for finite amounts of time.

Notebooks were empty. Pens were still. Brows were furrowed. I flushed as I watched Don write. I talked my thoughts as I saw them, trying hard to shift from a researcher's analysis of his approach to a teacher's running narration, noticing how his writer's patience withstood the pedagogical poison we had concocted.

"I was surprised to discover I HAD no favorite place and that I was already failing because of the implication that I SHOULD. I don't keep score that way," he remembers. He tried writing angrily about the beach, icy winters, and frozen seagulls, the rhythm of the tides at the North Shore. Then another twist: He tried describing his home office, a place he considers a favorite. Not bad, but so far not good. He continued to work.

Despite his valiant efforts as a professional writer, the Student Don was angry. When I asked him if he was ready to have a conference, he stiffened, resisting my interference. He complained that I was interrupting him. He grumbled at the words "favorite" and "New England" and was annoyed at the assumption that he would want to write something positive.

He said later that he was feeling a dishonesty that came from being forced into an attitude he didn't have and being asked to create an image he couldn't see. He was beginning to feel no favorite places, no activities to like. The more he worked on this assignment, the less the writing belonged to him.

"I don't have a favorite activity—or not one I would share," he explained later. "I was surprised at the tricks I had—'my unfavorite place'. I knew I had tricks, but I hoped I would have visualized something, thought something, felt something, and not run immediately to rhetoric."

An obedient student would not allow him/herself to take the risk of turning rhetorical tricks like playing against the assignment or finding an "edge" the way a clever journalist would do. Too dangerous (might not get an 'A'). Better play it safe and write something boring but acceptable.

The Writer Don might set this temporary failure aside to return to it later, allowing time and distance to help him find a new perspective. Or, maybe he'd choose to continue for another hour, catching a lead or a focus and playing it out, poking at another string of tension. But for the Student Don, the hour was gone, his time was up, and he had produced one sentence.

In a "process writing" classroom, he might get a grade or a check mark for this day's attempt, stash it in a folder with a few other pieces of writing, and know that tomorrow would present another chance. Like a professional, he might be able to go on to another piece of writing and return to this one. He might have a deadline to meet and face choices about which piece to finish and submit. Worse, he might be forced to continue at this one for another week of 50-minute periods. Worse still, in a different classroom he might not see this sentence again until the next "writing day," at which time he could pick up his failed 50 minutes from the week before.

If this had been a writing assessment prompt, prepared for a holistic scoring session by trained in-house readers, having written only one sentence, Don's score would be less than 1 and he would be placed in a special class. His parents might receive a notice suggesting remediation by sentence-combining, fluency practice with invention strategies, or disembodied pre-, during, and post-writing exercises to move his writing along.

Inside Our Assignments: What Do We Expect?

So what's in an assignment, anyway? What we experienced together in that classroom was a profound illustration of the dualities hidden behind writing assignments in school, and the assumptions that lie inside them, for teachers and for students.

No wonder Don couldn't write well about his favorite place in New England. He honestly couldn't, and he couldn't be honest. He might have chosen to write quite badly about it, in voiceless, oatmeal platitudes, with a topic sentence and lots of detailed support, mechanical perfection, and identifiable content. Dishonest, but successful. He wrote me later:

"I was surprised at how easy it would have been. . . . 'My favorite place is Ocean Park Beach in Maine where I used to run every summer morning when I was ten and where I now return to walk, not run, but to continue my study of the ancient rhythm of the tides.'

"Advanced placement at least. First, dishonesty in that it is not my favorite place; second, I have not returned to walk Ocean Park Beach; third, what I would—and have—written about is finding my first dead body washed ashore there."

With that one he could have had a holistic score of 5 on the state assessment and been placed at the top of the competency list, along with a referral to a counselor.

That same day during lunch at the conference, inspired by a question from a teacher friend, he gave *himself* an assignment he hadn't expected: "Who are your teachers?" For Don, this question became important enough to be the focus of the demonstration essay he is using throughout his new book, *Rewrite to Write* (Holt, in press). Why was this assignment so different? Because it came from a friend's honest curiosity? Because he assigned the topic to himself? Because it was an open assignment?

Of course there are assumptions in all assignments, open and closed, in designated writing time, in conferences, peer remarks, revision strategies, and editing choices. Perhaps we need to approach the creating of assignments with the same kind of caution we use to design our classroom environments. Even open assignments close options and make assumptions, consciously and unconsciously. We talk about learning to "act like professional writers" and want our students to understand their processes; yet, in our English classrooms and in our state and regional assessments, we ask students to write in ways professional writers would never be able to handle.

This story remains unfinished. We didn't teach Don Murray to write in that hour, but in observing his failure we came away with a lot to think about. At UNH, we're still talking about seeing what we didn't expect. As Don Graves observed later, even a writing period, a suggestion, or a pleasantly worded command carries its own expectations. And even though in many classrooms, armed with the technologies of chalk and voice, pen and notebook, computer and word processor, there is a lot of good writing going on (despite our unexamined assumptions and our unvoiced expectations), we are determined to think more now about the need to expect the unexpected, to allow our students the time and the room to "find the edges." We need to continue asking ourselves these questions:

- When is an assignment honest? When is it dishonest?
- What price does a student pay in honesty with each assignment he or she writes?
- What IS an assignment, anyway? Are we giving assignments even when we think we're not?
- Who owns an assignment after it's written?
- What assumptions do we make about students when we design assignments for them?

Bonnie Sunstein, Ph.D., Assistant Professor, English Education, The University of Iowa, Lindquist Center, Iowa City, IA 52242.

"Tricks" to Teaching Writing Well: Are There Any?

Jon Madian

"There are three tricks to writing well, but no one knows what they are."
W. Somerset Maugham

I sometimes like to say, "There are three tricks to *teaching* writing well, but no one knows what they are." But truthfully, I don't believe it. This article will focus on how we *can* teach writing well, with a particular emphasis upon revision.

Prewriting Stage

No good writing occurs unless students *want* to think about and express their ideas on a topic. Following that comes exploration, research, and discussion. Modeling is important to this process; Donald Graves has written extensively about the importance of modeling at all stages of the writing process. In "Investigate Nonfiction" he describes how, after deciding on the topic of whales for his research paper, he diagrammed in front of the class everything he knew about whales and then everything he wanted to learn—all of his questions. This is not modeling as an expert, but modeling as a student engaged in solving the kinds of problems that you want your students to solve.

Prewriting Conferences: Setting the Stage for Revision

Speaking is composing as surely as writing. When students talk about their ideas, images, themes, and feelings, they are composing. Barbara Smigala, a master teacher of the writing process at St. Louis Park High School in Minnesota until her untimely death two years ago, provided a strong model for teaching writing that continues to live.

Barbara's students worked in pairs at all stages of the writing process except the drafting and publishing stages. Here's how it's done:

At the prewriting stage students act as facilitators and recorders for each other. The facilitator interviews his or her partner (the writer) on the topic the writer plans to develop into a written piece. While interviewing and probing for details about the development of ideas and the relationship among those ideas, the facilitator takes notes that are then given to the writer. These notes serve as a prewriting map—an outline of sorts. This cooperative prewriting strategy sets the stage for the revision phase later on.

Drafting

Most students love writing at the computer, even if they're more efficient using a tape recorder, pencil, or pen. A frequently overlooked strategy for primary level writers is to have them work with cross grade tutors. Young students benefit by dictating their writing to older students, and older students gain a great deal as well. However the ideas are recorded, they need to find their way into a word processor for the revision phase. Here research and common sense agree: Even a very poor typist revises more efficiently using a word processor than rewriting by hand.

Revision

Most writing teachers feel fairly good about how they handle the prewriting and composing stages. The problems, it seems, occur at the revision stage. When thinking about this stage, I like to quote Mark Twain: "If we taught people to speak the way we teach them to write, everyone would stutter!" In teaching writing we need to accept and reinforce our students' original voices. Once students have confidence in their ability to express themselves in writing—to hear their own voice—we can then provide feedback to help them evolve and refine their skills.

Writing teachers need to distinguish students who are at the *fluency* stage in their writing, innocently offering their own ideas, from students who are at the *revision stage*, able to separate *what* they have said from *how* they say it.

It seems that students who have been writing often and naturally for about two or three years move naturally to the revision stage. Teachers can support students in moving to the revision stage by modeling revision on their own writing and by encouraging students to discuss what they like and dislike about a non-student-authored piece of writing. Although we find many third grade students at the revision stage, the paragraph below, written by an eighth grade girl, demonstrates that the fluency stage can be found at any age. This example is taken from a book titled *Me the Flunkie: Yearbook of a School of Failures* by A. Summers (Greenwich, CT: Fawcett, 1970). The writing prompt: "Write about what you want most."

Verbs

What I want most is strong verbs. Teachers all say I got weak verbs. I got no strong verbs. I always have a tuff time in school cause of that. I been pushed aroun and hounded to much aboit them verbs. Always then verbs! If I git strong verbs maybee teachers will leaf me alone. Other that that I wood like probly a hamboger and da malt. Porter sez he eat at 1215. Do I eat at 1215 are 1230? I steal dont now when I eat?

This student clearly is at the fluency stage and needs her sincere and wonderful writing, which contains an original and innocent sense of voice, to be accepted and appreciated. She won't learn from a lesson on keeping to one topic per paragraph or any other revision suggestions. At this very sensitive fluency stage, students feel that what they say is what they mean. They are developing their own voice and it is very important that we not offer suggestions or corrections, because we cannot correct or improve a writer's voice except by encouraging (with our appreciation) direct, honest, passionate expression.

Revision strategies at this stage involve asking for more information, more details: Help me, the reader, to understand what you, the writer, are seeing and saying. There are no issues of right or wrong, better or worse. Only requests for more information and more details. These requests show a sincere interest in the writer and make him or her feel appreciated, not judged—accepted, not corrected.

For years, at the revision stage, we have asked students to consider their writing with a view to adding more adjectives and adverbs. We have dealt with the impact of a piece of writing based upon grammatical considerations when in fact, good and great writers don't think about parts of speech when they revise. They focus on the intensity of their images and ideas, the energy and meaning behind the language. Students need practice in visualizing, imagining, feel-

ing, sensing, thinking, and intuiting about the whole of their written language.

This leads us directly to the issue at the heart of the revision stage: How do we create a nonjudgmental, supportive environment in the classroom in which everyone can be honest and sensitive about how ideas are expressed in order to help each other refine the experience of writing?

First, we need to respect everyone's ideas, expressed in writing or verbally. The classroom has to be a harbor, a safe place for everyone, and it is the teacher's job to create and nurture this environment.

Next, we need to talk about writing and look at it to see what makes it interesting or boring. If a teacher is going to inspire students to think about what makes good writing, he or she has to care a great deal about good writing and want to share good writing with students. Such a teacher will ask: Why is this passage by Salinger interesting? Why is this paragraph in this textbook boring? How can we rewrite Salinger to make him boring? How can we rewrite this passage from the textbook to make it interesting?

Writing teachers need to distinguish students who are at the fluency stage in their writing, innocently offering their own ideas, from students who are at the revision stage, able to separate what they have said from how they say it.

Barbara emphasized the importance of modeling for students. She had a small platform, a stage, in her classroom, where she did lots of role playing with her students. Then she and the class watched other students role play the things she modeled.

In modeling revision, begin by asking the writer what parts of the writing he or she likes best and least. What ideas does the writer have for improving the portions identified as weak? Then the peer editor might point out what he or she likes best and where the writing was unclear.

When the peer editor is the person who originally took the notes at the prewriting stage, he or she will have lots of ideas and expectations regarding the piece. Having the same students paired for a long period, working together through all stages of several compositions, helps them learn to communicate with each other at a deep level about their writing. Talking about how clearly and fully ideas are developed is a very sophisticated and creative skill. Two peer editing sheets are helpful: one generic and one specific to the particular assignment.

Directed Revision Practice

With the current emphasis upon learning in the context of writing in real situations, is directed practice beneficial? I think so. For example, before students write this year's essay on Martin Luther King, Jr., consider using last year's essays. Before passing out a "model" essay from last year, revise it, emphasizing the kinds of mistakes you suspect students will make this year and modeling the good writing you hope for. Give students a printout that is double-spaced with wide margins. Let them work alone and then in small groups to improve the writing. Then, using a computer and projection device, or simply an overhead and transparency, work through the piece together. When the class goes to the computer lab, have them bring up the same or another template that needs similar revisions.

If your emphasis is upon literature-based writing, you will find that sentence combining and other rewrite strategies that use word processing are excellent for helping students explore a writer's style and help your students develop their own style. For example, ask students to choose a favorite paragraph by Jack London and rewrite it so it reads like Hemingway. Turn Conrad, Melville, or Shakespeare into contemporary writers. Rewrite some of Aesop's fables into short, stubby sentences and have students rewrite them into longer, more descriptive narratives.

Evaluation

Many writing teachers evaluate both the peer reviewer and the author. The students turn in their writing along with all prewriting notes, peer review sheets, and all drafts. Students write until they feel they've done as well as they can. Only the final product is graded.

I recommend assigning grades to as few pieces of writing as possible—just enough to be able to defend a final grade. Students should, of course, know all grading criteria in advance and have an opportunity to rewrite a piece in order to improve their grade. They also are invited to write persuasive letters defending their right to the grade they want.

I like to use numbers on a scale of 1 to 10 or 1 to 100. I suggest grading for several things, depending on the assignment. A partial list might include voice, originality of language, originality of ideas, organization, logic, and mechanics.

Summary

How many tricks are there to teaching writing well? My list looks something like this:

1. Help students to find themes and topics upon which they want to write and rewrite;
2. Explore ideas verbally and nonverbally;
3. Be supportive;
4. Model both process and product at all stages of the writing process;
5. Involve students in discussing what makes good writing;
6. Provide lots of time for revision;
7. Use grades as infrequently as possible;
8. Be sure students know the criteria upon which they are being evaluated; and
9. Allow students to revise after grading to improve their score.

Perhaps W. Somerset Maugham holds the key to writing after all. He had this succinct advice for young writers:

If you can tell stories, create characters, devise incidents, and have sincerity and passion, it doesn't matter a damn how you write.

Jon Madian, Humanities Software, PO Box 950, Hood River, OR 97031.

Ken Kesey's Writing Classroom:
Computer Aided Apprenticeship

Carolyn Knox-Quinn

This past year, Ken Kesey and a group of University of Oregon graduate students wrote a novel together in a year-long writing class.

During a conversation with Carolyn Knox-Quinn, in the Kesey's red barn home in the Willamette Valley countryside near Eugene, he describes a process approach to writing, starting with a group design of plot and characterization. Using the computer as a medium, his students watched him and each other in the act of writing and rewriting.

At the end of the conversation, Kesey and two of his students discuss the power and immediacy of using a word processor with a big screen monitor to model the process of the artist at work to apprentices.

The novel, Caverns, **authored under the group name O.U. Lavonne, is published by Viking Press.**

By Ken Kesey:

One Flew Over the Cuckoo's Nest (New American Library, 1962; Viking, 1973).
Sometimes a Great Notion (Viking, 1964).
Demon Box (Viking, 1986).

Ken, can you give us some background on this very unique class?

Started out there were two rules in the class. One was that you couldn't tell anybody what the plot of the novel was until it was done. The other one was that I made up half the class. If it came to an argument about something, I was 50% of the class. I knew that we wouldn't have to go into a lot of democratic discussion. Nothing hampers creativity like too many cooks. We needed to move like a team with a quarterback. The more we did it, the more it was like a team.

When I first went into the class I explained to them that I had no idea what the plot was, who the characters were, where it was going to be located, what time frame it was going to be in, anything at all. We were starting from the beginning. Then we went a number of months doing what they call in jail "scoping each other's credentials." We talked literary blather (he laughs) to get comfortable with each other. That's fun, but talking writing is a lot different than writing. It's like talking basketball. You can talk basketball forever. It's different to pick up a ball. In the future, I think I'd pick up the ball right away and we would go right into the plotting and begin to make decisions.

How did you go about plotting the novel? Were there any ground rules?

The way we plotted it was this. I said "Start from character" and "Let's not do it about this time in history." The other thing I said was "Move out of Oregon. Let's go somewhere else. Let's write about something we don't know anything about."

What were your reasons for setting these conditions?

So many people write about things they're familiar with . . . they're all bound up emotionally with it. It becomes psychotherapy instead of writing. I just finished reading about Robert Burns' *Tam-O-Shanter*. It's about ghosts and boogie-ies and all sorts of stuff that he knows nothing about. He never saw any of that stuff. He had to go and research it (he laughs). It frees you from yourself.

So, we launched out into an area that I think is relative to the present but doesn't take place in the present. I read a part to Rebecca Preston from National Public Radio. As soon as it was over she said, "Oh, I see, this is about the New Age." "That's right!" I said. It's about the New Age only we've moved it. Instead of writing about now, we're writing about back then when it was at its heyday in the 20s and 30s. But she picked up on it right away. She understood why it would have been a mistake to write about it in the present. To write about El Salvador, for instance, it would be better to write about Montezuma and have that reflect on El Salvador.

How did you use the computer?

As time went by we came up with the third and most important rule. We changed things so that we didn't do any composition out-side of class. I found that when people wrote outside of class they began to go their own directions and into their own prose styles. Doing it in class really made a difference. Suddenly we started hearing a lot more and a lot better prose. This third rule was enacted when we were about a fourth of the way through the book. And, as you read the book, the early part is by far the weakest part. When we hit our stride and began to compose in class, the computer became important. I think this is the way to teach writing.

I think the way to teach writing is by *writing*. When you teach wrestling you have kids get out and wrestle. You teach basketball by having them play basketball, and you teach writing by having them sit and write. And I've had another interesting thought recently. You don't learn to write just to publish. You learn to write so that you can *write*. You can *feel* it flowing through you.

We would sit down around the table after we had drawn lots and would start in writing our little sections. This was only a half-hour period, and boy, you could hear the brain cells poppin', 'cause we knew we had to write and what we wrote had to fit in with the other pieces. You couldn't be too much yourself. Had to try to fit it into the tone of the novel, and then you had to read it aloud in front of this jury of your peers.

Can you back up just a bit? What were you drawing lots about?

We divided the chapter into increments 1 to 14. We designed the chapters . . . I wonder if it's still written on one of those blackboards . . . anyhow, we designed it up there (pointing to an imaginary blackboard), "Gabby gets up, walks outside, has a cigarette, and thinks about her past." That's number one (the first lot for someone to draw). Then, "She meets somebody and talks

to 'em, and they go to breakfast." That's number two. We put those lots in a hat and we drew 'em.

So we'd write and when it came reading time, we'd read our particular section in order into a tape recorder that we passed around the table. It gave people a chance to hear what the person had written before them and to make a few alterations in what they were writing. Then we transcribed it on the computer.

Did you read it as a class?

Sometimes we did. But by the time the class was really going well, people were coming in all the time and reading whenever they could.

Could they change it? Could anybody change anything?

Yeah, it was open for work. We would go through it and make

large editings on the computer, but then, during the next phase, each member of the class had a chapter that they had to work on and rewrite to make all those seams fit together and to take out discrepancies. Adjustment, I call it.

How did you decide on the characters?

(Aside to Bennett and Chuck) How did we do that?

(Chuck) Well, you told us to come in with a character . . .

(Bennett continues) on a card, describing some character's need or something like that.

(Chuck) We all came in and read them.

(Kesey) I studied Stanislavski's *My Life in Art*. He says that when you're studying acting what you do is try to find out what the character's need is. What's Richard the Third really trying to get? What's he really want? What's he going to do? Everything springs from that spine, he calls it. I think that's the same way a writer writes. The cards gave us a really simple way to create characters. Then you try to figure out a plot that will bring all the characters together so they all get to go somewhere and be together.

The necessity of bringing the characters together dictated the plot, which is really the way it is in life. People are people and they get together, and they have to do something and just what may surprise you. Whereas, if you make up the plot and then make up the characters to go into it, you've got puppets. Our characters, they did stuff none of us ever expected . . . said things that we couldn't have made up. And, they had *life*.

Here's a good example. We knew that we were going to need an archeologist, because of the theme of what we were doing. I had just assumed the archeologist was going to be a man. When the class went to design the characters, they brought back the archeologist and turns out she's a 50-year-old woman who's been studying the Anasazi's. It was not something I would have thought of. Having her be a woman changed all sorts of relationships that would happen naturally among the characters. It changed the tensions.

By the third term we did another thing that I think was really important. We reserved Gerlinger Hall for the reading. This was to be the class recital. It's different than sending a novel off to an editor, different than ending a class. It means that you're going to have to make a presentation . . . up in front of people. You could just feel the nervousness increase in the class. So we decided to wear 1930s garb! I don't remember who came up with that. It was a great idea.

If you're going to practice the violin steadily day by day for years and years, you might as well get it in your head that one of these days you're gonna have to take it on the stage. Have people out there listening to you play. Goethe said it: "Don't act. Compete." This doesn't mean to be competitive. It means you're going to be out there in a win/lose situation. As soon as that happens, as soon as you walk up on stage or send a piece of writing in to be published, you've risked something. You can be hurt. The people who don't ever put anything out there and that don't get hurt—they are never fully alive. People that play it safe end up, you know, driving Volvos (laughter).

I'll do this again some day, and I think that we'll do a play instead of a novel. Then, at the end of the year, instead of a reading, we'll put on a play—it's *made* for presentation! Publication really means just that . . . getting something in print is one form, but actually *presenting* it to the public is very important.

You've been talking a lot about people writing about what they don't know about, but finding out in the process—learning about it while they're writing about it.

Yes! and you know, when you do that, the books are gonna just show up in the library! *Caverns* takes place in 1934. We kind of arbitrarily picked that—a time almost nothing is written about. Then we thought, where can we take the people in the novel that isn't already beaten down by other novelists? So, we made it in the desert area of Idaho, Utah, and Wyoming. My brother took us all over to Bend so we could go down in a cave. Get down in there and turn all the lights out. Get a feeling what it's like.

We found out we had to learn about bats. We had to do this so we would all be current with each other. Then we got into Joseph Campbell like you couldn't believe. There was that whole series broadcast last year—exactly when we needed the information—that had to do with primal images found in caves. It was wonderful.

You were writing this novel with the students in your class. That doesn't happen very often in a class. Teachers assign students to write, they don't write!

Oh, gosh, yes. When I sent this book off to Viking, my heart was in my throat like nothing else I'd ever done. When we did the reading over there in Gerlinger Hall, I perform a lot, but this was a risk. I felt more under the hammer than I remember feeling in years and years.

The computer was essential to the process. We found in the rewrite that three people, maybe four, could work on one part on the computer. We finally tried a large screen. I focused the video camera on the screen and ran a line from the camera to my big TV so you could see the stuff this big. Ideally you'd have a large screen and people sitting in close enough contact that everybody could watch it.

This is how, as a professional writer, I can teach. I couldn't teach writing without *doing* it. I have to be writing. People have to be looking over each other's shoulders at the monitor . . . see, this phrase here is redundant, and this one is bad. In teaching writing, general abstractions don't work. You need something specific—a real context.

The other thing about this group style is that some days you just don't have any new sparkling stuff. But with 11 people, somebody always has something neat and it's as though somebody on your team is on and you're off. That old team effort. We keep hearing so much about the pride is back, stuff that's all muddied up by Budweiser beer, but it still works when you have a good team working together.

Do you think that the age of students would make a lot of difference? Can you imagine junior or senior high school teachers writing in this way?

I think if I had a high school class, I would sit them right down and say "Okay, right now, take your pencil and put it to this piece of paper. I want you to fill that piece of paper with words. You've got 15 minutes. Do it. Don't think about it. Do it." And when it's over, "Now stand up and read it out loud." And do that again the next day and the next day. By the end of a certain number of months those kids will be able to write.

Earlier you were talking about the students coming in with their own work and there being some competition. Is there a contradiction between competition and creativity?

Well, in this situation we competed with each other instead of competing with gravity and inertia. The real foe in teaching right now is not other kids. It's Coke commercials, it's the lethargy. Because this kind of class is an end run around the conventional kind of teaching framework, I'll bet you could take any bunch of kids in the school and by the end of the year, you would have a work. And they all would have contributed, and they would all be proud of it. The very fact that you don't let them tell others what it's about (rule number one) draws people together into a little cult. It's far out enough that they can see themselves being a little bit rebellious. Just step over the current trends. Step over!

Would several computers in the room change how you work?

Yes, it would be much easier, although still only two or three people would edit or rewrite at a time. The others would be at monitors, talking about various parts of the story, but without access to the keyboard. I think two keyboards might work, but if there were many more than that, people would just be fussing with each other.

You know, it became tremendously complicated working on this story. It was necessary to have people over the shoulders of other people, reminding them of what was going on, saying, "We can't do that—remember, he lost that in the last chapter." Usually when you're writing you have all that in your mind. In this class we had to have it *all* in *all* our minds—the class mind.

(Chuck) Working with Kesey was one of the really high points, with all of us sitting there together. That's something you never really do. That was the most valuable thing I got out of it . . . doing the rewriting . . . looking over his shoulder . . . doing the actual composing together right there . . . having him read his writing along with us.

It reminded me of Leonardo and Michelangelo—they studied under people. They were apprentices. And they got to learn by watching and working with masters and then they went out and had their own school and people learned from them. This class reminded me of that. We had a chance to see someone who has been doing this for 20 years and to learn by doing it along with him.

(Kesey) It's like what Chuck said—you're where the statue is being chipped. You're watching the hammer move and the chips fly and you get a chance every so often to chip some of the statue yourself. And as a teacher, the only way you're going to teach somebody sculpting is to have a hammer in your hand. You can't just look at their stuff and criticize it. You have to be working and have them see you do it. We're too used to the other form.

Someday somebody will do a thesis on this style. That's why I've kept all this stuff, so that somebody can go through and look at it . . . not in terms of whether the book is a great book, but as a way of teaching, an important way of teaching.

When the interview ended, it was dusk. The cows needed to be fed. Chuck, Bennett, and I were able to make ourselves useful throwing bales of hay off a flat wagon bed as Ken drove his tractor through the fields, past herds of cows and one faded, but once brightly painted, old bus, sinking quietly in the Oregon mud.

Carolyn Knox-Quinn, Ph.D., 180 E. 33rd, Eugene, OR 97405.

Enhancing the Reading-Writing Connection: Classroom Applications

Lynne Anderson-Inman

Writing is usually viewed as the process of putting meaning *onto* the printed page (production) and reading as the process of getting meaning *from* the printed page (reception). Although this view is certainly not incorrect, it is somewhat superficial. When one explores what a writer actually has to do in order to put meaning onto a page, it is clear that a tremendous amount of reading is required in order to write well. First, there is the reading that writers do in the process of becoming familiar with good writing, its various types of discourse and important stylistic conventions. Second, there is the reading that writers do in order to check on the clarity and meaningfulness of what they are writing. Successful writers are able to put themselves in the shoes of their intended audience and read as if reading with *their* eyes.

What the reader has to do in order to gain meaning from the printed page involves skills not unlike those of the writer. To comprehend what has been written, the reader must construct meaning from the writer's words, looking for relationships among the different parts of the text. This is not a passive endeavor, but rather one in which the reader works to combine his or her own background knowledge on the subject with the ideas presented by the writer. Thus, reading comprehension, like writing, is an active process of creating meaning.

Because the skills required for good reading and writing are related, instruction in one process can be beneficial to the other. This is where the computer can play an important role. The computer, with its capacity for word processing and ability to prompt and respond to reader interaction, can provide an environment for communication that enhances both reading and writing skills. This article presents an overview of three ways that the computer can help bridge the gap between reading and writing instruction: (a) the use of word processors in the Language Experience Approach, (b) programs that enable writers to combine text and graphics, and (c) programs that facilitate interactive reading and writing experiences.

Language Experience Approach

The Language Experience Approach to reading and writing instruction uses students' own language to create reading materials. Originally, stories were dictated to teachers by a group of students and recorded on the chalkboard or on large chart paper. The strength of this approach is the use of students' own oral language as the foundation for both reading and writing. Students quickly learn that thoughts can be translated into speech, speech into writing, and that one's own words can be read. This approach can be facilitated by using a word processing program for recording students' stories, along with

a large monitor or projection system so that groups of students can work together.

Use of a word processor has three advantages over the traditional method. First, language experience stories can be efficiently recorded and printed. Typing sentences into a computer takes less time than writing by hand in large print, and electronic printing of multiple copies takes less time than recopying. Second, stories can be easily revised. Inserting new words and altering a sequence of story ideas are easy to accomplish with a word processor and communicate an important message to students about writing; that is, that stories are not static, but rather are entities which can be molded to achieve better communication. The third advantage is the possibility for individualization. The teacher can easily personalize stories by inserting different students' names. Multiple story lines may also be developed at the same time.

When choosing a word processor to use in recording language experience stories, it is important that the program be simple to use and able to project text that can be read by a group of students. *Magic Slate* (Sunburst) works nicely because it can be set to write with only 20 or 40 characters per line, resulting in letters large enough to be read by a group of students using a single large monitor. *FrEd Writer* (ISTE) and *MECC Writer* (MECC) also work well. The *Language Experience Recorder* (Teacher Support

Software) is a program developed specifically for this purpose and has the additional advantages of providing word counts, readability estimates, and word banks for later study.

The increased availability of word processing programs with synthesized speech adds another dimension to the use of computers in the Language Experience Approach. A talking word processor can provide immediate auditory access to what has been written, so students can read and reread these stories on their own. When a word or phrase is problematic, the computer can repeat it as often as necessary. Word processing programs with speech synthesis include *Talking Text Writer* (Scholastic), *KidTalk* (First Byte), and *FirstWriter* (Houghton Mifflin). With the eventual addition of voice recognition and speech-to-text capabilities, the computer may free even very young students to both write and read language experience stories with total independence.

Combining Text and Graphics

Students have been enlivening their writing with hand-drawn pictures since the advent of crayons. The computer brings an electronic touch to this process and adds a look of professionalism to the final product. Software to support the production of illustrated, student-generated materials can be loosely classified into three categories: (a) build-a-book programs, (b) electronic books, and (c) desktop publishing programs.

Build-a-book software. This software prompts writers through a series of questions, generally about themselves, their family, and friends, with the answers used to personalize a story already on disk. The story is printed out, often on specially provided paper, and materials are included to add graphics and bind the pages into a book. The stories found on build-a-book software programs are highly motivational to children and may play a significant role in motivating young and reluctant writers to produce personalized materials. Early examples of the build-a-book software are programs in the *Playwriter* series (Woodbury) and *Build-a-Book* (Scarborough). A more recent example is the *Story Tailor* library (Humanities Software), which provides a whole collection of poems and stories to be personalized.

Electronic books. This software allows students to combine text and

---

By providing an environment in which the learner moves back and forth between the role of reader and the role of writer (or even plays both roles simultaneously), the computer promotes a recognition that reading and writing are interrelated events.

---

graphics to create electronic books (i.e., books that are meant to be read on the computer). The computer screen becomes the "page" and the writer is provided with electronic tools for writing and illustrating stories, reports, and text materials. Most of the available programs foster story writing, some with recognizable characters from cartoons and television, others with a more open-ended set of graphics. Examples of the former are *Kermit's Electronic Storymaker* (Simon & Schuster) and *Create with Garfield* (DLM). Examples of the latter include *Story Maker* (Scholastic), *Cotton Tales* (MindPlay), and *Bank Street Storybook* (Mindscape).

Some of the more recent programs present completed pictures and/or stories to modify and write about. For example, in the *Explore-a-Story* series (William K. Bradford), the student reads a richly illustrated story provided on disk (as well as in soft cover format) and then is encouraged to alter the characters, setting, and objects and write and print out a new story.

The addition of speech synthesis capabilities to some programs lets young writers experience yet another dimension to their creations. For example, in the "Story Maker" module of *Dinosaur Discovery Kit* (First Byte), students complete a partially written and illustrated story and may then choose to have the story read aloud by Zug the Dinosaur. Similarly, in *Monsters & Make-Believe* (Pelican/Learning Lab), students are provided with electronic tools for creating a monster, giving it speech, and writing an accompanying "monster myth." New programs are being designed to build on the capabilities presented in *HyperCard* (Apple). For example, using *ElectroText* (Enabling Technologies), the user can create hypertextbooks complete with illustrations, sound, and text supported by vocabulary instruction, background information, and study questions.

Desktop publishing programs. Desktop publishing programs can promote understanding of the literary conventions in journalism and recognition of text structures conducive to effective reporting as students create a class or school newspaper. Furthermore, publishing for a real world audience motivates writers to refine their writing. *Newsroom* (Springboard) was an early desktop publishing program for students. *The Children's Writing &*

Publishing Center (The Learning Company) is a more recent and easy-to-use program that lets children as young as second grade produce professional looking reports, stories, and two-column newspapers. There is a large databank of graphics to choose from, and words will wrap around pictures placed in the text. The program even supports color printers. At the secondary level, students and teachers are more likely to adopt professional desktop publishing programs for the Macintosh computer (e.g., *Ready, Set, Go* (Letraset), *Page-Maker* (Aldus), and *Publish It!* (Timeworks).

Interactive Reading and Writing Experiences

Interactive reading and writing experiences help to break down the distinctions between reader and writer. By providing an environment in which the learner moves back and forth between the role of reader and the role of writer (or even plays both roles simultaneously), the computer promotes a recognition that reading and writing are interrelated events. Such recognition is the first step in promoting the transfer of good writing skills to students' reading and the transfer of critical reading skills to students' writing. When readers see themselves as writers and writers see themselves as readers, both roles are enhanced.

For example, in the program *Suspect Sentences* (Silver Burdett and Ginn), students elect to take on the role of either "forger" or "detective." It is the forger's task to insert a sentence into an existing paragraph with such skill that it is indistinguishable from the original sentences. It is the detective's task to correctly identify the forged sentence. To be a successful forger, the reader/writer must construct the forged sentence so that it matches those in the original paragraph in content, style, tone, and complexity. This requires careful reading and skillful writing. The same level of analysis is required to be a successful detective, a role that makes clear the need to read like a writer.

Although several different types of software provide interactive reading and writing experiences, two of the most widely used for educational purposes are "branching stories" and "prompted stories."

Branching stories. In branching stories the reader proceeds through an adventure, responding to choices presented and thereby determining the plot and outcome of the story.

When readers see themselves as writers and writers see themselves as readers, both roles are enhanced.

Sometimes these choices are presented at specific points in the story in the form of multiple options from which the reader/writer selects. In other programs the options are continuously available and the student can freely move around in the story environment, choosing certain actions and ignoring others. In both types of programs the act of reading the story and making choices is also the act of writing the story. Since different choices can be made on subsequent readings of any given story, one basic plot can lead to many variations in outcome.

The Story Teller (Educational Activities) exemplifies this multiple-choice format. Set within the context of a personalized magical fantasy, readers/writers are confronted with critical decisions in each chapter. Their decisions are recorded and the story, as developed by the student, can be saved, printed, and illustrated.

Many of the best examples of branching stories are those used to provide simulated adventures for learning content-area material. For example, *Grizzly Bears* (Advanced Ideas) provides learners with four stories about grizzly bears and is tied to a database of related information. The reader plays the role of investigator with the overall task of designing strategies for saving the grizzly bear. Options selected by the reader determine the success of these efforts, throughout which the user is encouraged to take notes. Another program, *Hidden Agenda* (Springboard), exemplifies a more open-ended format. Here the learner plays the role of a Central American leader whose decisions determine the fate of a small country named Chimerica. Options are continuously available, including holding a press conference; appointing, consulting, and dismissing ministers to the cabinet; meeting with influential people to discuss important issues; making decisions about important matters of state; and reading reports from the domestic and international press.

Using software such as *Story Tree* and *Super Story Tree* (both from Scholastic), learners can create their own branching stories or adventures. *Story Tree* carefully prompts writers through the process of conceptualizing and recording stories with multiple branches and story lines. Each page of a *Story Tree* story has three parts: a title or descriptive name (used for accessing the page), a text portion (one or two paragraphs), and the branching connections that link it to other pages in the story. *Super Story Tree* adds graphics and sound features. On a graphics page, writers have control over background illustrations, clip art, speech, music, and special sound effects. Both programs help to blur the distinctions between reader and writer and thus enhance the reading-writing connection. Writers of branching stories have to read and reread their creations to maintain internal consistency and readers of branching stories become writers by virtue of the choices they make at the end of each page.

Emerging as another form of branching story is a genre known as "hyperfiction." Using the capabilities of hypertext authoring systems such as *HyperCard* (Apple), hyperfiction stories offer the reader multiple links from any given page, often presented as graphic images to be clicked on and "opened." Although early examples of hyperfiction have relatively little text (e.g., Amanda Goodenough's *Inigo Stories* (The Voyager Company) and *The Manhole* (Activision/Mediagenic), great potential exists for using the hypertext medium for both reading and writing complex, multi-linked stories.

Prompted Stories. To encourage creative writing, teachers frequently provide students with a "story starter"—the first paragraph of an adventure, or a stimulating picture to spur the writer's imagination. Software to enhance the reading-writing connection builds on that idea, adapting it to the electronic age. Prompted stories provide writers with an environment that elicits their ideas and helps them to put those ideas into an appropriate form. For example, *The Writing Adventure* (DLM) provides readers with screens of graphics presenting an adventure through a cave. The reader/writer makes choices within

the adventure and is required to record observations for later retrieval. In the final scene the main character is left trapped in the cave, and the student is challenged to use his or her notes to write a story describing the adventure and creating an appropriate conclusion.

The Railroad Snoop (Sunburst) is another excellent program which uses the interactive capabilities of the computer to prompt creative writing. Students become involved in mysterious happenings in a railroad yard and record entries about their observations into the Snoop's journal. In the process of completing ten lessons designed to improve their word processing and creative writing skills, students emerge as authors of a railroad mystery. *Scoop Mahoney* (DLM) also challenges students to adopt the role of investigator, in this case a magazine reporter, practicing reading comprehension skills while collecting information for an assignment. Information is recorded in the form of story notes and their success as a magazine reporter is based on the

quality of those notes.

The software described in this article barely touches the surface of the computer's potential for enhancing the reading-writing connection. And yet, considerable progress is being made by software developers in the creation of educationally appropriate programs that capitalize on the interactive capabilities and word processing features of the computer. Future applications will hopefully move toward computer-learner interactions that are increasingly substantive and which focus attention on specific reading and writing skills within a real world context.

This article is a condensed and updated version of two earlier articles by the same author appearing in *The Computing Teacher*: "The Reading-Writing Connection: Classroom Applications for the Computer" Part I (November 1986) and Part II (March 1987).

Dr. Lynne Anderson-Inman, Associate Professor, College of Education, University of Oregon, Eugene, OR 97405.

SPORTS
Football
Oval, brown,
Passing, running, falling,
Shoulder pads, knee pads, bat, glove,
Hitting, running, laughing,
Round, white
Baseball.

PRAIRIE
Brown, grass,
Laughing, farming, loving,
Grasslands, farm, water, wet
Swimming, sailing, glistening,
Blue, green,
Ocean.

by Adam, 6th grade, Ponderosa Elementary School

On the "Write" Track:
The Writing Process at Work in a First Grade Classroom

Deborah Domsky

When my class enters in September, with faces freshly scrubbed and wearing back-to-school clothes, I hear the same questions that all first grade teachers hear: "When will we learn how to read?" followed closely by "When will we get to write?"

Although children in my school have lots of opportunities to experiment with print in kindergarten, they know that when they enter first grade there will be a structured writing time each day called writer's workshop.

Every child has a story to tell and ideas to express. That need to express ideas and be heard is what makes the writing process so meaningful to the children. They come to first grade with a wide range of skill levels, and I allow them to create their own spelling conventions before being bogged down by spelling rules. I encourage them to spell out what they hear, understanding that what each child hears and puts down will vary. By appreciating their expression, by questioning their content and ideas, I can help them elaborate on their language. As I teach phonics skills during other times of the day, the children begin to carry these skills over into their writing. Phonics and spelling instruction are not taught before they write, but *as* they write. Then, as they learn to read they begin to remember the conventional spellings of many of the words they see in books. In the meantime they've been allowed to develop freedom of expression and more complex, thoughtful language.

The structure of writer's workshop is a predictable one for the children. They know that we will write each day. If we don't, they're disappointed. This consistency is important. Every day after recess we meet on the rug for a whole group lesson. Some days I just ask them to share what they're writing about so others can get an idea for a topic. I once asked the children to brainstorm a list of how they thought of ideas for their stories. Their responses ranged from "I think about it when I'm lying in bed at night" to "I just get the idea when I am drawing the picture."

> **"Miss Domsky, I think my published book is a HUGE success! Everyone keeps reading it!" ... a good reminder that the writing process does not end when the book is published.**

The important thing is that they are thinking about their own process. I've found that, in general, their ideas come either from their own experiences or from stories they've read or have heard read aloud to them.

Another day, the group lesson might introduce a new skill that I think they're ready for—perhaps a lesson on putting a period at the end of a sentence or a look at descriptive words. I often use their writing to illustrate a point. For example, first grader Nell used a lot of description in her story, "The Journey to the Desert." I shared with the class her description of the "long, eventful journey" and the "hot red earth." We talked about her use of imagery in saying "It looked like there was fire on the sand" as a fresh, surprising way of saying that it was hot. Although the whole class is exposed to a new skill or concept, they don't all pick it up immediately, so many lessons bear repeating.

Every so often a child writes a sentence that is extraordinary. I read these sentences aloud to the class. Michael once wrote, "The glittery snowflakes went by and the silver moon was high in the sky on Christmas eve." After that I saw lots of variations on his words in other students' writing—it seemed that everyone had a glittery snowflake or silver moon in their story! It's important to understand that children learn from mimicking what's modeled for them until it becomes their own. In many ways it's more powerful when the modeling comes from a peer rather than from the teacher.

On many days I simply read a story before the children begin to write. By exposing them to quality literature and by studying the styles of well-known authors and illustrators, they begin to use these books to structure their own writing. As they compare "professional" writing with their own, and as I juxtapose the writing of Maurice Sendak or Eric Carle with the children's, they are further encouraged to see themselves as authors.

One day Nick wrote a story that included some of his classmates as characters. He said, "I'm being just like Tomie de Paola! He has Strega Nona in lots of his stories. I have Jeff and Alex in lots of mine!"

Whether the mini-lesson is a skill lesson, a story, or a discussion on choosing a topic, I keep it short. Then the children get started writing. While they're writing, the room is full of talking as they get up to get paper and supplies and as they conference with each other and with me. Questions that I ask them in the beginning, such as "What is this about?" "What will happen next?" "Does this make sense?" are ones that they later begin to ask each other. The ultimate goal is for them to internalize these kinds of questions so they begin to ask them of themselves as they work on their own writing. When I'm conferencing with a child, I often purposely let the other children at the table hear our conversation and sure enough, I begin to hear those children using the same words and questions with each other as they work. I love hearing one of my students say to another, "I like the way you have a beginning, middle, and end" or "That's a good description."

My role as teacher during this time is simply to step back and watch them work. Sometimes it feels as though they don't need me at all. But they do. They need me to be an audience, to listen to them, to bolster their confidence, and to guide them simply by saying "This sounds good. I'll be back in ten minutes to see how you're doing."

At the end of writing time, one child shares his or her work with the class during what we call "author's chair." The author sits on the teacher's chair. It's a privilege to be the one to share.

During this time the class is learning how to be a good audience as well as learning respect for their peer's work. I model questions, and they begin to learn the difference between constructive questioning and just stating opinions. They focus on the development of a story and the process of writing as they comment and question the author's ideas and intent.

In first grade I encourage the children to think about whether the story makes sense. Laura was reading a story about a little girl in an orphanage wearing a "silk, blue dress and diamond shoes." Alexandra asked her why an orphan would be dressed like that, to which Laura quickly replied, "Well, she was in an orphanage until her grandparents came and got her and gave her the shoes and dress for her birthday!" The audience was placated. (In first grade, I find that the children rarely go back and make this level of revision in writing.)

Sometimes a child comes to the author's chair and will end with, "This is what I have so far. Does anyone have an idea of what I could do next?" The children are eager to supply ideas—and the author feels comfortable in deciding to try an idea or in saying, "No, that isn't really what I had in mind."

Children critique each other's writing in different ways. Some notice the illustrations, others the message. Some give specific praise, while others give more global approval such as "I think that story deserves a Caldecott!"

For the last step in the process, the children must decide what to do with a finished piece. I discuss possible options, but they make the decision. It might be published, thrown away, put in their finished folder, or shared with a friend. One day Christian came to me and said, "Miss Domsky, I think my published book is a HUGE success! Everyone keeps reading it!" This is a good reminder that the writing process does not end when the book is published.

Each child's finished writing needs to be accessible. Kelly, for example, spent her writing time one day looking through all of her writing from September through March. She came to me excitedly and a little out of breath, exclaiming, "Look at this! At the beginning of the year I made all my S's backwards. And do you remember how I used to think that I had to finish a story in one day?"

Teaching writing has its ups and downs. Some days my students seem to be creating brilliant stories and other days it seems they'll never write coherently. But it's all worth it when one child comes in, like Christy did after the long winter vacation, and said (before even taking off her coat), "I REALLY missed my writing. Can I take out my folder?"

Deborah Domsky, grade 1 teacher, Greeley School, Winnetka, IL.

A BUTTERFLY
by Hank

**Wings all aflutter
Colors soft as butter
Colors of blue,
Peaceful as dew,
That remind me
of kindness from you.**

Computers in a Whole Language Classroom

Cathy Gunn

Open any current journal on writing, reading, English, or computers, and you will find the phrases "whole language," "process writing," "reading strategies," and "computers and writing." Kenneth and Yetta Goodman, Don Holdaway, Donald Graves, Lucy Calkins, and Marie Clay, among many others, give teachers a base of information on reading and writing instruction geared to a whole language philosophy. Although fewer sources provide practical information to teachers interested in combining whole language with computer use, the topic is being discussed regularly in educational journals such as *The Writing Notebook* and occasionally in other journals, such as the October/November 1989 issue of *Writing Teacher*.

Whole language is described by Dorothy Watson (1988, p. 4) as follows: **Linguistically**, whole language includes "*all* systems of language" involved in any literacy encounter. **Curricularly**, "students—not textbooks or preformed guides or tests—are the heart of teaching and learning"; children read and are invited to write their own whole stories, poems, and books. Language is learned as students "use it in reading, writing, listening and speaking about science, math, social studies, literature, sports, and anything else that interests them." **Culturally**, students' "beliefs, lifestyles, interests, values, and needs are valued and are a source of information and joy. Students of all cultures and all subcultures have a place in the society of the classroom, and their contributions are celebrated." **Socially and psychologically**, whole language encourages peer support and interchange

as children learn language in context. **Instructionally**, real language with real thought is emphasized and includes hypothesizing, risk-taking, organizing, getting it wrong, getting it right, categorizing, summarizing, pondering, changing—instead of fragmented worksheet drills, fill-in-the-blanks, and a "get-it-right" atmosphere. **Politically**, whole language means that "teachers, through knowledge, become empowered, and they pass on that power to students, parents, and other teachers."

Some software companies provide variations on a literature with reading and process writing activities theme—exciting news for a teacher interested in combining the unique capabilities of a computer with whole language instruction.

To look at how the computer can help teachers use real language, make meaning, and empower children, it's important to understand the unique capabilities of this tool that separate it from paper and pencil or from traditional instructional tools like the chalkboard or overhead projector.

Several word processors use larger 20-column primary print or 40-column print (e.g., *Magic Slate* [Sunburst], *Bank Street Writer III* [Scholastic], *FrEdWriter* [public domain]). These programs can display

readable screens on VCR monitors or projection devices, which aid the modeling of writing and reading comprehension strategies in large group sessions. *Bank Street Writer III* and *FrEdWriter* also contain a writing feature that allows teachers to prompt students through writing activities on the screen. Text can be added, inserted, deleted, moved, and saved for future writing and can then be printed out (without the prompts) in a form that is easy to read and share.

Software companies are improving their reading and writing programs. *Write On!* (Humanities Software), *Explore-a-Classic* (William K. Bradford) and *The Creative Writing Series* (Pelican Software) provide variations on a literature with reading and process writing activities theme—exciting news for a teacher interested in combining the unique capabilities of a computer with whole language instruction. Although limited access to computers may make actual writing with computers by children an unrealistic goal, even with a one-computer classroom, many teachers are making good use of the technology available to strengthen their teaching of reading and writing.

A Linguistic Perspective

According to Watson, all systems of language, including meaning, grammar, and sound-symbol relationships, are involved in literacy acts. In the normal course of growing up, children acquire language with little thought about how it works; they learn by discovering connections that make sense to them (DeHaven, 1988). Modeling the strategies described below with children is one way teachers can help their students to be cognitively aware of language.

• **Story Schema.** Considerable research supports observations that readers have a story schema, and that readers use their knowledge of story structures to guide their expectations, understanding, recall, and production of text (Fitzgerald, 1989). This knowledge of text structures helps children in their own writing, because they have predictable structures in their mind to build on as they write themselves. Knowledge of the structure of stories also aids comprehension by helping the reader decide whether a portion of a story is complete or incomplete, or to predict what type of information might be forthcoming (Strickland, Feeley, & Wepner, 1987).

There are many comprehension strategies, as well as a variety of methods for teaching those strategies. The skills required for both reading and writing are similar, and instruction in one context can impact performance in the other. The computer provides excellent opportunities for students to experiment with various ways to organize texts as they write, predict, move text, and continue to experiment with their own organization. As students actively collaborate through predicting, journal writing, discussing a story structure, or constructing semantic maps, they interact with different text styles. If access to computers is too limited for students to use them for actual writing, teachers can use the computer to model the writing process with students.

• **Sentence Combining.** O'Hare suggests that sentence combining exercises may improve students' composing and comprehending abilities (cited in Strickland et al., 1987). The process of sentence combining can be demonstrated in large group sessions with a large screen monitor or projection device. This demonstration technique models both the practice of sentence combining as well as word processing features that make writing, as well as

combining and revision, easier for the writer. Using the word processor to practice sentence combining also provides opportunities to use real text from a variety of subject areas that pertain to material students are currently reading and studying.

Teachers and students can work through activities together to develop reading and writing strategies, with the material written determined by the teacher and children. Because the text is viewed by the entire class and can be changed, a teacher can talk through each strategy and model how each one is important in the reading and writing process. Although these same strate-

---

As skill instruction is incorporated within the context of students' own writing, these skills become part of the writing process rather than a set of isolated facts to be memorized. Teachers also can model writing and reading strategies at the same time they demonstrate word processing functions.

---

gies can be modeled using the blackboard, the computer allows for more versatility in moving, saving, and printing text; it also allows the text to be written before class time and continued or built on at a later time.

• **Cloze Passages.** Cloze exercises can be used to teach reading comprehension strategies. In cloze passages, students fill in blanks to complete parts of a story, including the setting, plot, and characters. Using the word processor for cloze passages provides a distinct advantage, because actual text that children have been using in reading or other subject areas may be used, taken from basal selections, con-

tent material, literature, or stories written by the children.

Social and Psychological Factors

Peer support and interchange are encouraged in a whole language classroom. They interact and support each other through reading, writing, listening, and speaking, using whole stories, poems, and books they write in a community setting. Alfred Bork (1986) states that learning must be active if ideas, methods, and concepts are to be internalized. The classroom teacher with access to even one computer and a VCR monitor or projection device has a valuable teaching tool to complement and reinforce active learning. Students can brainstorm, write cooperatively, and see their ideas take shape on a large screen, with the added joy of seeing their final product printed out and shared. With access to an easy-to-use desktop publishing program such as *The Children's Writing & Publishing Center* (The Learning Company), students can work together to create a newspaper on any subject representing any period in history!

Instructional Strategies

Whole language uses real language with opportunities for real thought in hypothesizing, risk-taking, organizing, categorizing, and summarizing, according to Watson. The replacement of worksheet drill and practice sheets with a word processor encourages these higher-order thinking skills. For example, upon completion of a story, the word processor can aid in the reading/writing process as an outline of the story is displayed on a large screen for discussion. Information can be added or deleted as the teacher types student responses. Predictions can be recorded and used for discussion and writing activities, and comparisons made among the outlines of several books in the same genre as patterns become apparent.

As students write their own stories, their knowledge of text patterns and structure is used as a framework. Using a large screen monitor makes the computer an active demonstration device. While the teacher types in the text on the word processor, modeling the writing process through "thinking out loud," students can collaborate on a group story and revise and edit as needed.

Young students enjoy writing sequels to the story of Miss Nelson, the missing teacher. Using what they know about story structures and about the structure of *Miss Nelson is Missing* in particular, they can collaborate on a new version, practicing story writing in a supportive environment with the teacher verbalizing strategies. For example: "We have two small sentences here. How can we combine them to make one good sentence? If I use a connecting word like 'and,' I can combine them like this. I'll read the sentence. Does that make sense? We have an extra word here that doesn't belong now, so I'll delete it by placing the arrow to the right of the word and pressing the DELETE key for each letter. Now let's read the sentence. Does that sound like a good sentence? Does it put both thoughts into one sentence? Sometimes in your writing you will want to take short sentences and combine them."

Older students reading chapter books can use what they know about story structure and continue the story through a new chapter, using a large group story writing process similar to the one described with younger children.

As skill instruction is incorporated within the context of students' own writing, these skills become *part* of the writing process rather than a set of isolated facts to be memorized. Teachers also can model writing and reading strategies at the same time they demonstrate word processing functions.

Curricular Implications

Modeling and verbalizing strategies for reading comprehension and the writing process are useful when applied across content areas where the language is real and serves a purpose for students. During science class, students can write a group lab report to describe an experiment and synthesize the results. Teachers can type the report as students direct the writing. Vocabulary can be developed and included in the report. Concepts that cause confusion can be further discussed, as retelling indicates comprehension of the activity as well as previous reading material. Questioning strategies also can be modeled, with students asked: Is the answer right there, do we have to think and search, or do we have to find the answer on our own? (Raphael, 1986).

Science reports written by fourth grade students in Springfield, Illinois, were enhanced by one computer and group writing. Each student chose one planet to research and brought a list of facts about their planet to the computer. As students discussed the planets, planet names were typed in a list on the computer by the teacher. New planets were added and moved around according to their distance from the sun, and the teacher was able to reinforce information read and discussed in a previous class. Information based upon each child's research was added under the planet name, and sentence combining was modeled as the teacher verbalized the process of combining similar information into one sentence. This information was saved and printed out for each student to use as a reference for a science report they were to write. Not only did the students have their own researched material, but they were able to benefit from new information from other students, as well as information the teacher incorporated into the lists through the discussion. Most important, the children were truly the heart of this teaching and learning experience.

Political and Cultural Relevance

In a whole language curriculum, children learn language as they use language in real literacy events and includes four elements: real roles for the learners, real purposes for the learners, real messages and content, and real situational contexts (Goodman, Smith, Meredith, & Goodman, 1987, p. 399). Exciting new telecommunications writing programs such as AT&T's Learning Circles, for example, give students around the world a real audience for their writing as they collaborate and share thoughts, stories, and information of interest to them. We are beginning to see how cooperative learning, literature-based instruction, and technology together can help provide appropriate and exciting curriculum that is culturally relevant and which is " . . . essentially social, communal, and empowering of all individuals" (Madian, 1989, p. 13).

Cathy Gunn, Ph.D., Assistant Professor, Northern Arizona University, Center for Excellence in Education, Flagstaff, AZ 86001.

References

Bork, A. (1986). Computers and the future: Education. In Board of Regents of the University of Wisconsin Systems (Ed.), *A book of readings for next steps with computers in the classroom* (pp. 86-91). Dubuque, IA: Kendall/Hunt.

DeHaven, E. (1988). *Thinking about language*. Glenview, IL: Scott, Foresman.

Fitzgerald, J. (1989). Research on stories: Implications for teachers. In K. D. Muth (Ed.), *Children's comprehension of text: Research into practice* (pp. 2-36). Newark, DE: International Reading Association.

Goodman, K., Smith, E., Meredith, R., & Goodman, Y. (1987). *Language and thinking in school: A whole-language curriculum*. New York: Richard C. Owen.

Madian, J. (1989). Cultural artists in the information age. *The Writing Notebook*, Jan/Feb 1989, 13-14.

Raphael, T. (1986). Teaching question-answer relationships, revisited. *The Reading Teacher*, February, 516-522.

Strickland, D., Feeley, J., & Wepner, S. (1987). *Using computers in the teaching of reading*. New York: Teachers College Press.

Watson, D. (1988). Reflections on whole language: Past, present and potential. *Oregon English*, *11*(1), 4-8.

Electronic Maps:
Evaluating Higher Order Thinking Skills

John Boeschen

Studying a map can be as revealing as marveling over Mihtat's signature. No two maps are ever the same and each provides insights into students' problem-solving thought processes— insights as revealing as individual fingerprints or signatures.

Mihtat was grinning from ear to ear. I had asked the class of seven Turkish agricultural engineers to describe on paper who they were.

"Tell me who you are inside—the real you," I had prodded them. "I want to be able to look at that writing and say, 'Yes, that's the very essence of you.'"

I wasn't able to express myself to these young men quite as elaborately as the words above might indicate. I was the first English as a second language teacher they had ever had. And I had only been in Turkey a couple of months as a Peace Corps Volunteer—my bare bones Turkish was no better than their English. But they grasped the idea.

Mihtat's inked response caught me off guard—a face in caricature. "What is this, Mihtat?"

"It's the face of John Bartok, Turkey's greatest soccer player."

"That's nice, Mihtat, but I asked you to write about yourself, not draw a cartoon."

Beaming that sly, Cheshire-cat smile of his, Mihtat explained: "You must look closer, teacher. His ear is the first letter of my name, his nose the second letter, his chin the third. . . ." Mihtat had written his name so that it looked like a caricature of John Bartok.

"If you want to know who I am, who I would really be, just look at my signature."

Graphic Insights into Student Thought Processes

What's the connection between Mihtat's insightful signature and the theme of this issue of *The Writing Notebook*— Writing to Think Across the Curriculum?

The connection has to do with an evaluation strategy that graphically reveals students' "higher level" thinking skills (just as Mihtat's signature revealed a higher order of his personality). The technique I have in mind graphically portrays students' problem-solving patterns like a road map, a map you can follow easily, evaluating students' problem-solving skills as you proceed from idea to idea. The technique is electronic clustering.

Consider this hypothetical student assignment (call it a test if you prefer):

Imagine that you are the new Vice President of Quality Control in a community hospital. For your first assignment, your boss has asked you to prepare a presentation for the next management meeting. The topic of your presentation: What effect will the thinning ozone layer have on hospital operations and the local community? If there is a problem, what steps can hospital employees take to minimize the impact within the hospital? —within their own homes? Make your presentation as convincing as possible.

The time you set aside for the assignment can be one to several class periods. If I were the new VP of Quality Control, I'd want to collaborate with as many people as appropriate to create my presentation; thus, you may want to encourage teams of students to work

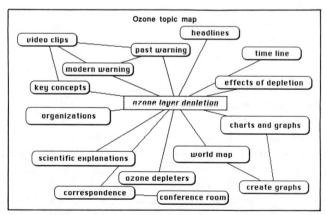

Figure 1. Student brainstormed maps are the "executive summaries" that give you an instant overview of their problem solutions. Clicking on the idea boxes that make up the map can lead you to a range of information expressed in different media: text, graphics, video, and sound.

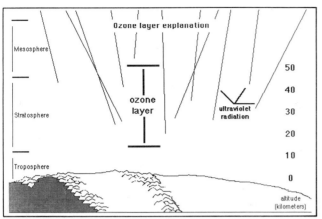

Figure 2.

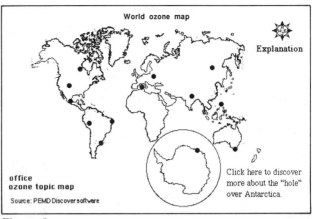

Figure 3.

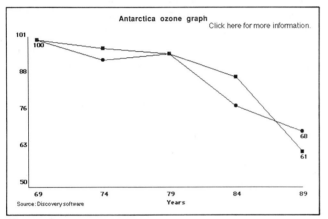

Figure 4.

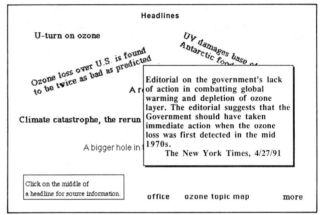

Figure 5.

Figures 2-5. The core of the information students use to solve their problems is already in the MindMap collection. Their goal is to create a network of links that takes you on a journey through that information. If they have been successful, by the time you've traversed their pathways you will have understood the purpose of the journey. As students create their informational pathways for you to follow, they're able to modify and add to any of the information types they use, including text, graphics, video, and sound.

together on the assignment. Whatever the time allocated and the size of problem-solving teams, one element remains constant: Students brainstorm and map their solutions for you to evaluate. The environment in which they map the assignment is a previously prepared MindMap collection containing information on the thinning of the ozone layer. Whether you purchase the collection commercially or create it yourself, the information in it can be displayed in different formats; for example, charts and tables, graphic representations of scientific principles, explanatory text, sound

from recorded newscasts, and appropriate videodisc clips.

Brainstorming Maps

Students brainstorm solutions on their own MindMap screen. Ideas they create can be filled with their own words or they can link those ideas directly to data already in the MindMap collection. If the collection was used in class prior to the assignment, students will be familiar with its content and flow. They'll be able to more quickly link into the data they feel is important to their solution. Otherwise, they'll rely more heavily on MindMap's directory and key word index to help them discover and navigate the information in the collection.

As students discover relevant information, they create links from their ideas to that information. With links in place, a single mouse click on a brainstormed idea takes browsers directly to information screens that support the hypothesis of the clicked-upon idea. Students can add more credibility to their hypotheses by creating additional links from those supporting data screens to other relevant screens. Along the way they can customize any MindMap screen to more accurately reflect their thinking. Very quickly, students begin to weave together sophisticated webs of knowledge.

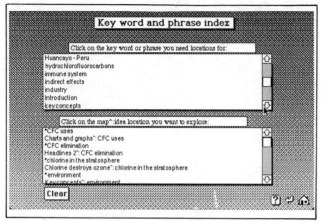

Figure 6. MindMap's index provides a quick way for students to discover the main concepts covered in the original collection. The index also can give you electronic clues to the key words and phrases students considered in their own problem-solving strategies. By comparing their list of key terms with the data to which they eventually navigated, you can determine if they used their chosen concepts appropriately or if they made omissions that needed more detailed explanation.

Evaluating Student Solutions

As students create their knowledge webs, they leave behind an electronic trail that you can follow and evaluate. The ''executive summary'' of their solution is the original one-screen brainstormed map. This map provides a quick overview of their solution in a single field of view. Studying a map can be as revealing as marveling over Mihtat's signature. No two maps are ever the same and each provides insights into students' problem-solving thought processes—insights as revealing as individual fingerprints or signatures.

With the overview of the solution in hand, your next step is to follow the actual trail through the data. Does the data support the group's claims? Are the selected video clips relevant to the solution? Do the words they wrote accurately describe each element in the journey?

The key words students chose to explore during their quest provide another set of evaluation clues. Mind-Map stores student-selected words and phrases in its index screen. Clicking on key words in a student index list takes you to the MindMap screen in which the words appear. If students opted not to include a particular concept in their final solution (you know they considered the concept because it appears in their key word list), should they have? Could this omission be something to mention in your evaluation?

Following electronic clues through a knowledge web may be uncharted territory for many teachers, but the adventure can reveal insights into students' thought processes hard to track down elsewhere. While your first trip through a web can be as unnerving as a precipitous descent on a Santa Cruz boardwalk roller coaster, each succeeding ride becomes less intimidating. Evaluating student maps becomes as intuitive and powerful as signing your own name.

John Boeschen, 25 Valley View Ave., San Rafael, CA 94901.

For more information on MindMap, see Vol. 8(4), pp. 16-19. MindMap is available from William J. Bradford Publishing Co., 310 School St., Acton, MA 01720.

Portfolio Assessment

Linda Polin

. . . tests widely used today are fundamentally incompatible with the kinds of changes in educational practice that are needed to meet current challenges. (Resnick & Resnick, 1989)

Portfolio assessment is a "hot topic" for the 90s. Portfolios are being discussed as an alternative to the use of standardized tests of multiple-choice items in the large-scale assessment of educational progress. While much of the conversation about portfolios is coming from evaluation specialists and testing agencies, most of the practical investigation and effort is coming from administrators, teachers, and state leaders concerned with the quality of large-scale assessments. Teachers and administrators have long questioned the validity of multiple-choice standardized tests, arguing that they (a) don't match up well with the local curriculum; (b) emphasize the recognition of facts, rather than the understanding of concepts; and (c) are a waste of instructional time because they provide teachers with little meaningful information about their students or their instruction.

Why Portfolios?

Just as a standardized test is intended to "sample" bits of knowledge from the larger domain of instruction, a portfolio offers a sample of student work representing the quality and diversity of that student's work over the school year. Standardized test items limit student response to the recognition and recall of information; portfolios give students latitude to display their intellectual processes and produce more complex responses. To appeal to a wide variety of school districts, standardized tests avoid ties to any particular local curriculum. The contents of portfolios are deeply embedded in local instructional contexts. Standardized tests tell us little about the nature of instruction students receive; portfolios provide a sample of the very tasks students experience.

Collecting Portfolios of Work

Portfolios contain a selective variety of students' work in a number of formats. While there is not complete agreement about whether these pieces should reflect the student's best work or a typical (representative) sample, the majority argue that it ought to be the student's best work.

By providing students with alternative representations of knowledge and alternative forums for the display of expertise, portfolios avoid the literate bias of schooling and align more closely with "real world" work.

The portfolio should offer as much variety in task and subject as possible, but should be selected carefully. No one wants an overflowing folder of all student work. Most portfolio users suggest a modest 6 to 10 pieces in each student's portfolio, some work from earlier in the year or semester, and some from later on. All portfolio advocates require the inclusion of a "reflective" piece, written by the student, in which he or she comments on the collection. Some require that a "common" task be included in everyone's portfolio; others require an individual's report and work from a group project.

Everyone also agrees that the included pieces should not be single products, but should have attached to them all previous work leading up to the final product. This may include outlines, notes, drafts, and other elements from the planning and revising process. Many portfolio specialists also require the teacher or student to include a description of the task and the resources available to students to complete it.

Portfolio advocates all agree that the contents of the portfolio may take many forms, including video and audio tapes, papers, computer printouts, reports, letters, sketches, semantic maps, paintings, snapshots of constructions, and so on. Buried in this odd assortment of formats are many advantages for students, especially students sometimes labelled "at risk" or "low achieving." Also, the independence from written English documents may allow a more accurate assessment of achievement or progress for students for whom English is a second language. By providing students with alternative representations of knowledge and alternative forums for the display of expertise, portfolios avoid the literate bias of schooling and align more closely with "real world" work.

Who should select the work? Every possible response has some support behind it: students only, teachers only, students and teachers together. The majority argues for student selection in conjunction with the teacher. After the student makes initial choices, the teacher and student discuss those choices. The teacher may suggest a piece he or she feels is very strong, which the student may have overlooked because it is not a favorite. In fact, reports of pilot tests of portfolios reveal that where decisions are made together, students may start out selecting favorite pieces, but soon recognize the value of ''less interesting'' but well executed work.

The Power of Personal Reflection

In gathering material for their portfolio and reflecting back across the accumulation of work, students gain an enlarged view of what they've learned and the progress they've made. Requiring students to include preliminary and draft work as supporting documents for their final pieces sends a message to students about the importance of process as well as product. Over time, reflected in the contents of their portfolio, students can compare early and later versions of their thinking and working processes and come to see that the changes reflected in their products are a result of their intellectual development. In the Pittsburgh Public Schools, Project PROPEL portfolios ask students to ''. . . [take] up the stance of an informed critic or autobiographer, noticing what is characteristic, what has changed with time, or what still remains to be done'' (Wolfe, 1989).

Reflecting on one's work and discussing it with someone else seems to lead students to a greater sense of pride, self-confidence, and responsibility. After some time in this system, students begin to internalize criteria for judging their work and recognize their own style and taste. If these are inevitable consequences of the portfolio process, than we have finally found an assessment strategy that doesn't waste students' time and functions as a very sophisticated learning experience.

Teachers also learn from perusing and discussing students' portfolios. Those who have used portfolios in their classes report that the experience offers them insights into the efficacy of their instructional methods as well as into the individual instructional needs and problems of their students.

Sample Portfolios

To create a middle school language arts portfolio, Linda Rief (1990) asks students to select two ''best'' pieces during each 6 weeks of a 12-week trimester for inclusion in their portfolios. Students may select work done for other courses, such as a social studies report. At the end of each trimester, students rearrange their work in order from most to least effective and add their self-evaluation of processes and products reflected in the chosen pieces. The portfolio from a typical student might contain 10 items: 3 poems, a narrative, a character sketch, a letter,

---

The quality of the portfolio experience is tempered by the quality of the instructional experience. A teacher who offers little diversity in his or her instructional tasks will not have portfolios that contain multiple formats displaying students' expertise, and will lose the opportunities that diversity offers.

---

a drawing, a play, an essay, and an acrylic collage interpreting a book the student had read. Attached to each item in the portfolio are items that ''contributed'' to the final product. To ensure an adequate supply of writing for students to choose from, Rief asks for five rough draft pages each week and demands a half-hour of reading each night.

To write their end-of-trimester reflective piece, Rief asks her seventh and eighth grade language arts students to address the following questions: What makes this your best piece? How did you go about writing it? What problems did you encounter? What makes your most effective piece

different from your least effective piece? What goals did you set for yourself? How well did you accomplish them? What are your goals for the next semester?

Math and language arts are commonly the subjects in which portfolios are being tried out. Some of the more systematic work on large-scale use of portfolio assessment comes from math and science educators struggling to find ways to get children to reveal their math and science knowledge in problem-solving situations by writing about them. To ignore their work in portfolio assessment simply because it isn't from the field of language arts is a real mistake.

The California Assessment Program (CAP), in conjunction with UC Berkeley and UC Irvine, initiated study of the use of mathematics portfolios for assessment. Based upon those experiences, CAP produced a set of guidelines for selection and scoring of math portfolios (CAP, 1989). The portfolios should contain from six to seven items of particular kinds, with some latitude for additional pieces. Teachers, rather than students, choose the materials to include in the portfolios. The portfolios must contain a minimum of four pieces of individual student work accompanied by student writing, an individual's report on a 3- to 5-day group project, and a ''reflective'' piece. Student work may take many forms: drawings, tables, graphs, writing, sketches, or other systems of representation. The reflective pieces are described as ''math autobiographies'' written at the beginning and end of the instructional period (e.g., semester). Teachers are encouraged to ask students to respond to questions such as ''What do you know about addition?'' To help math teachers, CAP guidelines were revised to specify how they might create writing prompts for math tasks that would allow students to display more clearly their thinking processes and abilities. For example, ''Imagine you are in a country that uses base five instead of base ten.

Describe aspects that would seem strange to you.''

Scoring Portfolios

There is no hard and fast rule on the scoring of portfolios. CAP suggests that math portfolios be scored or ranked on the basis of three characteristics: (a) mathematical thinking, (b) breadth and richness of experience, and (c) mathematical disposition. Teachers may choose to add other criteria to the list such as the student's facility with the math tools and resources. In Vermont, where portfolio assessment in math and language arts is a statewide commitment, portfolios will be scored by trained teams of teachers (Mills, 1989). Rather than collect and score portfolios from all students, Vermont will use a sampling procedure. The teacher teams will examine the sample and write a detailed description of student progress. This report will be disseminated to the public. The state also hopes to encourage local publication of samples of students work from their portfolios. No doubt this will provide parents and community with a better grasp of their students abilities than will a single percentile score from a standardized test.

Are portfolio assessments as good an indicator of student performance as the usual assessment? The only research study I could uncover seems to be a dissertation study undertaken by Jay Simmons out of the University of New Hampshire (Jongsma, 1989). Simmons randomly selected 27 fifth-grade students for two tasks. Students gathered up three pieces of their best school writing and also took a classic version of writing assessment— a timed test in which they wrote to a given prompt. Simmons scored the writings holistically and gathered additional data on length and time spent on the portfolio pieces. He also collected teacher and student comments. His analyses revealed that students who scored the lowest on the timed writing sample scored statistically significantly better on the essays in their portfolios. The quality of portfolio and timed sample essays of the average and above average students were not significantly different. This seems to suggest that portfolios offer important advantages to children who are most often the target of additional testing.

A Few Caveats

Of course, the quality of the portfolio experience is tempered by the quality of the instructional experience. A teacher who offers little diversity in his or her instructional tasks will not have portfolios that contain multiple formats displaying students' expertise, and will lose the opportunities that diversity offers. A teacher who provides few occasions for writing or constructing other products will restrict the choices students have available and thereby stunt opportunities for students to reflect on progress. Without an instructional emphasis on process, students will have little supporting documentation for the products they generate and restricted access to their own intellectual strategies. In fact, students and teachers in programs in which instructional goals are not clearly articulated will have difficulty selecting appropriate work. In such instances ". . . portfolios have the potential to become unfocused holding files for odds and ends, or worse, a place to collect more isolated skills tests'' (Valencia, 1990).

It is also critical to recognize that that students and teachers are not used to student involvement in evaluation. And, the self-selection and self-evaluation process students go through in constructing their portfolio collection can lead to ''intimate and often frighteningly subjective talk with students'' (Wolfe, 1989).

Who's Doing It?

Most of the talk about portfolio assessment is still talk, although there are at least three key places in the country where educators are putting portfolio assessment to the test. The Pittsburgh Public Schools have teamed up with Project Zero at the Harvard Graduate School of Education to establish a districtwide process for the use of portfolios in assessing student work in the arts and humanities. The entire state of Vermont has made a major, long-term commitment to the use of portfolios to assess math and language arts achievement with other subject areas slated to be included later on. In California, the California Assessment Program (CAP), in conjunction with UC Berkeley, UC Irvine, and UC Santa Barbara, has been pilot-testing the procedures for the statewide use of math portfolios. In addition, a number of schools and teachers are undertaking portfolio assessments on their own (Rief, 1990). Look for articles from them about their experiences in practitioner journals.

Resources

The projects mentioned in this article can be reached for additional information at the addresses below. Most publish quarterly or other periodic newsletters. An additional resource of interest is the Northwest Evaluation Association, a group which has established itself as a clearinghouse on information about portfolio assessment. These folks have annotated bibliographies on the subject and information on upcoming conferences being held around the country on portfolio assessment.

Mathematics Portfolio Project, California Assessment Program, PO Box 944272, Sacramento, CA 94244-2720

ARTS PROPEL, Project Zero, Harvard Graduate School of Education, 13 Appian Way, Cambridge, MA 02138-3752

Vermont Portfolio Assessment Project, Vermont State Dept. of Education, Montpelier, VT 05602

Portfolio Assessment Newsletter, Northwest Evaluation Association, 5 Centerpointe Dr., Suite 100, Lake Oswego, OR 97035

Portfolio Assessment Clearinghouse, c/o Sanguito Union High School District, 710 Encinitas Blvd., Encinitas, CA 92024

References

California Assessment Program (1989). *Draft of guidelines for the mathematics portfolio, Phase II pilot.* Sacramento, CA: California State Department of Education, California Assessment Program.

Jongsma, K. S. (1989). Questions & answers: Portfolio assessment. *The Reading Teacher, 43*(3), 264-265.

Mills, R. P. (1989). Portfolios capture rich array of student performance. *The School Administrator, 46*(11), 8-11.

Resnick, L. B., & Resnick, D. P. (in press). Assessing the thinking curriculum: New tools for educational reform. In B. R. Gifford & M. C. OConnor (Eds.), *Future assessments: Changing views of aptitude, achievement, and instruction.* Boston: Kluwer Academic Publishers.

Rief, L. (1990). Finding the value in evaluation: Self-assessment in a middle school classroom. *Educational Leadership, 47*(6), 24-29.

Valencia, S. (1990). A portfolio approach to classroom reading assessment: The whys, whats, and hows. *The Reading Teacher, 43*(4), 338-340.

Wolfe, D. P. (1989). Portfolio assessment: Sampling student work. *Educational Leadership, 46*(7), 35-39.

Linda G. Polin, Associate Professor of Education, Pepperdine University, Graduate School of Education and Psychology, 400 Corporate Pointe, Culver City, CA 90230-7627.

Ever So Carefully

by Marissa

Look Carefully,
Every so
      Carefully
At the shattered stones—
      For what was once green and lush
Is now bleached
        as bone.

Speak Quietly,
Lest you break the silence
      Although the stones have no ears—
And sit
      Quietly
Ever so Quietly
      In Defiance.

Walk SLOWLY
Through the hollow caves
Deep
Down
Where the future
      Lies—
And see the glimmering pool of Joy and Hope
    Draining Slowly
     Ever so Slowly
     And Quietly
    Ever so Quietly
      Slowly
      Quietly
      AND
      Carefully—
      (ever so)
      Until dry.

from Pomergranate, the Granada High School literary journal

Software Review
Kristi Kraemer

Writer's Helper Stage II

Gr. 8+; $135; Apple II, Macintosh, IBM-DOS, Windows; Network version available
CONDUIT
The University of Iowa
Oakdale Campus
Iowa City, IA 52242

Writer's Helper Stage II provides older students with support in both the prewriting and editing stages. Nineteen rewriting Tools (with 9 new activities in this second edition) cover a range of thinking and writing styles and can be selected or modified for individual writers and situations; the 20 Revision Tools with 9 new activities include a variety of sophisticated checks to help students reflect on how their choices in style and diction will affect their intended audience. By using the Customize menu, teachers can modify most of the preprogrammed activities or develop new ones to reinforce specific tasks or skills.

Prewriting Tools

Writer's Helper provides writers with ideas throughout the prewriting stage, from the earliest search for a topic through the process of precomposing, selecting, connecting, and organizing a "map" of the content to be included in the rough draft.

The very first set of Prewriting Tools helps writers Find or narrow topics about which to write. The set includes activities appropriate for writers who enjoy free choice, as well as activities to serve as catalysts for students working on assigned topics. Although many of the activities in this group, such as brainstorming, listing, and answering open-ended questions, have long served to inspire writers and teachers, one less well-known synectic activity also is included. Synectics, strategies used in business and in writing, aid in the discovery of new and creative connections between ideas or bits of information. William Wresch, author of **Writer's Helper**, describes the Idea Wheel as a "slot machine of ideas." Writers are presented with three columns of words: subjects, verbs, and objects, which are "spun" to present some oddly interesting sentences. Like other activities in **Writer's Helper**, the specific words in the program can be changed to reflect current topics of class discussion. This rolling, random presentation can help writers find ideas to develop even if the topic is very new to them.

For writers who already have a topic in mind, the next set of tools helps them Explore their ideas, information, and insights in an informal fashion. Several of the activities ask direct, open-ended questions about the topic or about the audience who will be reading the piece; others prompt the writer to look at the topic from a variety of perspectives; and still other activities help the writer to compare their topic with other concepts and topics. Some of the activities are open-ended, allowing the student to explore, unfettered by thoughts of a future product; others are more focused, asking the writer to consider long-range goals for the piece.

One of the most interesting activities in this section asks writers to make Connections among various aspects of their topic. First, they are asked to write 20 phrases about their subject. A student working on a paper about *The Great Gatsby*, for example, might include phrases such as "all those

Prewriting Tools

Find	Explore	Organize
Starters	Crazy Contrasts	Trees
Idea Wheel	Three Ways of	Debating an Issue
Associations	Seeing	Structure Guide
Questioner	Audience	Goals
Lists	Random Revelations	Compare/Contrast
Brainstorms	Connections	Outliner
		Develop a Paragraph
		Five Paragraph
		Theme

Revising Tools

Structure	Audience	Checks
Outline Document	Readability Index	Usage
Paragraph Coherence	Diction Level	Homonyms
Paragraph Development	Transitions	Gender
List by Sentence	Prepositions	
Sentence Lengths	References	
Category Match	"To Be" Verbs	
Subordinate Clauses	Sweet or Stuffy?	
Word Frequencies	Audience Summary	
Structure Summary		

shirts," "the parties," "the light on the dock," "Meyer Wolfsheim," and so forth. When completed, phrases from the list are paired at random and presented with a prompt asking the student to write about the possible connections among those phrases. In exploring the connections between "all those shirts" and "Meyer Wolfsheim," the student might recall that at one point in the book, Wolfsheim mentions that he had shown Gatsby how to dress and how to act, and that he is greatly satisfied with his creation. At this point, a potentially interesting thesis might present itself; if not, another spin of the columns might help.

As they work with these first two sets of Prewriting activities, identifying topics, developing controlling ideas or theses, and collecting and connecting ideas and information, students' notes are recorded on the NotePad in the program. Although a somewhat cumbersome procedure, these notes can be exported to another disk for use in writing the first draft or may be printed for later reference.

The last set of Prewriting Tools helps writers Organize their material, identify any gaps in logic or information, and focus on the potential final draft and its audience. Here too there is a mix of familiar and unfamiliar approaches, some of which encourage the writer to choose the form that will be most effective in communicating the content, and others that will help focus the content to fit a more formulaic structure such as a lab report or article for an academic journal. Some of the activities help the writer decide how to inform, others help structure persuasion; some are open, others are highly directed.

The mix is vast, and writers unsure about where to start with their topic, how to proceed, or how to end will surely find at least one of these activities helpful. Teachers working with specific domains of writing such as problem/solution, reflective essay, or firsthand biography can either modify existing activities or design new ones to help their students focus their thinking more effectively.

Revising Tools

Although **Writer's Helper** includes the NotePad to record notes throughout the prewriting process, the program is not designed to serve primarily as a word processing system. Writers are encouraged to transfer notes to another disk or to print them for reference, and to seek feedback from friends, classmates, and other readers as they write and revise their drafts. When the piece is ready for polish, the Revising Tools will be of great value. They are designed to help the writer focus beyond mere correctness to the reasons for it, and to look at choices in style, diction, and density to determine the most effective way to present his or her ideas to the audience.

As a high school teacher, I wish all my students had access to *Writer's Helper*; it would allow me to spend more time collaborating with them as they think through and write their papers and would boost their confidence as writers who are capable of effectively presenting their ideas and insights to the world.

The first set of Revising Tools helps the writer "re-see" the Structure of what has been written by listing key concepts and by looking at the texture of the writing through checks of sentence and paragraph length, subordination, and types of words used. These checks allow students to quickly review their work for the kinds of important but subtle details about their writing that are often elusive. Writers can select the checks they wish to run, and the procedure automatically teaches them about structure and logic at a time when they can immediately apply the information to their own writing. This solves the eternal teaching quandry of either having to hurry through instruction to "cover it all" or having to carefully time instruction on specific revision strategies for maximum effect, when most (but never all) of the students have drafts in hand.

The second set of Revising Tools helps the writer assess how the writing style might affect the Audience by reviewing the syntax and diction of the piece. These activities reinforce many of the "grammar" lessons taught at the secondary level, including "to be" verbs, un- or mis-referenced pronouns, overused prepositional phrases, missing transitions, and inappropriate vocabulary—the kinds of things often taught but rarely revised, because finding and fixing the problems is such a cumbersome task. Most of these checks take less than five minutes using **Writer's Helper**, and each check provides the writer with not only an analysis but with suggestions about how to improve the draft. Since each individual's problems are unique, the Revising Tools provide the kind of individualized instruction impossible in a classroom of one teacher and 30 or more students.

The final set of Checks reviews the writer's use of "problem words" such as accept/except, "alot," there/their/they're, its/it's, and other banes of an English teacher's existence, along with a quick check for possible gender bias in the piece.

As a high school teacher, I wish all my students had access to this program; it would allow me to spend more time collaborating with them as they think through and write their papers and would boost their confidence as writers who are capable of effectively presenting their ideas and insights to the world.

Because the variety of activities is so vast, multiple copies of the program are needed to fit the needs of any group of writers; fortunately CONDUIT provides both discount Educator Packs and special prices for groups of 15 students or more who wish to purchase their own copies.

I wonder . . . are the roles of teacher and salesperson antithetical to each other?? □

Becoming Writers

Beth Cox

"Wow! I've gotta do this!"

That's how I felt after reading "Ken Kesey's Writing Classroom: Computer Aided Apprenticeship" in the September/October 1989 issue of *The Writing Notebook*.

But with which class? Honors 12? I use the term loosely —academically these kids are just average. However, there are only 13 in the class. I could work with that number on a project like this.

After reading the article, Greg, the class clown, immediately asked, "So what are we going to do with this?" Always suspicious of my motives, he knew that everything I present in class turns into a project.

"You're all going to create a character to bring to class tomorrow. We'll listen to the descriptions and vote on which ones will be in our class short story."

Moans and groans followed. As usual, Danielle asked, "How are we going to get graded on this?" I explained that journal entries as well as numerous drafts of scenes would make up the bulk of the grade. A quiet frown covered Tony's face, but Meaka, the winner of a local writing contest, was eager to begin. "This sounds like fun!" The rest of the class treated it like any other assignment.

I was shocked when every student had a character description the next day. Everyone jotted down notes on the characters, trying to select a few for the story. Everyone, of course, was convinced that theirs was the best. However, Kesey's discussion of the writing process, as well as a review of the book, *Caverns,* indicated the necessity of limiting the number of characters.

"Look at all the characters and try to develop an interesting relationship between two or three of them. We'll need to vote on just two or three who will be the main characters in our story."

"Patricia and Corrine sound like they should be girl-friends," mumbled Tameka as she scribbled notes in her writer's journal. "I think Danny should be the romantic influence," interjected Danielle, who had modeled her character after her boyfriend. "Adolf and Igmund make a better pair," said Shane, thinking his and Greg's characters were the best.

But, Joe's character, Gavin Antonio, and Lisa's Corrine won as the romantic couple in the story. And John, the journalist, was proud that his Andrew was selected as the antagonist. I'll never forget hearing, "This is fun! When are we going to write the story?"

The next homework assignment was to outline a possible plot for our characters. Again, everyone completed the assignment. Half of the class, mainly the boys, led by Greg and Shane, thought for sure that Shane's idea would win out, but Tameka's was chosen.

"I like my idea better," insisted Shane.

"Yeah," added Scott, one of his followers. "Tameka's won just because the girls outnumber the guys." John tried to encourage the dissent, but I was firm. The class voted, and democracy prevailed.

During the next session I worked with the class to divide the plot up into 13 scenes so everyone could be responsible for one, but it didn't work out. We only came up with 12 scenes, so John and Danielle volunteered to write the ending. The class agreed.

I requested that students write the first draft of their scenes on dittomasters. I ran off 13 copies of the scenes for

---

I only expected them to read the story aloud as a finale. I only expected them to enjoy hearing their work completed. Instead, they persisted in revising. . . .

---

the whole class. This time Greg, Shane, and Meaka didn't have their scenes done on time. The story was missing Scenes 3, 5, and 11, but I didn't let this stop the process.

"Tomorrow we're going to revise Scene 1, Tony's scene, on the computer." The class had been using the computer for writing since October and it was now January. So after the class read Tony's draft from the ditto, they were ready to contribute to the second draft.

Tony stationed himself in front of the computer while I encouraged everyone to participate in the rewrite.

"I think Vinnie should be eating calamari," insisted Danielle. "That's a more interesting Italian dish than spaghetti and meatballs." Scott disagreed. "What's wrong with spaghetti and meatballs?"

And the revision progressed with nonstop comments from all 13 students. This session was loud and heated. Everyone was exhausted at the end of the period, and we still needed another period to complete this scene, because everyone became involved with the story and needed sufficient time to make their views known.

There was no way that I could have completed the rest of the story in this manner. It was exciting, but not time efficient. For the rest of the scenes, I divided the class into groups of three. "Joe, you wrote Scene 2. Who would you like to work with? Remember, Shane, Diane, and Greg will be working on their scenes." Joe chose Tony and Tameka.

For the next two class periods, the students worked in the computer writing lab. One student typed while the other two sat on either side and all three rewrote the scene. I moved from station to station and attempted to answer miscellaneous questions. "How do you spell Vinnie's last name?" "Which is more expensive—a mini-van or Chevy Cordoba?" "How long should Andrew stay in New York?"

Amelia, probably the hardest worker in the class, came up to me after one of these sessions. "I can't work with Greg. He doesn't do enough work."

"Is he fooling around?" I asked.

"Not really. He's working on his scene, but he gets off the track too easily." I gave Amelia the option of working in another group, and this solved that problem.

Another day Tony confided, "Nobody listens to me. Every time I make a suggestion, nobody likes it." I realized that the class had many strong individuals who overpowered Tony's quiet personality. I suggested that he try to work with Amelia, who was one of his best friends. But there were times when he had to work with a group of students who were not sensitive to his suggestions.

When Joe handed me his disk after his scene had gone through three drafts, he admitted, "I like my first draft better. Everyone else's ideas changed everything. It's not the same story anymore."

But Meaka interrupted him. "You're crazy! It's better this way. I love having other people help me write."

Lisa agreed. "I'm learning that not everyone thinks the way I do. And I think that all the different opinions and writing styles help to produce a more creative piece." This, from the best writer in the class.

Once the scenes had gone through at least a second draft, I reproduced a copy of all the scenes for the class. Joe selected two more students to work with, this time editing his scene for the final copy. I emphasized the importance of having smooth transitions between each scene and being alert to discrepancies in the plot.

The cooperative spirit was growing. "People help you with your mistakes," voiced Tameka. "I couldn't do this well on my own."

Greg agreed. "I'm learning how to describe more. Meaka and Danielle are really descriptive. I usually leave out the detail."

And, added Scott, "Diane is really good with the mushy stuff."

Once all drafts were completed, I sent the manuscript to the district printer. Two art students worked on the cover, and I included a title page as well as an introduction. The class also wrote a brief paragraph about themselves as writers for an author page at the end of the story.

They were all excited to see their names in print. The day finally came. The story ended up to be 17 pages.

"This looks GREAT!" exclaimed Meaka.

"I coulda drawn a better bullet," said Greg.

I had the class read the story aloud, assigning parts to everyone. Joe, of course, was his character, Gavin. Lisa insisted on being her Corrine. But John, who rarely says anything in class, asked Scott to read Andrew.

As they read, they automatically continued to revise.

"Shouldn't 'began' be 'begin'?" asked Lisa.

"Joe, you forgot to change Teresa to Corrine. Remember, we decided not to change the name?"

"Oh yeah, I forgot."

I only expected them to read the story aloud as a finale. I only expected them to enjoy hearing their work completed. Instead, they persisted in revising, a trait found in professional writers. There were problems with the collaboration. There were problems with the story itself. But the end result was obvious—during this project these 13 students had become writers.

Beth Cox, 108 Bradbury Road, Brookhaven, PA 19015.

A Sheet of Fear

"Did you say something?"
"Yes."
"What did you say?"
"Oh, never mind."
"No, you said something about fear."
"Yes, but it wouldn't make sense now."
"Why wouldn't it make sense now?"
"Because it's something I fear a little bit."
"What is it?"
"You."
"Me! Why me?"
Only when I first come face to face with you."
"Why?"
Because that's when you're a blank sheet of paper."
"Oh."

—*Tenley McCune*
Sophomore, Holmes High School
(From "Prewriting Strategies to Ease Fear." The Covington Writing Project, Ken Spurlock, Director, Covington, KY)

Comedy Grabs at the Smile

Darling child pantomime,
your silent voice echoed
        through satire and pathos.
Awarded for generous contributions,
        still you were tortured by self-doubt.
You were the blooming butterfly;
humor was within your soul.

Napoleon you never played,
but you overflowed with flowering humanity
and an individual freedom.
        "The Vagabond."
Wasn't serenading Edna enough?

        The beauty possessed
        through your silky, jet hair
        and perfect olive face
        came from the drumming,
        bright heart enhanced
        within your musical soul.

In England you were "Charlot,"
but the tragicomedian you always resembled.
Oh, Charlie, the circus clown,
you are my Lancelot,
my knight in shining humor.
You, the "shy and diffident,"
portrayed "the perfect clown."
Baggy pants,
enormous shoes,
a bowler hat,
and carrying a bamboo cane,
you portrayed the "Charlie"
that enlightened the quiet screen.
        "Little tramp."
        "Jazz boy, Charlie."
You were a man of many talents.
        You composed background melodies,
(musical rainbows that floated through the air),
produced and starred in films that sparkled
with your comic flare.

People adored the mustached man.
When you marched near, crowds shouted,
        "Charlie arrives!"

        Oh, "little tramp,"
        how much you shone.
        Your sweet style
        and candy coated qualities
        left the world aware
        of "a silhouette forsaken
        for the love of vanilla ice cream."

Comedy grabs at the one with the smile.
        "God love you!"

Michele Meza

Daniel Nguon
from the Stylus, Volume 17, Jordan High School, Long Beach, California

Laptops: An Organizing Tool for Writing

Sharon Franklin

The word processor is an excellent tool for writing. Unfortunately, with or without a computer, student writing all too often simply takes off, wanders for a time, and then ends—without ever really coming together.

At Hazel Valley School in Seattle, Washington, Mike Porter's sixth grade students use Tandy laptops at the beginning stages of the writing process to help outline and organize their thoughts. The skills Porter teaches his students begin as a very structured process that students individualize over time.

In Mike Porter's classroom, the writing process is ALIVE and well. Both students and ideas move freely around the room, along with their Tandy laptop computers. To an outsider it's an environment filled with the sound of energetic conversation over plots, characters, and endings. To Porter it's a sure sign that his students are thinking hard about their writing.

Sometimes Porter assigns a topic; other times students select their own topic and type it in. The examples presented in this article are from an assigned topic: "a mystery/adventure story involving one or more animals."

Students are given a series of **comment lines** to help them focus as they brainstorm ideas. The comment lines vary depending on the writing assignment. If a specific form or style of writing is the focus, Porter typically gives his students several "keys," or patterns, for writing in that genre. Other times, students brainstorm the elements they consider to be important for their report, article, or story. They discuss together how a writer might weave those elements into a good piece of writing.

Porter gave students six comment lines to help them begin their animal mystery/adventure story:

> **Prologue**
> **Setting**
> **Introduce main character(s)**
> **The problem**
> **The solution**
> **The ending**

Comment Lines as Idea Generators/Organizers

When students work on a structured assignment, they begin by typing in all the comment lines; typically they are typed in capital letters, along with a series of asterisks *** or other symbols. As time goes on, however, many students develop their own techniques for when and how to use comment lines.

After typing in the comment lines, students begin to type in their ideas under each one. Most students add and revise their ideas under each heading many times before beginning a rough draft. The flexibility of the laptops is apparent during this prewriting process: Students often pass their laptops back and forth, generously adding their own suggestions to the ideas of the main author. If the author likes an idea, it's kept in the story. If not, it's deleted.

Student Writing Using Comment Lines

The writing that follows shows the process in action.

Zac began his story by typing in one sentence following the first comment line, ***PROLOGUE.

***PROLOGUE
1938 was the year the private eyes Zac Bedell and Greg McClellan started the first detective agency in Burien.

When he finished typing in his initial ideas under PROLOGUE, he next considered the SETTING.

***SETTING
The time was 2:44. I was sitting on the beach minding my own business when a mangy old hound dog came up from behind and licked my face. I had never seen the dog before and in this small town thats a rarity. The dog had a collar on that looked like it had dimonds on it but in fact they where fake. The dog sitting next to me was as far as I could tell was a basset hound.

Next, Zac considered the characters in his story. As he continued his writing, note his decision to include two additional comment lines (THE PHONE CALL and THE CONFRONTATION) to help him further organize his ideas.

***INTRODUCE MAIN CHARACTER(S)
By the way my name is Zac Bedell private-eye my code number is 0.0.6 (double 0 six).
***SETTING
At my office
***THE PHONE CALL
***THE PROBLEM
***THE CONFRONTATION
***THE SOLUTION
***THE ENDING

The next time Zac returned to his writing, he continued to work on the PROLOGUE, SETTING, and CHARACTERS. Three revisions later, here's how his story progressed. Notice that the comment lines no longer appear.

1938 was the year private eyes Zac Bedell and Greg McClellan started the detective agency in Burien, WA. Their prime objective was to stop Harold Manny, the leader of a gang named the TIGERS. 1938 Zac's house burned to the ground. It was also the year the TIGERS got started (then it was a small club) but they still managed to burn somebodies house down.

Zac had seen Harold in his frontyard on his way back from church. Later Zac's house burned down to the ground. He swore he would get his revenge. After trying for six years Zac never got Harold back for it.

But now it was 1941 the time was 2:44 p.m. I was sitting on the beach minding my own business when a mangy old hound came up and licked my face. I had never seen the dog before and in this small town that's a rarity. The dog had a collar on that looked like it had diamonds on it, but in fact they where fake. (The diamonds would look real from a distance.) The dog, sitting next to me, was as far as I could tell a basset hound. It had no tags so I took it back to the office with me. And so ''Charlie'' was our new mascot.

By the way my name is Zac Bedell private eye ball. My code number is 006 (double 0 six). My partener's name is Greg McClellan, (Agent 42), but Greg and I call each other by our code numbers.

Another person you might want to know about is Harold Manny; his name may sound a bit weany but truthfully he is a master in every martial art you can think of. Harold is also the leader of the only gang in Burien . . . the TIGERS. They are the prime reason Agent 42 and I started this business.

Comment lines encourage students to enter their story more completely, to move through their characters, and to imagine their story more vividly as it unfolds.

We where in the office just playing some 1941 style NINTENDO when . . . the phone rang. It was the usual deep mysterious voice that I always get and so I new exactly who it was . . . Harold Manny. He said,
''Give me the dogs collar or the dog gets it.''
Then the usual dial tone afterwards.
. . . .

Zac is the first to point out that his story is not yet finished. Even though he has found and corrected several spelling and grammatical errors in each successive revision, the process of ''writing between the lines'' helps him to concentrate primarily on the substance of his story at this point. Just as it should be, says Porter. Zac will pronounce it a final copy only after several more content revisions and a thorough last check for spelling, grammar, and punctuation errors.

Comment lines encourage students to enter their story more completely, to move through their characters, and to imagine their story more vividly as it unfolds. In the following writing sample, you can begin to appreciate students' individual writing styles as shown in how they use the comment lines. Alix's story, unlike Zac's, progresses rather dramatically from her comment lines to her rough draft:

***SETTING
A cool summer day, in the month of May, with grass as green as an emerald, with the willow trees with just a slight breeze blowing their peddles around. A flowing stream tumbling down over pebbles and sticks to its destiny. Humming birds singing there toon so merry.

***MAIN CHARACTERS
A Kuvasz dog named Dutch with an ivory white coat sweet and yet a dangerous spirit he has. His best friend an Arabian stallion, his name is Secretariat, all black like the night with the same spirit as Dutch. His other good friend, Mike, a little field mouse timid and shy, a little gray thing he is.

***PROBLEM
Their owners are the worst and meanest people ever to own a animal! I mean they feed them unbalanced, unhealthy meals (except for the field mouse), they also don't pet, brush or pay attention to them. So they're making a plan to do something about it.

***SOLUTION
They (the dog and horse) tell the mouse to pack his bags because they're running away.

***ENDING
They find a little cove with every satisfaction of their dreams.

"It's a very flexible writing system, and the laptops are extremely well suited to this process. I encourage individualization—the tools shouldn't hinder the writer."

Here is the beginning of Alix's rough draft. Notice where and how she embeds her original ideas in the story. She already has deleted the comment lines.

The Great Escape from Catastrophe
Once upon cool summer day in the month of May a dog, horse, and a little field mouse sat under a willow tree with just a slight breeze blowing their blooms around, talking listening to the tumbling stream. The dogs name Dutch an ivory-white was he, his friend a horse as black as night his name Spirit. There little friend timmid and shy a little field mouse was he, his name was Mike and he was all gray except for a little black dot on his nose.

They were remembering once long ago when they were living in a persons home, oh he was so mean, they were mistreated and were fed unbalanced, unhealthy meals or sometimes no meal at all!

So one night when they were out grasing in the not so welltreated pasture they made up their minds to run away the next night. When Mike came that night they explained to him that tomorow night they were going to have the little mouse in the old run-down barn unlatch their chains and they would quietly sneak out and travel through the dark deserted woods and find a place to live.

The next day felt like a century, but finally it was time to leave. That night Dutch called to the little mouse and told him to unlatch the chains. The little mouse did so and Dutch thanked him. Finally they were on their way. . . .

Christie, unlike Zac and Alix, uses the comment lines more as an outlining tool to refer to as she writes.

***SETTING
Military Base

***INTRODUCE MAIN CHARACTER:
Buff the Bull Dog
Sico the Shnouser
Hendrixon the Hound
Lt. Commander Lenard J. Newton
Private Patrick Foster
General Gregory Shirwood

***THE PROBLEM
Buff, Sico, and Hendrixon have to guard the gate while Lenard, Patrick, and Gregory go to inspect the land for a top secret project. Resulting in some crazy mishaps.

***THE SOLUTION
To get the base cleaned before the general gets there.

***THE ENDING
Lenard, Patrick, and Gregory come back to camp. knowing nothing of the goings on in their absence.

In her next draft, she begins to write sentences and paragraphs from her notes:

Buff's Afternoon
The day started off slowly as Buff the bull dog ate his breakfast, consisting of two large beef basted bones. His day would begin relaxingly and progress in chaos. But for now he would streach out of his doghouse and lay down on the asphalt as the burning sun beat down on his shining, glossy, black coat.
. . . .

Porter encourages his students to use the computer initially as a tool to help them organize and express their ideas. Later in the process the computer becomes a tool for editing as they go back and make final changes in spelling, grammar, and punctuation. Many students find this organizing technique so helpful that they use it to complete reports in their social studies and science classes.

"It's a very flexible writing system, and the laptops are extremely well suited to this process," Porter explains. "I encourage individualization—the tools shouldn't hinder the writer. I've met very few adult writers who work in the same way. I respect the right of my students to work also in the way best suited for them."

With thanks to Mike Porter and his students at Hazel Valley School.

Works in Progress: The Gentle Art of Revision

Sharon Franklin

This editorial appeared in Volume 9(2).

The revision articles in this issue contain excellent ideas on how to encourage students to revise their writing. Even so, it occurs to me that the concept of revision carries implications that transcend a classroom setting.

Perhaps one reason our students are often loathe to revise their writing is that they see themselves as singled out for this punitive task—simply because they're kids. I mean, when do they ever see adults revise anything? What they see, mostly, is at least the illusion of finished products. The idea of a "work in progress" is pretty foreign.

This myth of the "finished" product is symbolized perfectly in the books children have before them. It's hard to know that these stories came out of the minds of real people through much hard work and many revisions. I remember once sharing with my students how Mercer Mayer began creating his version of *Beauty and the Beast* on airplane napkins as he was flying. I had photos of the napkins to show them—my students were amazed that such a gorgeous finished product actually came from a bunch of scratches and doodles!

We, as teachers, can make our own process explicit to students by modeling what we go through in planning a unit, including identifying the goals, listing possible resources and activities to include, arranging the schedule, and selecting guest speakers. This means thinking out loud in front of the class (with your students as collaborators) instead of in the privacy of your own home. It helps dispel the magic and reinforces the idea that (a) revision is hard work and (b) that it's done by real adults in everyday life.

Now, move the idea deeper, to a personal level. It helps kids immensely to hear us as adults share how we struggle with the issues that confront us: maintaining balance in our lives, finding time for ourselves, or resolving conflicts with our own parents, children, co-workers, or friends.

So why is this important? Why is "revision" important? I believe it has a lot to do with what we are ultimately trying to teach our students. I had the honor recently of talking with Howard Zinn, author of *People's History of the United States* (Harper Perennial, 1990). His book retells (i.e., revises) history through the voices of people whose feelings and perspectives traditionally are not heard. (In my mind, this book should be required reading for everyone over about the age of 12.)

Zinn makes the point that all accounts of history have a definite perspective; history is never neutral. Imagine a revision activity where students take one event from history, research it carefully, identify the perspective, and then retell it from the point of view of people who were present but not represented in the original telling.

Now we're at a level of revision with implications that far surpass a specific writing assignment. Imagine, ultimately, students who understand that no writing, no opinion, is carved in stone; that all writing, including their own, reflects a particular viewpoint and perspective at a specific moment in time. Imagine students who come to value *process* at least as much as product. Imagine a generation of students for whom the concept of revision is so deeply embedded that they feel entirely comfortable in looking critically, not only at their own life and ideas, but also at the words and ideas of politicians, world leaders, journalists, published authors, and other "experts" of the twentieth century and beyond. Imagine students who therefore have the courage to see themselves and their world as "works in progress," which makes it possible for them to be active participants in life, rather than paralyzed by complexities and numb to their own power.

The 3 R's of Revision: Review, Reread, React/Reshape

Rose Reissman

Have you ever read your students' work or heard students read their writing aloud and thought how much stronger it could be with some revision? Student-centered revision, independent revision, the core of the writer's art, has always been the hardest part of the writing process to "sell" to my junior high writers. To my surprise, I found an unexpected key to revision in a half-finished assignment on mystery stories.

It began in my 5th period class, where students were using the computer lab to maintain files of their own mystery stories developed from news clippings of unsolved cases. We were all busily engaged in writing when an unannounced fire drill interrupted the class. By the time we returned to the lab, the period was over and my class dashed off to their next class with their interrupted mysteries still on the screen.

The 1st R: PEER REVIEW
When my 6th period class came rushing in, I suggested that they begin by reading the mystery stories left on the monitors. I asked that they write the authors notes detailing the strong points so far and suggesting any possible changes or new directions. The students worked intently and, in fact, asked for more time. They signed their comments with their initials and class.

Before they started their own mystery writing, I asked them what they found so interesting about this task. They said that they liked getting to "see" and "comment" on the other students' work. One young man said it gave him ideas about what to do with his own story. Another student made everyone laugh when she said it gave her ideas for what *not* to do. She added, however, that she had been as positive as possible with her comments.

After students finished their own writing, they asked if the 7th period class could review *their* work, and I realized I'd experienced the first R of Revision: peer review.

The 2nd R: REREAD
The next day my 5th period class opened their mystery files and were surprised to find they had been reviewed by an initialed 6th period student. I explained what had happened and how much the 6th period class had learned from the experience.

After reading the comments, I gave them the remainder of the period either to respond to the reviewer in a short note in their file or to try out some of the revisions, "just to see how they would look on the monitor." At their request they also were given the 7th period students' stories to review. I began to see that the experience of being both peer reviewer and writer enhanced the writing process with an energy that was not there before.

The 3rd R: REACT/RESHAPE
Once students reread their pieces on the monitor and responded to the reviewer's ideas, I had them leave their files and go on to another writing task. When they asked why they couldn't work longer on their stories, I told them that often a writer needs to get away from the piece for a time and then return to it later in order to see it "fresh."

After a day's rest the students returned to their writing, read their original work, the reviewer's comments, and their own reactions or reshapings. They then rewrote more or, in some cases, wrote lengthy notes to the reviewer, explaining why they disagreed with their suggestions.

Reflections on the 3 R's from an English Teacher's Perspective
The computer facilitates peer review and revision in several important ways. First of all, it enhances the professionalism and productivity of these student writers. They quickly move beyond the handwriting problems of their peers to the core content of the writing. Second, both writer and reviewer are able to read and respond to the text on the screen without face-to-face extraneous discussions or potentially embarrassing exchanges. Both the writer and reviewer can shape the text in ways that the fastest "by hand" revising can't come close to touching. Finally, the ongoing file of each writing assignment offers my students and me an open record of their revision process.

Although I have access to a writing lab, this technique can be adapted easily to an individual classroom. Based on our experience, my students and I encourage you to "revise" your own classroom revision strategies.

Rose Reissman, Magnet Specialist District 25, Community School District 25, 70-30 164 St., Flushing, NY 11365.

REVISING: An Approach for All Seasons

Peter Adams

Since one view of our task as writing teachers is to help our students become stronger writers, we must convince our students to spend more time revising. But spending more time in itself will not produce better writing if the student is an ineffective revisor. So the task of a writing teacher is two-fold: to encourage students to spend more time revising and to ensure that whatever time they do spend is spent effectively. Of course, an emphasis on revision in the writing classroom is greatly enhanced when students are using word processors.

This article is written from the standpoint of the teacher as principal reader of student writing. However, these strategies could be used equally effectively with peer editing groups.

There are five revision principles that most students need to learn:

1. While all writers do some revising as they create a first draft of a paper, most writers produce better drafts full of better ideas if they postpone as much revision as possible until after they have completed that draft.

2. Revision is more than just correcting errors in punctuation and grammar—it includes reviewing the overall structure of the paper for unity, organization, development of ideas, and coherence.

3. Sentence-level revision (editing or proofreading) should be postponed if possible until after the major changes have been made.

4. Editing should be a sequence of rereadings in which the reader looks for only one category of problem at a time.

5. The editing process should be experimental, even playful; it should be a search for the most effective way of saying things, rather than merely a search for error.

A Process of Revision

As teachers, we need ways to encourage more effective revision by our students. One way to accomplish this is to *require* that papers be revised, and revised several times.

Most of us have required revision only when a student has turned in a particularly weak piece of writing. This encourages students to think of revision as punishment, as something that ''good'' writers don't have to do. Certainly not the message we intend.

If we require all students to revise papers regularly, we are encouraging students to view revision as a normal part of *everyone's* writing process. Furthermore, if we require that they revise in a series of steps instead of looking at everything at once, we will help them become more effective revisors.

The editing process should be experimental, even playful; it should be a search for the most effective way of saying things, rather than merely a search for error.

One way of accomplishing this is to give students comments on only one feature of their writing at a time. I use the following sequence with my students:

1. Thesis/unity/organization
2. Development of ideas
3. Coherence
4. Expression
5. Grammar/punctuation/spelling

I make comments on only one level of revision each time I see a paper. This means that the first time I see a paper I look first for problems with thesis, unity, or organization. If I find problems in this area, I write a comment about the problem and return the paper for revision. The next time I see the paper, I once again pay attention to the thesis, unity, or organization. If there are no problems, I then look at the development of ideas. If I find problems, I write a comment and return the paper for another revision. If there are no problems there, I move on to the next level. I don't comment on grammar, punctuation, or spelling until all other problems have been cleared up.

One result of this technique of multiple revisions is that students view my comments on their writing in a new light. In the past I've often worried that students were not reading my comments—that they just glanced at the grade and then threw the paper in the trash. Then I read Mary Hayes and Donald Daiker's article on using protocol analysis to study student reactions to teacher comments (*Freshman English News*, Fall 1984) and began to hope that my students *wouldn't* read my comments! Hayes and Daiker catalog a series of student misinterpretations of teacher comments. For example, one student read the comment, ". . . fragment, but it works stylistically, quite well in fact" and interpreted it as ". . . a fragment. Uh, I think it means that . . . it isn't really related to the preceding sentences. It's just . . . out of place." This, even after the class had worked on fragments. Another student, reading his teacher's comment saying that he needed more analysis of the text, concluded that he was rambling too much and should merely summarize the text. In both cases, the teacher comments did more harm than good.

Because I now require multiple revisions of papers, both my attitude and my students' attitudes toward comments have changed dramatically. They read them carefully as suggestions for revision (rather than as the final judgments they seemed to be in the past). And, I now make my comments in a different way. I couch everything as a suggestion for revision rather than as a criticism of a mistake—and not because of some dishonest pose that I assume; my comments really are suggestions for revisions.

Furthermore, I now know whether I am communicating my thoughts clearly or not. When I read the next revision, it is quite obvious whether or not the student understood my comments.

A student in my class may revise a particular paper four, five, six, or even more times. And I check each paper a corresponding number of times. Unrealistic? Too much work for student and teacher? Not necessarily. Notice, for example, that each time I check a paper, I am making comments on only one level. Once I discover a problem with organization, I write my comment and return the paper; I don't check anything else. The result is that I see each paper many times, but only briefly each time.

What about the amount of work required of the student? Remember that my students are writing on word processors. When they revise a paper, they make changes and reprint; they do not retype the entire paper. If your students do not have access to a word processor, you can still use this technique, but perhaps with only two or three papers in the course of a semester.

Having said all this, I must admit that multiple revisions do take more time—for teachers and students. But this is no reason not to adopt the technique. It may just mean that students write fewer papers. However, fewer papers is not the same thing as less writing. They do more writing, but much of it is revising rather than writing new drafts. Before adopting multiple drafts, I had my students write eight papers per semester; now they write and revise six.

The Final Step

I said earlier that I don't comment on grammar, punctuation, or spelling until everything else is in fairly good shape. That's so, and the way I comment on grammar is quite different from what I used to do.

When everything else looks good, I go through the paper and mark the number of errors in each paragraph. I also may indicate that the errors are punctuation or agreement problems or something else. I then return the paper to the student for revision. If the student does not correct all the errors, I next indicate which sentences have errors and give a more explicit description of the error. On the next draft I will indicate the exact location of the remaining errors and ask the student to correct them. When there are errors that the student simply cannot correct or errors that crop up time and time again in a particular student's writing, I make a very specific referral to the Writing Center, where the student works on that particular skill.

The result is that the student gets practice in error correction that (a) makes use of actual writing rather than numbered sentences, (b) is tailored to his or her individual weaknesses because it includes only errors the student has actually made, and (c) trains the student to become more proficient at both locating and correcting errors. This procedure puts grammar in its rightful place—at the end of the revising process.

Requiring multiple drafts is a general approach that shows great promise for improving students' revision skills as well as their ability to produce writing with a reduced number of errors.

_____

Peter Adams, English Dept., Essex Community College, Baltimore, MD 21237.

TWO I's and BRASS KNUCKLES: Successful Revision Strategies!

Elane Polin

TWO I's

This strategy accompanies one of the first writing assignments I give my sophomore writing class, planned for early October. I ask students to write from the voice of an animal. I start with a first person narrative, because it is usually fun for students and they are able to use previous knowledge and experiences so it's not hard to write more than one paragraph.

My students meet in a room with 28 computers, 6 printers, and tables and chairs arranged in groups of four—enough for all my students when they are not using the computers. This class meets every day for a semester, and every day there are students using the computers. They use them in the beginning for prewriting, either clustering or "jot listing." When they finish they share their work with the other students at their table. Next comes a rough draft. After printing a hard copy of this draft, they return to their table group.

Here is the beginning paragraph from one student's first draft:

> I wake up one morning and I feel a hunger. I want a rabbit. I growl to wake myself up. I stretch out every little inch of my body and start to hunt for a rabbit. I speed through the forest like a yellow blur. I run for miles and I finally reach my prey. I drool down my fur as I look at it with hungry eyes. I jump it but the rabbit is fast. It seems like I chase him for eternity. He begins to lose his momentum and I slaughter him.

At this point I collect all rough drafts and choose several to read. It's not a random selection: I purposefully choose three that have many I's in the first paragraph, like the example above. I read in a tone that slightly exaggerates the I's. The students soon catch on, commenting on the repetition of the word "I." I hand back their papers and tell them that two eyes are all that an animal has, and two I's are all I want to read in their papers! I joke about the record set last year with 65 I's! They circle and count the I's in their papers and discover who has the most and who has the least. The former usually gets applause and the latter cries of disbelief.

They moan about the impossible task of reducing the I's to two. Now I know they are desperate and ready to learn! Working collaboratively, they begin trying to eliminate the I's. One student—if I'm lucky, sometimes two—at a table are able to do this. The knowledgeable students share their strategies and examples with the class. We look for clues in their model sentences.

Students should handle language until it becomes putty in their hands.

How did they omit the I's? Usually the first pattern students discover is the participial phrase. "When I woke up I went to the pond" becomes "Waking up, I went to the pond." There are examples of dangling participles to warn against. I try to provide humorous examples: "Racing through the undergrowth, the roots tripped me."

Students discover that changing from passive to active voice helps. "I was bitten by the bear" becomes "The bear bit me." Phrases become subjects: "Carrying him through the jungle made me think about how delicious he would be." We look for prepositional phrases, changing "I feel hungry. I want a rabbit" to "I feel hungry for a rabbit."

91

The more experience the student has with language, the more sophisticated the sentences become. We find examples of adverbial clauses and add key words (e.g., "after," "when," "until") to our sentence pattern banks. (Whenever we find or learn something that can be used again in our writing, we put it in a bank. Students have sentence pattern banks as well as different types of word banks.)

Does this sound suspiciously like sentence combining? Of course it is, with one important difference. These are not isolated sentences, made up for the purpose of a lesson or taken from someone else's writing and cut into artificial parts. These are real sentences created to communicate a story to a real audience of peers. These are ideas and sentences that students own and care about.

Does this sound like an old-fashioned grammar lesson? Perhaps a little, but I never mention grammatical labels. It's important for the teacher to know the grammatical concepts and be able to model them and analyze them from his or her own writing, from students' writing, or from the literature they're reading. It's important for students to be able to play in the truest sense of the word, to fool around with words, trying different combinations, changing words and wording, subordinating and coordinating ideas, without puzzling about compound, complex patterns. Students should handle language until it becomes putty in their hands.

I must warn you that the writing that results from this is often forced, stuffy, awkward, even unclear. But since they have a hard copy of their original rough draft and a copy of the TWO I's revision, students can now combine the best of the two. Here's what happened to the rough draft quoted above:

> The hunger for rabbit woke me up from a long peaceful sleep. A growl from a good night's rest bellowed out of my lungs, and I stretched every muscle and bone in my body. My hunt started as my legs carried me through the forest like a lightning bolt. My fur coat made me look like a yellow blur. My eyes spotted rabbit. Drool dripped down my mouth as the chase went on. The rabbit turned and dodged away from me, but it was no use. After an eternity, he began to lose momentum. My teeth snatched at him and the race was finally over.

A final tip. This strategy sounds so simple. It has a touch of whimsey, a cuteness about it that is deceptive. But it works! It works because I write too. I find I's in my writing. It works because when asked for help, I sometimes say, "Gee, I don't know. Let's fool around with it," and others gather to help. It turns out that the best sentence usually comes from the student whose paper it is. It works because I truly care about my students' writing—students know this is not just busy work.

So here we are, my students and I, playing with language. Sometimes I ham it up and call our "showing, not telling" papers SNTS (pronounced "snits"). That makes them more palatable.

When we're revising for more exact and fresh vocabulary words, we use another strategy, called "Brass Knuckles."

BRASS KNUCKLES

This title originated from a student. He told me we were looking for "brass knuckle" words, so we could get power and pack a punch. This image really appeals to many of my students. Students have individual word banks on their own floppy disks, in addition to the public domain class data-based word banks. We have skill drills that use the word "get" in 20 different sentences. Students work in pairs to try to replace the word "get." (Do you get the idea of this lesson?) Students write skits, sometimes acting them out, using different forms of the word "walk" (e.g., "limp," "lurch," "amble," "saunter," "skidaddle") or "said" ("screamed," "bantered," "whispered," threatened"), both designed to give their writing a greater preciseness and vitality.

The TWO I's and BRASS KNUCKLES may be just what you need to encourage your students to play with language and refine their writing skills.

Elane Polin, West High School, Torrance Unified School District, Torrance, California.

Revising on Computer in the High School

Jo Zarro

I've found several ways for my 11th and 12th grade students to take advantage of the computer at the revision stage of their writing. Most of my students have some computer skills, either through taking an Introduction to Computers class or having used the English/Language Arts Writing Lab in the 10th grade.

The most common and least complicated way for them to revise is to:

1. Run their writing through the spell checker, which cleans up the most obvious mistakes and typos, and print a hard copy;

2. Pair up and read each other's printed drafts;

3. Discuss the strong and weak points of the writing;

4. Ask questions about unclear passages;

5. Edit mechanical errors; and

6. Exchange partners and repeat the process, following specific guidelines for each type of writing given to students at the beginning of a unit or writing assignment. (See Figure 1 for an example set of guidelines created using Hypercard.)

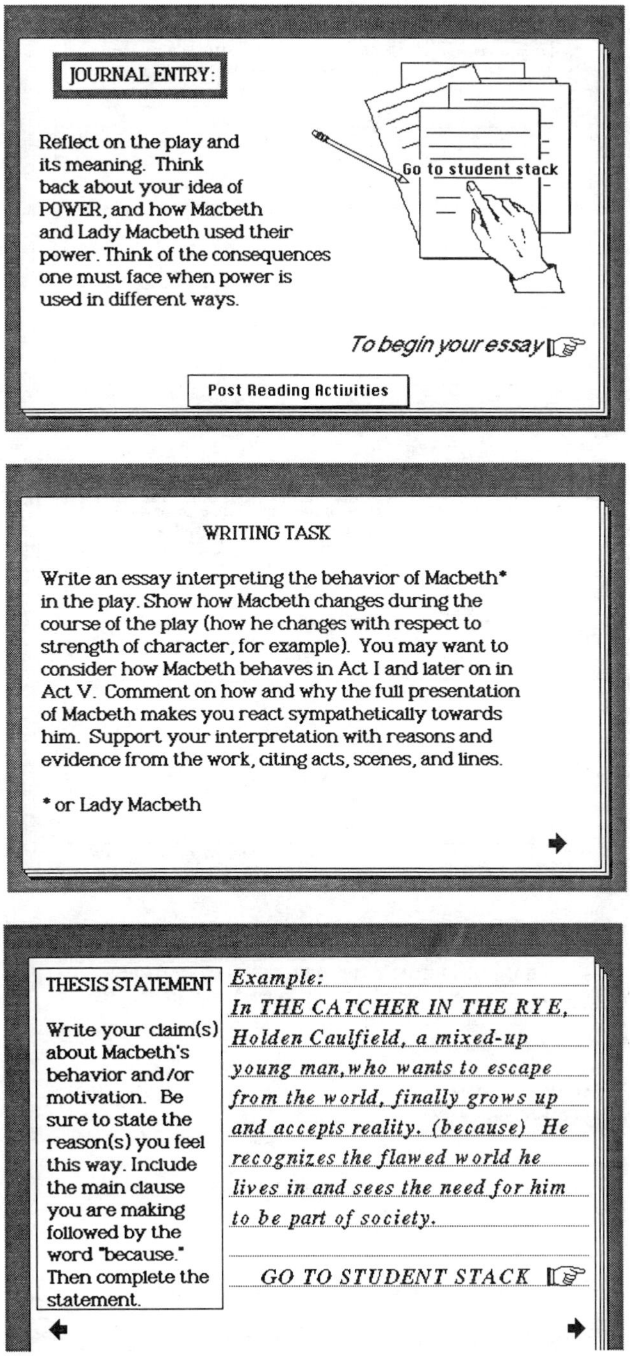

JOURNAL ENTRY:

Reflect on the play and its meaning. Think back about your idea of POWER, and how Macbeth and Lady Macbeth used their power. Think of the consequences one must face when power is used in different ways.

To begin your essay

Post Reading Activities

WRITING TASK

Write an essay interpreting the behavior of Macbeth* in the play. Show how Macbeth changes during the course of the play (how he changes with respect to strength of character, for example). You may want to consider how Macbeth behaves in Act I and later on in Act V. Comment on how and why the full presentation of Macbeth makes you react sympathetically towards him. Support your interpretation with reasons and evidence from the work, citing acts, scenes, and lines.

* or Lady Macbeth

THESIS STATEMENT

Write your claim(s) about Macbeth's behavior and/or motivation. Be sure to state the reason(s) you feel this way. Include the main clause you are making followed by the word "because." Then complete the statement.

Example:

In THE CATCHER IN THE RYE, Holden Caulfield, a mixed-up young man, who wants to escape from the world, finally grows up and accepts reality. (because) He recognizes the flawed world he lives in and sees the need for him to be part of society.

GO TO STUDENT STACK

Figure 1. General instructions for a writing assignment.

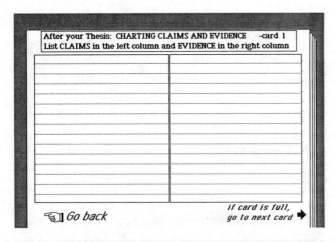

After your Thesis: CHARTING CLAIMS AND EVIDENCE   -card 1
List CLAIMS in the left column and EVIDENCE in the right column

☞ Go back   if card is full,
                                            go to next card ➤

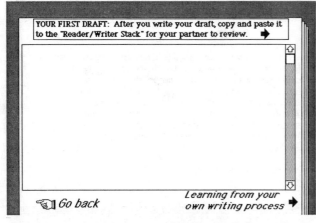

YOUR FIRST DRAFT: After you write your draft, copy and paste it
to the "Reader/Writer Stack" for your partner to review. ➤

☞ Go back   Learning from your
                                            own writing process ➤

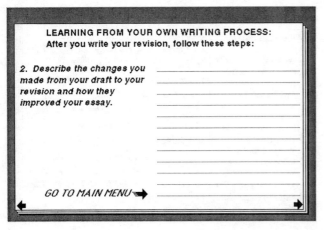

LEARNING FROM YOUR OWN WRITING PROCESS:
After you write your revision, follow these steps:

2. Describe the changes you
made from your draft to your
revision and how they
improved your essay.

GO TO MAIN MENU ➤

Our writing lab houses half Apple IIe and half Macintosh computers. We only have two-week blocks of time in the lab, since classes rotate through it. Although the above process worked well in many ways, it did waste paper and sometimes valuable time, so I recently made a change. Now, after students enter their drafts into the computer, they follow this procedure:

1. As before, students run their essays through the spell checker.
2. Students pair up and read their partner's essay, but now this is done *on screen*—before the rough draft is printed.
3. Students discuss the strong and weak points of each other's papers.
4. Then, as before, students find 2-4 new readers for their papers and go through the same process, again working off the computer screen. Then they print out a hard copy.

This process works very well with students using the Apple IIe's. Students using the Macintosh have some interesting additional options available.

Revision on the Mac

A more efficient method of revising is available to Macintosh users. I use Microsoft Word because I can open multiple windows. Here's how it works:

1. Students complete their first drafts on floppy disks, and use the spell checker.
2. They pair up and exchange disks.
3. The reader opens up the file and shrinks the window to cover only the upper half of the computer screen.
4. Then, he or she opens a New file, shrinking it to cover the lower half of the screen. On a Mac it's easy to click in and out of each file.
5. The reader then makes comments in the new file as he or she goes along, again following the guidelines I have set up for them on a separate paper.

Revision Using HyperCard

Here's a way to encourage student revision on the computer using HyperCard. To begin, I made a Reader-Writer stack of about 10 cards (see Figure 2).

- The first card asks the reader to ''copy'' the writer's essay into the stack. This means that the writer must have made a file of his or her essay, either on HyperCard or using another word processing application.

- Once the essay is read, card buttons lead the reader through a series of cards, each asking specific questions about the essay.

- The reader answers right on the cards in the sections provided. A return button allows the reader to access the essay at any point during the process.

- After completing the review, the reader prints this stack for the writer to consider in the final revision.

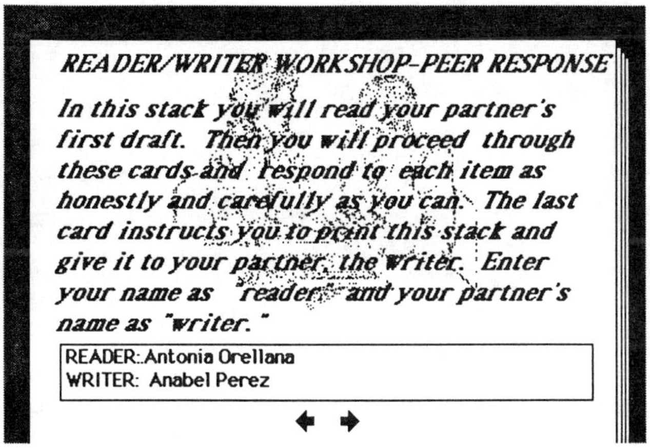

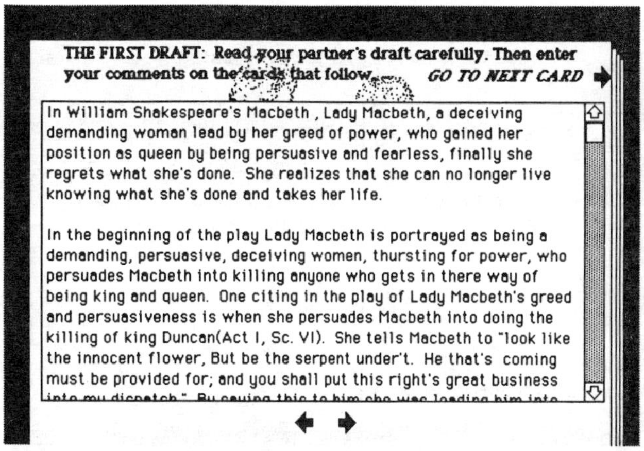

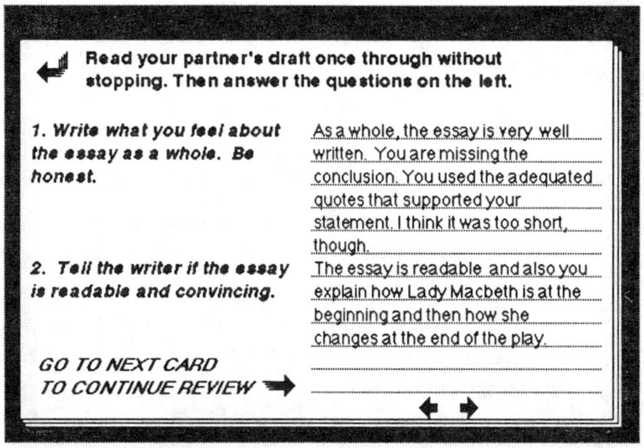

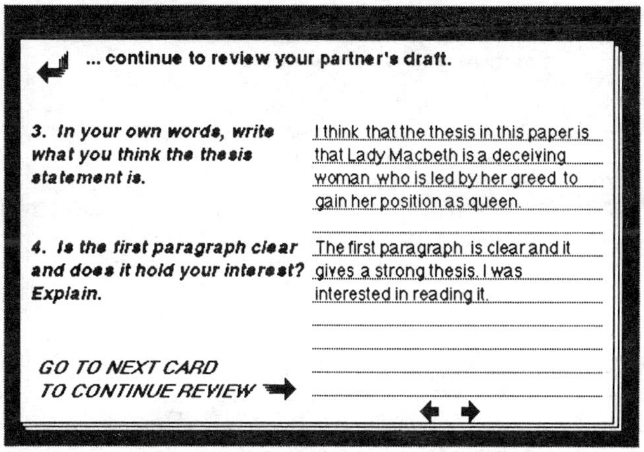

Figure 2. Reader/writer Hypercard stack with student responses.

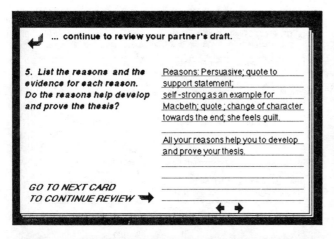

... continue to review your partner's draft.

5. List the reasons and the evidence for each reason. Do the reasons help develop and prove the thesis?

Reasons: Persuasive; quote to support statement; self - strong as an example for Macbeth; quote ; change of character towards the end; she feels guilt.

All your reasons help you to develop and prove your thesis.

GO TO NEXT CARD TO CONTINUE REVIEW ➡

... continue to review your partner's draft.

6. Are any sentences too long? Are there some sentences that need to be revised?

There is part in the second paragraph that I couldn't understand. I think that the screen was different. Your first sentence seems too long. Maybe you could make it two sentences?
I don't understand this sentence: She knew that in order to convince Macbeth out of this. (middle para)

GO TO NEXT CARD TO CONTINUE REVIEW ➡

... continue to review your partner's draft.

7. Check for subject-verb agreement, verb tense forms (is the tense the same?), and pronoun reference.

I fixed one. realize needed an "s"

GO TO NEXT CARD TO CONTINUE REVIEW ➡

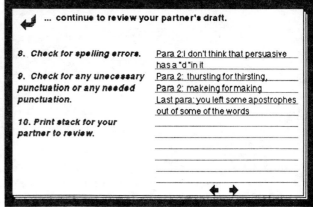

... continue to review your partner's draft.

8. Check for spelling errors.

9. Check for any unecessary punctuation or any needed punctuation.

10. Print stack for your partner to review.

Para 2:I don't think that persuasive has a "d" in it
Para 2: thursting for thirsting,
Para 2: makeing for making
Last para: you left some apostrophes out of some of the words

---

Witnessing my students' enthusiasm about this process of revision is truly gratifying. They enjoy peer review using the computers: It's faster, it's challenging, and, not to be taken for granted, students feel good knowing they're using "up to date" technology.

Jo Zarro teaches 11th and 12th grade at Manual Arts High School in the Los Angeles Unified School District. She is a member of the California Literature Project Macintosh Multimedia Institute at CSU Dominquez Hills.

Conference Guidelines—Advanced

CONFERENCE GUIDELINES: Listening with a purpose in mind

(Feel free to start at Step 3 if you like.)

1. Read your draft to your partner.
2. Let your partner tell you what he or she remembers the most about your piece (i.e., what was interesting or what sounded good).
3. Read your draft again, but this time ask your partner to listen for Conference Questions #_____ and/or #_____.
4. Let your partner respond to what you asked him or her to listen for. Your partner may give you other worthwhile suggestions. Listen carefully.
5. Remember, you are the author. Suggestions that others give you may be helpful, but they may not be. Change only those parts of your draft that you feel need changing.

CONFERENCE QUESTIONS: A few possibilities

1. Listen to my opening line(s). Does my lead interest you? If not, how might I improve it?
2. Do you think I need more information anywhere? That is, are there places in my draft where you would like me to get more specific? Where?
3. Do you ever get lost while reading/listening to my draft? When?
4. Do I get too wordy in my draft? That is, have I put in too much detail ("dead wood")? Where?
5. Have I mentioned things in my draft (for example, people, actions, or situations) that are hard for you to picture, that you wish you could picture? What are they?
6. Do you think that the sentences/paragraphs in my draft are in the best order possible? If not, which sentences/paragraphs would you move around? Why?
7. Do you think I should let my feelings/inner thoughts show more in places? Where?
8. Do I stay on my topic?
9. Do I have a good ending? If not, do you have a suggestion for how I might improve it?
10. Does my title fit my draft?

Other Possibilities

11.
12.
13.

From *Classroom Strategies That Work: An Elementary Teacher's Guide to Process Writing* by Nathan, Temple, Juntunen, & Temple (Portsmouth, NH: Heinemann, 1989). Reprinted by permission.

Oh Goody, Revision Exercises!

Linda Polin

I knew you'd see it my way. Now don't just sit there—do them!

Revision, or reseeing, is not necessarily a natural act. It draws on a different source of energy, the energy of anticipation.

. . . children need to write every day and receive a response to their voices, to know what comes through so that they might anticipate self-satisfaction and the vision of the imprint of their information on classmates or the vision of their work in published form. It is the forward vision, as well as the backward vision, that ultimately leads to major breakthroughs in a child's writing. (Graves, 1983, p. 160)

Occasion, the Prerequisite of Revision

In order to revise, the would-be revisor must see something that needs adjusting and be able to adjust it. But that notion of adjustment is based upon some sense of effect and effectiveness. Very sophisticated writers can conjure up the effect their writing will have on its intended readers. They can revise or rework their writing toward some vision of how it should be. Novice writers often have trouble conjuring up their readers and their readers' response to their writing. In fact, some student writers are clearly oblivious to the fact that someone must "make sense" of what they have written based solely upon the words on the page. Thus, it would appear that an important element of learning about revision is learning about readers. Indeed, most research and theory on the writing process, of which revision is an element, emphasizes the notion of audience. Unfortunately, most school writing tasks given students offer no clear audience other than the teacher-as-evaluator.

Finding an Audience

Most of the time your students write for you. Even if they share their writing in peer read-around groups or take it home to their parents, they still know that they will turn it in to you, and you will read and judge it. They are used to it; they expect it. As a result, you cannot simply "assign" an audience other than yourself and have it taken seriously. There must be another honest, for-real audience, preferably one with whom your students are quite familiar.

Do you publish your students' work and then make it available to other students, in the school library, for example? Do your students submit essays or creative pieces to newspapers or magazines? When students write "to their peers," do you require their peers to respond and the writers to respond again? That is to say, is it a complete exchange? Is the topic one that is really for that audience of peers, or are they acting as surrogate teachers?

Exercise 1: Audience Check

Take a piece of paper. Fold it in half lengthwise. In the left column write the prompt or task description of the last four writing assignments you dished out to your students. In the right column, directly opposite each assignment, note the audience (i.e., the reader[s] of the assignment and their purpose). This means the *genuine* reader(s), not the "pretend" ones. Are all four writing tasks for the teacher-as-evaluator? Think carefully: For whom are your student writers revising?

Finding a Purpose

Just as important as the writer's sense of audience is the writer's understanding of the communicative intent or purpose for writing. Teachers usually do not respond to students' school writing as a message from the writer, but as a demonstration of knowledge about the content area or about writing in general. Even when we allow students to do "creative writing," it is not because *they* have something they want to write about, but because it is "time" to do creative writing.

So now we have forced messages we expect students to deliver to unclear or bogus readers. No wonder our students aren't excited about revising. No wonder they can't figure out what to revise. Okay, I can hear some of you saying, as my dad used to say, "Sometimes you have to do things you don't want to do." And sometimes you have to write academic responses to "bogus" audiences. Of course you do. However, it's not the best way to learn to write (and when I say "write," I mean it all: draft, reread, plan, revise, edit).

If you want to be more successful in teaching writing generally, and in teaching revision specifically, then you and your students must find, create, and sustain genuine occasions for writing, complete with a writing purpose (message) and a real audience. If you find them, they will write.

Genuine occasions for writing "scaffold" the writing process for novice writers by providing a wealth of cues about what and how to write. Such occasions may be difficult to discover; we are generally out of practice at recognizing them, and many of us do not write much ourselves anymore.

Teaching Revision

After your students are doing genuine writing to a genuine audience that provides genuine responses to their writing, you're ready to "teach revision." There are some skills, tricks, and tips they can learn and you can teach.

Out of curiosity, do your students think you teach revision? One of the things students are quick to learn in school is that if it isn't graded it doesn't count. Do you have a column in your grade book in which you record revision grades? What about one for planning? -for editing? -for drafting? How do you give students evaluative information on the success of their attempts at revision? -on editing? -on drafting? -on planning? If you asked your students, would they say you grade their revising or their writing?

Revise for Meaning: The Desire to be Understood

Are you a persistent revisor? (Take the test at the end of this article to be sure.) If so, your writing lifestyle is different from those who don't revise. You have the need to be understood exactly as you intended. Other people, especially students, may not experience that need with their writing. Why not? Maybe they don't view their writing as communicating an urgent message or sharing an idea that is important to them.

If you want your students to choose to revise you must create conditions that lead them to care about the clarity and effectiveness of their written message. There are at least two motivations for caring about the quality of your writing, and hence about revision: the need to communicate successfully and the desire to entertain effectively. Donald Graves says, "What should never be forgotten . . is that the force of revision, the energy for revision, is rooted in the child's voice, the urge to express."

Revise for Effect: The Desire to Entertain

Wouldn't you just love to get your next piece of writing back from a reader with some of these comments splashed about the margins? So would your students.

very funny, delicious, action-packed blast, suspenseful, a masterpiece, classiest thriller in years, a non-stop flow of knockabout comedy, the feel-good comedy of the season, spellbinding, brilliant, holds your interest with the passion that's powerfully felt, better than the first, a bold endeavor that deals with some important ideas in a refreshing and entertaining way, larger than life, a jewel

These comments were lifted from an odd assortment of Wednesday movie advertisements in the *Los Angeles Times*. They refer to the entertainment quality of a variety of movies and are mostly excerpted from reviews of those movies.

We don't often talk about revision to improve the style or entertainment value of writing. Usually we're too busy trying to get students to write clearly, in an organized fashion, with sufficient detail. I believe, however, that encouraging students to improve the aesthetics of their prose may provide a more appealing inducement to revision. After all, most students are entertainment junkies and would love the idea of being entertrainers themselves. Ask them, expect them, to write entertaining prose.

Ahh, there's a catch. To be entertaining, you've got to know your audience. What are their tastes? -their relevant background knowledge? Have you ever seen a comic die on stage because the audience doesn't get his jokes? Weather jokes in Los Angeles are very different from weather jokes in Seattle. And, one man's art is another man's pornography. If you're applying for a grant from the NEA, you'd better know your audience.

Speak the Lingo; Build the Culture

One of the smartest things I've heard said about children's difficulties with mathematics is that they lack a language to talk easily about mathematical ideas with each other (Papert, 1980). The language of writing, as taught in school, is not common English either. Give your students the vocabulary to communicate more specifically with you and each other about the writing process and about prose itself. Encourage your students to use these words when they talk; use them when you talk. Anchor new concepts to analogous familiar ones.

Build and use a common vocabulary for talking about writing. Make it cool to know these terms. Talk about "grabbing the audience" in the opening—you know, the part of the television show that comes on even before the first commercial and the opening credits; the part that helps you decide whether or not to stay tuned. Talk about metaphors, or whatever terms you want them to know and use. Use blue pencil instead of red. Give students blue pencils; tell them what they're for and why they're blue.

Establish a classroom culture for revision. A culture is a set of shared values and beliefs that are embodied in customs, rituals, and social norms. A culture is a self-reinforcing system. People continue to interpret each other and events in light of particular beliefs and values they hold. Make writing and revising part of the norm. Build expectations to revise. Build revision rituals such as the blue pencil. Stop just short of sacrificing virgin paper to the goddess of revision.

Exercise 5: Connecting through Analogies

Editing is like getting your car washed at the drive-through car wash; revising is more like getting your car detailed.

Now you make up an analogy, right now, before you lose your nerve. Later, try it out in class. Then have students generate some. Let them select the ones they like best. Post them in the room. As new concepts come up in class, build and collect new analogies. When you've gotten through a few of these, take some time to talk about the power of analogies. Who knows, they may start showing up in students' papers.

Evangelize Revision

"Evangelism is the process of convincing people to believe in your product or idea as much as you do. It means selling your dream by using fervor, zeal, guts, and cunning" (Kawasaki, 1991). You must evangelize revision. You have to believe revision is important and convince others. You have to "get it" yourself. You have to do it too.

Exercise 6: Are You a Revisin' Fool? The Ten Warning Signs

1. Do you list your files by date so you can figure out which is the latest version of the document you were working on?

2. Do you fish papers out of the trash because you think maybe the first version was better after all? (Actually, Macintosh users can still fish "papers" out of the "trash.") Have you ever climbed into a dumpster to search through a plastic bag of trash?

3. Do you have word processing files labeled temp1, temp2, temp3, or scraps?

4. Have you ever spent more than 15 minutes hiking through pathways in your on-line thesaurus because of your reluctance to use the word "very"?

5. Do you make your spouse or significant other read it or listen to it before you are willing to consider it done?

6. Do you agonize over titles, trying to capture the essence of your message with rapier wit?

7. Do you make changes in the document after it's been distributed to its intended audience?

8. Is your experience of the recursive writing process akin to that of an indecisive motorist caught in a traffic circle?

9. Have you ever pasted the same paragraph in three different places at once, trying to decide where you think it works best? Do you rearrange the furniture in your home repeatedly?

10. When you find yourself in the throes of a disagreement, do you keep re-explaining your idea or position on the belief that if the other person just understood you clearly he or she would have to agree with you?

Linda G. Polin, Associate Professor of Education, Pepperdine University, Graduate School of Education and Psychology, 400 Corporate Pointe, Culver City, CA 90230-7627.

References

Graves, D. H. (1983). *Writing: Teachers and Children at Work.* Portsmouth, NH: Heinemann.

Kawasaki, G. (1991). *Selling the Dream.* New York: Harper Collins.

Papert, S. (1980). *Mindstorms: Children, Computers, and Powerful Ideas.* New York: Basic Books.

Unleashing Creativity: Revision by Computer

Rae M. Bruce

Three years ago my students began to revel in revision. Instead of avoiding any kind of revision, they began to attack their writing using their word processing skills. Now the lists of revisions they clip to the top of their stories read like those of professional writers, not reluctant students. They include major changes—adding new scenes, using white space creatively, deleting scenes, adding characters, and even changing the point of view. Learning the basics of word processing has expanded their understanding of the writing process and has unleashed their creativity.

Nine Drafts

Examining the writing process of some of my students shows clearly the extent of their revisions.

Hilary ended up putting her story "Upside Looking Down" through nine drafts that included both detailed and sweeping revisions. In her story the main character, Murphy, awakes in the morning to find "everything upside down. Somehow he had fallen out of bed . . . and landed on the ceiling."

With each draft new details appeared, making the specifics of life on the ceiling more interesting. His pajamas fall to the floor, and when he needs to use the bathroom he goes "limping into the kitchen . . . dodging the chandelier," and finally has to use the sink. Adding such details over a period of two weeks would have been extremely frustrating for a student writer who had to recopy each time a sentence or two was added. By pressing two computer keys, Hilary accomplished these revisions with ease and produced a story in which the world of the character was consistent and believable.

Adding a Scene

When Ken suggested to Hilary that Murphy's problems weren't severe enough to justify his anger at the end, she decided to add a scene in the middle of the story. Returning the next day with two and a half handwritten pages, she placed her cursor in the middle of page five, pressed Return, and inserted a scene that begins in the garage:

It [the garage] was freezing, arctic, and Murphy knew it. He also knew he was stark naked and Mrs. Perkins, the next-door neighbor, was an old bat who liked to peep into people's houses and report things to the police.

With two keystrokes, Hilary not only inserted this scene into her story, but also added the character of Mrs. Perkins to fuel Murphy's frustration.

Using White Space Creatively

As students used the word processor, they began to see the value of white space on the page. "Blind Date," a dramatic monologue that appeared in the school's literary magazine, illustrates the implicit meaning of white space. Here is a portion of the monologue, set in a restaurant, without the paragraphing:

Yeah, I went to college, one year at Estella's Beauty Academy. I'm a manicurist. Thanks, I do my own nails! Look at that, one of them's chipped! Huh? I don't see a sign that says no painting nails! Listen, if I don't paint it now, I'll forget all about it! . . . Now what? It's a proven fact that soaking your nail in cold water helps it dry. Oh, sorry, take my water glass. I thought this one was mine.

When Linda's writing group had trouble understanding the way this dramatic monologue reflected the words of the speaker's listener, I suggested paragraphing. Here is the result:

Yeah, I went to college, one year at Estella's Beauty Academy. I'm a manicurist.

Thanks, I do my own nails! Look at that, one of them's chipped!

Huh? I don't see a sign that says no painting nails! Listen, if I don't paint it now, I'll forget all about it! . . .

Now what? It's a proven fact that soaking your nail in cold water helps it dry.

Oh, sorry, take my water glass. I thought this one was mine.

In this way students come to understand that white space is a silent signal to the literate that the speaker changes.

Shaping Poetry

Even students with learning disabilities get turned on to writing free verse when they use word processing. A computer printout gives their work dignity and meaning. The words of Leslie's poem, "The Beach," remains the same regardless of spacing, but compare these two versions:

"The Beach" No two are alike glistening in the summer sun radiating inner beauty, star-like in shape, but not in distance. It's hard to believe I'm looking at a single grain of sand on my beach towel.

The Beach

No two are alike
   glistening in the summer sun
Radiating
   inner beauty
Star-like in shape,
   but not in distance.

It's hard to believe
   I'm looking at a
   single
   grain
   of
   sand
on my beach towel.

Writing free verse includes using white space to enhance meaning.

When Leslie arranged her poem on the computer screen, she emphasized words by their placement. She sharpened the image in her first group of lines by putting "Radiating" and "Star-like" out to the left margin and emphasized the uniqueness of each "grain of sand" by placing each word alone on a line. In so doing, the writing *looks* like the poetry that it is.

Without word processing skills, a student like Leslie—and many students without learning disabilities as well—would be reluctant to experiment with line formation. With word processing skills, Leslie finds this kind of revision a form of play.

White Space as a Transition

Using white space to indicate the passage of time is another silent signal to the reader. In Kathleen's paper, "In the Middle," she tells what led her to refuse to be put between her parents as they discussed divorce. As she described her writing problem, "I've already written about this for another class, but it was a *telling* paper. How can I *show* what happened?"

"How many scenes do you need to show it?" I asked.

"Well, I'd need to show my mom and me when she first told me about it, and then my dad and me, and finally the time when I stood up for myself. She hesitated. "But how do I get from one time to another?"

I showed her some stories that use white space to signal the passage of time. She rewrote her story, shaping it into three scenes separated by white space.

> I turned around again and left him [her dad] standing in my room. I wanted to turn back, to tell him everything would turn out okay, and everything else he wanted to hear. But I couldn't.
>
> I had been in the middle too many times.
>
> Two months passed, and I sat on the couch watching reruns.

Kathleen picked up the pace of the story by avoiding the boring details about life in the two months in between scenes. Student writers often get bogged down in unimportant interim scenes, become discouraged, and decide they can't write the story. But Kathleen completed this revision merely by pressing Return twice. Teaching students to use white space as a transition helps to focus their writing and encourages good revision strategies.

Doing a Complete Rewrite

Even the best student writers balk at a complete revision. Here again, word processing skills make such extensive revisions a feasible option.

Mary had already written her story about Bud, a teenage murderer, twice when she came to me for a conference. The first time the gruesome details had made it unacceptable for her audience, a school publication. So she centered her second draft on Bud's trial. As the conference started, she slumped into her chair and said, "It's boring. I hate it."

"Read me the first page," I suggested. What followed was a scene written in third person and full of trial cliches.

She hung her head. "See what I mean?"

We sat in silence for a moment or two. Both of us knew she could do better.

Eventually I asked, "Whose story is this? Is it Bud's? His parents'? His friends'?"

Another silence.

"I guess if I knew one of my friends had committed a murder, I'd be really upset. I wouldn't know what to do." She thought again, then smiled suddenly and went back to her seat.

By the next class Mary had completely rewritten her story from the point of view of Bud's friend Josh. She threw out the trial scene altogether and began her story with Josh wondering why Bud was acting so strangely. She carried the story through Bud's revealing himself as the murderer and Josh's indecision about what to do, and ended with the beginning of the trial.

Her classmate, Alan, asked, "But Mary, didn't you write past the ending?"

Returning to the computer, she punched in delete commands, bringing her story to a climatic ending: The murderer chases Josh into his house and stands banging on the locked screen door as Josh calls the police.

> "Los Angeles Police Department. May I help you?"
>
> "Yes," Josh breathed, "I'd like to report a murder."

In the course of Mary's two rewrites, she changed the point of view, deleted the ending, and made numerous other editing changes. She executed all these creative leaps by using word processing skills so simple that the class spent less than two days of the semester learning them. As Mary's classmate Hilary put it, "Word processing gives me more real creative time to solve writing problems."

Freed of tedious recopying, my students now seek out sophisticated revision strategies instead of avoiding them. They print out copies and pass them around to their friends for comment. Peer conferencing takes place both in and out of the classroom. Eagerly discussing their own work and offering suggestions to their classmates, they relish the ease with which they revise by computer. Never again will the limits of pencil and paper stymie these students. Word processing has unleashed their creativity.

What's "Whole" in Readers Theatre?

Terrell A. Young

Laughter and applause thundered as fifth grade students finished a Readers Theatre performance based on Barbara Robinson's *The Best Christmas Pageant Ever.* The students smiled at one another with radiant pride. These students had entertained their teachers, peers, and parents. And, since there were only a limited number of parts, they were the stars! These weren't typical "stars." They were students their teacher chose because he thought they needed the opportunity to prove themselves to their fellow students, their parents, and, most important, to themselves. As you will see—and hopefully experience for yourself, the magic of Readers Theatre can transform a classroom and its students.

Readers Theatre, a presentation of prose or poetry that is expressively and emotionally read aloud by several readers, is a Whole Language strategy. It is quite similar to a play; however, the participants read their parts, rather than memorizing them. While costumes, movement, and props are not generally associated with Readers Theatre, simple costumes, props, sound effects, and movement may be used to enhance the performance.

Readers Theatre is an activity useful not only in the language arts program, but in the content areas as well. To bring energy and stimulation to any subject area, teachers and students prepare scripts from books and stories with exciting characters and expressive dialogue. Moreover, Readers Theatre is effective with students from the primary grades to postgraduate school. Thus, in many subject areas and with students of various ages, Readers Theatre is dynamic and fun for both the participants and the audience.

Older students can work in collaborative groups of five to seven to select and adapt one of their favorite books, poems, or stories to a Readers Theatre script. Choosing their own text for a script adds to the motivational nature of Readers Theatre and helps students feel ownership of the activity. They also learn to select books that suit their interests, needs, abilities, and audience. With young students, however, the teacher may want to choose class favorites and adapt them to Readers Theatre scripts.

Picture books are often very effective for Readers Theatre scripts, since they were written to be read aloud. Here are just a few examples of picture books that make good Readers Theatre scripts: *Strega Nona* by Tomie de Paola, *Hattie and the Fox* by Mem Fox, *Why Mosquitoes Buzz in People's Ears* by Verna Aardema, *Arthur Goes to Camp* by Marc Brown, *Alexander and the Terrible, Horrible, No Good, Very Bad Day* by Judith Viorst, and *Lon Po Po* by Ed Young.

There will be times when students can't agree on a text for the script; thus, a compromise must be reached. Give students the opportunity to discuss their book, story, or poetry choices and their reasons for preferring that text. Some students will likely agree to save their favorites for another time.

A group of sixth graders rewrote *The Three Billy Goats Gruff* from the point of view of a jovial troll who was misunderstood by some nasty goats who couldn't take a joke. Students learn a great deal about revision and writing as they adapt and write texts for Readers Theatre scripts.

After students have chosen the text, they are ready to adapt it to a Readers Theatre script. Usually the dialogue itself requires little adaptation. When students use an episode from a book for a script, they often write either a prologue or an epilogue (to be read by narrators) so the episode is self-contained. Students may also write narrator parts to provide effective transitions from one scene to another. Here is a sample prologue that was written by a college student and a group of fifth graders planning to perform a script based on an episode from *The Lion, the Witch, and the Wardrobe* by C. S. Lewis.

Narrator 1: This story began when Lucy found a secret doorway through a wardrobe into the land of Narnia. Every day is winter in Narnia due to a spell cast by the wicked White Witch. Lucy is protected and befriended by a Faun named Mr. Tumnus during her first visit to Narnia.

Narrator 2: During her brother Edmund's first visit to Narnia, he meets up with the evil witch and falls under her spell after eating the Turkish Delight she gives him.

Narrator 3: Our friends have returned to Narnia and discovered that Mr. Tumnus has been arrested for hiding Lucy and showing her the way home. While searching for a way to rescue Mr. Tumnus, the children are first led out of the forest by a robin and then meet up with Mr. Beaver.

Narrator 1: Mr. Beaver takes the children home to his house where his wife prepares dinner for them and they talk about the coming of Aslan.

Narrator 2: At this time, Edmund slips away to warn the White Witch of Aslan's arrival and to tell her of the whereabouts of his brother and sisters.

Narrator 3: The children and Beavers notice Edmund's absence and realize that they have been betrayed. They flee for their lives and rush toward Aslan. On the way to Aslan they notice that there appears to be a spring thaw. The snow begins to melt and the weather turns warmer.

Narrator 1: Now, Peter's First Battle.

Students also may rewrite the text from another point of view. For instance, after reading *The True Story of the Three Little Pigs* by Jon Scieszka, students may want to rewrite other fairy tales from a different (often the antagonist's) point of view. A group of sixth graders, for example, rewrote *The Three Billy Goats Gruff* from the point of view of a jovial troll who was misunderstood by some nasty goats who couldn't take a joke. Students learn a great deal about revision and writing as they adapt and write texts for Readers Theatre scripts.

In Readers Theatre, as in other Whole Language strategies, students are not grouped by ability. By allowing students of differing abilities to work together, the poor readers have the good readers as models. All students can make a meaningful contribution, since they have ample opportunities to practice their parts and a meaningful reason for reading a text more than once. Furthermore, the teacher and other students can work with members of the group to facilitate clear, expressive reading. The quality of their oral reading improves a great deal as students learn how to use their voices to alter delivery, tone, pitch, and volume.

The collaborative nature of Readers Theatre enhances students' social and personal growth. They develop confidence and improved self-esteem as they work together, experience success, and entertain an audience.

In Readers Theatre, students read a whole poem, book, story, or a self-contained episode from a story. This is crucial. Students need to understand the text at a level where they can live into and understand the characters' motives. If the text has no meaning to the students, then the time spent in Readers Theatre will not be beneficial to them. However, reading a whole text is not the only way that Readers Theatre facilitates comprehension. Rather than emphasizing acting ability, Readers Theatre focuses on a fundamental reading skill—interpretation. Because students have a purpose for reading—they need to learn to make inferences, identify moods, interpret characters, and to understand the author's purpose—comprehension is further enhanced.

Involvement in Readers Theatre can result in improved listening and listening comprehension as well. Students must listen carefully to each other as they plan and discuss the selection, adaptation, and presentation of their script. They listen to each other practice reading as they determine how best to present their script. The performances themselves can be quite enjoyable and entertaining. Students are introduced to many different types of literature, and since characterization is conveyed by the readers rather than by costumes, action, and props, the audience learns to listen critically and appreciatively. For many students, Readers Theatre also has the added benefit of expanding their recreational reading. Students who enjoy listening to a Readers Theatre presentation of an episode from a book often want to read that book.

Students who have had little or no experience with Readers Theatre may need some teacher assistance for the first few practice sessions. However, as students become more experienced, they can direct their own practices. Videotaping practices further helps students prepare for the actual presentation; watching themselves on tape makes them aware of areas they want to improve.

As students perform, they can sit or stand in a semicircle. This arrangement allows students to make eye contact with each other and with the audience. They may also enjoy expanding their performance schedule beyond the classroom. Readers Theatre performances are fun and appropriate for presenting to other classes, parents, PTA, or community groups.

Readers Theatre is a Whole Language strategy that you owe yourself and your students to try at some point during the year! You *and* your students will be glad you did.

Terrell A. Young, Assistant Professor, Washington State University, 100 Sprout Road, Richland, WA 99352.

Pow! Zap! Ker-plunk! The Comic Book Maker

Grades K-12; $49.95—school version, $99.95—lab pack
Apple IIGS, IBM compatible
QUEUE/Pelican Software
768 Farmington Ave.
Farmington, CT 06032

Pow! Zap! Ker-plunk!, the newest addition to Pelican's Creative Writing Series, is a new twist on an old, familiar format—the comic book. Comics provide a unique writing environment for satire, symbolism, sequencing, and combining text and graphics to communicate ideas. Recall Boss Tweed's era with Thomas Nest's political cartoon editorials on Tammany Hall, or the many other serious social concerns expressed through symbolic cartooning. Cultural superheros and superheroines like Spiderman, Wonder Woman, Batman, and Superman provide a modern day context for life lessons, messages, and communication. **Pow! Zap! Ker-plunk!** brings this art and communication form to writers in a **pow**-erful way.

The program begins with a Main Menu that is easy to highlight and select. Choose Create a comic, Write about them, or Read previous comic collection stories. Students combine text and graphics using a variety of fonts, page layouts, and clip art. The clip art designed for the **Pow! Zap! Ker-Plunk!** school version is very different from the consumer retail version. The school version is highly recommended as it includes school scenes and artwork more appropriate for school settings. It is clear that the designers had the important issues of cultural diversity and equity firmly in mind—the clip art includes a wide variety of multiethnic kids and kids with disabilities. One girl, for example, has a secret identity where she turns into a Superkid with rockets on her

> **Comics provide a unique writing environment for satire, symbolism, sequencing, and combining text and graphics to communicate ideas.... *Pow! Zap! Kerplunk!* brings this art and communication form to writers in a *pow*-erful way.**

wheelchair and a cape that appears to give her extraordinary powers.

Students start by designing their graphic panels. Backgrounds are chosen and clip art selected and "stamped" on the panel. The clip art can be placed, flipped, or removed. All other Pelican clip art and utility disks are compatible as well, which extends the possible content to science, social studies, dinosaurs, monsters, and robots.

Speech bubbles for talking and thinking are treated like clip art except that a little line (cursor) appears for writing. Text boxes are stamped like the bubbles on the top

or bottom of the panel. You can edit the text or remove the entire bubble or box and start again.

The limited writing space presents its own unique writing challenges for students that include purposeful word choice, succinctness, and how to create an impact with more than words. If longer narrative writing is wanted, printing out the graphic and writing on the hard copy should be planned.

Finally, a speech option, if you have an Echo (IIe) or Cricket (IIc) speech synthesizer, provides talking capabilities. This should have special appeal for whole language, preschool, ESL, bilingual, and special education classes. The utilities program has an Edit Speech feature to customize pronunciations. Be sure to save these changes with the story.

When ready to print, writers select a print style: miniature, standard, tall, short, skinny, or poster size. The variety of styles creates many different looks and uses. Print a Comic Page will let writers choose a layout for their comic book combining more than one of their panels. There are four page layouts provided, as well as a normal or outline choice. Printouts can be in color (normal with color ribbons) or black and white (normal with regular ribbons). Printing in outline form will save ribbons or allow coloring after printing. The Utilities option lets classrooms use a variety of printers. (Make sure writers SAVE their work before printing. The program will freeze if the printer settings are incorrect.)

Pow! Zap! Ker-plunk! offers a unique writing tool that will appeal to all ages. Reading and writing in the Information Age has moved beyond print. Creating graphics and text messages require high level thinking skills, symbolic awareness, and graphic design qualities often missed in classrooms today. Writers using this program will experience the richness of what the authors of Spiderman, Garfield, Wizard of Id, or Cathy experience as they creatively bring philosophical snapshots of life to us every day.

Reviewed by Bernajean Porter

Comic Curriculum Craziness

- Create comic books for new students explaining school rules, what to expect, or who's who in the building.
- Create comic books on science, history, or math topics having students explain new information researched or what they understood about material covered.
- Create a graphic design unit giving student teams the same topic and debriefing how their information was packaged, why they made their design choices, and what was most effective/detracting about their message.
- Create a school hero and heroine and publish a monthly cartoon page about your school for parents, community, and students.
- Rewrite classic literature books for varied audiences like younger children or non-English speaking readers.
- Model contemporary cartoonists' styles with new characters and settings.
- Create storybooks or coloring books on important issues like "Saying NO to Strangers," "Being New in School," "Learning to Drive," "Going to Court," or "How to Be a Friend."
- Make comic book posters to advertise books, school slogans, classroom rules, or school functions.
- Make comic book posters to illustrate content like propaganda techniques, making a science lab report, the stages of the American Revolution, or how to. . . .
- Make personalized Big Books to welcome new students, say good-bye to old friends, or generate interest in special topics.
- Make mini-books for content review.
- Create coloring books on your community, family, friends, or school.
- Create stationery, puppets, bookmarks, achievement awards, mobiles, or holiday cards.

KIDS WRITING COMIC BOOKS: LESSONS FROM THE PROFESSIONALS

George W. Chilcoat, Terrell A. Young, & Christine Kerr

A San Antonio, Texas, teacher commented, ''My kids have been asking me if they can write comic books. There must be something that I can tell them besides 'make boxes and draw pictures.' ''

Our response is definite and emphatic. Yes, there is much more that a teacher can tell students about writing comic books! This article provides tips for comic book writing that have been gathered from actual comic book authors. These tips can be used in mini-lessons for your writing workshop.

You may want to introduce the comic book by sharing commercially produced comic books. Ask your students to examine these comic books and make note of the techniques used for writing and illustrating. Here are some of the techniques students may discover:

- Compactness. Every word counts.
- Onomatopoeia. It's often used to present sounds. POW! BAM!
- Exaggerated facial expressions.
- Different balloon styles used to represent conversation and thought.
- Simple backgrounds.
- Speed lines used to show rapid motion and action.

After your students have identified several techniques used by professionals, it's a good time to share a student-authored comic book with them in order to show how a story is adapted to comic book form.

We've found it useful to focus on five specific components of comic book writing: (a) plot development, (b) layout, (c) drawing, (d) narration, and (e) the cover page.

Plot Development

Plot development involves the telling of the story. The following steps can help students create the plot for their comic book:

1. Introduce the characters.
2. Establish their situation.
3. Introduce the events surrounding the characters.
4. Build suspense if it is important to the story.
5. Show some type of resolution or ending.

When the plot is complete it should be written down in outline form and divided into the number of scenes that represent each panel of drawings (see Layout below). Each scene should be listed in sequence, with its setting, action, characters, and their speeches, if any. Writing out the plot in this manner gives students a handy way to check for inconsistencies and errors of action and sequence before creating the drawings.

Layout

A comic book is made up of pages comprised of units called *panels*. Each panel is a bordered illustration that conveys one scene of the story in visual form. Together these panels tell the complete story. A single page may have one panel or as many as the author wants to include without making the story too difficult for the reader.

Two types of panels may be used. One type is called the ''splash page''—a one-page panel that introduces the story. It usually contains the beginning scene with any narration running at the bottom of the page, the title of the story at the top of the page, and author credits somewhere near the bottom (see Figure 1).

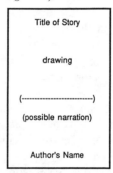

Figure 1. Splash Page.

The second type of panel is a set of four panels per page (see Figure 2). You or your students may also decide to change the layout to fit a specific project or topic.

Figure 2. Four Panels Per Page.

Each comic book panel relates to the one before and after it. The logical arrangement of these units forms a larger unit called a *sequence*. Sequences can be as brief as two or three panels or they can stretch out over several pages, depending on the length of the story. Your students may want to determine how many panels are necessary to illustrate the plot before determining the panel sizes.

Drawing

The purpose of the project is not to see how well students can draw, but to practice conveying meaning in a visual form. Only two requirements are absolutely necessary: (a) Draw each panel as realistically as possible, and (b) use color.

However, to help add variety to the drawings, students can draw a panel from whatever angle they choose. A scene can be viewed head on, upwards, downwards, sideways, far away, or close up. There are three basic shots (although using a number of combinations can help move the story along). Each of these shots tends to convey a certain kind of information as described below:

1. *Long shots*, also called "establishing shots," are good for conveying setting or for establishing a locale. They are also good for showing objects or events of great magnitude.
2. *Medium shots* sometimes are referred to as "action depth" shots. These show full figures or objects with no parts hidden by the panel border and are good for showing action. Most televised sporting events are shown almost entirely from this depth for that reason. They are also good for giving an overall view of a person or object.
3. *Close-ups* include any shots closer than action depth. If any part of the subject of the picture is cropped by the panel border, the picture is a close-up. Generally, close-ups are used for faces or expressive gestures. They are good for showing reactions, emotions, and feelings. Close-ups also can be used for showing what a character's face looks like or for showing the detail on an object.

Some students may want to replace the drawings with photographs to create a "photocomic." To make photocomics, students develop their plots and then stage costumed characters for the pictures. The actual pictures can be used with balloon stickers (available at most photography stores). The photographs can be photocopied or scanned into a computer.

Narration

Narration is used chiefly as a means to convey essential information and to carry the plot forward. There are two basic types of narration: the *runner* and the *balloon*. The runner is a block, or strip, at the top or bottom of a panel to provide information about the direction of the story. This information describes what is taking place in the panel. See Figure 3 for an example of runner narration.

Figure 3. Runner Narration.

The balloon is a dramatic, graphic device inside the panel that provides dialogue for any character who is speaking or thinking. By using the graphic elements of the balloon, such as its shape or lettering within the balloon, students are able to translate any emotion or aspect of language: tone, pitch, rhythm, and accent. The types of balloons that one might incorporate can be seen in Figure 4.

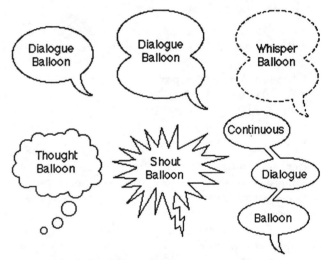

Figure 4. Balloon Narration.

A general rule to follow when writing dialogue in balloons is not to overcrowd the dialogue. A cartoon panel is to be read from left to right so that a character on the left side of the panel is talking and the character on the right side is responding. The balloon going to the character on the left is higher than the balloon going to the character on the right. This will indicate that the person on the left is speaking first.

Cover Page

The cover is a very important page of the comic book. It catches the eye of the reader and entices him or her to read further. The cover usually combines a full page of illustrations with the title of the comic book at the top. The illustration highlights the basic story line and is not a blown-up drawing of one of the panels inside the comic book. Normally there is no runner or dialogue, but only the title of the story somewhere at the bottom (see Figure 5).

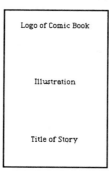

Figure 5. Cover Page.

Students should draw a preliminary rough sketch of each panel based on the division of the story. Using 8½ x 11 white paper divided into four equal panels is easiest. It's helpful for students to share their preliminary drawings with a group of four to six students. This group of their peers can provide helpful information on story development, graphic description, or expression. The preliminaries are also useful for experimenting with the right color combinations. Generally, contrasting colors are effective. Then students are ready to make the necessary changes and draw the final copy in color.

Technology and Comic Books

The comic book is a format well suited to technology. Indeed, comic book program software is available (e.g., Pelican Software's *POW! ZAP! KERPLUNK! The Comic Book Maker!* or Foundation Publishing's *The Comic Strip Factory*). However, students do not require a comic book program to use the computer to produce comic books —they can use drawing programs, clip art, and scanners.

Conclusion

Comic books are a long-time, popular, reading genre with students—and they can be written by kids. Comic book writing is a fun activity that can make writing interesting and appealing for many students. Moreover, students can collaborate on comic book writing. The collaboration allows students to share their insights as writers with their peers. Furthermore, teachers can implement the suggested tips to guide students in comic book writing as a learning tool across the curriculum.

George W. Chilcoat, Associate Professor, Department of Elementary Education, Brigham Young University, Provo, UT; Terrell A. Young, Assistant Professor, Literacy Education, Washington State University, Richland, WA; & Christine Kerr, Student, Teacher Education, Department of Elementary Education, Brigham Young University, Provo, UT.

Curriculum Applications

Language Arts
Episode of a Favorite Book for Book Sharing
Stories
Autobiographies

Science
Illustrate Scientific Principles
Science Reports
Space Exploration
Life Cycle of a Butterfly
Migration of Whales
Dinosaurs
Global Warming

Social Studies Reports
States
Countries
Historical Events
Civil Rights Movement
Wars
Immigration
Westward Expansion
Women's Suffrage
Biographical Sketches
Family Histories

Health
How White Blood Cells Fight Disease
The Effects of Smoking on the Human Body

Math
Biographical Sketches of Mathematicians
How Math is Used in Occupations
Survey of Students in School

References

Barrier, M., & Williams, M. (1981). *A Smithsonian book of comic book comics.* New York: Smithsonian Press.

Buckler, R. (1986). *How to become a comic book artist.* Brooklyn, NY: Solson Publications.

Eisner, W. (1985). *Comics and sequential art.* Tamarag, FL: Poorhouse Press.

Lee, S. (1978). *How to draw cartoons the Marvel way.* New York: Simon & Schuster.

POW! ZAP! KERPLUNK! The Comic Book Maker [Computer program]. Farmington, CT: Pelican/QUEUE.

Shooter, J. (1983). *The official Marvel tryout book.* New York: Marvel Comics Group.

Suid, M., & Lincoln, W. (1988). *Recipes for writing: Motivation, skills, and activities.* Reading, MA: Addison-Wesley.

The Comic Strip Factory [Computer program]. Prior Lake, MN: Foundation Publishing.

Design Elements in Desktop Publishing

Part 1

Sharon Franklin

The advent of desktop publishing finds many of us in a domain for which precious few of us were trained. Prior to desktop publishing, all design decisions were the property of graphic artists and art directors. Back in those days, ''we'' were simply in charge of text, giving it happily to someone else to arrange nicely on the page.

Desktop publishing has changed all that.

It is now common for many of us, whether teachers, students, consultants, writers, or administrators, to design products that range from flyers to newsletters to books. In addition, many teachers are now in the position of guiding their students through desktop publishing projects.

The good news is that desktop publishing tools are becoming increasingly friendly and downright fun to use. Even better, there really are no hard and fast rules of design to memorize and follow religiously.

If you find yourself in the position of designer as well as writer these days, this three-part article will provide you with some general guidelines and a bit of philosophy from which to start. Over the next three issues we'll look specifically at:

- Typefaces
- Spacing
- Titles and headings
- Column width
- White space
- Text: Justified, ragged, word wrap
- Callouts
- Layout
- Graphics placement
- Screens and other additions to text
- Filler
- Headers/footers/table of contents
- Resources

Trust Thyself

One good way to begin to trust your own ability to make decisions about design is to look around. Find examples of printed material that you like. Ask yourself what it is that you especially like, and why. When you get a newsletter or flyer in the mail, even if you have no intention of reading it, take a moment to notice the headings, the layout, and the overall effect. How were graphics and text combined on the page? Or make a trip to your favorite bookstore (as if you needed a reason!) and look through the magazines and journals for examples of layout and design that you really like. (Yes, I have been known to stand in the magazine section with my yellow pad and sketch article layouts!) Between my sketches and actual examples of things that come to me in the mail, I now have a folder of ideas that I can refer to for ideas for specific projects.

Typefaces

No doubt about it, there are plenty of typefaces to choose from.

And, you've undoubtedly seen and perhaps even created at least one newsletter that looks as if it were done by someone who was making up a sampler of all the possibilities! It's good to keep one perfectly horrible example close at hand in your folder. Refer to it periodically, and *especially* when you're tempted to use four or five of the brand-new, just-arrived typefaces available to you—all on the same page.

Instead, try this. You'll notice that typefaces generally fall into two categories, called *serif* and *sans-serif*.

Serif fonts have decorative ends on the letters. On the typeface used in the body of this article, for example, notice the little feet on the bottom of the most of the letters and on the tops of letters such as "l" and "b." Serif typefaces include Times, Bookman, Pasquale, New York, and Venice.

Sans-serif typefaces lack these decorations, so the letters look much less "fancy." They include Geneva, Chicago, Helvetica, Triumvirate, or Avant Garde.

Generally speaking (you'll hear this a lot!), it's best not to mix serif typefaces. So, if you're doing a newsletter, start by picking a font for the body copy, which most often is a serif typeface (because the ends on the letters help "lead" the reader's eye to the next word more easily). In selecting a typeface for the body copy, think about the purpose of your document and how easy you want it to be to read. If there are large amounts of text, you will probably want to stick with a serif typeface. If you have very small amounts of text, a sans-serif typeface may work equally well.

Now, pick a sans-serif typeface for the subheadings, and keep them

. . . experiment and try something new every so often . . . every once in a while you will find you have designed a truly elegant page—some with bold exceptions to these "general rules."

the same throughout. A good example in this issue is the article on //Write. The body copy is a serif typeface similar to Times, and the subheadings are in a bold sans-serif font. Often, as in the article on //Write, the typeface chosen for the subheadings is carried through in the heading (title) as well.

Once in a while there are some good reasons for adding a third typeface, but I prefer to think of them as exceptions. For the most part, they can easily "muddy" your newsletter or flyer, with all the attention suddenly shifting to all the typefaces and diverted away from the ideas you're trying to communicate. For now, suffice it to say that a third typeface can sometimes work well for a boxed-in chart or graph.

Now that you've selected the main typefaces, a word of caution about all the ways they can be modified using italics, bold, underline, shadow, and so on. **Use them sparingly!** Italics may be used to draw attention to a particular term when it is referred to for the first time in the text, to underscore the importance of particular words, in citations, and sometimes to identify software programs, books, or publications.

Keep a Style Guide of decisions you make regarding italicized and boldface words and other style issues (data base or database, for instance), or have your students create a guide for their publication. There are many decisions to be made in the course of doing a publication; it's helpful not to have to make the same ones over and over, and it enables you to be consistent over time.

Boldface is used in headings and subheadings and to emphasize certain words or phrases. It is particularly useful in breaking up large chunks of text (which is why subheadings in articles are so nice). Depending on the project, you may decide to put all poetry titles in bold, or all pieces of software reviewed by your district committee in bold. If so, make a note of it in your Style Guide, so you can refer to your decision at a later time.

Underline is tricky to use in text, mainly because it often runs too close to the line of type below it. For a cleaner look, try using italics instead.

Spacing

As you make decisions on the text, consider also the *leading*. Leading (rhymes with wedding) refers to the amount of space between each line. (In the past, most type was cast on a linotype machine, which used a process of casting hot lead into letter molds. To add more space between lines you added more lead; hence, the term leading.)

If you want a feeling of more space or "air" within the page, *increase* the leading. If you want a two or three line title to be read easily as a unit, *decrease* the leading.

If you run into a problem with too much or too little space for a particular article, for example, experiment with changing the leading as well as the size of the type in order to increase or decrease the amount of space as needed.]

Titles and Headings

If you're creating a newsletter, bulletin, or other publication that will come out periodically, take some time to design the masthead or heading. Often a masthead has a graphic of some sort along with the name. Keep working until you find something you really like, because you will probably live with it for some time.

If instead of a newsletter, perhaps you'd like to show students how to create titles for articles. Again, look at the print materials that cross your desk and notice the titles. Which ones catch your eye? Some titles may be placed in the center of the page, while others may run word by word down the left or right margin. Some titles may read across two pages. Would any of those ideas fit your purposes? If so, file them away for future reference. Take a minute to look through this issue of **The Writing Notebook**. You will more than likely find three or four different heading formats.

Sometimes students may want to make their story titles "fit" the meaning of the words. My 10-year-old daughter, for example, stairstepped the words of the title to her story, *One Step Up From Broadway!* on the computer to look like this:

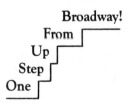

Column Width

When you begin to lay out a publication, whether it's a flyer, an article, the high school annual literary journal, or a newsletter, the width of the columns is one of the first decisions you will make.

Again, refer to the printed material you receive in the mail. I suspect that most of it will be 3-column format (like this article). Generally speaking, 3-column formats are easiest to read, because the eye doesn't have to travel so far across each line. (Another advantage to 3-column formats, which will be discussed later in the series, is the flexibility in placing graphics, charts, tables, and other visuals.) Mixing 2- and 3-column widths on a page also can be very striking, and remember too that introductions to articles can be done effectively in full-column width. Many desktop publishing programs come with templates for different column formats that will help you.

About "General Rules"

At the same time you are taking these guidelines to heart, remember to take some risks as well! Experiment and try something new every so often. The worst that can happen is that you'll vow *never* to do that again and as a further reminder you will add it to your file for future reference! The best part is that every once in a while you will find you have designed a truly elegant page—some with bold exceptions to these "general rules."

At that moment desktop publishing is no longer intimidating—it's a whole lot of fun!

[In the January/February issue we'll talk about the use of white space, callouts, and decisions regarding text.]

Sharon Franklin, The Writing Notebook, 2676 Emerald, Eugene, OR 97403.

Design Elements in Desktop Publishing
Part 2

Sharon Franklin

White Space

I can almost remember the day that I discovered white space. The idea that I could do something *other* than fill every square inch of the page with type came as a tremendous surprise. It is still, for me, one of the most satisfying issues in laying out a publication.

White space serves some very important functions. First and foremost, it gives "air" to the page—and allows the reader to rest (or to continue the analogy, *breathe!*). White space adds contrast by setting off text and graphics every bit as profoundly as a box or screened text, and many times more elegantly. The problem is that all too often the costs of publishing demand that no space go unused. I understand this issue, but I still urge you to fight the tendency. If you use white space effectively, you will have a publication that looks designed rather than packed together.

Below are some examples of how you can add white space to a page. Try some of these ideas in the next printing of your school literary journal or school newsletter and see what you think. Remember to keep a folder of possibilities to refer to when you're working on subsequent projects. It will save you lots of "starting from scratch" thinking time.

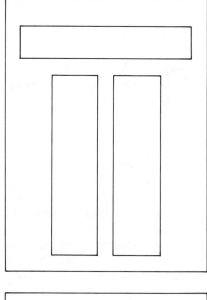

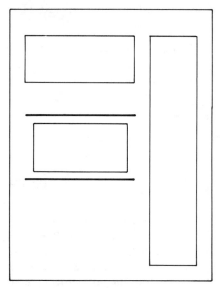

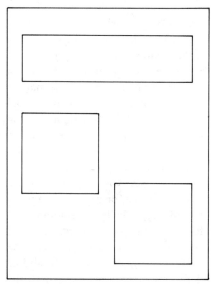

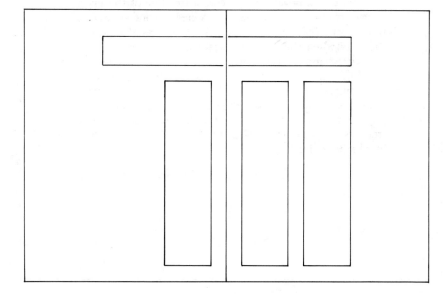

Text

We'll assume you've already decided whether the text for your publication will run full width, 2- or 3-column, or a combination of these. Will you **justify** the right margins (each line runs right to the end of the line) or opt for **flush left/ragged right** (where the end of each line may be a different length)?

Consider: Ragged right text adds white space to the end of lines. It is less formal, generally, than justified text. It also prevents some of the tracking problems seen in so many desktop publications; namely, the overly wide spaces between some words in justified text. Also, ragged right text has few or no hyphenated words, which makes it easier to read.

Justified text can look very tidy. With 3-column width, it's particularly nice, since the space between the columns will be uniform. Just make sure that you pay attention to the tracking (space between letters) and kerning (space between characters) when justifying text, tightening up space or hyphenating when necessary. The results will look much more professional.

Tabs and indents are an important part of structuring your piece of writing. If your students, in particular, are not using a desktop publishing program, they will gain much more uniformity if they always set tabs rather than spacing over *x* spaces. On the other hand, programs such as *PageMaker* help to streamline many of these decisions, something that's particularly helpful when doing similar projects (e.g., different issues of a class newspaper) over time. After naming and setting the specifications for different parts of your copy (e.g., headline, body text, or captions), you can use the Style Pallet to automatically format your copy according to the specifications you set.

Bullets (•), along with tabs and indents, are all ways of adding both emphasis and white space to your copy. If you're using a desktop publishing program, you have the option of wrapping the text around an unusually shaped graphic. **Wrap-around text** also visually connects the graphic with the text.

Callouts

If you are not using callouts in your newsletter at this point, I suggest you begin. The age we live in is an age of rapid reading. So much print material comes across our desks and into our mailboxes that callouts become one way of quickly scanning the material to see whether or not we want to read it. By planning your callouts careful-

ly, you can give your audience a good "preview" of the piece, whetting their appetites for more.

Callouts can be structured in several ways. Sometimes the first few sentences or the first paragraph of an article can act as the introduction. If so, put it in bold and begin the article that way, moving from there into the regular text with paragraph 2. Other times you may find quotes from the article that stand out when you're reading it; if so, "pull" them out and structure them as callouts.

Callouts are usually in boldface, italics, or bold italics. The size will vary, but callouts always tend to be larger than the text. They may be placed anywhere within the text. Here are a few possibilities:

- Begin an article that will run one or more pages with a callout in full-page width.

- Center each line of the pull quote, and place it close to where it appears in the text of the article.

- Begin the article with a bold callout, flush left, ragged right, in the same column width as the article.

- "Float" the callout in 2 of 3 columns, or wrap the text around it.

- Set it off with a thin line (hairline) top and bottom, or let it appear in a shaded box.

One last thing: Try increasing the leading (the space between lines) in callouts. They will be easier to read.

[Next time we'll look at some general layout issues, placement of graphics, screens and other additions to text, and several design resources.]

Sharon Franklin, The Writing Notebook, 2676 Emerald, Eugene, OR 97403.

Literary Timelines

Timeliner from Tom Snyder Productions gracefully allows students to build timelines of their lives or the history of science or the Roman Empire. A nice approach to integrating literature into other content areas is to have students create a timeline of a novel. First, create a timeline of the main characters that includes when they were born and key events in the story. Ask questions such as "What was going on in the story when the character was your age?"

Then expand the timeline by asking questions about the world that are relevant to the time and setting of the story. For example, if students are reading a biography of Thomas Edison, adding details about the history of science, engineering, and inventions to Edison's personal timeline would help students understand the place of his inventions in the world in which he lived.

Jon Madian, Humanities Software, P. O. Box 950, Hood River, OR 97031.

Tom Snyder Productions, 90 Sherman St., Cambridge, MA 02140.

Design Elements in Desktop Publishing
Part 3

Sharon Franklin

Layout

In laying out the text of your publication you will probably choose either one-, two-, or three-column format. Each has its strengths and drawbacks. One-column format (full-width text) often is used for introductions, with the text that follows in two- or three-column width. It is generally used sparingly, because it is more difficult to read text when the eye has to travel so far across each line.

Two-column widths often are used in newsletters. Two-column width is sometimes just right when you have graphics or poems that are a bit too wide for three-column format.

Three-column format is probably most often used. It is the easiest to read, and it gives the most flexibility in placing graphics, charts, and tables because you can run a graphic over two of the three columns if desired. When placing callouts (or pull quotes), three columns are also advantageous, because you can place the callout in the center column, which becomes the focal point of the page.

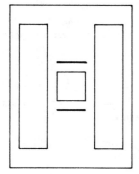

There are many variations on these themes that you or your students may want to play around with at some point; for example, formats that combine two- and three-column widths on

a page. Sometimes it may be desirable to "float" one column of text on a page. This means that the text will not run from the left to the right margin; instead, it floats in the middle with slightly wider margins on both sides. This works well to set off a one-page article or feature that is actually too short to fill an entire page in one-, two-, or three-column widths.

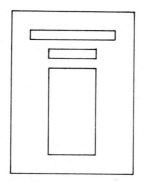

Graphics, Filler, and Other Additions to Text

For better or worse, reading in a nonlinear way is becoming second nature to most of us. Newspapers like *USA Today* have taken it to heart (and some would add, to an extreme), literally cramming their paper with short "mix-and match" items. Although the degree may be offensive to some, it's not a bad idea to loosen up your newsletter or other publication—a little—with short, eye-catching items. You can accomplish this in a number of ways AND do it with style.

Try placing important sentences as callouts to help focus the reader's attention on a particularly important point or to introduce what is to come. Wherever it is placed, the bold print (or italics) helps to visually break up the page.

Look for ways to present tangential information apart from the text. Boxes work well for this purpose. You can use screened (shaded) boxes, or simply set off the related boxed text with a different font. You will find examples of both in this issue. Think about why these items were placed in a box. How would the article have looked and read had that information simply been added to the body of the article?

When you elect to present information in parts, the relationship to the text must be absolutely clear. Perhaps you too have experienced the frustration of trying to figure out how to "read" an article when the text has not been organized in a logical way. It makes for cranky readers, and it is not good layout. Boxes, screens, lines, reverse type (white type on a black background—used sparingly), or a different font can all help to distinguish material as clearly separate from the rest.

A different challenge arises if the material is truly "filler"; that is, it bears no relationship to the rest of the material on the page. It may be an advertisement or perhaps a short news item that fits perfectly in an otherwise empty space. In such a case, you have a responsibility to your readers to clearly define the situation visually.

If the material to be added is "filler," it is helpful to add a vertical or horizontal line between the article copy and the miscellaneous item. This will help to set it off, so readers won't spend valuable time trying to figure out how it relates to the article.

The bottom line here is ease of reading, comfort, and logic. Remember: Reading your newsletter should not be a personal challenge in problem solving—you want your readers to concentrate on the content!

Photographs

Most of us have taken great photos of our children and pets, but there is another standard altogether for photos that will be reproduced in a publication. Stand back and look at the photo in question as the *only one* most people will see—and with no prior knowledge of the classroom, for example, that is portrayed. Is there anything memorable about the photo that will stay with readers? Does the photo convey an idea, a feeling, or *energy* that cannot be expressed easily or as well in words? If so, then go on to the technical questions. Look carefully at the quality of the photo, and if possible, get the opinion of a professional photographer on these and other questions: Is the lighting and contrast sufficient that all dark objects won't simply blend into the background? Are you sure that the light from the window won't wash out most of what you know is there? Is there a way to crop the side of the computer that now takes up 90% of the foreground? If the answer to these questions is no, opt for a good graphic or "filler" instead.

Headers/Footers/ Table of Contents

Headers or footers identify the name, date (month and year), and page number of the publication. (This is especially helpful in identifying the source if a page is duplicated.) You will need to decide whether to use headers, footers, or both; the information to be presented; and whether it will appear on the outer or inner corners of each page (or both).

Designing a Table of Contents is fun! Think of it as the introduction to your publication or book. Make another trip to the bookstore or library to look at examples. Note any ideas you especially like, use some of the techniques mentioned in this series, and have at it. Think also about the placement. Will the Table of Contents appear on the cover or on the first inside page? There are good reasons for both: On the cover it gives readers an instantaneous look at what they will find inside. Academic journals often place the contents on the cover. Placing the contents inside leaves the cover open for logos, graphics, and more eye-catching design that entice the reader to venture inside.

Summary

In this three-part series, I've tried to give you some easy-to-follow design guidelines as you enter the world of desktop publishing, alone or with your students. I hope you will be inspired to:

1. Look at the material that you receive in the mail with an eye to the design. Keep a file of formats, fonts, and layouts that you especially like and incorporate them into your projects and publications.

2. Take some risks. Make a note of your successes as well as those things you will not do again.

3. Consider carefully the purpose of your publication. With that in mind, make the presentation as interesting, yet uncluttered, as possible. Remember the virtues of white space in a busy, crowded world!

4. Make a conscious decision about how you will lay out each page. About 15 years ago I received some of the best advice on writing I have ever received from an editor who cautioned me by saying: "Don't let the words write themselves." Come to think of it,

the same holds true for page design. Don't let the pages fill themselves.

5. Above all, HAVE FUN!

Resources

Listed below are a few of the many desktop publishing resources available.

Beach, M. (1982). *Editing your newsletter: A guide to writing, design, and production.* Portland, OR: Coast to Coast Books. *This book contains many example layouts and is a good introduction to design.*

Felici, J. & Nace, T. (1987). *Desktop publishing skills: A primer for typesetting with computers and laser printers.* Reading, MA: Addison-Wesley.

Parker, R.C. (1987). *The Aldus guide to basic design.* Seattle, WA: Aldus Corporation. *This tiny 68-page guide will be the perfect resource for many people, with chapters titled Basic Concepts, Establish a Format, Add Emphasis Where Needed, Apply the Finishing Touches, and Review the Four Steps to Success. Almost every page contains sample layouts, and a short reference list is included. [This guide is available for the reasonable price of $6.95 from Aldus Corporation, Attn. Customer Relations, 411 First Ave. South, Seattle, WA 98104-2871.]*

Parker, R.C. (1988). *Looking good in print: A guide to basic design for desktop publishing.* Chapel Hill, NC: Ventana Press. *This 221-page book is probably one of the best resources around. It is highly readable, includes many examples, and contains a good bibliography as well as sources of additional information.*

Sharon Franklin, The Writing Notebook, 2676 Emerald, Eugene, OR 97403.

FrEd Writing
Compiling for Publishing

Bruce Fleury

Extend the possibilities for publishing your students' work by assembling the best writing selected from many compositions.

Publishing is recognized as an important step in teaching the writing process. The purpose for writing becomes real, with the audience no longer hypothesized for a classroom exercise. As a result, student motivation is higher and the whole writing process is enhanced.

But how often do we truly "publish" student writing in the ordinary sense of the word? How often do we actually "go to press," "give out," "print," or "issue" student writing? Because of the time, energy, and money involved in actually publishing student writing, often we simply share it within the classroom, frequently by posting work on the bulletin board.

Compiling for publishing can extend the possibilities for publishing your students' work. By assembling the best writing selected from many compositions, you can minimize the expense, both in time and money, of publishing.

The idea is simple. Many writing students work on the same assignment, each one completing a composition. Then, the most successful parts of each composition are selected, organized, and published as a product of the entire group. A word processor facilitates this task.

Let me demonstrate with an example from one elementary school. The following student work was compiled from student compositions written in three classrooms, using FrEd Writer and Computer Organized Writing Templates. The most successful parts of each composition were selected and duplicate ideas were represented only once.

The resulting compiled writing of more than one hundred students was "published" on the back of one page in our school newsletter.

WHEN I WAS LITTLE . . .

When I was little my first teacher was my mother.

When I was a baby my brother taught me how to get out of my crib from the corner. He would also roll me down the stairs to see if I would get to the bottom without getting hurt. Then he would blame it on the dog.

When I was two I would tear off my diapers. So, my mom would put me in my carriage and I would cry like a baby.

When I was two I cracked an egg on my Dad's head. I got another egg and cracked it in the bathtub with water in it. By the time I was three I could skate. I could do a single sowcow and a single flip.

When I was little I used to go to the street and sit in the middle of it.

When I was a baby, I used to eat glue and paper. I used to throw food over the table to my brother.

When I was little I would cry, my Grandpa would come in my bedroom and give me my bottle and lay me in my crib. Then he would sing to me and I would go to sleep. My Grandma has fake teeth on the top. She would leave them in a glass to wash and I would get scared.

When I was little I would go around the house with a bottle in my mouth. I would get into the cupboards. Once I climbed out of my crib and fell on my head.

When I was about two, my family went on a camping trip. My brother caught a big fish and showed it to me. I was so scared I yelled, but by the end of the trip I could touch a live fish without screaming.

They say when I was little I would hit my dad's car. When we went to the mountains I ate snow. My dad and I had snow fights, but I never won. I used to bite my Dad.

When we went to the store I would get lost.

When I was little I would lie. I would say, ''Mom, help! Call the Fire Department! Somebody's house is on fire!''

They say when I was little I would play with the animals at the zoo. I also liked to throw peanuts to the monkeys.

I played in the mud.

When I was little, I would get on my grandmother's bed and start crying because I was hungry. They also say when I was little, I would go outside and run up and down the street.

My mom said that I would yell at the priest in baby talk. My aunt also said when I was little I would try to breakdance.

My birthday party was at the park. I was asleep when we got there. My mom woke me up so the other kids could hit the pinata. I cried while they were breaking it.

When I was little, my mom said sometimes she would take me to the store and I would read the prices. I would even get some right.

Once when I was little, my mom was making pizza. When she turned around I burned my hand on the wire rack of the oven.

My grandpa would bring us treats. He would bring candy, pizzas and ice cream.

When I was little I wore Mickey Mouse glasses.

When I was four I used to tap dance and was in a show.

They say I would cry more than my little sister. When my sister came from the hospital, she slept alone.

When I was little I was kind of a daredevil.

When I was little I would chase my mom around the house in my walker and when she stopped I would crash into her.

When I took a bath I would splash water everywhere.

When I was three and my sister Ricky was one, I would take her bottle and hide with it under the covers in the corner of my bed and drink it. Sometimes I would put the bottle back so my mom wouldn't know that I took it. I remember that.

When I was little I had nightmares.

I told my brother that an egg was cooked, so he cracked it over his head.

When I was little I pushed the swing. It came back and hit me in the head. I had to get eighteen stitches.

When I was little I would eat dirt and then cry for my mom. One time I climbed up the TV antenna outside and my mom had to come up and get me.

When I was little I would call my cereal ''dooy-bats.''

One time my brother and I rolled toilet paper all around the house while my parents were sleeping. One time we climbed up the a tree and got on our garage roof and we couldn't get down.

When I was real little my brother actually liked me.

Bruce N. Fleury, Ed.S., Ed.D., Johnson Ave. Elementary School, El Cajon, CA.

Cultural Currents:
Computer-Supported Newspaper Investigation

Rose Reissman

As an avid newspaper reader, I spend time each day evaluating various newspapers. Recently I have had strong reactions to the quality of coverage of ethnically and culturally diverse groups. Both as a concerned citizen and an English teacher, I wanted to sensitize my multiculturally diverse students to this disturbing current.

How could I best encourage my students to explore cultural issues and racial coverage that often probed highly sensitive and potentially explosive concerns? By using the computer as a report analysis notebook, student teams could work together to examine touchy headlines, content, and graphics, using a scanner. Then, from the objective notes they compiled on their monitor and printed out, they could begin to evaluate how the coverage celebrated or jarred the multicultural mosaic of our community.

To begin, I asked students to bring a newspaper to class. I suggested that they include in their selection foreign language newspapers read in their own homes. (Over 40% of my students are from Hispanic, Chinese, or Korean backgrounds.)

Before using the computer lab, I divided students into teams of two or three. In the lab, I asked each group to sit down at two adjoining computer stations. Then I listed the following racial/ethnic groups on the board: African American, Hispanic, Chinese, Japanese, Korean, Jew, Indian, Native American, Haitian, Dominican Republican, Puerto Rican, Greek, and Irish. I asked students to work together as "Eyewitness News Reader" teams to make predictions on how many news items newspapers would devote to a particular group and in what sections of the news these groups would appear. I gave the groups five minutes to confer and come up with their predictions. I requested that each team appoint a recorder to enter their predictions on one of their computer monitors.

After students had entered their individual predictions on the monitors, each team shared their predictions. Once all the teams had presented their ideas, they were given time to modify their predictions, based on what we had discussed. Then I distributed the Cultural Currents Computer Investigation sheet.

Each group selected one student to enter on the second of their computer stations the actual number of references.

Name_____ Class_____

**CULTURAL CURRENTS
NEWSPAPER INVESTIGATION**

Date of Newspaper Surveyed _____

Newspapers used _____

I. Analysis/Survey

As you go through the newspaper, list all references to the target ethnic or cultural groups by news section, classification (story, ad, graphic, photo) and by effect (positive, negative, neutral).

Target Group: _____

II. References

	News Section	Classification	Effect
1.			
2.			
3.			
4.			
5.			
6.			
7.			
8.			
9.			
10.			

III. Evaluation

Based on this date's survey, I find that the coverage of my target group is:

_____ valid

_____ perpetuates a favorable stereotype

_____ perpetuates a negative stereotype

_____ provides insufficient data to make a statement

My reaction to my findings is:

I would like to see coverage of this target group:

_____ changed

_____ remain the same

_____ stopped

because:

Since we had a scanner available, one team member also cut and scanned relevant photos and graphic references.

Students worked intently for 30 minutes. As I circulated through the lab, I watched them scrolling through their entries and listened to earnest discussion about whether the reference to a particular group was positive, negative, or neutral.

Rather than having students share their findings in a group discussion as I would in my classroom, I asked teams to switch stations in order to review another team's findings. They were given time to enter their own comments under their names on the team's file they were examining. As I wandered through the lab during this exchange, I noticed students intently reading each other's entries and then adding their own evaluations of the references. When I asked if they needed more time, many nodded, so I allowed them to continue. Since the bell rang in the interim, we saved our findings and predictions file until the next session.

When students returned they went back to their original stations with two tasks: They were to review the comments made on their evaluations and then to check and confirm their original predictions, which they had saved on one of their two stations. I encouraged them to comment on the accuracy of their predictions.

When we shared our findings, consensus was reached by students on the following items and entered by one student on a large-screen monitor:

- With the exception of one team out of ten, each team greatly underestimated the number and diversity of cultural references.

- The images and citations of African Americans in the news was mostly negative. Many visual/verbal references to African Americans dealt with crime, low academic scores, and poverty. There was only one positive story, which featured an athlete. Was this a trend that would be confirmed through weekly examination?

- Although there were references to Hispanics, Indians, Greeks, and Native Americans, they were too few to provide sufficient data to make a judgment on the affect of the media coverage on these groups.

- Some groups such as the Chinese were covered favorably, but with an emphasis on academic success and artistic ability. Was there such a thing as ''too positive'' coverage, so that the expectations of success for people in that group would be too high? Was that kind of coverage as bad as a denigrating stereotype? On the same theme, did every Dominican Republic student have the ability to be a star athlete?

- Was Japan bashing in the news a topical theme only after the President's disastrous January 1992 trip, or would it continue in the next few months?

- Was every reference to Israel a reference to Jews? Were Italians always linked to the Mafia in the news?

- Were racial bias crimes the media equivalent to the ''flavor of the month,'' or was it accurate coverage of an alarming trend?

Students wanted to pursue these questions. They asked if they could continue to add to their files and make a database of specific target groups. Several students said that entering the data, scanning graphics, and comparing files diffused potentially volatile issues into relatively objective words and photos they could evaluate. Some students said they liked working in small groups and said they felt comfortable entering their views into the computer, whereas voicing them would have been very difficult. Two students suggested we use the online headlines available on our BBS and set up a student discussion group called ''Cultural Comments.'' They especially wanted to get online responses from students who were from schools and neighborhoods involved in racial bias cases. As one student explained, ''Don't you see? Online they have visual anonymity—they can speak openly and freely!''

I do see. Using the computer to support this kind of investigation provided students a way to share, exchange, and examine concerns that touched a controversial but significant social terrain. We can use technology as a channel for increased cultural communication.

Rose Reissman, Magnet Specialist District 25, 70-30 164th Street, Flushing, NY 11365.

Art: The Telling of History through Technology

Whether dating from 20,000 years ago or in the year 2,000, whether primitive art or technologically generated art, visual history possesses magic and wonder. Creating, communicating, and visually interpreting Primitive art, Egyptian art, African art, Japanese art, and Native American art from different periods in history will capture the imagination and hearts of students, and is a joyful way to expose students to art, cultural history, and present day technology.

Computers provide a unique link between past, present, and future artistic and historical visions. Software programs such as *Dazzle Draw* (Broderbund), *816 Paint* (Baudville), *Paintworks Plus/Paintworks Gold* (Mediagenic), and *Deluxe Paint* (Electronic Arts) use tools, icons, and options that allow students to create imagery of the past as well as the future. In your study of history and culture through art, you can use the computer to simulate prehistoric animal images; Egyptian hieroglyphics; African masks; Japanese tapestries, poems, and prints; and Native American pictographs, blankets, and rugs.

PREHISTORIC ART

Art and visual history may have begun 20,000 years ago in the French caves of Niaux, Lascaux, Rouffignac, and the Spanish caves of Altamira. Cave dwellers, wishing for a successful hunt, relied on skilled artisans to draw, paint, and model pictures of mammoths, bison, horses, wild goats, and even rhinoceroses. Sticks, clumps of fur, hollowed bones, clay, and soft chalky rock, ground into colors of brown, orange, and red, transformed cave walls into a gallery of historic documentation and ecological record keeping.

Off-Line Prehistoric Art and Writing Activities

1. Using red low fire clay, make an 8'' by 8'' clay slab (approximately 1'' thick). Use three fingers to make swirling designs in the clay, replicating the swirling designs once made in the wet clay cave walls by cave dwellers in France.

2. Grind charcoal or earth tone chalk in a mortar and pestle or between two stones. Dip cotton balls into small amounts of vegetable oil and then dip into colored powders. Draw animal images on 12'' by 18'' manila paper or large pieces of brown butcher paper. Use smooth brushing strokes to duplicate the brushing strokes used by cave artists as they took ground stone powders and pieces of animal fur and animal fat and mixed them together to create cave paintings of various animals.

3. Use twigs and ink to draw delicate contours of bison, deer, and mammoths.

4. Use straws and watercolor to "spray paint" the contour of hands. (Cave artists often "sprayed" clay water over hands that were touching cave walls. The remaining image resembled a hand silhouette.) Record thoughts about prehistoric times inside hand contours. Use twigs and ink to write simple concepts.

5. Make a clay slab and then use sticks or fingernails to etch a poem about prehistory.

On-Line Prehistoric Art and Writing Activities

1. Select the thinnest drawing point from a software program such as *Dazzle Draw*, *816 Paint*, or *Paintworks Plus*. Sketch a bison, horse, cow, or mammoth.

   Use the EDIT COLOR options on *816 Paint* or *Paintworks Plus* to change or mix the earthtone colors: yellow ochre, burnt umber, or raw sienna. Select a thick line or point to draw sweeping strokes of color to recreate the moving forms of prehistoric cave art. After the animal forms are printed (using a color ribbon and color printer), add detailed lines, outlines, and contours using pen and ink or fine-line markers in black or brown.

2. Use the SPRAY PAINT options in *Dazzle Draw*, *816 Paint*, or *Paintworks Gold*. Draw a stippled or spray paint contour of a handprint.

   Use white wrapping paper to make boiled paper, which can simulate cave walls. Put crumpled paper into a pan of hot coffee and boil for five minutes. Rinse in cold water and squeeze all the water out. Spread on a tinfoil tray to dry.

   When the boiled paper is dry, place it in the printer. Set printer for "heavy" paper and reproduce the handprint onto the simulated "cave walls."

3. Use SPRAY PAINT and FRISKET/MASKING *(Paintworks Gold)* to make an airbrush hand silhouette. Print on brown butcher paper and then crumple for texture.

4. Select FONTS on your favorite word processing program, choosing one that reflects ancient lettering. Imagine the wonder and magic of creating those first cave paintings and clay reliefs. Make a prehistoric diary. Include five written entries and five illustrations.

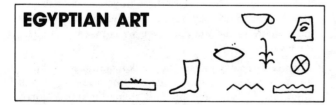

EGYPTIAN ART

Five thousand years ago Egyptian artists were designing and building the pyramids, the oldest stone buildings in the world. Other Egyptian artists were using their technological skills to make paper called papyrus. Originally, papyrus was a kind of plant that could be cut into long, thin strips and placed side by side in a vertical pattern. A second layer of horizontal strips would then be added to the top of the first layer. The layered papyrus strips were held together with a muddy clay paste. When dry, the papyrus paper was ready to preserve the artist's picture language, called hieroglyphics.

Off-Line Egyptian Art and Writing Activities

1. Use 8" by 10" strips of aluminum foil as drying trays. Dip 1" to 6" strips of newsprint paper into a glue/starch solution (about half and half). Place the strips side by side in a vertical pattern on a foil drying tray. Repeat with more strips and place in a horizontal layer on top of the first layer. This will simulate a simplified version of making papyrus.

   Paint Egyptian hieroglyphic images and stories on the dried "papyrus."

2. Create a hieroglyphic chart for writing and story ideas.

On-Line Egyptian Art and Writing Activities

1. Look at examples of early Egyptian art. Notice that many "flat" images of Egyptian royalty and workers are portrayed in profile. Using a favorite drawing or painting program, make an Egyptian profile portrait. Use FLIP HORIZONTAL or REVERSE IMAGE to create a different sense of balance or a reverse perspective image.

2. Use the CUT, PASTE, and COPY options to MOVE, DUPLICATE, and REUSE computer drawn hieroglyphics. Use the same option to make an Egyptian Counting Book or Word Problem Book.

3. Make a hieroglyphic story using a favorite drawing program. Print the story on computer paper or brown butcher paper. Wipe the story paper with a light coating of vegetable oil (use a cotton ball). Press the story between two sheets of manilla paper for seven days. When the story is removed, it will be water-proofed and will resemble the texture of parchment or papyrus.

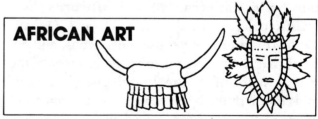

AFRICAN ART

African artists used mask making about 300 years ago to assist with the telling of oral history and family stories. Tribal artists were skilled at using clay, wood, straw, fibers, shells, feathers, animal skins, and gold for mask construction. Various tribal masks represented life, death, youth, love, judgment, and animal forms. Color, form, line, and texture were juxtaposed together to support the formation of masks that helped interpret societal values and carried on oral traditions.

Off-Line African Art and Writing Activities

1. Collect a variety of materials such as feathers, beads, shells, yarn, tree bark, animal fur. Decide which of these materials would tell something about the location of a tribe in Africa, or what the people of the tribe might do to make a living. For example, if a mask is made with seashells, it might suggest that the tribe lived on the coast of Africa. If the mask is made with feathers, it might mean that the particular tribe farmed. If the mask is made with beads and fur, it might mean that the tribe hunted and traded to make a living.

2. Talk about symmetry in art, history, mathematics, and science. Fold a piece of drawing paper in half (9'' by 12''). On one-half of the paper draw an eye, eyebrow, half of a nose, half of a pair of lips. Take the drawing paper to a window, put the drawn half of the paper against the window and trace the other half of the face onto the unprinted side of the folded paper. Open the paper up and a symmetrical mask/face will appear!

3. In African art history, a long mask is usually a judgmental mask. A black wooden mask is often the image of a man. A small oval or round white mask represents a woman. A white mask with thin, tightly closed eyes means death. Masai masks were once decorated with straw and cattle horns, reflecting their cow-herding community and nomadic life style. Masks with familiar animal shapes or masks decorated with antlers and stylized antler horns were once used as part of a hunting ceremony. Colors, lines, textures, and wooden burned tattoos all helped to identify different tribal masks. Select a shape for a mask. Write and describe the reason for selecting the shape of the mask. Select other materials for the mask and continue to describe the purpose for its use.

On-Line African Art and Writing Activities

1. Use *816 Paint* or *Paintworks Plus*. Select MIRRORED SCREEN (half split), which will allow for the development of a perfectly symmetrical mask. Use COLOR EDIT or MIX COLOR to reduce the intense color values often found on a multicolored color ribbon. Attach other materials (feathers, tree bark, shells, beads) to extend the art qualities and to suggest the function of the mask.

2. Using *Dazzle Draw* or *816 Paint*, draw only the symmetrical contour of a mask, and then select a font and write a series of riddle descriptions inside the contour of the mask. Use descriptions to define what the mask might represent. For example: "I am large and heavy. I have one hairy tusk or horn. I like the water. It supports my body weight. What am I?" Duplicate the masks for students to decorate after the riddles have been solved.

3. Use the color version of *ComputerEyes* to digitize student portraits using the computer and video camera. Use *816 Paint* tools combined with the digitized portraits to make self-portrait original art masks.

JAPANESE ART

Japanese artists of the 15th, 16th, and 17th centuries used wood block carvings, ink, rice paper, and silk fabric to illustrate important historical events. Tidal waves, snow-covered mountains, palaces, wild cranes, cherry blossoms, and weathered trees decorated precious scrolls—keepers of poetic calligraphy and visual expression. The partial rolling and unrolling of the scrolls prevented the possibility of ''bad luck.''

Off-Line Japanese Art and Writing Activities

1. To simulate a Japanese wood block print, use a 9'' by 12'' piece of styrofoam mounting board (styrofoam board laminated between two pieces of paper). Look at Japanese textiles, and research different Japanese watercolor prints and scrolls. Use a pencil to draw a picture on typing paper or tracing paper. Tape the picture to the mounting board. Trace the picture with a primary pencil, pressing the line image into the styrofoam while the picture is being traced. After tracing/outlining, use the primary pencil to add line or dotted textures on the remainder of the board. Remove the drawing from the mounting board. Wet the board with water. Paint black tempera over the etched ''plate'' (mounting board) using a 3'' wide foam rubber brush. Place a 9'' by 12'' piece of drawing paper, rice paper, mulberry paper, or colored construction paper on top of the painted plate surface. Rub the paper in a circular motion with your hand. Remove the paper from the plate and a print of the plate image will remain on the paper. This can be repeated many times.

2. Take a simulated wood block print and glue it in the middle of a 12'' by 18'' piece of construction paper. Write a haiku or cinquain poem on the left side of the print. Glue a 20'' dowel on the left and right side of the construction paper. Roll each side of the paper to the center, creating a treasured scroll.

On-Line Japanese Art and Writing Activities

1. Follow the directions for making simulated wood block prints using computer drawings.

2. Look at 14th through 17th century Japanese scrolls such as *Lady Murasaki's Diary*, *Landscape* by Sesshu Ashikaga, *Burning of the Sanjo Palace*, and *Animal Scroll* by Choju Giga. Using *Dazzle Draw*, *816 Paint*, or *Paintworks Gold*, create a painting in the Japanese scroll style. Use Fotoware heat sensitive paper to transfer the colored computer paintings onto 12'' by 12'' cotton fabric using a hot iron. Attach wooden dowels to the top and bottom of the fabric. Attach bead weights and tassels to the bottom.

3. Using *816 Paint*, draw five images that represent YOU. Using selected fonts, write a Haiku poem for each image.

   Design an 8'' by 10'' Japanese fabric pattern using *816 Paint*. Observe the various patterns found in Japanese kimonos. Print the pattern on white rice paper or mulberry paper.

   Roll the YOU images and poems in the Japanese patterned paper and tie with embroidery thread.

NATIVE AMERICAN ART

Eighteenth century North American Indians illustrated their history through pictographs, using clay, bone, stone, plant dyes, and animal hides. Artists etched designs and symbols into clay pottery and wove patterns into baskets, blankets, and rugs. Pictographs decorated rocks, canyon walls, and caves. The environment provided the most treasured icons in Native American history, for these were natural extensions of the artist's spirit.

Off-Line Native American Art and Writing Activities

1. Take a 12'' by 18'' sheet of light brown construction paper or butcher paper. Crush the paper into a small ball (the size of a golf ball). Unroll and repeat crumpling the paper about 50 times. The fibers and sizing will break down after the paper is repeatedly crumpled. It will shrink about 1/4'' and will have the texture of soft deer hide.

   Use this simulated deerskin as a writing surface. Select various pictographs to write or tell a story.

2. Make a pictograph writing chart.

3. Make clay pinch pots and decorate them with pictographs.

4. Make clay slabs and write a story using pictographs.

On-Line Native American Art and Writing Activities

1. Simulate a deerskin pictograph story: Dip a 12'' by 12'' piece of cotton fabric into boiling (a) tea or walnut shells (for brown), (b) yellow onion skins (for yellow ochre), or (c) red onion skins (for maroon). Remove and air dry.

   Use *816 Paint* or *Paintworks Plus* to draw a black line pictograph.

   Print the pictograph images on computer line-fed paper, using a *black heat transfer ribbon*. Now turn the artwork face down on the fabric and press with a dry, hot iron. Pull the paper off and the pictographs will remain on fabric. This will simulate a deerskin pictograph story.

2. Use MIRRORS to duplicate beautiful Native American rug patterns. Print on fabric using a color heat transfer ribbon.

3. Look at the designs found in different Native American pottery or weavings. Use the computer to design a summetrical composition with patterns of Native American origin.

   Print the black-line composition with using a black ribbon. Run the composition through a thermofax machine.

   Take the purple-inked side of the thermofax and press into a 12'' by 12'' terra cotta clay slab. Remove thermofax after rubbing the image against wet clay. The purple ink image will transfer to the clay. The clay is now ready for etching with ceramic tools or an orangewood stick.

Nancy Scali, Arroyo School, 1700 East 7th St., Ontario, CA 91764.

Bibliography

Prehistoric Art
McGowen, T. (1987). *Album of Prehistoric Man*. New York: Checkerboard Press.

Nougier, L. (1979). *Prehistoric Times*. Englewood Cliffs, NJ: Silver Burdett.

Rius, M., Verges, G., & Verges, O. (1988). *Prehistory to Egypt*. Hauppauge, NY: Barrons.

Egyptian Art
Ancient Egyptians activity book. (1981). Cambridge, MA: Cambridge University Press. (Parts of this book can be copied for use within the school for which it was purchased.)

Cosner, S. (1984). *Paper through the ages*. Minneapolis, MN: Carolrhoda.

Weeks, J. (1971). *The pyramids*. Cambridge, MA: Cambridge University Press.

African Art
Gillon, W. (1988). *A short history of African art*. Gretna, LA: Pelican.

Musgrove, M. (1977). *Ashanti to Zulu*. New York: Dial.

Japanese Art
Clement, C. (1986). *The painter and the wild swans*. New York: Dial.

Seattle Art Museum. (1987). *A thousand cranes: Treasures of Japanese art*. San Francisco, CA: Chronicle Books.

Native American Art
Baylor, B. (1972). *When clay sings*. New York: Aladdin.

Museum of New Mexico. (1988). *I am here: Two thousand years of Southwest Indian art and culture*.

Ortiz, S. (1977). *The people shall continue*. New York: Children's Book Press.

Computer Art
Friedhoff, R. M. (1989). *The second computer revolution: Visualization*. New York: Abrams.

Integrating Technology into an I-Search Unit

Judith Zorfass & Shira E. Persky

MAKE IT HAPPEN! is a research-based approach to integrating technology into the middle school curriculum. Developed by Education Development Center, Inc.[1], MAKE IT HAPPEN! guides interdisciplinary teams of teachers to design and implement an inquiry-based curriculum unit called "I-search." This article describes the I-search process, discusses ways in which technology can be integrated into an I-search unit, and illustrates how teachers field testing the approach in four middle schools creatively and meaningfully used technology to benefit student learning.

The I-Search Process

The underlying educational goal of an I-search unit is for students to engage in inquiry oriented learning. Using a variety of materials, tools, and procedures, students explore or investigate topics that are personally meaningful (thus the importance of the "I" in the search process). Over time, working both cooperatively with peers and alone, students gather and integrate information to make meaning out of what they are learning. Based on the work of Ken Macrorie (1988), EDC adapted the I-search process so that it has four phases of instruction lasting approximately 8-10 weeks as shown in Figure 1.

I-SEARCH PROCESS: FOUR INSTRUCTIONAL PHASES

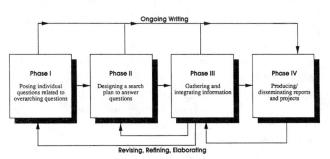

Figure 1.

In Phase I, teachers immerse students in the unit topic (e.g., American Immigration, Human Body Systems, Dispelling the Myth of Africa as a Dark Continent). Teachers elicit and build background knowledge as a way of providing students with the foundation they need to delve into the topic and find some aspect or issue that intrigues them personally. By the end of Phase I, students are ready to pose their individual search questions.

During Phase II, each student develops a search plan; that is, how he or she will go about gathering the information needed to answer the question posed. In developing a plan, each student is able to draw on experiences from Phase I, since many of the activities geared to immersing students in the topic also model a variety of search strategies (e.g., surveying, interviewing, using a data base).

In Phase III, students gather and integrate information. They carry out their search plans and make modifications as needed. They are encouraged to use a variety of sources of information and not to rely solely on textbooks. Interviews, for example, can be a rich source of information for students. As one student explained in his report, "I found I learned a lot more from people than from books."

During Phase IV, students write and disseminate an I-search paper, which deviates in format from a traditional research paper in several ways. An I-search paper has five sections:

- *My Search Questions.* Here the student states his or her question, how they chose their questions, and the starting point for the search for information.

- *My Search Plan.* The student describes the chronology of the search or the quest for information in a narrative format. Students explain how one step led to another, which avenues were fruitful, and what challenges they had to overcome.

- *What I Have Learned.* In this section of the paper, students present the content and the information that answers the search questions.

- *What this Means to Me.* Going beyond the presentation of content, this section allows students to inter-

> **Going beyond the presentation of content, this section allows students to interpret, evaluate, and reflect on what they learned. As they write this section they should be thinking:**
> *How does this change my way of thinking or what I do?*
> *What impact does this information have on my life?*

pret, evaluate, and reflect on what they learned. As they write this section they should be thinking: How does this change my way of thinking or what I do? What impact does this information have on my life?

• *References.* Here students list, in typical bibliographic form, the materials they used to gather their information.

The arrows in Figure 1 represent the recursive nature of the process. The arrows along the top indicate that the writing process is ongoing throughout the unit. Students do not begin to write in Phase IV, but in Phase I—as soon as they identify questions. The arrows along the bottom show that the search process in not a linear one. For example, students may find that they need to refine their question because it was too narrow or too broad only after they are enmeshed in the information gathering phase.

Integrating Technology into the I-Search Process

The I-search unit provides an excellent vehicle for using a rich variety of technology applications that help students to:

• gather information
• organize, analyze, and relate information
• produce reports and projects

For example, in Phase I of the unit, teachers can use simulations, data base files, videodiscs, and videos to help students build background knowledge. In Phase II, students can use time lines (e.g., *Timeliner* from Tom Snyder Productions) to show graphically the intended sequence of their search plan. In Phase III, simulations, data base files, CD ROM encyclopedias, and videodiscs help students gather information. Data base programs, mind-mapping software, and graphing software are effective tools for integrating information. To produce and disseminate reports in Phase IV, students can use graphing programs, desktop publishing, and multimedia packages. Word processing is useful throughout the process.

EDC recommends that teachers create individual computer files (a template) for each student with headings cor-

responding to the different sections of the I-search paper as shown in Figure 2. Students can return to this file repeatedly as they construct their report over the course of the unit.

Sample Uses of Technology in I-Search Units

During the field test of MAKE IT HAPPEN!, participating teachers used a variety of technology applications in their units. Below are three descriptions which highlight actual uses of technology during Phases I (Posing Questions), III (Gathering and Integrating Information), and IV (Producing and Disseminating Reports).

Phase I. The following Phase I activity represents one link in a longer chain of activities that culminated in an I-search paper about Africa. The overall theme of the unit challenged the myth that pre-colonial Africa was a "dark continent," devoid of culture. After studying a novel, *Things Fall Apart* by Chinua Achebe (1959), which discussed various social customs, students designed invitations to an African celebration of a social custom (e.g., a wrestling match, a prenuptial party, a storytelling concert, or a wedding). To do this, students used MacPaint, a Macintosh program with graphics and text capabilities. The MacPaint activity required students first to choose a social custom to illustrate, to conceptualize the image and its relationship to the surrounding text, and then to carry out the design process itself on the computer. Students' drawings depicted symbols, pictures, and original drawings showing the various types of celebrations. One student created an invitation to a funeral. She drew a half-open casket with the words "rest in peace" on the bottom. In the text, she described the deceased and how his death was commemorated with the traditional beating of the drums. Another student created an invitation to the feast of the new yams, a tribal tradition he discovered in his reading (see Figure 3). The graphic showed a tree and a nearby African hut. The text read "Come one, come all, to the feast of the new yam. Be at the great field of the feast at dawn. Bring some new yams."

Phase III. During Phase III of this unit, several students used *Inspiration*, a piece of software that helps students organize their thinking, allowing them to be generative, creative, and structured at the same time. It helps students create mind maps or outlines for writing by first creating a web of their thinking. One student, Marjorie, used *Inspiration* from Series Software to help her link ideas for a report on slavery and the development of the triangle trade in Africa. While the student had already gathered information from an interview with an aging relative whose grandparents recalled the days of slavery, she had trouble seeing how one fact related to another and thus how to organize and sequence her information. She needed help in integrating her ideas. Marjorie booted up the software

REPORT OUTLINE

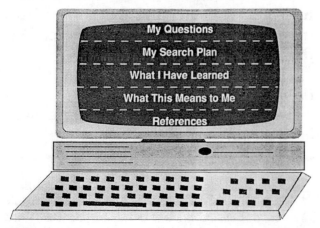

My Questions
My Search Plan
What I Have Learned
What This Means to Me
References

Figure 2.

Figure 3.

realized that in the past 10 years alone, the total assets of Milford's Cooperative Bank had doubled.

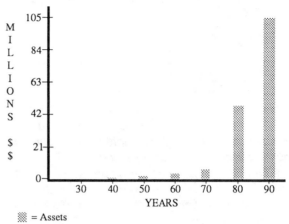

Figure 4.

and typed in some of her notes about slavery. The computer arranged these in a web form. She then went through her written notecards to see which ones related to outcomes of slavery. When she typed these in, the computer arranged and resequenced what she had written to include the new information. When Marjorie completed typing in the information from her notes, she had the program create both a web and a standard outline of her information, which she then printed out and used repeatedly throughout the rest of the process.

Phase IV. During Phase IV, students are to produce and disseminate their reports. The example that follows shows how one student used a graphing program to help him illustrate his findings. The unit in this case dealt with the history of the town, specifically the changes in architecture, economy, and population. The student's search question was: How does the economy affect the businesses of Milford?

Todd, a student with special needs, was writing a report which showed the growth of Milford's Cooperative Bank over the past 100 years. In the gathering information phase, he had interviewed the bank president and found out that the bank's assets reached $105,000,000. Since his teacher had required that all students include at least one graph in their reports, Todd decided to use MECC's graphing software to display what he had learned. The program created a bar graph depicting the assets in millions of dollars in 10-year intervals (see Figure 4). The graph allowed Todd to interpret his information in a new way; he

Summary

An I-search curriculum unit creates a context for using a variety of technology applications to help students gather, integrate, and analyze information and convey what they have learned to others. Many teachers want to use technology to promote problem solving and critical thinking but may have difficulty knowing how. MAKE IT HAPPEN! shows how technology can be used meaningfully within a strong, inquiry-based curriculum unit.

Judith Zorfass, Senior Project Director, & Shira Persky, Research Assistant, Technology Integration Project, Education Development Center, Inc., 55 Chapel St., Newton, MA 02160.

References

Achebe, C. (1959). *Things fall apart.* NY: Ballantine.

Macrorie, K. (1988). *The I-search paper.* Portsmouth, NH: Boynton/Cook.

[1]Funded by the U.S. Department of Education, OSEP, this 3-year project was carried out in collaboration with TERC in Cambridge, MA.

The Great Junk Mail Project

Jeff Golub

Have students take a good look at the mail that is delivered to their homes. (You might want to bring in examples for students to choose from, also.)

They can work in cooperative groups to complete this project, either using the word processor during all stages of the writing process, or instead completing their brainstorming and first drafts using pencil and paper. When all groups have completed their analyses, have them share their findings with the class.

As a follow-up, students may want to write to the companies involved and share their evaluations.

Instructions to Students:
ANALYZE THE PERSUASION TECHNIQUES USED IN ONE PIECE OF JUNK MAIL.

Your analysis of the junk mail should include a discussion of these items:

The Envelope

Are there pictures on the envelope? What are they? What are they designed to do? Any slogans? Other words?

Choice of Words

Point out examples of words used to make the item seem as attractive as possible. What words are used to describe the product?

Doublespeak Techniques

Look for weasel words, unfinished comparisons, vague words. Also look for places where they "compliment the consumer" and say we're "different and unique."

Look at the Pictures

Do the pictures represent doublespeak? Is the item shown actual size? How do the pictures make the product look appealing and attractive?

How Much Will It Cost?

Look at the order blank. How much exactly will you have to pay to get this item? What exactly are you signing yourself up for if you decide to say "yes"?

Evaluate the Junk Mail

In a separate section, give your own opinion about how good a job the advertisers did in trying to sell the product. What did they do that was particularly clever? What did they do that you thought was sneaky or unfair? Even if you are not persuaded to buy the product, do you think that many other people might be tempted?

YOUR PROJECT WILL BE EVALUATED IN THREE AREAS:

- **Your analysis**
  Did you make important, appropriate, and insightful comments about the envelope, the choice of words, doublespeak techniques, the cost involved, and the pictures?

- **Your organization**
  Clear (your explanations are easy to understand)
  Complete (you covered the major areas and items)

- **Your presentation**
  Suitable for display
  No spelling or editing problems

Jeff Golub, Shorecrest High School, Seattle, WA.

Writing to Learn:
The Diary of Anne Frank

John Powers

The Diary of Anne Frank *offers junior high school students a rich literature experience closely tied to an historical period. In a sense, this is part of the dilemma of using such a work: Students need to understand the plight of the people hiding in the secret annex in the context of the Holocaust without losing the sense of immediacy of the everyday struggle of living in such quarters in constant fear.*

Young people need to be prepared for works such as this in two ways: historically and emotionally.

Historical Preparation

Black and white film images of the dead piled up in concentration camps often brutalize students or fail to engage them because of their distance in time. One effective way to prepare students for the enormity of this tragedy is to use numbers in different ways to try to comprehend "6 million."

I begin by stacking ten poker chips on my desk and asking a student volunteer to measure the stack. With this information, I have the student calculate the height of 100 chips, 1,000 chips, and so on up to 6 million. The homework that night is to make a poster illustrating 6 million in a visually understandable way.

The results range from how long one could play a particular video game with 6 million quarters to how many jars it would take to hold 6 million dill pickles.

After the posters are displayed and shared, students move on to the next phase. In this exercise they must visually represent 6 million people. Many of these representations are whimsical, such as the number of square feet needed to provide a beach for that many people. When these posters also are displayed and shared, I make the grim announcement: This was the number of human beings systematically killed during the Holocaust. Students are stunned and confused. Why was this done? How could something be accomplished on such a scale? I answer some of their questions and refer interested students to the library to seek answers to others. At this point I have students write their thoughts down in journal form as the first in a series of writings they will do on the play.

Emotional Preparation

To prepare students emotionally for the play, I give them each a grocery bag. I explain that to avoid being sent to a concentration camp, many people went into hiding. Often they could take with them only what they could carry. The homework assignment that night is to choose the items they would take into hiding. The items they choose must fit into the bag. They are not to actually fill the bag, but to list the objects on the bag itself.

After students share their lists, I have them write about the items they could not fit into the bag, as well as the reasons for choosing the items they did. The explanations are often startling, showing the complexity of naivete and growing maturity that characterizes young adolescents.

With this historical and emotional preparation, we begin to read the play aloud. Throughout the reading I have students pause, either to reflect on what they have read or to write to a particular prompt. Below are several prompts I have used successfully:

Writing Prompts

1. Before beginning the reading, have students write letters of farewell to best friends that they may never see again.

2. At the halfway point in the reading, have students write letters to the same friend, explaining daily life in the annex and what they miss most.

3. At various points in the reading, have them write interior monologues for different characters at particularly dramatic scenes.

4. Occasionally, have students create diary entries that Anne might have written at a given point. Compare these entries to the actual entries from Anne's diary at the same point.

5. At the end of the reading, have students describe how they would spend the day with Anne if she could be transported from the play to the present.

The writing that students produce during this period is some of the best and the most moving that I receive all year. There is the constant hope that Anne will not become one of the grim statistics of the posters they created. Through their writing they come to terms with conflicts they have with their parents, relationships with the opposite sex, and often ponder questions about man's inhumanity to man. Their learning experiences come primarily from their writing and show incredible diversity. When I have access to a computer lab, students keep all their writing on the same disk. Without their names and with their permission, I exchange the disks with other classes and have them make comments of their own.

With proper preparation and guided writing assignments, students can learn a great deal from any work of literature—*The Diary of Anne Frank* is just one example. When I see my former students years later, many can still remember what they had written about the play years before, and how the world validated many of the ideas they had.

John Powers, Magonia High School, 2450 West Ball Road, Anaheim, CA 92804-5298.

Pearls of Wisdom:
Acquiring and Sharing Information via Computer

Elaine Coulson

I have a confession to make. Writing is easy for me—most of the time. Even as a student I was rarely at a loss for words, because I had an opinion about most topics and was eager to share my pearls of wisdom on paper. But sometimes, when those pearls wouldn't form, writing became a loathsome task ending in dismal failure.

Quite simply, my failure was the result of having nothing to say. My writing lacked purpose and commitment. I wasn't absorbed in my topic. In fact, I lacked even the most basic information upon which to begin writing. And without information, how could I synthesize, analyze, interpret, or evaluate anything? Without thoughts, ideas, or opinions, pearls can't form.

At the middle school level, not having anything to say is a major hurdle in the writing process, especially for lower ability students. In my teaching experience, I have come to realize that writing is first a function of how much information the writer knows about the topic. Although most teachers try to assign what they think are appropriate writing topics for students, it isn't always easy to find a topic about which all students have some knowledge, especially in today's heterogeneous classrooms.

One way to circumvent this problem is to design a common classroom experience that enables all students to acquire and share information together. Of course, structuring a common classroom experience isn't a new strategy for writing teachers. Teachers routinely use movies, novels, poetry, and short stories as common experiences for writing. But it is only recently that teachers have had the opportunity to use the computer as the common experience from which good writing flows. Computers can become the catalyst for pearl formation.

Too often the computer is used only as a word processing device in the writing process. It certainly serves this function well, but to stop there denies students the exciting opportunity to use the computer to gather, synthesize, analyze, interpret, and evaluate information *before* using its word processing capabilities to capture their thoughts, ideas, and opinions—the pearls—in writing.

Using the computer as a source of information has two benefits. First, it helps students to understand how computers are used as a tool to gather and work with data. Second, it provides students with the added bonus of learning information within a specific subject area together—information that is then used as the basis for their writing. I have found two software programs particularly useful for such shared experiences: *GeoWorld* (Tom Snyder Productions), a social studies/science simulation, and *Food for Thought* (Sunburst), a nutrition program.

GeoWorld

GeoWorld is an accurate, living data base of 15 natural resources with a simulation of geological exploration.

At the middle school level, not having anything to say is a major hurdle in the writing process.

Students become researchers and geologists as they search the world for a particular resource. I always select oil as our resource because of its particular importance. Other resources include aluminum, chromium, coal, cobalt, copper, gold, iron, lead, manganese, nickel, silver, tin, uranium, and zinc. During the simulation, student geologists conduct geological tests to help them decide where resource deposits are most likely to be found. The results of each test are presented as meters, charts, or diagrams. Students can determine which areas should be further examined and tested by interpreting these results. When they have gathered strong evidence of a resource, students test their research by mining or drilling. *GeoWorld* then keeps

a record of their findings.

After experiencing the simulation, my students write a field report that includes information about how oil is formed, the importance of oil to society, steps used in the exploration process, exploration results, and a discussion of current environmental, economic, and political issues. *GeoWorld* does not provide all the information students need for this report, so outside resources including science books, encyclopedias, atlases, and newspapers also are used. Since much of this outside information is written at levels that are too difficult for my students to read and understand, I have rewritten many of them. Some information has even been entered on *Bank Street Writer* and stored on data disks as reference materials for students. All information in the shared experience is presented to everyone in the same way and is discussed by the whole group so that each student has the same opportunity to gather, synthesize, analyze, interpret, and evaluate the information before writing the field report.

Too often the computer is used only as a word processing device in the writing process. To stop there denies students the exciting opportunity to use the computer to gather, synthesize, analyze, interpret, and evaluate information.

Clearly, *GeoWorld* and the supporting resource materials provide much more than a common experience upon which to base a writing assignment. Students have the added bonus of learning about geology through the simulated geochemical test, core samples, and diagrams of rock formations. Since they learn the scientific explanation for how oil is formed, they understand the necessity of looking for oil in sedimentary rocks with marine fossils. They also learn to identify particular rock formations such as anticline deposits, faulted anticline deposits, faulted deposition deposits, and salt dome deposits.

In addition to geology, students also acquire geography skills as they travel through the world exploring for oil. They quickly learn to identify the Persian Gulf countries, since they center much of their oil exploration in Saudi Arabia, Iraq, Iran, and Kuwait. They also identify other countries with oil reserves: Venezuela, Mexico, the United Kingdom, Canada, Libya, Nigeria, and the Soviet Union. Printouts list resource deposits by longitude and latitude readings, giving students further opportunities to practice map-reading skills.

Critical thinking and problem solving skills are learned as students interpret information from maps, meters, charts, and diagrams; record and organize their information; compare and contrast information; make predictions; and develop strategies while considering alternatives and weighing consequences.

The simulation also offers a perfect opportunity to teach economics. An explanation of how the supply and demand for oil affects the price is the topic of at least one period of classroom discussion. Furthermore, the economic implications of Iraq's recent invasion of Kuwait are better understood after their firsthand experience in drilling for oil in Kuwait or Saudi Arabia. All information gleaned from newspapers and magazines on the economics of oil is discussed as a group, since most students have a poor foundation in economic concepts. Newspaper articles on oil spills and offshore drilling also provide opportunities to discuss environmental issues and concerns. After a few weeks of work and discussion, pearls of wisdom form quite naturally for students, and they are ready and eager to share their knowledge and opinions with others.

I especially recall what one student wrote last year about averting a new energy crisis.

"I think we should have a tax on imported oil, because higher oil prices would force people to use less and conserve. Then, if the U. S. could switch some of its energy needs to nuclear energy, solar energy, or other power sources, we just might be able to satisfy our own energy needs."

Perhaps these pearls of wisdom should have been part of a national energy policy.

Food for Thought

Food for Thought (Sunburst) provides the basis for a shared experience in a different content area. This software program includes a nutrition database containing 17 fields of information on 331 foods. With this database students can locate nutritional information for a particular food or they can direct the computer to scan the list to locate all foods with a specific nutrient content. Sunburst also provides a variety of activity sheets for students to practice data base skills.

After completing and discussing these worksheets, students take the role of dieticians working for Food For Thought, Inc. Their job is first to analyze the dietary habits of Ms. Eda Wrong in relation to U.S. RDA standards for vitamin A, vitamin C, thiamin, riboflavin, niacin, calcium, and iron and then to determine her areas of deficiency. The student dieticians explain the importance of these nutrients and recommend foods to help Ms. Wrong reach 100% of the U.S. RDA in each deficient area. All of this information is related to Ms. Wrong through a written report. Since the data base does not include all information needed for the report, I again provide students with other resources, including a fictitious, one-day log of Ms. Eda Wrong's dietary habits for them to analyze. There is also the opportunity to bring in the most recent research on nutrition. Sunburst provides student handouts on the importance of nutrients to the body.

Just as with *GeoWorld*, *Food for Thought* gives students more than a common writing experience. Although health and nutrition topics are covered in physical education and home economics classes, this is the first time that most students have used the computer as a source of information about nutrition. They see that data bases are useful tools for gathering, synthesizing, analyzing, interpreting, and evaluating information.

I have used *GeoWorld* and *Food for Thought* for two years and I am very pleased with the results. Because students acquire so much information, I no longer hear the most common of all writing complaints: "I don't have anything to say." Since all students share the same experience, they can discuss their information and help each other. Working in cooperative learning groups is an especially useful approach. Even students previously labeled as "poor writers" write three-page reports. For them, this is the first time they have had so much to say, and it's because they know so much. The computer has a unique ability to stimulate the growth of pearls and provide students with the opportunity to display their lustrous gems to others

Elaine Coulson, Ladue Junior High, 9701 Conway Road, St. Louis, MO 63124.

Tom Snyder Productions, 90 Sherman St., Cambridge, MA 02140.
Sunburst Communications, 39 Washington Ave., Pleasantville, NY 10570.

Making a Pop-Up History Book with Young Children

Nancy Scali

Kindergarten is a delightful grade level! Five-year-olds are ''fresh,'' they believe they can do almost anything, and they are anxious to be successful!

Although continuums, frameworks, and grade-appropriate sequencing exist for kindergarten children, not all students can be placed easily in a niche. Fortunately, the computer is a tool that eases students into a variety of subject areas, provides positive self-esteem, and encourages good cooperative learning skills.

These Arroyo School kindergarten children are studying about important individuals in United States history. They have used the library for ''research,'' and they have listened to stories that provide equitable representations of historically significant women and men. Each day, three students work at the computer during center time, creating their illustrations for a class pop-up history book. Students not working at the computer are busy at the writing center, completing simple descriptions of their chosen individuals.

The students have access to one Apple //GS computer and *816 Paint* (Baudville). *816 Paint* is easy for the children to use. Although pulldown menus do exist, young students can draw and paint simply by using the self-explanatory icon images that appear at the bottom of the screen. They print their final artwork on an Imagewriter II color printer. (It takes two weeks for all 28 students to create illustrations on the computer, and eight hours to print 28 pieces of art.)

At the end of two weeks, the students are ready to make their pop-up history book. The process is lengthy and requires a great deal of small group cooperation. The final results, however, are fantastic, and the students receive tremendous satisfaction.

The children's book is titled *Important Individuals in United States History*. It has a table of contents, a title page, and is divided into three sections: Past, Present, and Future. Although the visuals accompanying this article all represent women of the past, present, and future, the book itself included both women and men. For the Future section of the book, the children did drawings of themselves, along with a sentence about what they would do as an adult.

Included also are some of the children's pop-up drawings. These delightful drawings must be seen in all their 3-dimensional and multicolored splendor to be truly appreciated. A couple of explanations must be added: Clara Barton is holding a thermometer in her right hand and a bottle of pills in her left. Nancy Reagan is wearing a fancy red dress with green, yellow, purple, and blue polkadots and two different colored shoes.

Clara Barton was born in 1812. She was a good nurse.

I am going to be a doctor. Kristen

Sally Ride was the first woman in space.

Rosa Parks was black so she had to ride in the back of the bus. One day she decided not to ride in the back. People and judges said she was right.

133

How to Make a Pop-Up Book

1. To make the first page of the pop-up book, fold one sheet of 12" x 18" construction paper in half.

2. Make two perpendicular cuts on the FOLDED EDGE of the paper.
2a. Make each cut 3" long, with 3" between the two cuts.

3. Open folded paper and PULL newly cut strip FORWARD, away from the 12" fold.
3a. A pop-up BASE SUPPORT is now created.

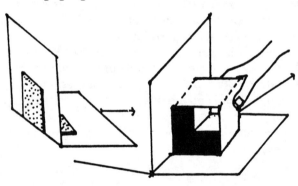

4. Computer artwork (5" x 7" or smaller) can now be glued on the pop-up support.

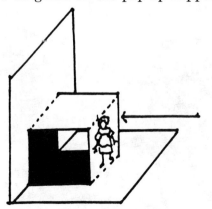

4a. Written information can be glued on the TOP SIDE of the 12" fold.

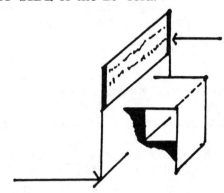

5. When the two sides of the FOLDED PAGE are CLOSED TOGETHER, the pop-up support and computer artwork will fold FORWARD and FLAT.

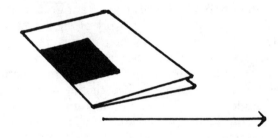

6. To make a POP-UP BOOK, glue the BOTTOM SIDE of the first page to the TOP SIDE of the next folded pop-up page.

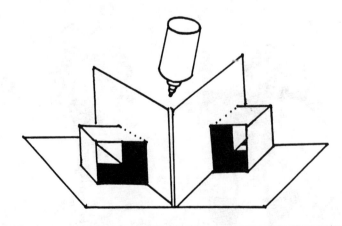

6a. GLUE ENTIRE 9" x 12" BOTTOM SIDE of folded first page to the ENTIRE 9" x 12" TOP SIDE of the next folded page.

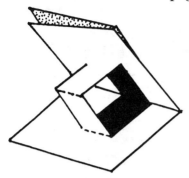

6b. GLUE as many folded pop-up pages together in a BOTTOM-TO-TOP fashion as you need to make a complete book.

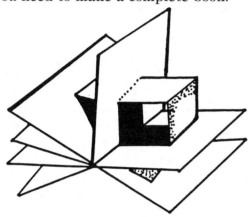

7. BIND folded edges of pop-up book with masking tape or strapping tape.

8. GLUE a 13" x 19" piece of construction paper to the outside TOP and BOTTOM of the tape-bound pages to create a book cover.

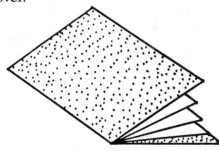

Pop-up books are great fun for children of **all** ages (adults included!). (Older students can type in their text on the word processor.) Consider a pop-up book as the culmination to any of these units of study:

POP-UP BOOKS

Pop-Up Book	Subject Area or Unit
Animals	Endangered species
Characters from favorite children's books	Caldecott or Newbery Award books
Gods and goddesses along with a retelling of the myth	Mythology
An alphabet book (in another language, perhaps incorporating facts about that country or culture)	Foreign language, social studies, or language arts
A science experiment presented step by step	Science
A pictorial presentation of math concepts learned	Math
A favorite fairy tale, real or ''fractured''	Language arts, library/media
Safety rules for the home, classroom, or playground	Primary safety unit

And finally, let it not be said that you can't also think **BIG**! Imagine, if you will, creating a pop-up book of large enough proportions to sit on the floor of your classroom or the library/media center!

Nancy Scali, Arroyo School, 1700 East 7th Street, Ontario, CA 91764.

POCAHONTAS SAVED CAPTAIN JOHN SMITH's life in 1614.

Mrs. Nancy Reagan helps children say 'NO' to drugs.

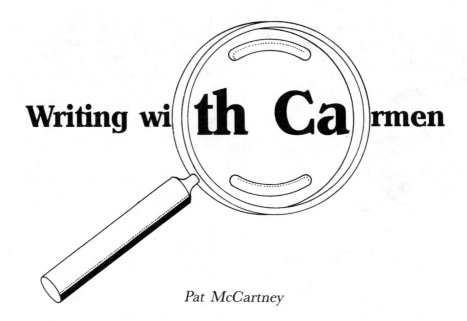

Writing with Carmen

Pat McCartney

Here's how to enhance the benefits of using a well-known educational software program with your students by building in generous amounts of creative and fun writing activities.

When planning for the effective use of *any* computer program in your classroom, several initial questions should be asked:

- How can I best integrate this program into my classroom?

- In addition to the primary curriculum this program supports, what other curriculum and skills is it going to reinforce or teach?

- Can the program best be used individually, in small groups, or as a whole class activity?

- What activities should the class do to prepare for the effective use of this program and what activities can be done after this program is used?

- What writing activities can be created to use with this program?

The Carmen Sandiego series (Broderbund), which includes *Where in Europe is Carmen Sandiego?*, *Where in the USA is Carmen Sandiego?*, *Where in the World is Carmen Sandiego?*, and *Where in Time is Carmen Sandiego?* are being used successfully in many fourth through eighth grade classrooms. They also lend themselves easily to writing activities. In all

of the Carmen programs, students must unravel clues that require a knowledge of geography, history, or politics. As they chase Carmen around the world or through time, students must also chase down specific information from encyclopedias, atlases, and other reference sources. Besides teaching history and geography, these programs also encourage higher order thinking skills and can be used effectively with individual students, small groups, or an entire class. The Carmen Sandiego programs provide a perfect opportunity to create some writing activities that will stimulate your students' imaginations and encourage their ability to communicate through writing.

Journal Writing and Carmen

For starters, ask students simply to keep a journal—a detective's diary—as they search for Carmen. It's a very effective way of getting students to organize and communicate their ideas. However, if used too often, it can get boring. Adding another dimension to the activity can create renewed interest, introduce other perspectives, and provide further opportunities to practice higher order thinking skills. If the program is being used with small groups, let one student keep a journal as the reporter who is following the detective in search of Carmen. Another student can be an informer for Carmen, reporting the activities of the detective. A third student can write from the point of view of Carmen's mother as she reacts to the rumors about her child. Each of these perspectives can be discussed within the group or shared with the entire class. They may lead to other writing activities such as newspaper articles or "The Memoirs of Mother Carmen."

Character Sketches and Carmen

Character sketches are an engaging writing activity to accompany any of the Carmen programs, again encouraging higher order thinking skills as students consider other perspectives. Each student must first establish a specific character personality and write a character sketch that includes childhood history, education, family, hobbies, physical description, habits, clothes, marital status, and type of car.

Involve the class in a discussion of detectives they're familiar with in literature, movies, and television. For example, the discussion might compare the styles of Miami Vice detectives, Angela Lansbury in "Murder She Wrote," and "Teenage Mutant Ninja Turtles." Begin by modeling a character sketch for the class for one of these characters and then have students create one of their own. After students finish writing their individual sketches, pose specific questions that ask them to relate moves in the game to their character. Some students may want to create a character sketch for Carmen and judge her moves accordingly.

The Carmen Sandiego programs provide a perfect opportunity to create some writing activities that will stimulate your students' imaginations and encourage their ability to communicate through writing.

Once students' characters are firmly established, their journals can be written from that character's perspective. Students could also assume secret identities and, through written clues given to each other or posted throughout the room, try to guess the identities of their classmates. As the game progresses, students can rewrite/revise their character sketches, probing deeper into the psyche of their character and clarifying their written explanations. These character sketches—and even accompanying graphics—can be posted or published, thereby completing the writing cycle from prewriting through writing and revising to publishing.

Letter Writing and Carmen

The Carmen series lends itself well to lots of letter-writing activities. Students can write letters to Carmen, trying to convince her to stop running. They can be written in defense of Carmen once she is caught. Students can write letters home, keeping their parents informed about the progress of the case. Letters can be written and sent to Broderbund, sharing their experiences with the program and any suggestions they have for improving it. Messages may be sent between detectives to help or confuse their search for Carmen.

In these activities, students practice RESEARCH SKILLS in order to gain the background necessary to write effectively; HIGHER ORDER THINKING SKILLS as they consider ideas from different perspectives; and THE WRITING PROCESS as they write, revise, and publish their letters.

Students can write to friends and relatives in various parts of the United States or Europe to learn about the areas where Carmen hides. For *Where in Time is Carmen Sandiego?*, each student can assume the role of a famous character from history and then write to the class, parents, Carmen, another detective, or another historical character who meets Carmen. In each of these activities, students practice (a) **research skills** in order to gain the background necessary to write effectively; (b) **higher order thinking skills** as they consider ideas from different perspectives; and (c) **the writing process** as they write, revise, and publish their letters.

Writing Books with Carmen

A travel book or encyclopedia can be written by each student or group of students in preparation for playing the game. Each student becomes an expert on one or two states, countries, or time periods, writing a report that includes the necessary facts to use the clues given in the program. Or, instead of becoming experts on a geographic area or time period, each student could become an expert on a subject such as the various languages of a region, types of currency, or agricultural products. Reference books included with the software provide important information, but you may prefer to have your students research the information themselves. These data can be compiled into a class-created resource book, or have students use a second computer and place all of this information into a data base, which teaches an important computer skill and encourages cooperative thinking and learning. As students learn to search for information on a data base, they will further improve their ability to analyze, compare, and synthesize.

Writing After the Simulation is Completed

After completing the game, give students the opportunity to discuss what Carmen should have done to prevent being captured and ask them to report their conclusions in written form. They might write an end-of-job report for the detective agency, explaining the steps they took to find Carmen and an analysis of their process. It's also great fun for students to justify their expense account entries as a part of this end-of-job report! Besides necessitating some math thinking, it also gives students the opportunity to consider the cost of living in various countries or time periods, as well as daily travel expenses.

Writing activities that extend the usefulness of a quality software program enhance the value of both the machine and the software.

The class may wish to take Carmen to trial, with students playing the roles of lawyers for both sides, the judge, witnesses, members of the jury, and reporters. Let each student write a speech or report as his or her character: the lawyers write opening and closing statements to the jury, the judge reports his or her justification for punishment, jury members individually or collectively report their beliefs in Carmen's guilt or innocence, witnesses write about their

knowledge or involvement in the crime, and reporters write their stories for a newspaper or television newscast. All of these can be compiled into a book, using a desktop publishing program and including text and graphics from each student or group of students. One possible title might be ''The Rise and Fall of Carmen Sandiego.'' Your students will have many other ideas.

Other Software Possibilities

The Carmen Sandiego series represents just one example of how you can use quality educational software programs to encourage your students to write. Other programs that can be extended in creative ways to maximize your students' learning include: *Moptown Hotel* and *Gertrude's Puzzles* (The Learning Company), *Cross Country USA* (Didatech Software), *The Oregon Trail* (MECC), *King's Rule* (Sunburst), and *Science Toolkit* (Broderbund). It's likely that you can add many more to this list.

And . . . a final note. While students need to become computer literate, all computer education should *not* be aimed at that goal. Like the blackboard and the overhead projector, the computer will achieve its greatest success in education when it becomes simply another *invisible* tool to be used, not because it is the latest fad, but because it makes learning more effective. Writing activities that extend the usefulness of a quality software program enhance the value of both the machine and the software.

Pat McCartney, Education Technology Senior Consultant, Colorado Department of Education, 201 E. Colfax, Denver, CO 80203.

References
Broderbund, 17 Paul Drive, San Rafael, CA 94903-2101.
Didatech Software, 3812 William St., Burnaby, BC V5C 3H9, Canada.
Minnesota Educational Computing Corporation, 3490 Lexington Ave. North, St. Paul, MN 55112.
Sunburst, 39 Washington Ave., Pleasantville, NY 10570.
The Learning Company, 6493 Kaiser Drive, Fremont, CA 94555.

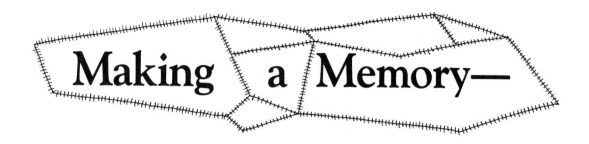

Making a Memory—

A Patchwork Writing/Art Activity for Young Children

Nancy Scali

Natalie raced into her kindergarten classroom, put her things away, and anxiously sat down, ready to draw her "favorite thing." She wasn't using crayons or markers—instead, she was learning to draw on the classroom computer using the mouse. Looking at the color palette and pen and brush selections, she chose her tools and soon a wonderful yellow-orange image appeared on the monitor. She explained:

"It's Sara. Sara's my bear. She gots a thing on her back and you can wind it up and it makes a song. She's so cute. She only has one eye and you can see the pink fur inside her ears and you can wiggle her ears and she's soft. I even sleep with her and I like her."

Over at the writing table, Joshua was dictating a story about his favorite thing.

"I like dump trucks! Someday I want to be a truck driver. I used to have a dump truck at grandma's. I played with it a lot. I used to put dirt in it. It was black and I could dump the dirt."

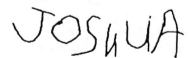

Eventually all the children completed their pictures and stories about their favorite things. The pictures were placed on cupboard doors as the dictated stories were read. Each picture was special, each shared something in common, and together they represented a patchwork of memories and pleasant visions.

The idea came: Could we make these drawings into a real quilt?

Making a Classroom Quilt

The software program, *T Shirt* (Spinnaker Software) proved to be a tremendous tool for this project. *T Shirt* includes a variety of images that may be printed on heat sensitive paper using an Apple Imagewriter II Color Printer. To transfer the printed image to the fabric, the sensitive paper is placed on a t-shirt (artwork face down) and pressed with a hot iron. Using this idea, heat sensitive paper was ordered from Foto Ware, Inc. The students' original computer art was printed on the heat sensitive paper and the picture images heat-transferred to 12'' x 12'' white cotton squares. The squares were then sewn together to make the quilt.

We also wanted our stories and pictures to be a classroom book. Using *Paintworks Gold* and an Apple IIᴳˢ computer, the students' artwork was reduced 50%. (For older students, this provides a good math challenge.) The smaller pictures then were printed on heat sensitive paper and transferred to two 16'' x 16'' cotton squares using an iron. To make the binding/cover for Our Favorite Things stories and artwork, two 14'' x 14'' pieces of cardboard were covered with cotton batting (using 1/2'' layered sheet and white glue) and then covered with the decorated fabric. Heavy colored railroad board was glued to the inside of the fabric-covered cardboard. We used *MultiScribe* to print the stories and *816 Paint* to draw the artwork.

Our classroom quilt is very special. Many children discovered quilts for the first time through this activity!

Some families had special quilts. The children found exciting quilt stories in the library. After reading *The Keeping Quilt*, students decided that the classroom quilt could be used for special occasions or to conjure up the joy of a favorite thing. (Most students thought wrapping themselves up in the quilt would be tremendously wonderful.) Currently, the quilt is a coverlet for the reading table and the Favorite Things book remains the most popular and tactile book in our class library.

Nancy Scali, Arroyo School, 1700 East 7th Street, Ontario, CA 91764.

Foto-Ware, Inc., P. O. Box 1040, Grand Rapids, MN 55745; ph. 1-800-346-0021.

A Bibliography of Quilt Books

Johnston, Tony. (1985). *The quilt story.* Illus. by Tomie de Paola. New York: Putnam.

Jonas, Ann. (1984). *The quilt.* New York: Greenwillow.

Martin, Jacqueline. (1988). *Bizzy Bones and the lost quilt.* New York: Lothrop, Lee & Shepard.

Polacco, Patricia. (1988). *The keeping quilt.* New York: Simon and Schuster.

Roth, Susan L., & Phang, Ruth. (1984). *Patchwork tales.* New York: Atheneum.

Vincent, Gabrielle. (1982). *Ernest and Celestine's patchwork quilt.* New York: Greenwillow.

Puppets Across the Curriculum

Nancy Scali

Children and adults have been fascinated by puppets for thousands of years. Archaeologists have found puppets in the ruins and tombs of ancient Egypt, Greece, and Rome. During ancient times puppets may have represented gods, idols, or sacred images. Imagine watching a statue or idol "come alive" with head, arm, leg, or eye movements, with the manipulation secretly known to only a select few. The Middle Ages was a period of widespread illiteracy. In order to educate the people and teach Biblical stories, a kind of puppet called "Little Mary" was created, which translated to "marionette." In Japan during the 1700s, many dramatists were eager to write plays for a unique rod puppet called "Bunraku." Today many people in Indonesia enjoy performances of the rod puppets called "Wayang Kulit" (leather puppets). They are held behind a silk screen with the puppet rods operated from below the floor; a strong spotlight at the back of the stage casts a shadow on the screen in front of the puppets.

There are three types of puppets: the **hand puppet**, which consists of a glove or cloth body that slips over the hand; a **marionette**, which is controlled by strings or wires; and a **rod puppet**, which is manipulated by one or more rods or sticks.

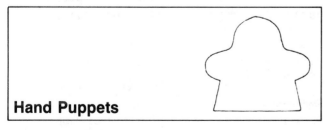

Hand Puppets

Using *816 Paint,* a color monitor and color printer, have students make a puppet using FULL SCREEN (8½'' x 11''). The figure may have the shape of a thumb-less mitten, or instead may have a head, two arms, and waist-length body.

Try making overhead outline transparencies of the top, middle, and bottom third of a desired puppet shape. Tape each third on the monitor (one at a time), starting with the top (head shape). Students can then 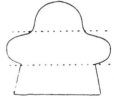 trace the transparency outline with a mouse, or work inside the outlined area to create one puppet section at a time. As the picture area shifts upward on the monitor, a new transparency section should be attached to the monitor screen. All three parts of the puppet should blend and join together easily. Upon completion, print the puppet image on heat transfer paper. Press the transfer image onto a 9'' x 12'' piece of cotton fabric using a hot, dry iron. Place fabric print onto a second 9'' x 12'' cotton fabric piece. Pin around the perimeter of the image, securing both pieces of fabric with straight pins. Leave a one-inch seam allowance on the sides and top of the puppet. Remember to leave the bottom open so a hand can be slipped in.

Hand puppets can be made out of paper using the overhead outline method. Simply glue the outside margin of the puppet image paper to its paper backing.

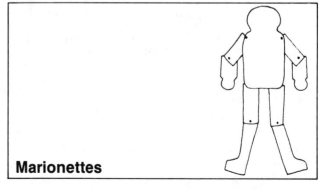

Marionettes

Using *Dazzle Draw, 816 Paint,* or *Paintworks Plus,* have students draw "parts" of a puppet: a body with head attached, two upper arms (rectangular), two lower arms with hands attached, two upper legs, and two lower legs with feet attached.

Print these parts on white construction paper. Glue on poster board and trim to size. Attach paper fasteners at elbows, knees, shoulders, and lower body (close to the left and right lower corners). Glue a 1'' x 20'' piece of balsa/wood molding to the back of the puppet. At the bottom of the puppet level on stick, screw in one tiny eye loop. Use heavy tape to attach one string to the center back side of each arm. Tape one string to the center back side of each upper leg. Put the four strings through the tiny eye loop, dropping them in from the top. Tie the ends of the strings together. Gently pull the strings, which cause the arms and legs to move.

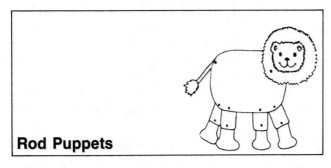

Rod Puppets

Using *816 Paint* or *Paintworks Plus*, have students create an animal character. A frontal view including neck is most successful. Design a body, four separate upper legs, four lower legs with attached feet, paws, or hooves, and a tail. Mount on poster board and trim to fit. Attach all parts with paper fasteners. Tape a 30'' (1/16'') dowel to the center of the back side of the body, and attach a 30'' dowel to the center of the back side of the head. The head and body will move when their respective rods are moved, causing the legs to appear to walk or run. This rod puppet may also be used as a shadow puppet.

Many students and teachers have discovered the joy of puppets. They can make special projects came alive, help a child overcome shyness—and some speech problems. They can assist in the teaching of difficult concepts and bridge language barriers.

Puppets can be used nearly any grade level and subject area curricula, and they are a beautiful way to integrate literature, writing, and computer technology. Consider:

- Animal puppets, computer drawn and pasted on paper bags, as part of an endangered species unit;
- Spider or insect marionette puppets as a follow-up to a science unit;
- Famous characters from literature puppets;
- Puppets to mark historical events;
- Puppets to tell students' original myths or folktales; or
- Puppets as part of the culmination of a study of Asian culture.

Now go even further. How about:

- Flower and plant marionettes with moving petals and leaves;
- Simple computer-drawn shapes made into stick puppets for students to "talk" about the properties of various geometric shapes as part of a primary mathematics unit;
- Fruit and vegetable rod puppets for a nutrition unit;
- Train or car marionette puppets for a study of transportation;
- Computer-drawn lungs, hearts, and brains (ironed on fabric, stuffed with cotton and used as stick puppets) for a unit on good health;
- If you have access to a digitizer, your students can digitize their own faces to make self-puppets! And older students may want to get really fancy and attach small battery-driven lights to the eyes, hands, and feet of their marionettes for an interesting effect with the lights off!

Making and using puppets is a dynamic, enriching experience. After an amateur puppetry experience in the classroom, students—and teachers—may wish to join the Puppeteers of America, a group of people from over twenty countries.

Nancy Scali, Arroyo School, 1700 East 7th St., Ontario, CA 91764.

References
Currell, D. (1975). *The Complete Book of Puppetry.*
Lasky, K. (1985). *Puppeteer.* New York: Macmillan.

Enriching a Study Theme with Visual Art

Nancy Scali

Claude Monet, a delightful French artist, began painting in the 1870s. His fascination with light, color, and nature was the basis for an art form called Impressionism. While in search of a new, creative way to introduce the change of seasons to my Kindergarten students, I glanced through a wonderful book, *Monet's Years at Giverny*. It isn't a child's art book, but the reproductions were so lovely that I decided to share some of Monet's seasonal naturescapes with my students.

Monet's *Poplars*

This sharing led to discussions about Monet and his family, art materials, artistic styles, and art as a career. The topic of Claude Monet, Impressionist Painter, branched out in many directions and provided opportunities for language, writing, literature, historical research, science, and visual art activities.

In the process I discovered a wonderful children's book, *Linnea in Monet's Garden*. This book addressed many of the questions my students posed regarding Monet's personal life. For example: "He loved children and had eight children of his own. He lived in a huge pink house in Giverny. He painted all year round, which allowed him to paint the same subjects over and over again with different colors or flecks of light, depending on the season."

Students painted, sketched, and colored pictures in an Impressionistic style. As an experiment, they forged ahead to try creating on the computer. Using an Apple IIGS and the software *816Paint*, students selected a favorite Monet painting to reproduce. The "sparkle" effect of Impressionistic light was achieved in three ways:

1. Using thick or thin brushes and the Spraypaint option, images were drawn on the picture area, using a mouse. Spraypaint left some pixels white and added color to others.

2. A second way to achieve an Impressionist "look" was achieved by some students using a Zoom option to paint each individual pixel with various colors.

3. A third choice involved filling some areas with solid color and then spraying secondary colors, lines, and textures on top.

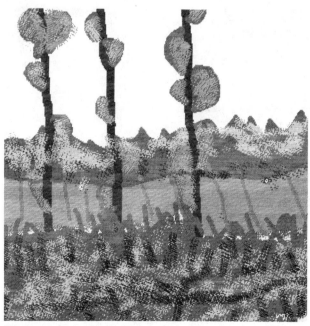

Kindergarten student's *Poplars*

Monet often painted the same subject during different seasons; thus, the subject would have many new and different color values. Color value and color value changes were accomplished by adjusting the color values of the standard color palette under Menu Selection.

Monet's *Walking Bridge*

So much excitement and enthusiasm was generated by this theme that the children moved from there to doing research on a female artist of the same period or one who painted in the same style. This research topic was challenging, since most women artists throughout history have gone unrecognized for their accomplishments. There are, however, two books that give recognition where it's due. *History of Women Artists for Children* by Vivian Sheldon Epstein provides brief histories of selected women artists. The artists included begin in about the 10th century. A chronological list of the artists and their styles is also included, which provides a foundation for further research. *Inspirations* by Leslie Sills also introduces early female artists and their accomplishments with an approach that lovingly entwines culture, family, and art-for-art's-sake.

In the course of their research, my students discovered Berthe Morisot, Marie Bracquemond, Rosa Boneur, and Mary Cassatt. They were able to compare and contrast the artistic styles and the personal interpretations of individual artists. In addition, students gained an awareness and appreciation of how difficult it was for these women to achieve comparable recognition to their male counterparts.

Kindergarten student's *Walking Bridge*

Visual art is an excellent way to enrich any study theme. It provides a very vital sensory approach to learning and adds meaning to the Chinese proverb, I HEAR, AND I FORGET. I SEE, AND I REMEMBER. I DO, AND I UNDERSTAND.

Nancy Scali, Arroyo School, 1700 East 7th Street, Ontario, CA 91764.

Writing and Art:
Tools for Self-Expression and Understanding

Nancy Scali

Staci's drawing of her brother.

Sometimes it is difficult for students to talk about very real problems in their lives. Many times these feelings can be expressed through writing, painting, and drawing, however, and in the process students can help increase the awareness and sensitivity of their classmates.

Bringing Difficult Issues to Light

In the late 1800s, French Impressionist artist Edgar Degas visited his uncles and cousins in New Orleans. At the time Degas was a fairly realistic painter and strived to tell stories through his artwork. When he decided to paint his favorite cousin, he was confronted with a dilemma. How could he paint her portrait without revealing her blind, disfigured eyes? Degas' solution became a visual story. First, the cousin was carefully seated on a couch to the left of the center point of the painting. She wore a long, flowing, white voile dress with large red polka dots. To the right of the picture area was a soft textured green wall.

The completed painting was very visual. The white dress with red polka dots appeared to "leap" out in the front of the picture and capture the visual focal point. The green textured wall carried the viewer's eye to the right because it was a complimentary color—the opposite of red on the color wheel. Last to be seen was a soft, subtle pastel portrait with blind, empty eyes. Degas' painting seemed to say, "My cousin is wonderful, delightful, and bright! Her disability is so insignificant!"

• **Encourage your students to write and draw about a special person in their lives. The writing and drawing below helped this young girl to communicate some of her feelings about her brother.**

When I was little my brother and me played all the time. When he was 5 I was 3. Mom put him on a bus to go to school but I walked to school. He grew and I grew but he couldn't do much like read and stuff. Dad moved away. Now he is big and I hate people looking at him and I don't know why he had to be retarded.

Identifying Feelings and Emotions in Works of Art

Mary Cassatt was an American artist. She lived in Paris and studied art with Degas. Cassatt loved to paint; her favorite subjects were friends and family. She wanted people to look at her work and share the feelings her subjects seemed to express.

• **Have students review various works of art on laser-disc (e.g., The National Gallery of Art). Using appropriate software, ask them to write or draw descriptions of the feelings and emotions they observe in selected works of art.**

I looked at this picsure of Vincent Van Gogh and his head and ear were covered with these bandages. It made me think about when I was little and I tried to cacht my sister and I fell down hard on the sidewalk. Dad put me on the kichen table and put this medacine on me and some bandaides. My Mom said he was dressing my hurts. I didn't know what she mint but I thot someone must have dressed Van Gogh too.

145

Special Treasures

In 1970, English painter David Hockney completed "Mr. and Mrs. Clark and Percy." In this piece the husband appears to be sitting casually in a favorite chair holding a white cat, Percy. Mrs. Clark seems to be looking directly at the viewer of the artwork. Both people are surrounded by objects that have meaning for them: a bouquet of flowers, a book, a Hockney print, a telephone, and an antique lamp.

• **Using computer software, have students create illustrations of themselves and their special treasures. A story that talks about the meaning and significance of the treasures could be written using the word processor.**

Multimedia Creations

Faith Ringgold is an American artist who was born in Harlem. Faith remembers her mother's beautiful storytelling. Aunts, uncles, and neighbors would gather around Faith's mother and listen to her vivid adventures. As Faith's artistic style developed, she decided that she would like her artwork to "tell stories" as beautifully as her mother's language had. She also decided that some of her work should include storytelling and simple dramatic productions. Not only would the viewer of the work enjoy *seeing* the images, but they would also have the opportunity simultaneously to hear singing, chanting, and stories.

• **Create a class mural around a particular theme of interest to the children, complete with their poems, stories, and music.**

Sharing the Stories of Our Lives

Ten years ago I was demonstrating how to fold origami birds to a group of third grade students. Three Vietnamese boys were in the group; they giggled and laughed as I clumsily folded the colored paper squares. In turn, they did a wonderful job of folding their birds and were kind enough to share their secrets. As they began to demonstrate their expertise, one of the boys began to fold a paper boat. As he folded he said:

> My parents take me and my sister to this place. I think it was very dark like in night. We get on this boat with this guy, I think he's like my relative or uncle or something. My sister say, "Wave!" I wave and I never see my parents anymore.

He pushed his paper boat across the table.

It wasn't painting, drawing, or writing, but through the process of creating, this young boy was able to share an important part of his history with us.

All of these ideas remind us that language, art, and writing—alone or in combination—can help our students to express their inner thoughts and feelings. Learning can be difficult when there is so much in a child's everyday reality that school does not seem to care about. No matter what subject or grade level we're teaching, it's important to honor our students' experiences by giving them both a place and the opportunity to express their feelings.

Nancy Scali, Arroyo School, 1700 East 7th St., Ontario, CA 91764.

References

Conner, Patrick. (1982). *Looking at art: People at home.* New York: Margaret McElderberry.

Sills, Leslie. (1989). *Inspirations: Stories about women artists.* Niles, IL: Albert Whitman.

Terrasse, Antoine. (1974). *Degas.* New York: Doubleday.

MY FATHER LOVES ME MOST IN RESTAURANTS
Juliet Feibel

a man's pride in his eldest
can be conditional,
based on her capacity
to handle supercilious service
and an unpeeled shrimp.

through crystal, ice, and wine
i talk of Florence while
his eyes rain money on me.

prayers for ex-lovers
Juliet Feibel

I   for sunblinded lakes of summers past
where we, the unloving, played hearts.
for one hundred springs to come
when i adore you in secret.

II   for these truths i now deny;
for the winter when he believes
the lies i told to stay in love.

from Crescendo, Volume XXVI, Horton Watkins High School, Ladue, MO.

Mathematics Portfolios

This was taken from Assessment alternatives in mathematics: An overview of assessment techniques that promote learning, a booklet prepared by the EQUALS staff and the Assessment Committee of the California Mathematics Council Campaign for Mathematics. (1989). Used with permission.

Student portfolios are well known in art and writing, but until now have rarely been used to keep a record of student progress in mathematics.

What's In a Portfolio?

A portfolio might include samples of student-produced:

- Written descriptions of the results of practical or mathematical investigations
- Pictures and dictated reports from younger students
- Extended analyses of problem situations and investigations
- Descriptions and diagrams of problem-solving processes
- Statistical studies and graphic representations
- Reports of investigations of major mathematical ideas such as the relationship between functions, coordinate graphs, arithmetic, algebra, and geometry
- Responses to open-ended questions or homework problems
- Group reports and photographs of student projects
- Copies of awards or prizes
- Video, audio, and computer-generated examples of student work
- Other material based on project ideas developed with colleagues

Advantages of Portfolios

Student portfolios can provide:

- Evidence of performance beyond factual knowledge gained
- Assessment records that reflect the emphases of a good mathematics program
- A permanent and long-term record of a student's progress, reflecting the life-long nature of learning
- A clear and understandable picture, instead of a mysterious test score number
- Opportunities for improved student self-image as a result of showing accomplishments rather than deficiencies

- Recognition of different learning styles, making assessment less culture dependent and less biased
- An active role for students in assessing and selecting their work

Student Attitudes

A portfolio may also incorporate important information about student attitudes toward mathematics such as

- A mathematical biography, renewed each year
- A student self-report of what has been learned and/or what is yet to be learned
- A description of how the student feels about mathematics
- Work of the student's own choosing
- Excerpts from a student's mathematics journal

Teachers and Portfolios

Teachers and their students should choose most of the items to include in the portfolio, since it gives a good indication of what is valued. Putting dates on all papers is important. First draft or revised writing should be acceptable, with a note about which it is. The names of group members should probably be on papers done by a group, or at least indicate that it was group work.

The definition and evaluation of portfolios are opportunities for teachers to share and learn with peers. Groups of teachers who have reviewed the contents together have found it an exciting and rewarding experience. Sharing with parents, administrators, and school boards will help emphasize student accomplishments.

Assessment of Portfolios

Educators should look at many portfolios before trying to establish a standard of assessment. Because portfolios should reflect the instructional goals of each situation, the ''rubrics'' (detailed descriptions of assessment standards) will vary.

For further information on EQUALS or on the booklet, write EQUALS, Lawrence Hall of Science, University of California, Berkeley, CA 94720.

Poetry for Homework

Marilyn Burns

Here is a problem to challenge 2nd and 3rd graders' thinking and reasoning, taught by Cheryl Liechty from Wildwood School, Piedmont, CA.

Shel Silverstein's book of poems, *Where the Sidewalk Ends* (Harper & Row) is a favorite for many children. Cheryl read this poem to her class:

Smart

My dad gave me one dollar bill
'Cause I'm his smartest son,
And I swapped it for two shiny quarters
'Cause two is more than one!

And then I took the quarters
And traded them to Lou
For three dimes—I guess he don't know
That three is more than two!

Just then, along came old blind Bates
And just 'cause he can't see
He gave me four nickels for my three dimes
And four is more than three!

And I took the nickels to Hiram Coombs
Down at the seed-feed store,
And the fool gave me five pennies for them,
And five is more than four!

And then I went and showed my dad,
And he got red in the cheeks
And closed his eyes and shook his head—
Too proud of me to speak!

Cheryl gave the children a homework question to answer: Did the boy get the good deal he thought he did? Explain why.

Anne, a second grader, wrote: *No because he is trading coins, and for instance, three is more than two, but if he traded like this: 1 dollar for two dollars that would be better. He got more <u>coins</u>, but less <u>money</u>.*

Victoria, also a second grader, wrote: *No. He was useing sense. But then again he wasn't. A Dollar is more than 50c. 50c is more than 30c and so on and when he comes to 5 pennies he thinks he's smart but is he? No.*

> no because he is trading coins, and for instance, three is more than two, but if he traded like this: 1 dollar for two dollars that would be better. He got more <u>coins</u>, but less money.

Another second grader, Lauren, developed her argument in detail. She wrote: *No. Because 2 is more than 1 but 50c is less then $1.00. And 3 is more then 2 but 30c is less then 50c. And 4 is more then 3 but 20c is less then 30c. Also 5 is more then 4 but 5c is less than 20c. So, Lou, Old Blind Bates, and Hiram Coombs are all smarter then that fool boy!*

Bert, a third grader, gave a brief answer: *Sometimes more is less and less is more.*

Reprinted with permission from The Math Solution newsletter, Fall/Winter 1989-1990. © Marilyn Burns Education Associates, 150 Gate 5 Rd., #101, Sausalito, CA 94965.

Mathimagine

Stephen Marcus

Mathimagine is a HyperCard stack that provides thinking and writing assignments based on the concepts of addition, subtraction, division, multiplication, and equivalence. Mathimagine plays with those concepts in both literal and metaphorical ways. I hoped it would invite thinking, writing, and discussion of the nature of those concepts while it encouraged students to write narrative, autobiographical, argumentative, persuasive, expository, and other kinds of prose. Mathimagine also tries to make familiar things strange and strange things familiar—all within a single overriding metaphor.

Mathimagine is part of a collection of writing activities called HyperShelf, a set of HyperCard stacks that I created to illustrate that teachers could develop some useful classroom materials with only a very little knowledge of HyperCard (see Figure 1).

Figure 1. HyperShelf, containing the volume Mathimagine.

As a stack, Mathimagine has an extremely simple design. There's a scrolling text field on the lefthand page that holds the equivalent of 8-10 pages of typewritten text. On the righthand page is a set of calculator-type buttons (see Figure 2).

Figure 2. A page in Mathimagine.

Pressing a button provides a "math problem" in a pop-up field. There's also an "X-Factor" button that can be used to throw in a new perspective. Each page has five writing assigments, and new pages (and assignments) can be added easily by teachers and students. Figure 3 illustrates a subtraction problem.

Figure 3. A subtraction problem in Mathimagine.

It was quite challenge to develop the "math problems" for Mathimagine. Here are a few examples:

- Describe a situation you know about where things just don't add up. (An addition problem)

- If boredom equals indifference multiplied by impatience, what is enthusiasm? Illustrate. (An "equals" problem)

- What would it be like if you were five times more of something? (A multiplication problem)

- Give an example of how "A house divided against itself cannot stand." And what's the remainder? (A division problem)

Mathimagine, like all the "volumes" of HyperShelf, was created with certain design features in mind, related to the software innerface. I wanted it to have a certain personality. I also wanted it to be informed by elements of challenge, curiosity, control, and fantasy. That is, Mathimagine tries to offer appropriate levels of challenge, to evoke curiosity, to give meaningful kinds of control over to the student, and to engage people's imagination and story-telling abilities.

As a small, friendly attempt to encourage writing and thinking across the curriculum, Mathimagine can serve as a design example for a variety of subject areas. The keys for development are a willingness to play with ideas and language, the use of connotations as well as denotations, an emphasis on visual and language metaphors, and a certain sneaky approach to things.

Note: A review of HyperShelf by middle school teacher Linda Nielsen appeared in *The Computing Teacher*, February 1991, pp. 45-48.

HyperShelf is now available from Intellimation, 1-800-3-INTELL.

Stephen Marcus, Ph.D., coordinates a HyperCard project for the South Coast Writing Project, Graduate School of Education, University of California, Santa Barbara, CA 93106.

Guess Our Number

A Lesson with 7th and 8th Graders Taught by Cathy Humphreys

Marilyn Burns

In this riddle activity, Cathy Humphreys' students combined their number sense and logical reasoning abilities. Working in pairs, students wrote clues to define a particular number. Cathy checked to see that students' solutions were correct and that only one answer was possible. Students then solved each other's riddles and checked their answers on an answer sheet that Cathy had compiled. Cathy reported that students' interest and involvement were high.

To introduce this activity, Cathy gave the class a riddle to solve. "I am thinking of a number," she said. "See if you can figure it out from these clues." Cathy wrote the clues on an overhead transparency. She showed the first two clues to the class.

Clue #1: *The number is less than 30.*
Clue #2: *It is a multiple of 3.*

"Talk in your groups," she told the class, "and see what you now know." It didn't take long for students to figure out that the numbers that fit these clues were 3, 6, 9, 12, 15, 18, 21, 24, and 27. Cathy showed the next clue.

Clue #3: *The number is odd.*

Groups huddled together and quickly eliminated the even numbers and agreed that the possibilities now were 3, 9, 15, 21, and 27. Cathy then gave the fourth clue.

Clue #4: *The number is not a square number.*

"So it can't be 9," Jon blurted out. The others agreed. Cathy showed them the last clue.

Clue #5: *The sum of the digits is 6.*

It now was obvious to students that the only possible solution to the riddle was the number 15.

"I'm going to give you another set of clues," Cathy then told the class. "This time, I'll show you all the clues at once. Work in your groups to solve the riddle."

Clue #1: *The number has two digits.*
Clue #2: *It is a factor of 60.*
Clue #3: *The number is not a multiple of 10.*
Clue #4: *The number is not prime.*

Cathy's previous experience taught her that two errors were typical when students wrote their own riddles—clues sometimes led to more than one possible answer, and riddles sometimes included redundant clues. To address these

possible pitfalls, Cathy purposely wrote her second riddle so it had these flaws. Both 12 and 15 were possible solutions and Clue #4 was unnecessary.

When they had solved the riddle, two groups arrived at the answer of 12, three got 15, and two groups discovered that both numbers were possible.

"My riddle is incomplete, then," Cathy said when the class agreed that two answers were plausible.

"Which one is right?" Kelly asked.

"The number I was thinking of was 15," Cathy responded. "In your groups, think of a clue that would make 15 the only possible answer."

The groups came up with several suggestions: The number is odd. The number is a multiple of 5. The number isn't even. Adding the digits gives 6.

"Although my riddle was incomplete," Cathy then said, "I also included a clue that wasn't necessary."

"Oh yeah," Nathan said, "you didn't need to say the number wasn't prime. We already knew that."

"How did you know?" Cathy asked.

Tami answered. "It couldn't be 2, 3, or 5, because you said it had to have two digits, and those were the only possible numbers that were prime."

"A clue that's unnecessary is called a redundant clue," Cathy told the class. She wrote the word "redundant" on the overhead.

Cathy then had students work with a partner to write their own riddles. "Be sure your clues lead to only one answer," she cautioned, "and check to be sure you don't have any clues that are redundant."

The students got to work.

Clue1: We are thinking of a number less than 20.
Clue2: It's a multiple of 2.
Clue3: It's Not Square, It's not prime
Clue4: Cre number has six factors.
Clue5: Are number is higher than twelve.

We are thinking of a number

clue 1: Our number is less than 40
clue 2: Our number is an odd number
clue 3: Our number is not a square number
clue 4: Our number is not prime
clue 5: Our number is not a multiple of 5
clue 6: Our number is a factor of 165

Marilyn Burns Education Associates, 150 Gate 5 Rd., #101, Sausalito, CA 94965.

Timed Tests

Marilyn Burns

Timed tests have long been used to monitor children's learning of basic math facts and skills. Even with a nationwide shift in mathematics education to a curriculum that calls for teaching for understanding—a curriculum that emphasizes children's thinking and ability to solve problems—timed tests still persist as standard classroom procedure in many school districts.

Teachers who use timed tests believe that the tests help children learn basic facts. This makes no instructional sense. Children who perform well under time pressure display their skills. Children who have difficulty with skills or who work more slowly run the risk of reinforcing wrong practices under pressure. In addition, they can become fearful and negative toward their mathematics learning.

Timed tests do not measure children's understanding. Teachers concerned with children's results on timed tests necessarily maintain a vigorous and steady program of drill and practice. The danger in this pedagogical focus is that an instructional emphasis on skill development does not guarantee the needed attention to understanding. As we all know, skills can be learned and maintained with little underlying mathematical understanding. (I remember being taught: "Yours is not to question why; just invert and multiply.")

Test results from the National Assessment of Educational Progress demonstrate that children's ability to perform arithmetic skills does not ensure their ability to use those skills in problem-solving situations. And, as stated in the California Mathematics Model Curriculum Guide: If a child does not have an understanding of the concept represented by a symbol, no amount of practice working with that symbol will help to develop that concept.

From a regimen of timed tests, children learn that it is not only important to be able to recall math facts and skills, but it is important to do so *fast*. Speed with arithmetic skills has little, if anything, to do with mathematical power. The more important measure of children's mathematical prowess is their ability to use numbers to solve problems, confidently analyze situations that call for the use of numerical

> **The more important measure of children's mathematical prowess is their ability to use numbers to solve problems, confidently analyze situations that call for the use of numerical calculations, and be able to arrive at reasonable numerical decisions they can explain and justify. Expecting any less is educationally foolish and short-sighted.**

calculations, and be able to arrive at reasonable numerical decisions they can explain and justify. Expecting any less is educationally foolish and short-sighted.

Lauren Resnick, co-director of the Learning Research and Development Center at the University of Pittsburgh, had this to say in an interview in response to a question about drill and practice and tests:

> *If you believe that mathematics is a collection of specific pieces of knowledge, it is very reasonable to build tests that sample that knowledge. . . . And those tests encourage teaching that emphasizes*

bits of knowledge because that's how you improve students' scores. With the kind of teaching those tests promote, children come to believe that mathematics is a collection of questions to which one can find the answer within about a minute, or not at all.

And that is contradictory to the goal of having children come to believe that mathematics is an organized system of thought that they are capable of figuring out.

Dee Uyeda told her class that they were going to take a test. Dee was interested in the progress the children were making in their math learning.

Tommy's hand shot up. "Is this a timed test?" he asked.

Dee hadn't intended to impose a time limit on the children and was surprised by the question. After talking with the children about their experiences with timed tests, she asked them to write about their feelings.

Jess wrote: *I don't like timed tests because the teachers never give you enough time and when I have a timed test I start to tremble with fear.*

From Emily: *I hate time test when I try to do them I think oh no the time is running out and I look at the paper next to me and it's half way done and I've only done one problem and after that I hate math.*

Elizabeth

Timed Tests

The teacher pases out the paper. Thats when the butterflys began. Your heart is in your throt. you want to get all the math promlems. But there is No time to think. There is a blur of prolbms to be done. Your head gets dizzy rushing. you try to finsh. No time to check over. It will have to do. I don't think I ever got all the prolmems in a timed test rigt. You get so nervs that you cant think, your palms svet. That feeling in your stomick is too bad for words. The dreoded time test...

Writing Questions From Graphs:
A Question for 4th-6th Graders

Marilyn Burns

This lesson was taught to a multi-graded group of 20 children in Westport, CT. To begin the lesson I had students record on a graph:

WHICH WOULD YOU RATHER BE? Mark an X.		
Younger	X X X	
The same age	X X X X X X X X X X X X	
Older	X X X X X	

I had introduced graphs in two previous lessons, modeling for the students how I drew conclusions, having them draw conclusions, and giving them questions to answer from the data.

This morning I gave them a different task. "For this graph," I told them, "you are to work together in your groups and write questions that can be answered from the information posted."

1. Which one was picked the most?
2. What fraction of the class picked younger?
3. How many more people picked older than younger?
4. What fraction of the class picked The same Age and Younger?
5. If you added the "older" with the "young How much would you get?
6. How many people picked the same age?

After the groups wrote their questions, they read them aloud to the class in turn. Before beginning I gave them instructions. "After you hear a question, decide if it can be answered from the information on the graph." In this way I involved students in listening and thinking about the questions.

1. What fraction of the class picked the same age? (lowest terms)
2. What would you get if you added the same & the older together and then times it by the younger?
3. How many groups of 2 are there on the graph?

It turned out that all the questions they wrote could be answered from the information. However, another issue arose. Some questions had no relationship to the content of the graph. This presented another thinking opportunity—to sort the questions they wrote into two groups: those that did and those that did not relate to the question asked by the graph.

1. How many more people chose the same age over younger?
2. If you plus all the x's on the chart, times it by 10 and divided by 5, what would the answer be?

To end the lesson I raised one more question: "Would it be a reasonable assignment for you to find solutions for all the questions posed by the groups?" Their response was a unanimous "yes." I think that doing work from problems they create themselves helps make students more willing learners.

> Doing work from problems students create themselves helps make them more willing learners.

Marilyn Burns Education Associates, 150 Gate 5 Rd., #101, Sausalito, CA 94965.

The Place Value Game

Marilyn Burns

Teachers often worry about repeating an activity that children experienced in an earlier grade. However, there is value in doing so, especially when an activity probes children's thinking and reasoning. The Place Value Game is an example of an activity that is appropriate for children at different grade levels.

The game relies on a combination of luck and strategy. The goal is to try and make the largest number possible. The digits in the number are determined by a die or spinner. Each time a number comes up on a die or spinner, all players write it in one of the places. Once a digit is written, it cannot be changed. There is an extra box that allows players to reject one number.

First and second graders can play the game with two or three-digit numbers. Children in grades three and above can play a four-place game.

Students play in groups. After each game, they read their numbers aloud to compare and see who has the largest.

I do not make a worksheet of blank gameboards for the children. Also, I do not tell students how to keep score or even if they should keep score. I feel that students benefit from organizing themselves for such purposes.

Beyond playing the game, however, it is valuable to have students think about the strategies they use. Samples of strategies from 3rd and 7th graders are included. The writing from the older students demonstrates the increased knowledge and savvy they bring to the game.

Work from 3rd Graders

After the children played the game for several days, I conducted a class discussion about what they had figured out about playing to win.

The children offered a variety of ideas. "It's a good idea to put a 6 in the first box." "I always put a 1 in the reject box." "I put a 5 or 6 in the thousands place." "You have to decide if you'll take a chance with a 3." I didn't comment or probe their ideas, but merely gave all who wanted the chance to talk.

"When people play games," I said, "they often have a strategy, a plan for deciding what to do." I wrote the word strategy on the chalkboard. I then explained that I wanted them to write about the strategy they used to decide where to play numbers as they came up.

> Our table got 9 all ties and 8 all in a row. One of them was all 1s. My stratagy was that if there was one I put it in the regect box. I put 6s in the thousands box. I put 3s in the ones box. I put 4s in the tens box. I put 5s in the hundreds box. I never won alone but I was in a few winning ties and a few losing ties. I was dissapointed when I lost but I know games are for fun not winning.

> I thought taking chances on low numbers like 2 is better than putting it in the reject box. Thats how I won a game. We all almost had the same stratege. Thats how we got 9 all ties. I lost three games from not taking chances. So I changed my stratege.

Work from 7th Graders

When having the older children write their strategies, I related the assignment to computers. "Imagine that you are programming a computer to play the game," I explained. "Describe how you would tell the computer to make the decision where to play each number as it comes up." This seemed to help focus them.

153

① Rolls of 1 and 2, put in reject box; if reject box filled, put farthest right as possible.
② In rolling a six, put it farthest left as possible.
③ 5 and 4 on first roll go in 100's place.
④ 4 on first roll or three on first roll go in 10's place.
⑤ 4 on second roll goes in 10's place.
⑥ on 4th roll, 5 goes to thousandth
⑦ 4 rolled after a four in the 10's place put in the 100's place.
⑧ rolling a 3 on other than 1st roll, put farthest right as possible.

Roll the die —
You must put the number you roll in a box and you may not change it to a different box after you roll again. Put the 6 in the top left box. If you get a 5 or a 4 put them in the hundredths or tenths box. If you get a 3, 2, or 1 put them in the ones box or the reject box. If the space of a 1, 2, or 3 is taken move it to the nearest right hand box. If the space for a 4, 5, or 6 is taken move it to the nearest left hand box.

After students wrote their decision-making strategies, they were interested in doing some comparison testing with them. We did this. I rolled the dice and each group played the number that came up according to the strategy they had written. It was not easy for all groups to make decisions based on what they had written. They also became aware that it was necessary to play many games before producing convincing indications that some strategies were more effective than others.

Reprinted with permission from The Math Solution newsletter, Spring 1988. © Marilyn Burns Education Associates, 150 Gate 5 Rd., #101, Sausalito, CA 94965.

Simple Pleasures

The white sun, glaring,
setting air on fire,
turning houses into ovens,
shooed the day into silence.

But I remember, too,
the shedding of shorts and shirts,
diving into delicious pond water,
sinking,
        sinking,
                sinking,

into icy bottom,
soaring,
        soaring,
                soaring,

to warm surface,
laughing at the sun...

The slipping into shorts and shirts,
(body still wet)
letting the wind and sun blow-dry the skin...

The carrying of sling shots,
chasing after birds
from tree
to tree
saying all the time,
"I almost got it!"
"I almost got it!"

I shall rise early tomorrow,
and just as the sun comes up,
I will ask him,
"Are you the same sun
I used to laugh at
when I was a kid
in Cambodia?"

Kimnee Chheang

from the Stylus, Volume 17
Jordan High School, Long Beach, California

Writing Down the Earth

Charlie Perry

As a member of the Central Coast Writing Project, I do my best to get across the point that writers simply need to keep their eyes and ears open and then comment on what they see and hear. *Earthwatch* magazine is a feast to look through and dream about, so it seemed an appropriate spark for writing.

Earthwatch is a nonprofit corporation that helps link scientific studies throughout the world with volunteer workers and benefactors. They publish a bimonthly magazine of the same name for their members nationwide. This 70-100 page publication generally includes scientific findings, feature articles, and listings/explanations of available volunteer positions in studies that range from digs in Israel to Arctic wolf observation to studies of the giant clams of Tonga. Since becoming an Earthwatch member, I look forward to each issue of the magazine—an adventure wish-list of the highest order!

I figured it might inspire a dream or two in my students, too, so I took a some issues to one of my English classes. The kids looked over all the possible adventures, formed into teams based on a shared interest in specific scientific expeditions, and then spent three days in the library gathering information on their topics.

We sent our work to Earthwatch to let them know what we had done, suggesting that English students should be solicited for scholarships to Earthwatch expeditions, as such students could capture in prose and poetry some of nature's magic. Earthwatch graciously sent us a thank-you note and honorary expedition patches. Then, in the October 1990 issue, they dedicated an entire page to our work!

Here are some samples of the writing my students did. "Last Song" by Amber Ramage also appeared in *Earthwatch*.

*My stocky
shadow swiftly
tumbles from the sky,
grace, happiness
trickling through my
veins flooding my
heart with warmth.*

*The murmur of
calm seas is scarcely
audible through my
mighty song. I
emerge from waves of
dawn. The bright
hues in the sky dance
on my slick body, and
paint visions in my
head.*

*A large
shadow blocks the
sun, a sleek cold
metal rising sharply
upward clangs
hollowly in the
waves. Grim faces
squint down, a pang
of fear, a deafening
sound, a jolt of
pain, a mournful cry
and no more.*

*An echoing
song rippling through
the seas with muted
power, smoldering,
withering . . .
finally dying as I
did, forgotten.*
—Amber Ramage

Untitled

*Across the snow
The hunters stalk their prey
Shadows on the ice
Paws stepping
Tongues licking
It is the hunters
With their guns
Killing
Blood across the ice
It's murder
Killing for the sport of it.
Packs of wolves killed.
If a cub is lucky it won't be shot
But it will die
eventually*

*No food
No Mother
Father
How can people do this?*
—Wes Benica

Last Song

*I rise with
the roaring tides
overtaking miles of
rugged crests
dotted with foam. I
lunge into the
lonesome depths,
releasing the strong
chains of fear.*

Charlie Perry, Los Osos Junior High, 1555 El Moro Ave., Los Osos, CA 93402

For more information on Earthwatch, write Earthwatch Expeditions, Inc., 680 Mt. Auburn St., Box 403, Watertown, MA 02272. One-year membership: $25 (U.S.), $35 (overseas). Illustration © 1990 Christopher Bing. Used with permission.

The RAIN FOREST Book

Nancy Scali

Our children are exposed on a daily basis to environmental issues that may someday affect their lives in very real ways.

Kindergarten students at Arroyo School have begun to broaden their knowledge base about the few remaining rain forests in the world and are being encouraged to develop a sense of conservation for these complex ecosystems.

Confronted with information about the decline in rain forests, the kindergarteners posed this question: Do we need rain forests? Responses were provided through a "Yes" and "No" graph, along with home, school, and library research. The hypothesis reiterated the research and graph conclusions that we do indeed need rain forests. In addition, the procedures the students used as part of their research provided wonderful opportunities for learning they won't soon forget.

STEP ONE:
Students collected materials to create a rain forest. They included:

- Small plants to represent trees
- Charcoal, to represent a layer of infertile soil
- Potting soil, to represent healthy topsoil
- A small, two-cup watering can for creating rain
- An aquarium/container for rain forest construction

1. Students constructed the forest together in a group, taking turns putting rain forest ingredients (charcoal, soil, and plants) into a container. Care was taken in the measurement of quantities of charcoal and soil. Analysis of color and texture characteristics of the plants, soil, and charcoal were made using a hand-held microscope, and data was drawn on a chart.

2. As plants were placed into the rain forest, close attention was given to the "roots." Exploration and observation with the magnifying glass and hand-held microscope indicated that the roots held clumps and clusters of soil together. As an extension, students held soil samples in their closed hands, imagining their fingers to be roots. Hands were turned upside down, but fingers grasped the soil tightly. Different hand and finger sizes held different quantities of soil together. Such

comparisons could be made with plant roots and tree roots of different sizes. A balance also assisted in the comparison of amounts of soil held by different hand and finger sizes.

3. After all the plants and trees were in place, a small finger-width river was dug through the forest. Once again it was observed how tightly the roots held the soil together, especially along the river banks.

4. Students added the ever-present rain to the rain forest model. It was measured (2 cups of water) and the pouring/sprinkling was timed (40 seconds). A new observation! The tops of the trees (plants) seemed to catch the heavy rain just like an umbrella (perhaps this is why the tops of rain forest trees are called umbrellas). The tree foliage slowed the rain down—it was a misty rain. (A spray bottle of water was used to demonstrate how the rain might feel under the tree umbrellas).

5. Slowly the topsoil moistened and the river filled with water.

6. There was no flooding because the tree roots gave strong support to the soil. The trees flourished. Students illustrated these factors and observations.

STEP TWO:

Materials were collected to make a rain forest without trees. Students were to imagine that all the trees had been cut down, burned down, or removed.

1. Students assembled the treeless forest together in a cooperative group.

2. Charcoal and potting soil were layered into a container, and students' analyses, investigations, and observations were collected.

3. A finger-width river once again wound its way through the forest.

4. Students added rain. It was measured and timed.

5. Suddenly there was massive flooding. The river bed disappeared, and the land filled with water. Nothing could be seen except water. Students clearly understood the value of the rain forest trees. Observations were made that there were no tree roots or trees to help hold the soil together and prevent the river bed from collapsing, overflowing, and flooding the land. Many students

expressed concern over the possible loss of animals and the destruction of animal homes in the rain forest.

STEP THREE:

The last step was to demonstrate how erosion, flooding, and the loss of topsoil would prevent plants from growing and how animal food sources and home-sites would disappear.

1. Students assembled a treeless rain forest.

2. Charcoal and potting soil were measured and layered. This time a layer of white sand was placed on top of the potting soil to represent topsoil. The white sand could be easily observed and identified.

3. A finger width river ran through the forest.

4. Rain was added.

5. Tremendous flooding occurred. The edges of the river eroded until they could not be defined. The topsoil (white sand) washed away and collected in the flood water.

6. The flood water was drained into a plastic bowl. The river bed was gone, the topsoil was gone and different sized fissures were left in the rain forest floor where rain had forcefully hit the ground.

The results demonstrated that plants could not grow without topsoil or protection from rain and flooding. Without trees or plants, animals would have few food sources. Constant rain and flooding would cause plants to die, animals would have no homes and they too would succumb to the environment. The conclusion supported the need for a healthy, balanced ecosystem in rain forests around the world.

Students did a great deal of research during this project. In order to find a niche for the collected data, the kindergarteners made a large (partner-size) book, rather than a science project display. When students found that 179 different kinds of trees grow in a 2½ acre area of rain forest and only about 7 tree varieties grow in that same size area in United States forests, diagrams were made—one with 179 different trees and another with seven different kind of trees. Coloring, cutting, glueing, and assembling the trees into equivalent areas made a clear visual image.

In other research it was found that one person needs the oxygen made by 500 trees in order to breathe for about one year. To show this, one child drew, colored, cut, and glued 500 trees onto a 25-foot long strip along with a self-portrait. This activity had a great pictorial and tangible impact and helped all students to understand this information.

In another activity, the children's computer self-portraits were drawn to scale to represent an average height of 4 feet, printed out double, and glued head to toe beside a 12-foot painted tree that represented an equivalent height of about 176 feet. This activity helped them to see and evaluate the enormous size of one rain forest tree. When it was discovered that half of the world's variety of animals live in rain forests, the children created computer drawings to illustrate this research. Data was later collected to identify animal species already on endangered lists and possible solutions for saving these animals and their rain forest homes were generated.

This study of the rain forest provided a wonderful introduction to the scientific method, along with a meaningful integration of language arts, science, social science, visual arts, and technology. It also gave children the opportunity to express caring concern for the future. The Rain Forest Book continues to be part of the classroom library and sparks ongoing natural conversation among the children about the animals, plants, trees, climate, and balance the rain forests provide to the world.

Nancy Scali, Arroyo School, 1700 East 7th St., Ontario, CA 91764.

BUT YOU DIDN'T

Remember the time
I wrecked your new car?
I thought you'd kill me,
But you didn't.

Remember when
I dragged you off to the beach?
You said it would rain
And it did.
I thought you'd say,
"I told you so."
But you didn't.

And remember that time
I flirted with those guys,
Just to make you jealous?
I thought you'd dump me.
But you didn't.

I loved you
And wanted to make those things
Up to you
When you came back
From Vietnam.

But you didn't.
—*Mary Anne*

SOME

Some of us look at the world
And see the color of the wind. . .
Dark and dripping with gray
Sunshine.

And we can hear flowers talk.

We see pain
As an old-yellow woman
Dancing to old-yellow tunes,
And we can hear clouds scream.

Some call us gifted.
Some call us insane.

We call ourselves . . . lonely
With nothing better to do than
Listen to flowers talk
And watch pain dance.
—*Paula*

from Horizons, Holmes High School, Covington, Kentucky

Writing as a Reflection of Student Thinking: One Field Experience

Heidi Imhof

Have you ever climbed a mountain, seen grizzly sows and their cubs play, and had some caribou come within a few feet of where you were standing? These are just of the few of the things we experienced at the science and writing camp this summer.

—two ninth grade students, Yukon-Koyukuk School Districk

Background

I was privileged to lead a summer experience in natural history and writing for a group of students from several villages within Yukon-Koyukuk School District (YKSD). YKSD serves an area in the interior of Alaska larger than the state of Washington. Headquartered in Nenana, it is composed of ten rural schools in villages along the Yukon and Koyukuk Rivers. Two of them are on the road system; the others are mosquito-sized plane rides away from Fairbanks, the closest urban environment. The district's population is more than 95% Athabascan Indian. The intent of the summer program was to enhance the academic programs of the district and to provide social interaction experiences for these ninth through twelfth grade students who are geographically isolated from the world beyond their immediate village sites.

I moved to Alaska for a consulting job with the Alaska Writing Program[1], a prompted writing environment on computers modeled after the Bay Area Writing Project. Our goal was to develop a program with hands-on science experiences in the outdoors that would lead to writing activities. Perfect! I had made the move for just this kind of opportunity—especially to teach in a generative[2], student-honoring way.

Four Critical Characteristics

To me there are four important characteristics of this style of teaching:

- **Teacher sincerity models student sincerity.** If I'm not interested in my subject, or in my students, why should they be interested? Being sincere as a teacher means that the word ''teach'' has an active voice; that is, showing rather than telling. With a penchant for the outdoors and field science, it isn't hard for me to be enthusiastic about being there.

- **Mental attendance for all.** I want it from my students, but I need to demonstrate my complete attendance as well—especially my own attendance as a learner. That means I start fresh, asking questions and looking for answers along with the group. We agree to a *mental meet*; that is, to be there together at the same time and in the same relative space.

- **Learning as a joyful individual and group experience that has real products.** As a teacher, I have the option—and responsibility—to provide much more than a funeral-dirge learning environment. I need to openly acknowledge the joy that comes from learning with others. When I learn new, meaningful skills that give me new tools for understanding the world, I increase my self-esteem and my life possibilities.

- **Processing group experiences requires individual reflection.** To get the maximum benefit from any group experience, individuals need time to process what happened for them, to sort out their understanding or their lingering questions. It's important to acknowledge the different ways of thinking about an event that occur when individuals have the opportunity to respond to what they have experienced. Writing activities, if structured carefully, facilitate reflective experience better than perhaps any other activity. Writing forces us to make our thinking public and to confront our personal muses. As such, writing becomes important as a tool for thinking and as an artifact of our ideas.

The setting in which to put these characteristics in place was one that many people only dream of: Denali National Park, part of the immediate environment of Nenana.

Setting the Stage

I continued to ask myself: How could I best prepare this group of students for a deep learning experience in Denali National Park? What could I do to capture their hearts, to maximize their ability to acknowledge and interpret what they would see, hear, touch, smell, and taste? YKSD students have an aptitude for nature based on very fundamental, instinctive grounds—their survival depends upon it.

I began with an introductory activity that gave us a chance to meet and get to know each other. I then introduced them to some basic tools that we would use to extend our senses: thermometers, hand lenses, binoculars, pH paper, length measurement devices, journals and writing instruments, working groups, and our own thinking.

Frequent Neighborhood Encounters

Armed with our tools, we began with morning trips in the field, focused closely on our immediate microworld—the symmetry of flowers and the larger vegetative and physical patterns in taiga and tundra habitats around us. On one rock expedition, in search of crystals and a better understanding of the formations in the area, we were surprised by and in turn startled a porcupine just a few feet from us. For several minutes we watched the porcupine's reactions to us, quills tensed and positioned in our direction; with relief we observed his gradual relaxation and slow lumbering movement away from us.

These field activities supplied a multitude of questions that we researched in the afternoons, either in an exploratory science lab-type setting or in a computer lab, where we wrote about what we had discovered. Additionally, the students spent evening study time researching and writing about large and small mammals of the area in preparation for our trip.

To encourage students to use their own words as they wrote about mammals, we got in the habit of "publishing" their evening labors by videotaping their live presentations of their written reports each morning. Students took turns as cinematographers for each other. While reviewing the videotapes, we used peer commentary—the praise/question/suggestion format—to offer positive critiques of their reports and their oral presentations. The added benefit, of course, was that students became knowledgeable about mammals they saw on our daily excursions or would see in Denali.

Thinking From a Wolf's (or Artichoke's or Schist's) Point of View

One important area of our study was a particular animal's sensory experience of the world—what that animal might comprehend and/or think about. Humans tend to consciously focus on the world in a visual way; wolves and dogs, on the other hand, are equipped with a much higher degree of olfactory sensitivity; their dominant sensory experience is through the nose and mouth. If you think about how well developed a wolf's or dog's nose is, watch them in action, or look at their skull, you can begin to understand how different their world focus must be. Organisms process the world as their sensory apparati dictate. Our human tendency is to interpret behavior based on our own experience, both in fiction[3] and nonfiction[4] writing.

To access other ways of thinking, we tried to imagine an animal's experience in the world. Which sense is dominant? What does the animal smell, taste, touch, see, or hear? Students were forced to step outside their initial interpretations—to bend, stretch, and apply their thinking about a particular animal, both in movement and in writing. Initially, we tried running in each other's footprints on a sandy riverside as we considered the gait of a caribou versus a moose. The satisfying consequence of this approach to learning is best illustrated in the simple, elegant questions one student jotted in his journal at the top of Mt. Healy:

"I wonder if [grizzly] bears come up this far? If they do, what do they eat?"

His questions reflect an assimilation of many important ideas about his alpine tundra perch and its lack of available moisture. Additionally, it's clear he comprehends some basics of Denali Park grizzly behavior[5], the lush plants they favor and the valley settings where those plants are found, and the volume of food grizzlies must consume during the summer to survive hibernation. His writing reveals his thinking, a real measure of his understanding. There are endless, obvious spinoffs of considering the world from another point of view[6].

The Denali Experience

After many half-day trips, we took a three-day field trip to Denali National Park. For some of the students, the 70-mile drive to the park and the 86-mile shuttle bus ride[7] in to Wonder Lake was the longest road trip they had ever taken; indeed, most of them live on the river in places that are not accessible by roads.

The hike up Mt. Healy on the second afternoon vividly captured students' thinking. Several of the following excerpts were taken from pieces they wrote at the top of the mountain and later shared out of their journals. The longer pieces were written from their journal notes in the computer lab, using several different prewriting programs from the Alaska Writing Program.

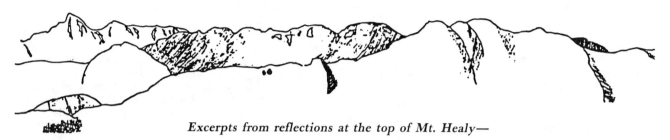

Excerpts from reflections at the top of Mt. Healy—

I could hear the wind roaring around me. . .
I hear an airplane flying over the wind,
the voice of Sharon,
and the sound of cars and trucks from down below.
Also I could smell the small plants.
I have no idea what these plants are,
but I guess I should describe them for you. . . .

Today was great. As I look out, there are mountains in every direction. Not too far off, I can see a mountain with two large glacial erratics. They look as big as houses and must weigh over 1,000 tons! About 10,000 years ago this whole place was covered by ice and snow. The glaciers that came through here a long time ago must have been enormous judging from the size of the erratics they left behind.

On the way up, I stopped a lot of times because the scenery was so beautiful that you can't help but stop to look. I felt a variety of different things, like the types of rocks, the moist ground from last night's rain, the cool of the grass and shrubs. I tasted the clean air, and the extreme dryness in my mouth.

From the top you can see the roads going around in circles, and all the cars on them look like little bugs. Also you can see the rivers, but they look like little streams. Right now, there is a plane burring around that looks like a fly. I guess it is just doing that to annoy everyone.

When I began to climb the steep part of the trail after Mt. Healy lookout, I felt a burning sensation in my legs. After a while I started to get out of breath, but I didn't want to stop. During the hike up, most of the time I could smell pine needles and moss. About ninety-five percent of the way up there were bushes and shrubs. As we approached Mt. Healy summit, the bushes began to disappear and we ran into alpine tundra. The wind began blowing harder and it was also colder the higher we climbed. As I kept hiking, I noticed a gross, stickly liquid in my mouth that tasted slightly sweet. It was probably caused by the residue of the iced tea I drank halfway up the mountain. The trail got even steeper near the top, and I began to get nervous because I was so high up on the mountain. When I got to the top and looked down to see what I had hiked, I was amazed. . . .

161

The shuttle bus into the park—

. . . We saw many wild animals on our journey through the park. The first creature we saw was the willow ptarmigan in summer colors, and the last was the dall sheep, a somewhat ugly animal. It was a pleasure to see so many caribou, almost one every 20 minutes! We also saw other wildlife, including ducks, bears, arctic ground squirrels, and a moose. Another kind of animal that interested the girls were the mountain men. These are just some of the exciting things that we saw, but we also learned many interesting things about the park.

. . . The shuttle bus took us through the scenery of the park, and it helped us realize how beautiful the landscapes are in our state. The most majestic thing we remember seeing was "The Great One" (Mt. McKinley). There were many other things we saw in the park, but the mountain tended to stick out in all of our minds the most. Using shuttle buses was a good idea because from it, we saw many things we might not have seen in a private car. It also keeps people from disturbing or in any way harassing the wildlife. When you don't have to think about driving you can really pay attention to the scenery around you. Also, you learn a lot more riding a park shuttle bus than you would if you were exploring the park on your own.

. . . Visiting Denali Park is important because everyone should see how wildlife behaves [when left wild]. It may also lead people to try to preserve the wildlife in their own area.

Students' words show best some of the images that they carried away from our two-week camp. It's clear in my mind that field science offers richly textured experiences for students to write about, and that the writing process allows them to interpret, understand, and remember those experiences.

—Written by Tawna Alexander, Russell Darling, John Ekada, Elizabeth Sam, Sharon Shrock, & Nakon Vent. Drawings by John Ekada, Sharon Shrock, & Nakon Vent.

Heidi Imhof, Alaska Writing Program, Yukon-Koyukuk School District, Box 309, Nenana, AK 99760.

Notes and References

[1]The Alaska Writing Program by Niki & Alan McCurry and Bill Wresch for Yukon-Koyukuk School District, Box 309, Nenana, AK 99760; ph. 1-800-478-5560 (inside Alaska); 1-800-348-1335 (outside Alaska). It is currently disseminated as a Title VII Academic Excellence Project.

[2]For one of the most complete discussions of generative, constructionist teaching, see Osborne, R. & Freyberg, P. (1985). *Learning in science: The implications of children's science.* Auckland: Heinemann.

[3]As cute and appealing as anthropomorphic fictional stories can be, they are told through a human's sensory screen. Amanda Goodenough's HyperCard story, *Inigo Gets Out*, is one excellent example. It is a charming visual story of a cat's escape from the house and its reactions to the world outside as seen through a human interpretation of house cat behavior. Equally creative would be to picture the world as Inigo might actually experience it, based on what we understand about a cat's sensory equipment. *Inigo Gets Out*, The Voyager Company, 2139 Manning Ave., Los Angeles, CA 90025.

[4]History and science are two obvious nonfiction areas where we write through our own perceptive. Consider, for example, the different ways that chemists and geologists might define the words "field" or "crystal."

[5]The grizzlies found in Denali National Park have a largely vegetarian diet. They are consequently smaller than the coastal grizzlies, whose diet is comprised primarily of fish. To make up for the protein difference, Denali grizzlies must consume a huge amount of the plant material—pea vine, grasses, and berries—available at lower elevations in the park.

[6]One excellent follow-up to any science study is to write a biography, letter, or story from the point of view of that organism or environment. It provides a creative and challenging application of the information students have learned. The writing they produce is far more revealing of their actual comprehension than any objective test could ever measure.

[7]With few exceptions, Denali National Park is closed to private automobiles. Park shuttle buses take visitors in and out of the park area, stopping for wildlife sightings and picture-taking. Visitors may get off and on the bus at any time and hike, although they are restricted to hiking the road in a few closed areas of the park. Often these areas represent prime denning areas. The result is wildlife settings and habitat unlike any I have experienced in \the lower 48. It was a pleasure to have such a pleasant alternative in the park's system's 75th anniversary year, when national park publicity focused on the overcrowding and traffic jams in Yellowstone and Yosemite.

The Work of Beatrix Potter: A Model for Integrating Fine Art, Writing, and Science Using Technology

Nancy Scali

For many students and adults alike, Beatrix Potter lingers as a true storyteller and illustrator for children, best known as the creator of Peter Rabbit. There is also a less well-known part of Beatrix Potter's life that can be used to stimulate interest and exploration in technology, art, aesthetics, writing, and scientific discovery.

As a young girl, Beatrix Potter received an excellent education that included the study of fine art, illustration, and the study of natural science. She took private drawing and painting lessons, enhanced by visits to art museums, galleries, and exhibitions. She also enjoyed nature and used a camera and microscope to help envision the intricate details for scientific illustrations.

After her introduction to the art of the Masters, Beatrix Potter began to keep a journal. Her journal entries reflect her desire to become a quality artist (''I will do something sooner or later'') as well as her personal valuing of individual artistic styles. She was cheered by the achievement of women artists whose work she saw at exhibitions, including Angelica Kauffman, Lady Waterford, and Rosa Bonheur.

Beatrix Potter analyzed many artists' work in her journal. Her aesthetic valuing of technique, style, composition, and design laid a foundation for her experimentation in modeling, drawing, painting, and etching.

A second interest, natural science, provided the subject matter for many of Potter's early paintings and illustrations, and additional sketchbooks and journals about fungi, insects, and animals were begun. Written commentary supported Potter's scientific observations, while the technology of the camera and microscopic enlargements enriched her illustrations. Visits to quarries, the arboretum, and the natural history museum expanded the subject matter to be studied and reproduced visually, thus providing continuous written information, personal perspectives, and scientific illustrations.

Students of all ages will love seeing Beatrix Potter's well-known books, whether for the first or the ump-

Artwork observation
Grade 5

teenth time. Take time to share other examples of her scientific illustrations as well as entries from her journal. Then it will be time to integrate technology, fine art, aesthetics, writing, and science. Three projects are presented here; you will undoubtedly think of many others.

Art History, Aesthetics, and Writing

Have students select a favorite artist and then create a biographical sketch on computer that includes the artist's creative style, period of time in which he or she lived and worked, the medium or materials used by the artist, and a discussion of which elements seem to dominate in the artist's work: LINE, SHAPE, SPACE, COLOR, or TEXTURE.

Next, have students study a variety of work produced by that artist and discuss in their electronic journal the artist's aesthetic values, influences, and conclusions.

Using a computer and selected art software, have students create a work of art based on their journal commentary. When the artwork is completed, they may then record in their journal how the artist's style and use of specific art elements influenced *their* artwork.

Japanese woodblock print
N. Scali

Use a videodisc player and The National Gallery of Art videodisc to recreate the National Gallery in your classroom. Have each student select three artists or artworks, using information found on the disc and in fine arts reference materials to create an outline about the artworks or artists. Students may then join together to become a team of docents and art historians, sharing their gallery, artist biographies, and artworks with other classes in the school. The docents and historians may wish to create a "National Gallery Catalogue," which details the selected artworks and artists' backgrounds, much like a gallery catalogue.

Natural Science, Illustration, and Drawing

Using *816Paint*, *DazzleDraw*, or *Paintworks*, have each student observe and illustrate a flower, bird, plant, insect, or spider. When the illustration is complete, students can select a font and point size to label the parts of their illustration, much like a scientific drawing.

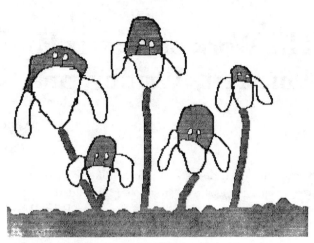

Scientific observation
Grade 6

For their second illustration, have students view the same specimen through a microscope and then illustrate it in its enlarged form. If a student observes and draws a moth, butterfly, insect, or spider, the Mirror option provides a split vertical screen to help create a symmetrical illustration. The Zoom option (much like an electronic microscope) may be used to enlarge the drawing in order to add fine details, texture, scales, hair, or joints. Have students discuss the details, differences, and new information observed about their specimen in their electronic journal.

Nancy Scali, Arroyo School, 1700 East 7th St., Ontario, CA 91764.

References

Epstein, V.S. (1989). *History of women artists for children.* Denver, CO: V.S. Epstein.

Hobbs, A.S. (1989). *Beatrix Potter's art.* London: Frederick Warne.

Nature takes shape. (1980). London: Ladybird Books.

Taylor, J. (1986). *Beatrix Potter.* London: Frederick Warne.

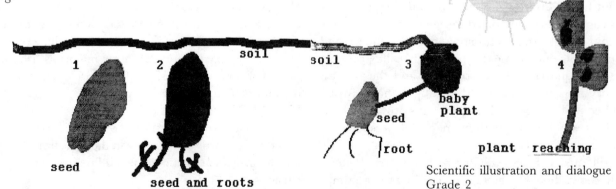

Scientific illustration and dialogue
Grade 2

CHAPTER 3
STUDENTS WITH SPECIAL NEEDS

The Indians long ago knew that music was going on permanently and that hearing it was like looking out a window at a landscape which didn't stop when one turned away.

—John Cage

Teaching Standard English: Whose Standard?

Linda M. Christensen

When I was in the ninth grade, Mrs. Delaney, my English teacher, wanted to demonstrate the correct and incorrect ways to pronounce the English language. She asked Helen Draper, whose father owned several clothing stores in town, to stand and say "lawyer." Then she asked me, whose father owned a bar, to stand and say "lawyer." Everyone burst into laughter at my pronunciation.

What did Mrs. Delaney accomplish? Did she make me pronounce *lawyer* correctly? No. I say *attorney*. I never say *lawyer*. In fact, I've found substitutes for every word my tongue can't get around and for all the rules I can't remember.

For years I've played word cop on myself. I stop what I'm saying to think, "Objective or subjective case? Do I need *I* or *me* here? Hmmm. There's a *lay* coming up. What word can I substitute for it? Recline?"

And I've studied this stuff. After all, I've been an English teacher for almost 15 years. I've gone through all of the Warriner's workbook exercises. I even found a lie/lay computer program and kept it in my head until I needed it in speech and became confused again.

Thanks to Mrs. Delaney, I learned early on that in our society language classifies me. Generosity, warmth, kindness, intelligence, good humor aren't enough—I need to speak correctly to make it. Mrs. Delaney taught me that the "melting pot" was an illusion. The real version of the melting pot is that people of diverse backgrounds are mixed together, and when they come out, they're supposed to look like Vanna White and sound like Dan Rather. The only diversity we celebrate is tacos and chop suey at the mall.

It wasn't until a few years ago that I realized grammar was an indication of class and cultural background in the United States and that there is a bias against people who do not use language "correctly." Even the terminology "standard" and "nonstandard" reflects that one is less than the other. English teachers are urged to "correct" students who speak or write in their home language. A friend of mine, whose ancestors came over on the Mayflower, never studied any of the grammar texts I keep by my side, but she can spot all of my errors because she grew up in a home where Standard English was spoken.

And I didn't, so I've trained myself to play language cop. The problem is that every time I pause, I stop the momentum of my thinking. I'm no longer pursuing content, no longer engaged in trying to persuade or entertain or clarify. Instead, I'm pulling Warriner's or Mrs. Delaney out of my head and trying to figure out how to say something.

"Ah, but this is good," you might say. "You have the rules and Mrs. Delaney to go back to. This is what our students need."

But it doesn't happen that way. I try to remember the rule or the catchy phrase that is supposed to etch the rule in my mind forever like "people never get laid," but I'm still not sure if I used it correctly. These side trips cost a lot of velocity in my logic.

Over the years my English teachers pointed out all of my errors—the usage errors I inherited from my mother's Bandon, Oregon, dialect, the spelling errors I overlooked, the fancy words I used incorrectly. They did this in good faith in the same way that, years later, I "corrected" my students' "errors" because I wanted them to know the rules. They were keys to a secret and wealthier society I wanted them to be prepared to enter, just as my teachers wanted to help me.

And we should help kids. It would be misleading to suggest that people in our society will value my thoughts or my students' thoughts as readily in our home languages as in the "cash language" as Jesse Jackson calls it. Students need to know where to find help, and they need to understand what changes might be necessary, but they need to learn in a context that doesn't say, "The way you said this is wrong."

English teachers must know when to correct and how to correct—and I use that word uneasily. Take Fred, for example. Fred entered my first-year class last year unwilling to write. Every day during writing time I'd find Fred doodling pictures of Playboy bunnies on his Pee Chee. When I sat down and asked him why he didn't write, he said he couldn't.

I explained to him that in this class his writing couldn't be wrong because we were just practicing our writing until we found a piece we wanted to polish, in the same way that he practiced football every day after school but played games only on Fridays. His resistance lasted for a couple of weeks. Around him, other students struggled with their writing, shared it with the class on occasion, and heard positive comments. Certainly, the writing of his fellow students was not intimidating. At that point this class was tracked—and Fred was in the lowest track.

On October 1, after reading a story by Toni Cade Bambara (1972) about trusting people in our lives, Fred wrote for the first time: "I remember my next door neighbor trusted me with some money that she owed my grandmother. She owed my grandmother about 25 dollars." Fred didn't make a lot of errors. In this first piece of writing, it looked as if he had basic pronunciation figured out. He didn't misspell any words. And he certainly didn't make any usage errors. Based on this sample, he appeared to be a competent writer.

However, the biggest problem with Fred's writing was the fact that he didn't make mistakes. This piece demonstrates his discomfort with writing. He wasn't taking any risks. Just as I avoid *lawyer* and *lay*, he wrote to avoid errors instead of writing to communicate or think on paper.

When more attention is paid to the way something is written or said than to what is said, students' words and thoughts become devalued. They learn to be silent, to give as few words as possible for teacher criticism.

Students must be taught to hold their own voices sacred, to ignore the teachers who have made them feel that what they've said is wrong or bad or stupid. Students must be taught how to listen to the knowledge they've stored up but which they are seldom asked to relate.

Too often students feel alienated in schools. Knowledge is foreign. It's about other people, in other times (Bigelow, 1990). At a conference I attended recently, a young woman whose mother was Puerto Rican and whose father was Haitian said,

> I went through school wondering if anyone like me had ever done anything worthwhile or important. We kept reading and hearing about all of these famous people. I remember thinking, "Don't we have anyone?" I walked out of the school that day feeling tiny, invisible, unimportant.

As teachers, we have daily opportunities to affirm that our students' lives and language are unique and important. We do that in the selections of literature we read, in the history we choose to teach (Bigelow, 1989), and we do it by giving legitimacy to our students' lives as a content worthy of study.

One way to encourage the reluctant writers who have been silenced and the not-so-reluctant writers who have found a safe and sterile voice is to encourage them to recount their experiences. I sometimes recruit former students to share their writing and their wisdom as a way of underscoring the importance of the voices and stories of teenagers. Rochelle, a student in my senior writing class, brought a few of her stories and poems to read to my first-year students. Rochelle, like Zora Neale Hurston, blends her home language with Standard English in most pieces. She read the following piece to open up a discussion about how kids are sometimes treated as servants in their homes, but also to demonstrate the necessity of using the language she hears in her family to develop characters:

> "I'm tired of washing dishes. Seems like every time our family gets together, they just got to eat and bring their millions of kids over to our house. And then we got to wash the dishes."
> I listened sympathetically as my little sister mumbled these words.
> "And how come we cain't have ribs like grownups? After all, ain't we grown?"
> "Lord," I prayed, "seal her lips while the blood is still running warm in her veins."
> Her bottom lip protruded farther and farther as she dipped each plate in the soapy water, then rinsed each side with cold water (about a two-second process) until she felt the majority of suds were off.
> "One minute we lazy women that cain't keep the living room half clean. The next minute we just kids and gotta eat some funky chicken while they eat ribs."
> . . . Suddenly it was quiet. All except my little sister who was still talking. I strained to hear a laugh or joke from the adults in the living room, a hint that all were well, full and ready to go home. Everyone was still sitting in their same spots, not making a move to leave.
> "You ought to be thankful you got a choice."
> Uh-oh. Now she got Aunt Macy started. . . .

When more attention is paid to the way something is written or said than to what is said, students' words and thoughts become devalued. Students must be taught to hold their own voices sacred....

After reading her work, Rochelle talked about listening to her family and friends tell their stories. She urged the first-year students to relate the tales of their own lives—the times they were caught doing something forbidden, the times they got stuck with the dishes, the funny/sad events that made their first year in high school memorable. When Rochelle left, students wrote more easily. Some. Some were afraid of the stories because, as Rance said, "It takes heart to tell the truth about your life."

But eventually they write. They write stories. They write poems. They write letters. They write essays. They learn how to switch in and out of the language of the powerful, as Rochelle does so effortlessly in her "Tired of Chicken" piece.

And after we write, we listen to each other's stories in our read-around circle, where everyone has the opportunity to share, to be heard, to learn that knowledge can be gained by examining our lives (see Shor, 1987; Shor & Freire, 1987). In the circle, we discover that many young women

167

encounter sexual harrassment; we learn that store clerks follow black students, especially males, more frequently than they follow white students; we find that many parents drink or use drugs; we learn that many students are kept awake by the crack houses in their neighborhoods.

Before we share, students often understand these incidents individually. They feel there's something wrong with them. If they were smarter, prettier, stronger, these things wouldn't have happened to them. When they hear other students' stories, they begin to realize that many of their problems aren't caused by a character defect. For example, a young man shared a passionate story about life with his mother who is a lesbian. He loved her but felt embarrassed to bring his friends home. He was afraid his peers would think he was gay or reject him if they knew about his mother. After he read, the class was silent. Some students cried. One young woman told him that her father was gay, and she had experienced similar difficulties but hadn't had the courage to tell people about it. She thanked him. Another student confided that his uncle had died from

---

As teachers, we have daily opportunities to affirm that our students' lives and language are unique and important. We do that in the selections of literature we read, in the history we choose to teach, and we do it by giving legitimacy to our students' lives as a content worthy of study.

AIDS the year before. What had been a secret shame became an opportunity for students to discuss sexual diversity more openly. Students who were rigidly opposed to the idea of homosexuality gained insights into their own homophobia—especially when presented with the personal revelations from their classmates. Those with homosexual relatives found new allies with whom they could continue their discussion and find support.

Sharing also provides a ''collective text'' for us to examine the social roots of problems more closely. Where do men/women develop the ideas that women are sexual objects? Where do they learn that it's okay for men to follow women or make suggestive remarks? Where is it written that it's the woman's fault if a man leers at her? How did these roles develop? Who gains from them? Who loses? How could we make it different? Our lives become a window to examine society.

But the lessons can't stop there. Fred can write better now. He and his classmates can feel comfortable and safe

sharing their lives or discussing literature and the world. They can even understand that they need to ask ''Who benefits?'' to get a better perspective on a problem. But still, when they leave my class or this school, some people will judge them by how their subjects and verbs line up.

So I teach Fred the rules. It's the language of power in this country, and I would be cheating him if I pretended otherwise (Delpit, 1988). I teach him this more effectively than Mrs. Delaney taught me because I don't humiliate him or put down his language. I'm also more effective because I don't rely on textbook drills; I use the text of Fred's writing. But I also teach Fred what Mrs. Delaney left out.

I teach Fred that language, like tracking, functions as part of a gatekeeping system in our country. Who gets managerial jobs, who works at banks and who works at fast-food restaurants, who gets into what college and who gets into college at all, are decisions linked to the ability to use Standard English.

So how do we teach kids to write with honesty and passion about their world *and* get them to study the rules of the cash language?

We go back to our study of society. We ask: Who made the rules that govern how we speak and write? Did Ninh's family and Fred's family and LaShonda's family all sit down together and decide on these rules? Who already talks like this and writes like this? Who has to learn how to change the way they talk and write? Why?

We make up our own tests that speakers of Standard English would find difficult. We read articles, stories, poems written in Standard English and those written in home language. We listen to videotapes of people talking. Most kids like the sound of their home language better. They like the energy, the poetry, and the rhythm of the language. We determine when and why people shift. We talk about why it might be necessary to learn Standard English.

Asking my students to memorize the rules without asking who makes the rules, who enforces the rules, who benefits from the rules, who loses from the rules, and who uses the rules to keep some in and keep others out, legitimates a social system that devalues my students' knowledge and language. Teaching the rules without reflection also underscores that it's okay for others—''authorities''—to dictate something as fundamental and as personal as the way they speak. Further, the study of Standard English without critique encourages students to believe that if they fail, it is because they are not smart enough or didn't work hard enough. They learn to blame themselves. If they get poor SAT scores, low grades on term papers or essays because of language errors, or fail teacher entrance exams, they will internalize the blame; they will believe they did not succeed because they are inferior instead of questioning the standard of measurement and those making the standard.

We must teach our students how to match subjects and verbs, how to pronounce lawyer, because they are the ones without power and, for the moment, they have to use the language of the powerful to be heard. But, in addition, we need to equip them to question an educational system that devalues their lives and their knowledge. If we don't, we condition them to a pedagogy of consumption where they will consume knowledge, priorities, and products that have been decided and manufactured without them in mind.

It took me years to undo what Mrs. Delaney did to me. Years to discover that what I said was more important than how I said it. Years to understand that my words, my family's words, weren't wrong, weren't bad—they were just the words of the working class. For too long, I felt inferior when I spoke. I knew the voice of my childhood crept in, and I confused that with ignorance. It wasn't. I just didn't belong to the group who made the rules. I was an outsider, a foreigner in their world. My students won't be.

Linda Christensen, Jefferson High School, Portland, OR 97211. This article first appeared in English Journal, *February 1990.*

References

Bambara, T. C. (1972). *Gorilla, my love.* New York: Random.

Bigelow, W. (1989). Discovering Columbus: Rereading the past. *Language Arts, 66*(6), 636-643.

Bigelow, W. (in press). Inside the classroom: Social vision and critical pedagogy. *Teachers College Record.*

Delpit, L. (1988). The silenced dialogue: Power and pedagogy in educating other people's children. *Harvard Educational Review, 58*(3), 280-298.

Shor, I. (1987). *Freire for the classroom.* Portsmouth, NH: Heinemann.

Shor, I., & Freire, P. (1987). *A pedagogy for liberation.* South Hadley, MA: Bergin.

Memories Of A When

Dancing on a moonlit beach,
turning corners to a dead end street,
holding onto a blood red rose,
a timid wave tickles my toes.
A whisper in the dark night air.
A phantom breeze plays with my hair,
A semi honks in the distance.

You cannot see my smile.
The city streets are filled with cars,
The country skies pinned up with stars,
Look down on the apple core,
the old newspapers, a crumpled shore.
The rose petals fall to the sand.
Their scent is gone.

I never cared much anyway,
I'm only here for a short stay.
I dreamt of cement again last night.
I hope the trees don't get too lonely.

—*Kathy*

from Pomegranate, Granada High School

Writing Partnerships: Teaching ESL Composition through Letter Exchanges

Nancy L. Hadaway

As children progress through school, writing grows increasingly important for academic success. Fostering and developing the writing ability of *all* students is crucial, and limited English proficient children are no exception. Second language learners need opportunities and hands-on experiences to expand their knowledge of the process of writing.

Recent research provides us with a broadened vision of writing, with a focus on holistic and process approaches. As with native speakers, findings indicate that "second language acquisition is facilitated when the target language is used in a natural communicative context" (Diaz, 1986, p. 169). Writing instruction should be centered around students' backgrounds and needs, rather than around rules and structures.

Many teachers of limited English proficient (LEP) students assume that if these children cannot speak English, then writing instruction should be deferred and/or highly controlled. Recent findings do not support such teacher actions. Hudelson (1984, p. 221) notes that "child ESL learners, early in their development of English, can write English and can do so for various purposes." Practice and research are demonstrating that children at all ages and levels of schooling and language proficiency can and *should* write and that through writing they can expand their language base and other language skills, especially reading. In fact, a host of researchers have found that for both native speakers and second language learners, writing may very well precede formal reading (Bissex, 1980; Edelsky, 1982; Hansen, Newkirk, & Graves, 1985).

Thus, like native speakers and writers of English, LEP children need opportunities to write, role models who demonstrate and value writing, room to experiment with language and make mistakes, and a safe and secure environment in which to practice and take risks in writing.

Letter writing proves to be an ideal activity for the second language learner. Through letters, children are provided a genuine audience, a real purpose for writing, and lots of nonconfrontational feedback about and response to their writing. The project described in this article involves a letter exchange linking university students preparing to become teachers with bilingual and English as a second language (ESL) students. The exchange, the results of the project, and implications for using letter writing to teach composition skills are discussed, along with applications of the computer in this process.

The Project

Over the course of a year, bilingual/ ESL students in grades 2 through 12 were paired with university-level teacher preparation students for a letter exchange. Forty-eight students were involved during the fall semester and 85 in the spring, with 40 of the 85 carried over from the fall semester. Eight schools from four separate school districts participated in the project. Each member of the bilingual/ ESL classes participated, so that all children, regardless of language proficiency, were writing and receiving letters. University students received their penpal assignments at the beginning of each semester and then initiated the first piece of correspondence to their partner. Writers were given no instructions or assignments about their letters except to write, and each subsequent letter after the initial introductory one from the university students was a response to a previous letter. In addition to letters, pictures and small gifts such as pencils and stickers were also sent.

Project Results

Although the logistics of coordinating such a letter exchange were tremendous, the linguistic and emotional benefits made it all worthwhile. The penpals overcame language and cultural barriers to get acquainted and, in some cases, bonds of real friendship and support developed.

Topics covered in the letters included school, coursework and studying, family and home, hobbies and interests, language learning difficulties, and moving and adjusting to a new country and/or a new school.

Limited English proficient children and university students shared cultural aspects of their lives that included holiday celebrations, recreation, language, and foods. Embedded within the school year were several holidays, which offered many opportunities to share vocabulary, family traditions, and customs. These were familiar and important happenings that elicited much language from the children. At the same time, the LEP students gained insight into university life and activities through their penpals' letters. They read about football weekends, sororities, dorm life, and academic majors. Some became curious about how one studied to become a teacher and what it meant to attend college.

The letter exchange fostered growing self-confidence. A critical need for writers is "ownership over their topics, a chance to feel a sense of control over their own ideas" (Jochum, 1989, p. 1). With the exchange of letters, children experienced the freedom to choose topics of interest to them. Even though they were aware of their responsibilities to their writing partner, the LEP child could still initiate new topics or change the topic completely. These tactics helped the second language writer to manage the linguistic difficulty and interest level of communicating. Indeed, the letters often centered around juvenile concerns. However, such ownership in the writing process kept the lines of communication open and provided valuable practice in writing for the LEP child, along with opportunities to share their native language with their writing partners. This opportunity to teach was indeed validating.

Perhaps the most successful aspects of the exchange from a psychological and linguistic perspective were the support and role modeling. University students served as native speaker role models, and their language was authentic, including slang, college jargon, and informal syntax, rather than complete and formal sentences only.

In addition, every letter extended understanding and support. University students encouraged LEP children to study and to master English. The children followed suit and began to encourage their penpals through the tough academic moments of college life. One fourth grader wrote, "You will do good on those tests. You just have to believe in yourself." Support was offered on the personal side as well. When one university student broke up with her boyfriend, her bilingual penpal sent an original poem entitled "Don't Be Sad."

Homesickness and language difficulties were another topic that proved to bring out the best of both correspondents. University students shared recollections of moving to a new city or school in the hopes of helping bilingual/ESL students in their adjustments. One university student had recently come to the U.S. from Taiwan, so she had firsthand knowledge and suggestions to share with her penpal.

Like native speakers and writers of English, LEP children need opportunities to write, role models who demonstrate and value writing, room to experiment with language and make mistakes, and a safe and secure environment in which to practice and take risks in writing.

Classroom Applications

Letters involve reading as well as writing. Not only do LEP students reread as they compose, but their penpal letters must be read in order to frame an appropriate response. Peer conferencing can greatly enhance this process. When letters are received, pairs of students can work together reading letters aloud, confirming comprehension and brainstorming possibilities for replies. As a group, second language students can share more about their penpals and have the opportunity to talk more about what they may write in return. This whole class interaction can even evolve into group brainstorming or content mapping exercises that will help many students to further develop vocabulary and language structures.

The letters themselves also can serve as a basis for instruction. In the spirit of process writing and whole language, here the child's own interests and language provide the material for lessons. In communicating with a penpal, the LEP child will be using familiar and meaningful words and structures. With copies of their own letters and their penpal's responses, the second language learner can identify words that are difficult to spell or focus on areas where a lack of vocabulary may have inhibited communication. The teacher may then take several areas of concern that are thematically related and develop a spelling/vocabulary lesson on a recurring topic such as family or pastimes. Through the use of vocabulary/semantic webs, the whole class can expand their vocabulary. For more individual problem areas, students can develop personal word lists from their letters, which can provide more than enough input for spelling and vocabulary work.

Letters can be used also as a source of content in other subject areas such as social studies or math. With each letter providing a rich source of information about culture, family, traditions, holiday celebrations, geographic roots, and much more, children can take information about their penpals and chart it for the class as a whole. Bulletin boards can be developed to display maps that note each partner's birthplace and hometown. This data can then provide the input for a math lesson on computing distance or a social studies lesson on map skills. As the writing partners share information about their families, interests, recreational activities, and pets, it can be incorporated into graphic displays (pie, line, or bar graphs) on all correspondents. In all cases the content of the lessons has meaning and personal interest for students.

Using the Word Processor

If second language learners are using a word processor to compose and/or type their letters, the use of spell checkers and thesaurus/dictionary aids can help them to work independently. For younger children especially, using a word processor will make their writing easier to read. The computer is also a real confidence builder and motivator. One yound second grade student who initially refused to participate in the letter exchange changed his mind after a brief introduction to word processing and subsequent composing via the computer. If school finances allow, networking via a modem also provides exciting possibilities for linking students in different parts of the country or world.

Summary

The more LEP children read and write, the easier those tasks will become. Letters are relevant and meaningful communication, and letter exchanges provide strong motivation to write as well as providing an emotional link with another individual who can serve as a role model of the target language. Students can choose and utilize realistic topics and language and will be encouraged to stretch their own language limits in order to communicate fully with their partner. Taking it one step further by using the LEP child's own words and interests to draw lesson content makes letter exchanges a teaching and learning opportunity not to be missed.

Nancy Hadaway, Assistant Professor/Assistant Director of Field Experiences, The University of Texas at Arlington, Box 19227, Arlington, TX 76019.

References

Bissex, G. (1980). *GYNS AT WK.* Cambridge, MA: Harvard University Press.

Diaz, D. M. (1986). The writing process and the ESL writer: Reinforcement from second language research. *The Writing Instructor, 5,* (4), 167-175.

Edelsky, C. (1982). Writing in a bilingual program: The relation of L1 and L2 texts. *TESOL Quarterly, 16,* (2), 211-228.

Hansen, J., Newkirk, T., & Graves, D. (Eds.). (1985). *Breaking ground: Teachers relate reading and writing in the elementary school.* Portsmouth, NH: Heinemann.

Hudelson, S. (1984). Kan yu ret an rayt en ingles: Children become literate in English as a second language. *TESOL Quarterly, 18,* (2), 221-238.

Jochum, J. (1989). Writing: The critical response. *Texas Reading Report, 12,* (1), 1/10.

For You

"If you ever, ever need my life, come and take it."
—*The Seagull,* Anton Chekhov

come & take it
from hands of silver
that have touched the heavens & been kissed
by the devil.
they've buried my life
in the sand for you.
i scream the tides to stay away;
only you can take my life.
my heavy hands are prepared to dig.
at the drop of your eyes they will jump to justice.
i hold my life for you.

—Karen Sherman
Horton Watkins High School, Ladue, MO

Sonnet 1
Doomed to the Pedestal

Placed on a pedestal, I have remained;
I am respected and adored by all;
From mentioning comfort, I have refrained,
Although I do often fear I will fall.
I am all that the others never were
And all that they never could be, some say,
But let me have what I'd truly prefer
And I'd choose a slightly different way.
No more epitomizing perfection,
In its stead I am a woman who errs,
Accepting some praise and some rejection,
Becoming someone who lives, laughs and shares.
Expectations are difficult to meet;
At least offer me a chance to retreat.

—Sue Tackett
Holmes High School, Covington, KY

Computerized Connections: Cluster First

Linda Lippitt and Guy Monroe

In 1977, Santa Fe Indian School became the first tribal contract boarding school in the U.S. to operate under the provisions of the Indian Self-Determination Act (P.L. 93-638). Since that time the 19 Pueblo governors of New Mexico have operated the school under policy set by the Indian School Board and guided by Superintendent Joe Abeyta from Santa Clara Pueblo.

The majority of the 500 students grades 7 to 12 who choose to attend are from the Pueblo communities, with many other tribes represented, including the Apache (Mescalero, Jicarilla, and White Mountain), Blackfeet, Caddo, Cheyenne, Choctaw, Comanche, Hopi, Kiowa, Navaho, Pima, and Ute.

Santa Fe Indian School has been the recipient of numerous awards, including the Presidential Award for Excellence.

Correct and effective communication of creative ideas is the goal of the Santa Fe Indian School (SFIS) Computer Writing Lab. The teachers in the language arts department created a computerized "web," which allows brainstorming, idea classification, and outlining with the use of a single graphics program. This prewriting exercise sets the stage for a well structured paper, with main ideas and supporting details easily discernible.

Students already should be familiar with the idea of brainstorming ideas, either as a group or individually. Clustering, sometimes called webbing or networking, allows the writer to classify the ideas into general categories, using color as a visual stimulus. The use of the mouse to circle and connect one idea to another adds a tactile approach that greatly benefits some students.

To introduce the concept of computer clustering, a graphics program that combines the use of color, freehand drawing, and keyboarding is needed. Students at the SFIS Lab have had great success with the Apple //GS and the program *816 Paint* (Baudville). Whatever program is used, explain what a graphics program is; show examples of drawings done with the program and samples of student clustering.

Once the program is booted up, show students how to select a tool, brush size, and color, and how to make menu changes. Choosing the keyboard option, type the subject in the center of the screen. Continue using the keyboard option and fill the screen with words and phrases that evolve from the original concept. The mouse will allow rapid placement of words around the page (see Figure 1). If you are using a system without a color printer, print the page of ideas and proceed with the next step using colored markers.

Read over the list and decide which words appear connected. (For example, seventh graders working on a cluster following a lesson on Custer's Last Stand decided that they had information on the tribes, individuals, and weaponry used in the battle.) Each category then is assigned a specific color. Change to the freehand drawing tool and select the color for one category. Using the mouse, draw a circle around each of the words that belong together. Connect each idea in the same color category with a line leading to the next idea. When the first category is complete, change colors and begin circling the next category of related ideas, as shown in Figure 2.

Some words or phrases may not fit in with the categories that were chosen. They can be easily erased, allowing students to select only the most relevant information and providing an opportunity to further develop critical decision-making and analysis skills. When combined with the following steps, this simple method of classification lends itself to the development of tight paragraphs with an identified main idea and appropriate supporting details.

Looking over the group of words and phrases in the category they wish to discuss first, the students decide on a name that reflects this subject. At the bottom of the page, they then draw a circle the color of this first general category. Students label this color-coded circle with the name they chose and proceed to organize the sequence of their composition by placing each colored circle and its category name in an appropriate order. Print a copy of the completed cluster and coding key for students to use as an outline for their compositions (see Figure 3).

This sequence is the basis for either a single paragraph or a combination of paragraphs on a single topic. Students can create a topic sentence that focuses on the word in the center of the cluster. Sentences to convey the main ideas are developed directly from the category names. Supporting details are chosen from the color-coded clusters. The concluding sentence can restate easily the main ideas of the paragraph, readily identified from the labels of the color coding.

Clustering becomes an organizational method to avoid repetition and provide smooth transitions from one

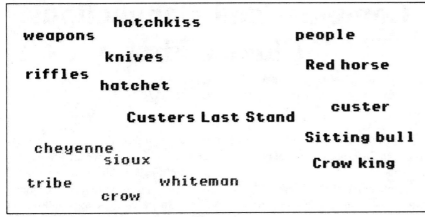

Figure 1

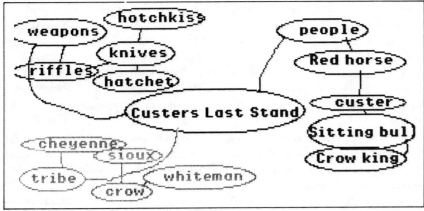

Figure 2

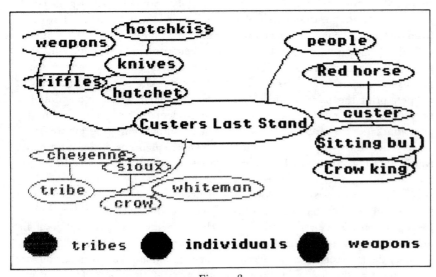

Figure 3

The clustering exercise is intended as one component of a broader lesson. It fits in especially well with a holistic approach to the learning experience, offering a bridge from a global personal understanding to a linear written process. Short compositions with illustrations can be composed directly on the graphics program. The combination of clustering with an easy-to-use word processing program containing a good spell checker and thesaurus offers students the tools to create correct and effective original compositions.

This model of structured composition has been used at the Computer Writing Lab for two years. A concurrent study of the learning styles of these Native American students has suggested a positive relationship between their generalized learning preferences and the use of computer technology. Students have demonstrated a high preference for analytic skills, small group work, and personal interaction during the learning process.

Computer assisted instruction can incorporate all of these preferences with the additional benefit of a multisensory approach. Manipulating the mouse and keyboard and having the ability to adjust the colors and contrast of the screen provide a degree of personal control of the learning environment. Computer assignments can be easily individualized according to student needs and lend themselves to small group work and peer interaction. Students receive guided practice, evaluation, and feedback in privacy—respecting traditional learning situations which afford the learner time to observe and practice alone. At the same time, they are learning new technical skills and sharpening the communication skills necessary for future success.

Linda Lippitt, LARC Project Director, and Guy Monroe, LARC Computer Writing Lab Proctor, Santa Fe Indian School, 1501 Cerrillos Road, Santa Fe, NM 87501.

fact to the next. Students create relationships, structure, and compositional design from a unique map of personal thoughts and reflections. The use of color, keyboarding, and the mouse provide additional modalities for learners who need supplemental stimuli. Practicing the flow from topic idea to completed paragraph can be a private exercise or a group activity, depending on the learning preferences of the individual student.

Samuels School: Celebrating Diversity

Sharon Franklin

At Samuels, diversity is celebrated. But such rich diversity in backgrounds and language skills challenges teachers and makes individualizing instruction more a matter of necessity than choice. Although precise teaching methods and writing instruction vary, teachers agree that the writing lab has enabled their students to experience an exciting level of success in writing.

"It was a long, arduous process going from first to final draft with pencil and paper," recalls bilingual teacher Lupe Leece. "Many students' handwriting can be difficult to read and the meaning challenging to decode. Then, by the time we made it through the revision process, they had to write it all again in final form. They were tired and often made more (and new) mistakes.

"The writing lab has changed all that. Kids can see their progress using computers. With pencil and paper, it can be difficult to see."

After introducing several genres of literature at the beginning of the year, Leece leaves the topics up to her students. They each write a contract to complete six pieces of writing per quarter and specify the types of writing they will do (e.g., two stories, two poems, one biography, and one historical fiction).

The computer allows teachers to spend more productive teaching time with each child, focusing on the precise skills they need and carefully tracking their progress. A writing folder helps Leece's students keep track of their work and the skills they're working on. They come to the lab armed with their folders which contain:

1. Their personal disk;
2. A list of the mechanics they know;
3. Their checklist of skills;
4. Their classroom literature book (referred to often in order to check how a professional writer handles a specific punctuation or style issue); and typically
5. The rough drafts of three works in progress.

Leece individualizes the writing process for her students. She may choose to focus first on sequencing with one student. Instruction, with references to many examples from familiar stories in the student's literature book, comes first; then it's time to begin writing. At the end of the writing process, Leece evaluates the final copy only for mastery of the student's ability to sequence. All other needed editing changes are made by her. In the next piece of writing, Leece would expect to see the student continue to demonstrate an understanding of sequencing. In addition, she might identify a new punctuation or spelling related goal as well.

Her Spanish speaking students learn the computer commands for accent marks, the tilda, and question marks in Spanish, with their bilingual classmates helping with translation

> Samuels School, located in southeast Denver, is a designated bilingual school for grades 3 to 5. One-fourth of the classes are taught in both English and Spanish, and many of the students read and write in both languages with varying levels of proficiency.
> The Samuels Writing Lab includes a Macintosh SE30, which functions as the file server, along with 14 Macintosh Plus computers, 3 ImageWriter printers, and 1 LaserWriter II printer.

and spelling in both languages when necessary. Leece is anxious to begin using the MacWrite II Spanish dictionary next year. Instead of waiting until they print out a rough draft to check their spelling, students will be able to refer to the Spanish dictionary while they're on the computer and get immediate feedback and help with their spelling.

If the computer has changed forever the process of teaching writing for Leece, it has also changed the nature of the final product for Gay Peecher's fifth grade students.

"If I could spend all day in the lab, I would," says Peecher. "These kids feel so good about themselves and their accomplishments. We are able to produce things that none of us thought possible."

Structured research projects begin with what Peecher terms "we search." After reading several articles out loud, her students (some with teacher help) take notes in English and then work in the lab to create sentences and paragraphs from their notes. After working in editing groups, it's back to the lab to make changes, print out a final copy, and add illustrations. A typical research assignment perhaps—except that all writing assignments in her class end up as professional-looking books, each bound in a different way.

Peecher has seen some of the greatest success in the lab by students with learning disabilities. Lack of finger dexterity can be a problem for many of these students, and marvelous ideas can remain largely unexpressed because it's so difficult for many of them to write by hand. Using the computer solved in large part the legibility problem. In addition, Peecher found that enlarging the print for these students makes a big difference in their ability to read their writing. This, in turn, makes them more willing to put in the time to work on their editing and revising.

Chapter 1 teacher Cheryl Dow experienced similar results with her students using *Talking Keys*, a software program that lets students hear their compositions read back exactly as they typed them in.

"When I would read my students' papers out loud exactly as written, many times I could not convince them that they had left out a word. They wouldn't believe me . . . but they believe whatever the program reads back to them and willingly make the necessary corrections! Their writing has just taken off."

When the Parent Advisory Group began to communicate on line with a group of parents in San Diego, the students became partners in learning with their parents.

All teachers are pleased to see the spontaneous cooperation among their students in the lab. They encourage this interaction and see it as increasing all students' bilingual proficiency. It's not unusual for a student writing in Spanish to ask a nearby student writing in English for advice on a sentence or paragraph. The English-speaking student will stop typing, read the passage on screen, suggest a change (switching to Spanish in order to help), and then return to his or her own composition.

This sort of cooperation and sharing now extends beyond the boundaries of the school in a telecommunications network that opens new vistas for parents as well as students. The network connects students with other students in Puerto Rico and Connecticut and parents with a group of Spanish and English speaking parents in San Diego.

Students may spend one lab day each week reading and writing pen pal letters. There is a good mix of Spanish and English speaking children in the three schools, giving all students good opportunities to stretch their skills in both languages at the same time they're learning about different schools and cultures.

When the Parent Advisory Group began to communicate on line with a group of parents in San Diego, the children were encouraged to accompany their parents to the meetings. The school draws from a wide range of socio-economic areas in Denver, with some parents unable to read or write. The students became partners in learning with their parents as they proudly demonstrated how to use the computers and, in many cases, solved the literacy problem by typing in the sentences dictated by their parents and grandparents about their community and the kinds of things they do with their children.

The confidence in writing exuded by Samuels students is exciting to witness.

"When these kids walk into the lab," explains Leece, "they *know* what to do. They are in command of their writing."

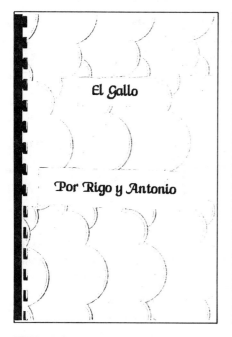

When these kids walk into the lab, they KNOW what to do. They are in command of their writing.

The Dialogue Journal: Empowering ESL Students

Terrell A. Young

"No one can empower another, and it is patronizing to think this way. Empowerment comes from within. One can only create a process which allows another to discover empowerment."

James Cummins (1986)

Dialogue journals give you the special opportunity to get to know your students on an individual basis, a luxury that often doesn't exist in many classrooms.

Learning to read and write in a second language is more difficult than speaking or listening to a second language. Thus, it is important to make reading and writing instruction natural, personal, and supportive for ESL students. The dialogue journal, a written conversation between a teacher and students, is just the vehicle for helping ESL students read and write in a second language. Writing in a dialogue journal helps students to see writing as a purposeful activity in which they can communicate their thoughts and ideas. Dialogue journals allow students to share privately their reactions, questions, and concerns about school and personal matters with teachers. The quantity and quality of ESL students' writing in dialogue journals may exceed that of their writing on other assigned tasks, perhaps because the topics are generated by them and deal with their concerns, interests, experiences, and questions (Peyton, Staton, Richardson, & Wolfram, 1990; Staton, 1987). Finally, ESL students are empowered as they think critically about their environment and express their feelings in dialogue journals. This article presents guidelines for introducing, managing, and responding to dialogue journals with ESL (and other) students.

Introducing Dialogue Journals

When introducing dialogue journals to students it is best to begin by talking with students about the excitement of receiving a letter. Explain how they will write to you and you will write to them. Staton (1987) provides some helpful guidelines in introducing dialogue journals:

1. Discuss the natural need to communicate with and understand each other in the classroom.
2. Talk about the importance of privacy.
3. Brainstorm possible topics and purposes for a journal.
4. Make a chart with four or five typical journal entries. Read the entries to students and discuss which they would most enjoy reading.
5. Stress that entries can vary in length, but set a minimum length (two lines of writing or three sentences).
6. Give students the opportunity to decorate the covers of their journals—it helps to establish ownership of them. (If your students will be journaling via computer, they might instead decorate a folder in which to keep their disk, any hard copy entries, word lists, etc.)
7. Don't worry about the content or mechanics of the first entries.

Managing Dialogue Journals

You may wonder how you will be able to respond to all of your students in dialogue journals. These guidelines, established by Staton (1987), may help:

1. Start gradually with a few students or with just one class. If you work with only one group of students at a time, it's good to work with them for at least three weeks.
2. Set a time each day for students to read your responses to their writing.
3. Create a special place where students can leave their journals when they are finished for the day.
4. Use positive reinforcement strategies to encourage regular entries by expressing interest in what they are writing.
5. Remember that it takes one or two months for

most students to get going and even longer for a few.

6. Some students will not like journaling and will do only the minimum amount asked of them. That is their choice.

Guidelines for Teacher Responses

Your responses should encourage and stimulate a continued dialogue when important topics come up. Gambrell (1985) and Staton (1987) provide these guidelines for responding to student entries:

1. Acknowledge your students' topics and encourage them to elaborate on their interests.

2. Affirm and support each student; the private dialogue is a great place for compliments about appearance or behavior.

3. Add new, relevant information about topics, so that your response is interesting to read.

4. Don't write much more than the student does.

5. Avoid glib comments like ''good idea'' or ''very interesting.'' These responses cut off rather than promote dialogue.

6. Ask very few questions. The goal is to get students to ask *you* questions.

7. Make your writing so interesting so that they will want to know more.

8. Respond to the content that is written and do not correct spelling and usage. Students will learn a great deal through teacher modeling of correct usage and spelling.

9. View journals as letters that need a response.

Computer Dialogues

If you have access to one or more computers, you and your students may want to use technology to create their journals, with students submitting their writing on disk. The same guidelines may be used for implementing, managing, and responding to the dialogues as in hard-copy journals, but you may find some added benefits: (a) In journaling via computer, you will find your response time greatly reduced; (b) many students will find added motivation in writing via computer; (c) some students may be interested in adding graphics to some of their entries; and (d) students may decide to publish a class anthology, compiled from one or more entries voluntarily submitted by each class member.

In choosing to begin dialogue journals with your students, you will have the special opportunity to get to know your students on an individual basis, a luxury that doesn't always exist in many classrooms. Through the use of dialogue journals, ESL students also are provided with a regular opportunity to develop the ability to express their ideas in writing.

Terrell A. Young, Assistant Professor, Washington State University at Tri-Cities, 100 Sprout Road, Richland, WA 99352.

References

Cummins, J. (1986). Empowering minority students: A framework for intervention. *Harvard Education Review, 56,* 18-36.

Gambrell, L. (1985). Dialogue journals: Reading-writing interaction. *The Reading Teacher, 38,* 512-515.

Peyton, J. K., Staton, J., Richardson, G., & Wolfram, W. (1990). The influence of writing task on ESL students' written production. *Research in the Teaching of English, 24,* 142-171.

Staton, J. (1980). Writing and counseling: Using a dialogue journal. *Language Arts, 57,* 514-518.

Staton, J. (1987). The power of responding in dialogue journals. In T. Fulwiler (Ed.), *The journal book* (pp. 47-63). Portsmouth, NH: Heinemann.

Build self-esteem through writing

One of the characteristics children at risk often share is low self-esteem, a perception that is, in part, fostered by children's judgment of what their peers think of them. Teachers can impact this affective need and simultaneously strengthen an academic skill through a simple, fun, and rewarding writing lesson.

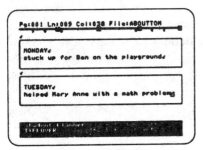

Planning boxes with student notes.

PREWRITING: Begin the activity with a class discussion on looking for good in others. What qualities do students value in their peers? Kindness? Athletic skill? Loyalty? As a class, brainstorm a list of characteristics and record them on the blackboard or a poster. Can students describe how words and actions show evidence of these characteristics?

For the next four or five days, each student will secretly watch another student (teachers should assign who watches whom) and then record positive observations about their subject. (If you are using *Magic Slate II*, have students use the planning boxes.)

During this observation process take a few minutes each day, as a class, to add more traits to the list. Can students draw upon examples from literature (*Charlotte's Web*, *The Secret Garden*, *The High King*) which have an underlying theme of recognizing good in people? Current

events (what criteria is the president-elect using to select his cabinet?), specific subject matter the class is studying (what qualities did the famous night-rider Paul Revere possess?), or even the actions of students (how does Jason, with his broken leg, make it to his second floor classroom without the help of his peers?) can also serve as a springboard for generating additional characteristics.

The list will grow, and the time used for discussion will serve as a daily reminder for students to both watch their subject and record their observations. (For *Magic Slate II* users, start a separate planner box for each day.)

WRITING: After four or five days, students will have a rich collection of notes, from which they can write a one-page "positive profile" of their subject. When students have finished composing, instruct them to print a double-spaced draft of their writing (this can be done in *Magic Slate II* with QUICK FORMAT). Double-spaced text makes it easier to revise and correct spelling, punctuation, etc.

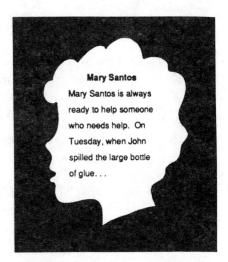

Mary Santos

Mary Santos is always ready to help someone who needs help. On Tuesday, when John spilled the large bottle of glue. . .

REVISING: Confer with each student during the editing step. Have they captured the spirit of the assignment? Do they like what they have written? Do they need to condense their writing to meet the one-page requirement? Help students understand that it can be just one idea or a combination of their observations that will result in the final essay.

Provide students time to edit their writing and make a new print-out. Encourage students to then swap their papers with friends to proofread before printing the final version of their "positive profiles."

PUBLISHING: Display the students' writing on a silhouette of the subject student. (You probably will want to integrate the actual making of the silhouettes during the entire writing process, as it will take time.)

Display the finished products – the written profiles mounted on the silhouettes – on the class bulletin board or in the hallway outside the classroom. What reactions do students have to their published positive thoughts? Do students believe that they measure up in the eyes of their peers?

Later, give your students their silhouettes to take home. They will become valued mementos of school life!

This writing activity, especially the prewriting stage, works well in a one-computer classroom, with students taking short turns at the computer.

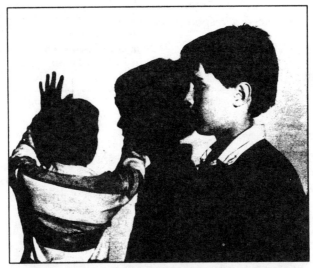

Silhouettes can be quickly produced using the light from an overhead projector to cast a shadow of the student's profile onto a sheet of newsprint or construction paper that is taped to a wall.

[Reprinted by permission from Sunburst Solutions, *Winter 1988.]*

A Brand New View: Language Development and Creative Writing for Elementary ESL Students

Anne Kenyon-Nord

School can be a very scary place for students who cannot read or understand what is being said around them. This lesson is used with elementary ESL students when they first arrive at school in order to help them feel more comfortable in their new surroundings. The goal: To introduce these students to simple vocabulary they can use in everyday situations along with the corresponding written words.

Software: *A Brand New View* (from the Explore-a-Story series developed by Learningways, Inc., and distributed by William K. Bradford.) In the Explore-a-Story series, children are motivated to read, imagine, write, and stage their own stories. They can watch the story as it unfolds on the screen, add characters, change the setting, alter the ending—or write a new story altogether and print it out.

Preparation: Review *A Brand New View* and develop a list of the vocabulary words that can be introduced over a one- to two-week period. About ten words were scheduled to be introduced each day. Although all ten words were not recognized or assimilated immediately, they were repeated daily. A data disk of the key words was developed by copying the student disk and pulling down from the menu or writing on the screen the vocabulary words to be introduced. Word files (recipe boxes with 3x5 cards) and flash cards were developed for each child, and labels posted on the actual objects in the room added further reinforcement.

Introduction: The first screen of *A Brand New View* was booted up. This scene shows a typical school building, an adult (labeled "teacher"), girls and boys, a sun, clouds, trees, flowers, a playground, and playground equipment, all previously labeled. We talked about some of the objects in the room and the name. I explained that we were going to begin to identify things around us and their names.

Instructional Activities: We began by analyzing each picture. Some students could readily identify the

objects in the pictures and were very helpful in explaining the pictures to other students. We pronounced the words as a group and then individually. I made notes to myself on those students who seemed to understand the pictures, words, and picture/word associations. We proceeded this way through the first four scenes, introducing new words when necessary and repeating those already identified.

We then went back to the first scene. I asked each student to identify something they thought they knew and to pronounce that word. If they had the picture/word association correct, they began to develop their word files by writing that word on a 3x5 card.

Practice Activities: The next day (session) students were asked to find words from their word file that matched pictures and words from *A Brand New View* as we progressed through the first four scenes. We repeated the words both as a group and individually, and students gradually completed the process of adding new words to their word files.

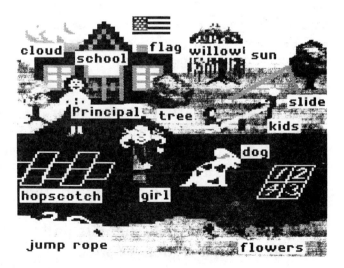

When I felt that students had enough words, I booted up another copy of *A Brand New View*. This time the pictures were not labeled, and students took turns typing in the appropriate labels. Each student identified the word being typed with the word from their word file. If they did not have the word in their file and could say the word, they added it to their file.

In this way we progressed through the first four scenes.

During another lesson I read the actual story that accompanies the program as students scrolled through the scenes. I showed them how words can be linked together to make sentences that others can read.

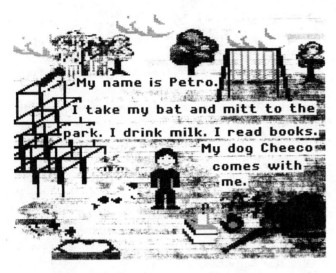

Booting up the first scene, I asked students to take out of their word file any words that described the pictures on the scene. We decided as a group that our first sentence would contain the word "school." I wrote on the screen "We go to school" and introduced the words "we," "go," and "to." Then I wrote "The boy goes to school" and "The girl goes to school." (It was necessary to explain the different tenses of "go.") They were then asked to write these sentences on a piece of paper and to add their new words to their word files.

I am always surprised at the variety in students' picture analyses, the development of reality to fantasy, and their compositions. Their attention span and motivation is very high, and I've found this format to be effective with at-risk students and other non-readers as well.

We continued this format over the next several days, progressing through the scenes in the story. Eventually students typed their own sentences, using appropriate vocabulary for the scenes. We chose some scenes to print out in color to post on the bulletin board and students printed others in black and white for them to color.

Extended Activities: The students were very pleased with their writing and became more familiar with the words for objects around them. They began to write stories of their own in groups of two or three, using the graphics from the program. Having a buddy to work with gave them more self-confidence and the stories were more fully developed.

Although the same graphics are used several times, I am always surprised at the variety in students' picture analyses, the development of reality to fantasy, and their compositions. Their attention span and motivation is very high, and I've found this format to be effective with at-risk students and other non-readers as well. I've now used several other Explore-a-Story titles, and I'm looking forward to trying some of Bradford's *Read, Write, & Publish* programs with older students using the same teaching format.

Anne Kenyon-Nord, Educational Consultant, Deep River, CT 06417.
William K. Bradford, 310 School Street, Acton, MA 01720; ph. 1-800-421-2009.

Software for ESL Students

Bernajean Porter

Students learning a second language benefit from exposure to many different language use situations, and technology can add an array of dynamic choices. When looking for software suitable for ESL populations, it's important to remember that many programs, while not *labeled* "ESL," can support language learning at all levels. Software programs that combine text and graphics, include speech, personalize text for students, promote interactive participation, and support electronic mail all provide interesting and valuable ways for students to learn language. This month's column provides a sampling of useful software along with ideas for using them in an ESL setting.

Combining Text and Graphics

Graphics software like *Create with Garfield* (DLM) allows students to start their language expression at the image level. Bring in newspaper comics for word usage, humor, and cultural discussions. After creating comic strips or posters of their own, students can orally present their stories to their classmates. Class books on thematic topics like being in a new country or school, the weather, foods, shopping, or families can be published and shared with classmates, parents, and younger siblings.

Slide Shop (Scholastic) uses sound, text, borders, and graphics to create fun and entertaining presentations. It provides another format for students to use for oral presentations to their classmates or to younger students on thematic topics.

The Print Shop (Broderbund) allows students to create a variety of interesting and useful items, including vocabulary posters, bookmarks, stick puppets for storytelling, advertising, party invitations, greeting cards, stationery, labels for their rooms at home, bumper stickers, or banners with favorite quotes or cultural expressions.

SuperPrint II (Scholastic) lets students make signs, posters, cards, banners, and even personalized calendars. Printouts range from miniature to mega size,

which allows students to design bulletin boards, big books, masks, rebus writings, new student coloring books, and customized activity sheets. [Note: *Clifford, the Big Red Dog* books can be combined with *SuperPrint II's* new *Clifford, the Big Red Dog* graphic pack.]

Certificate Maker (Springboard) creates documents like birth certificates, social security cards, driver's licenses, credit cards, and other "official" papers.

The Children's Writing & Publishing Center (The Learning Company) also gives students a chance to produce a newspaper on any topic, adding graphics where desired. Some students have written letters to relatives and friends, in this case in Hmong, a hill dialect of Vietnamese.

Ger Moua
6335 Humboldt #5
Eureka Ca 95501

Feb 14 1990

Nyob Zoo Txog Tus Phooj Ywg Leej
Kuv yog Ntxawg Muas
npawg Koj puas noj qab nyob zoo
niaj hnub nim no koj ua ab tsi
Lawm os! npawg koj puas nco txog
kuv lawm. kuv nyob pem no mas
kuv nco koj kawg li os! vim tsis
muaj leej twg nrog kuv ua si lawm
mas kuv nco txog thaum wb tseem
kawm ntawv ua ke wb tau ncaws
pob ua ke lom zem kawg tiam sis
nim no tsis muaj leej twg nrog
kuv ua si laum mas kuv nco txog
koj heev. wb sib ntsi li no xwb
lwm Zaus wb mam sibntsib dua.

Sau Npe: Ntxawg Muas.

Letter by Ger M.
Edith Fritzche, ESL Teacher, South Bay Union
School District, Eureka, CA.

Talking Software

Talking Textwriter (Scholastic) builds reading and writing skills with synthesized speech. There is a Talking Text Library with books and data disks already created, or personal files can be created as easily as using a word processor. Students can also use this unique word processor. It will read at the student's pace, repeat the words as often as the reader needs—and students can print out their stories to reread on their own and at home.

The Talking Text Spelling (Scholastic) is a complete basal spelling program using synthesized speech. The words are spoken in context, spelling tests with immediate feedback can be seen and heard on the computer, and printed copies of test results can be made. There is a record-keeping feature as well as the ability to customize spelling lists.

English Express, from Davidson & Associates, is a new multimedia tool designed especially for ESL students in all stages of language acquisition. The laserdisc version (there is also a CD ROM version) comes with two software products: Speech Master and Language Builder.

Other talking programs include *Monsters and Make-Believe Plus*, *Robot Writer Plus*, and *Dinosaur Days Plus* from Pelican Software. *Talking Numbers* (Weekly Reader), *Talking Stickybear Alphabet* (Weekly Reader), *Reader Rabbit* (The Learning Company), and *Talking Clock* (Orange Cherry) also are available if you are using an Apple //GS.

Personalized Software

Story Tailor (Humanities Software) automatically personalizes literature for students to read and reread, write and rewrite. There is a library of chants, pattern poems, plays, stories, rhymes, and literature that automatically inserts students' names from class lists. The poems, for example, are personalized and provide playful language practice in beginning decoding skills with a high level of peer interaction. The software is designed for students to insert their ideas into the text as well. Frames for student illustrations can be inserted prior to printing. *Story Tailor* integrates reading and writing while offering science, social studies, and math content.

Interactive Software

Adventure games provide interactive language experiences, with students working cooperatively to solve the adventure. This type of software can help build and reinforce skills in sequencing, cause and effect, vocabulary, and problem solving. Group discussions during the game will be the most valuable part of the experience. Adventure games also provide interesting settings for extended writing and oral speaking experiences; for example: "Write directions explaining to someone new to the game how to get to the shield room. . . ." The writer can then check his or her work by asking a classmate to follow the directions! Or dedicate a classroom bulletin board for hints written by students to other players. A few example adventure games for different ages include *Winnie the Pooh in Hundred Acre Land* (Walt Disney), *Swiss Family Robinson* (Windham Classics), *Cave of Time* (Bantam), as well as Microzines' *Twistaplots* (Scholastic).

Electronic Mail

The Electronic Mailbag (Exsym) uses one computer to simulate electronic mail for the classroom. With this program, students and the teacher can send electronic messages to each other. Messages are stored until a student accesses his or her electronic mailbox, reads, and prints out the letters. Teachers can also send messages to the whole class at the same time. *The Electronic Mailbag* is a motivating program that encourages communication skills that reinforce language learning. It can also be used within specific curriculum areas, giving students the opportunity to discuss in writing their responses to a poem, book, or science experiment, or share their thoughts on a current national or community issue. [Note: Exsym may be reached at 606/737-2312.]

Bernajean Porter is a senior partner with The Confluence International Group, a consulting firm for educational technology planning and curriculum development.

A RECIPE FOR DRIVING MOMS CRAZY

This recipe is simple to make,
All you do is take
One whiny little sister,
Someone to call her mister,
A little brother to scatter
his toys,
And a little brother's friend
to make more noise.
I think if you put anymore in,
Mother will come in with an
exasperated grin.

by Savi
Ponderosa Ele. School

Local Area Networks: The ENFI Project

Linda Stine

Ever since the technology was introduced, networking has had a strong psychological as well as pedagogical appeal for college writing teachers. It seemed to offer the chance to right some existing wrongs while helping students improve their writing skills. As Cynthia Selfe, director of the Scientific and Technical Communication program at Michigan Technological University (and co-editor of Computers and Composition) *summarized in her talk on "Computers and Politics" at the 1988 CCCC Convention, traditional writing classes typically have been environments in which*

- *Visible hierarchies of age, power, gender, and race exist;*
- *Activities involve high risk and traditional rules;*
- *The orally articulate are rewarded;*
- *The orally assertive are rewarded; and*
- *Women and minorities are silenced.*

Networked classrooms, on the other hand, offer an environment in which

- *Visual cues to student identity need not exist;*
- *Activities involve reduced risk and new rules;*
- *Written expression is rewarded;*
- *Contributors need not hurry to respond; and*
- *Women and minorities are demarginalized and given a forum.*

This month's column describes one networking project developed to empower a particular minority, students with hearing impairments, but which since has been adapted for use with traditional students as well.

Electronic Networks for Interaction (ENFI) at Gallaudet

Trent Batson, professor of English at Gallaudet University in Washington DC, a university for students who are hearing impaired, began the ENFI Project in 1985. Initially standing for "English Natural Form Instruction," the ENFI network was developed to expand the ways in which students who are deaf use written English. Typically these students produce written English only for school tasks and therefore have little feeling for English as a living language. In networked classrooms, however, English can be the sole means of communication, creating, in effect, a language-immersion program for students with hearing impairments.

An ENFI classroom contains computers linked by networks such as Novell or 10Net and supported by one of a variety of software utilities that allow group conversation such as CTC from CompuTeach of Washington DC. The unique feature of an ENFI network is that it is synchronous; it operates in real time rather than as a receptacle to hold stored documents for later retrieval. Students and instructor sit at individual terminals and compose messages on a private window at the bottom of their screen.

185

When they want to "speak" they press a key which sends their message, signed with their name, to the public window visible on all screens. Conversation appears on a first-come, first-served basis, and scrolls up as new messages appear. The entire transcript is stored and can be reviewed at any time or printed out for further use.

The Advantages of Real-Time Communication

Batson and his colleague Joy Peyton, from the Center for Applied Linguistics, (Peyton & Batson, 1986) describe ENFI and its promise for many kinds of students—basic writers, ESL students, youngsters just beginning to write—anyone who needs to increase fluency in written language.

As they point out, this real-time communication via writing shows great promise for language development. First, it offers the kind of non-threatening environment for self-expression that Selfe described above. Second, it forces participants to use writing in a wide range of contexts. Additionally, it provides continuing written interaction with an instructor who is using the language to give immediate feedback and to model. It encourages creativity as form of self identity, since students are known only through their written expression. It requires students to read and analyze continually, thus learning the relationship between the two activities. And finally, students practice writing to a real and quite diverse audience.

As Peyton and Batson (1986) conclude,

> The most radical and promising aspect of the use of local area networks is their potential to completely overhaul classroom practice. The classroom may become a place where writing does not occur only at that dreaded moment when a composition is assigned, but where written language is central to communication; where writing is natural, alive, and vital; where it is used to joke and play; to argue, reason, praise, and criticize; to tear apart and create. And that is how writing should be used. (p. 7)

The ENFI Consortium

Clearly the pedagogical advantages of this technology are not limited to students who are hearing impaired, and ENFI soon expanded beyond Gallaudet, helped by an Annenberg Corporation for Public Broadcasting demonstration grant in 1987. A consortium of five schools is now using the ENFI system: Gallaudet, Northern Virginia Community College, the University of Minnesota, Carnegie Mellon, and New York Institute of Technology. Batson (1988) acknowledges that it is unusual for an idea to move from special to mainstream education, but explains ENFI's growth by pointing out how well its philosophy —"conceiving of writing as a social act, not a solitary task; as a process, not a product; and as a collaborative endeavor" (p. 32) —fits current writing practices.

To get an idea of how ENFI is being used with traditional students, I spoke recently with Michael Spitzer, Dean of the School of Humanities at NYIT's Old Westbury campus. NYIT joined the ENFI consortium two years ago, with one networked classroom. This fall they will have eight ENFI classrooms on three campuses for all writing levels from developmental through advanced. The expansion has not been entirely trouble-free; last year there were technical problems with software compatibility and with a computer virus. In addition, teachers using the system have had to learn how to use it effectively, which means learning how to relinquish control and how to structure activities so that the dialogue among students does not deteriorate. Nonetheless, the opportunity ENFI provides for students to get in the habit of thinking about writing as comunication and to begin to appreciate written language in a new way has excited students and teachers alike.

NYIT writing classes are not conducted entirely on the network; a typical writing class might only spend one-fourth of its time using the system.

That time, however, is very special. "In the classroom, when the system is being used," Mike reports, "there's a kind of electricity in the air. When students are interrupted in a written conversation, they groan. That's not the reaction teachers are used to getting when they ask students to stop writing!" Mike speculates that this reaction comes from the sense of empowerment that ENFI gives the students, a sense of pseudo-anonymity, one in which what they write is separate from their personal identity, something between speech and writing, and thus freer.

As Batson (1986) wrote in EnfiLOG, the bimonthly newsletter for the project:

> Since [real time] communication—the ENFI approach—has the power to transmit the sense of teacher presence, the computer is not coming between the teacher and student but is instead opening up a whole new channel of communication; it is allowing people to connect in a way they never have before. It is this psychological dimension that is the key to the power of ENFI. By itself it is not a startling or even very sophisticated technological application, but the pedagogical implications are both. (p. 2)

Anyone interested in learning more about the ENFI project is invited to contact Trent Batson at Gallaudet (202/651-5494) or Michael Spitzer at NYIT (516/686-7720).

Linda Stine, Associate Professor, Lincoln University, PA 19352.

References

Batson, T. (1986, December 1). *EnfiLOG*, p.2.

Batson, T. (1988). The ENFI Project: A Networked Classroom Approach to Writing Instruction. *Academic Computing*, February, 32-33, 55-56.

Peyton, J., & Batson, T. (1986). Computer networking: Making connections between speech and writing. *ERIC/CLL News Bulletin, 10*(1), 4-7.

Selfe, C. (1988, March). *Computers and Politics*. Talk given at the CCCC Convention, St. Louis, MO.

Nontraditional Students—Nontraditional Needs

Linda Stine

Lack of access to culturally relevant software, as other articles in this issue suggest, presents a real problem for the instructor working with nontraditional students. However, when these students are commuters, as is often the case on college campuses, there is an even more basic concern: How can we ensure adequate student access to computers upon which to run any software? This month's column describes one approach to addressing this concern, in hopes of stimulating more discussion on both the problem and possible solutions.

Lincoln University in Pennsylvania is one of the nation's oldest historically black colleges. The Master of Human Services Program, in which I teach writing, serves a nontraditional student population made up of predominately minority students with an average age in the mid-30s. Since this is a program designed for working adults, classes are held on campus on Saturdays only. All students commute, some from a distance of 3 to 4 hours away.

Several years ago I designed a writing program to help prospective applicants raise their writing skills to an acceptable college level so that they could enter our graduate program. I wanted, somehow, to provide a curriculum in which students would be forced to write more than they had in years and yet do so in an environment which would free them from the fear of writing most carried with them from past school experiences. Computers seemed to be a promising tool. If students had access to word processing, they could reasonably be asked to write and revise more, with less worry about error. It was at this stage of my thinking, however, that I came up against the dilemma facing many adult, working students: The very people who most need access to the advantages computers offer are the least likely to have such access because of limitations both in terms of time and money.

The problem was not with our campus facilities—we have a lab equipped with 18 Apple IIe's, which is available on Saturdays for class use. However, I could not expect a student making a 2-hour commute and working all day to come to school on weeknights to use the equipment in our labs. And I certainly could not expect anything more than frustration to result if I showed students the wonders of word processing in our Saturday classes, but then sent them home to use the same old writing tools during the week when most of their composing and revising would take place.

Requiring students to purchase or lease a computer for the semester was not an option. Most of our students pay for school with a student loan, and any additional costs would put education out of reach for many of them.

Program Description

I decided that if students couldn't come to our computer lab, we should send the computer lab to them. With the help of some state funding available for the enhancement of our college curriculum, the university purchased 16 Apple IIc's (which would be compatible with our microlab equipment, but portable enough to move around easily) and 16 copies of *Appleworks* word processing software at a cost (in 1986) of about $14,000. These computers and the software are given to students for home use, free of

187

charge, for the semester in which they are enrolled in our new Pre-graduate Semester in Writing and Critical Thinking.

To protect our investment, we require each student to put down a $706 security deposit, which covers the full cost of the machine. This deposit, which most students finance through their student loans, is refunded in full when the computers are returned. However, the company from which we purchased the computers agreed to sell students a new IIc at the same cost it had charged the school; at the end of the semester, those students who return their computers and receive their refund can use that money to purchase their own equipment if they wish.

Classes meet Saturdays in the microlab from 9 a.m. to 4:45 p.m. Each week as homework, students complete a chapter of grammar exercises, keep an "electronic journal" (15 minutes a day for 5 days), and write a short (2- to 3-page) essay. Students bring these homework essays to class on disk, and we spend the day creating, editing, and proofreading text, using computers for all stages of the writing process. Students also review grammar at the computer, both by working on exercises I have prepared and put on a disk for them and by checking their own or peers' homework essays for possible problems with the grammar topic of the day.

Results

I've taught four semesters of this program so far, with a total enrollment of 48 students. At the end of each semester, all computers have been returned on time and in good working order. Tuition money has repaid easily the initial investment in equipment. In addition, students have been unanimous in their praise of the computer as a writing tool.

My students give three main responses when asked to describe how the computer affected their writing habits:

- Computers help make the emerging text more visible.
- Computers make editing easier.
- Computers motivate them to write.

If computer access enables writing teachers to teach more effectively and writing students to learn more quickly, then schools at all levels have a responsibility to examine the access problem and look for creative solutions, ensuring access where it is needed and not just where it is convenient.

Because these people are quite a bit older than the average college student and generally less technologically sophisticated, I think their acknowledgment of the motivational factor is most important. Students tend to write about their computer experience in such terms as "takes the worry out," "gives me a sense of mastery over the written word," and "it's an instrument of pleasure." These certainly are not sentiments I am used to hearing from my writing students. And these subjective comments have been borne out by their scores on a pre- and post-Daly/Miller Writing Apprehension test. Students in my first semester class, the only one for which I have completed statistics at this point, showed a 13.7 drop in writing apprehension, much of which I feel to be a result of the feeling of empowerment they gained from their new writing tool.

Cautions and Implications

Lest I paint too rosy a picture to be believable, I must report that there have been many times when I, as a teacher, have not shared the students' general enthusiasm. I have found it much more difficult to plan class time use effectively (especially in the beginning of the course), since students have very different levels of writing fluency and keyboarding skills. When a student with weak writing skills also has weak technical skills, he or she is often just beginning a class exercise when most of the others have finished it. (I've learned to make most in-class exercises group assignments during the first part of the semester, taking care to assign at least one good typist to each group. This helps ease the situation somewhat.)

I also have found that I need more patience in my computer and writing class than I was used to previously. It seems to take longer to see writing skills begin to improve, although students do seem to make at least normal gains by the end of the semester. I'm interested in knowing how much having to learn the technology interferes with the learning of writing skills and what we as teachers can do to minimize this interference. Furthermore, I'm concerned about the research that seems to suggest that computer use may reinforce the bad writing habits of weaker students. What must I do in the classroom to make sure the computer is an aid, rather than a detriment?

Nevertheless, my experience thus far suggests that computers are a powerful writing tool to put in the hands of the basic writer. If, as it seems, computer access enables writing teachers to teach more effectively and writing students to learn more quickly, then schools at all levels have a responsibility to examine the access problem and look for creative solutions, ensuring access where it is *needed* and not just where it is convenient.

Linda Stine, Associate Professor, Lincoln University, PA 19352.

Breathing Life into Reluctant Writers: The Seattle Public Schools Laptop Project

Sharon Franklin

Seattle Public Schools set out to improve the writing skills of a group of bright, verbally articulate, but at-risk students identified as "reluctant writers." Many of these "dysgraphic" students were unable to jot down a simple sentence, let alone complete assignments required of students their age. Their often illegible writing added to their difficulties, resulting in frustration and an assortment of related academic and self-image problems.

There is data to suggest that computers in general offer distinct advantages for these students. Using a word processor, students can read their own writing—some of them for the first time. Not only that, it can be read easily by their teacher and classmates. Because it is easier to identify errors and correct them, editing and revising becomes a routine part of writing rather than an insurmountable chore. Add to that the pride that comes with printing out a professional looking final copy, and it's easy to see why students who have not liked writing before find it palatable—and even fun—using a computer.

Laptops offer additional advantages. Students can use them in any location—their classroom, the school library, and even in their own homes. Carted around within a classroom or school, laptops begin to assume a comfortable familiarity of something between that of a loyal friend and an added appendage.

Used in conjunction with a modem, laptops allow students to "hand in" a paper from home as well as confer electronically with a teacher about their writing. Overall, the portability of laptops extends the idea of the computer as a tool one step further, since their use is not driven by location, time of day, or class schedule.

This article focuses on three exciting laptop programs within the Seattle Public Schools: Alternative School #1, Asa Mercer Middle School, and Middle College High School. Each program uses their laptops in very different ways. Together, they paint an exciting picture of the potential of laptops to impact the teaching—and practice—of writing in schools.

Alternative School #1

At Alternative School #1, an "experiential learning center for grades K-8," everything seems tilted toward enthusiastic, fun-filled learning. Students begin writing on the laptops in kindergarten, carefully copying letters and reading words on the screen that match those in their storybooks. Sixth through eighth grade students share their experience with laptops as they pair up with the younger

students to help them with their stories.

Some of the older students write ongoing books that resemble an historical diary. Whether students are asked to write on a theme inspired by a work of literature studied in class or a writing assignment given by the teacher, students relate the topic to their own life. The laptops add motivation as they put their writing into story form, adding illustrations if desired.

It's often hard for children to put their ideas and dreams into words. It's easy with the laptops.

The staff at AS #1 believes that students need to write about things of importance to them. Principal Ron Snyder gives an example of a student sent to him for discipline.

"Rather than asking him to write 100 times what he should or shouldn't have done, I asked him to write about how he felt about the war in Iraq. His response? 'I don't like to write.'

Sarah at work.

"We had just received our laptops. I gave him one, showed him how to use it, and suggested that he write a letter to President Bush expressing his feelings. He wrote an incredible letter, found that he liked writing using the laptop, and had the important experience of making his views known. To me, *that's* education.''

The school recently wrote a grant in partnership with the Seattle Group Theater. This exciting project involves an expert on multicultural dance, song, and stories, who will give a presentation each week based on a particular culture. After students hear the presentation, they will write their own individual stories based on that culture using the laptops. Next, an experienced mask-maker will help them create masks to help them tell their story. At the end of the year, the masks and stories will come together in a multicultural pageant.

As a follow-up, it is planned that these 25 students will form into groups of five. Each group will work cooperatively to create a playlet, again written on the laptops, that combines their five individual masks into one story. Rather than emphasizing the cultures as they did originally, now students will be challenged to focus their writing on the feelings they experience as they wear the masks of their characters.

''It's often hard for children to put their ideas and dreams into words,'' says Snyder. ''It's easy with the laptops.''

Asa Mercer Middle School

Kathy Pruzan teaches seventh grade language arts in one of the most extreme inner city schools in Seattle. She chose to be a writing magnet classroom using Tandy 102 laptops. This year 17 computers will be added to the 16 she now has, which will allow one laptop per student.

Pruzan's writing practice starts with simple sentences. From there her students begin to expand the complexity, adding more information, combining sentences, writing more sophisticated sentences, and finally, developing those sentences into paragraphs and then into papers. Laptops have not changed the content of her teaching, but they have altered the process and the outcome in significant ways.

''My laptop writing program doesn't sound particularly glamorous,'' admits Pruzan, ''but it *really* works!''

Students go through three basic steps:

Step 1: Keyboarding. Students are given a minimum of one week of training—enough to get them started.

Step 2: Cooperative Groups. Pruzan assigns her students to work in cooperative groups, often pairing a student with good academic skills with a student who has good computer skills. Students learn basic rules for working cooperatively.

Step 3: Language Arts Lessons. Students use their Tandy laptops to complete assignments from their workbook, *Analyze, Organize, and Write*. Sometimes students complete their assignments by writing directly in the computer. Other times Pruzan types up a lesson and puts it in their computers. Students learn word processing skills as they complete language arts assignments.

Cut and paste functions, for example, are learned as students practice punctuating or combining sentences.

Pruzan's students use the laptops at least three times a week. As many as 2/3 of their assignments are completed on the computer.

My laptop writing program doesn't sound particularly glamorous, but it *really* works!

The benefits? She sees several.

- A clean final copy is rewarding. ''Students care about the end product. Having a 'publishable paper' has become an important new goal for my students.''

- Students are more attuned to the subtleties of grammar and punctuation. ''Seldom would a student ask a question like 'Should there be a space before a semicolon?' when we wrote in longhand.''

- The laptops allow students to be more objective about their work. ''When students see their writing printed out, they're much more willing to correct it. For some reason, errors are not a personal affront to them.''

- It's much easier to correct their papers. ''Students' writing is legible, and they take more time initially in editing and revising their work.''

As soon as each of Pruzan's students has a computer, she plans to have them write their individual papers and essays on the computer as well.

Two Mercer students collaborate on a writing assignment.

''At that point, my students will be able to practice *content* editing and revising using the laptops. I'm looking forward to seeing how the laptops affect the composing process—and their enthusiasm for writing and publishing longer pieces.''

Middle College High School

Middle College High School (MCHS) opened in January

1990. Located on the campus of Seattle Central Community College, MCHS is a unique Seattle high school that seeks to recapture drop-out youth ages 15-20 in a quality high school completion program.

The core classes offered at MCHS are interdisciplinary, team taught courses: Natural Sciences includes mathematics and science; the Humanities course combines English and history. Writing across the curriculum is standard, and students are required to write research papers in all major classes.

Students feel more comfortable writing down things on the computer than they do on paper. For many of these students, being able to get their feelings out carries them a long way toward solving problems that prevent achievement.

MCHS recently introduced The Laptop Project to an already creative curriculum. Students who previously met with academic failure are stimulated and challenged to articulate their thoughts using this multisensory approach.

"We're finding that when students use laptops, they think alone and remain focused," says Laptop Project Coordinator Moses Howard.

All MCHS students use the laptops routinely to create, draft, and revise their writing, especially in the area of science. Students carry them to the library to take notes for research reports. Nineteen percent of MCHS students attend college classes as well and find the laptops extremely useful there for taking notes.

Juan, Kinh, and Quang pool their efforts to complete a science project.

In addition to their use in the core curriculum, laptops have become an important tool for students to use *whenever* they want to communicate in writing. Recently, a student requested a laptop. Not an unusual request in itself, but the result was an emotional journal account of a very difficult personal experience. The laptop was an immediate and unbiased tool, available on the spot, which allowed the student to look at her experience from many different vantage points. Most important, it allowed her to verbalize her feelings, for which she expressed relief.

"Students feel more comfortable writing down things on the computer than they do on paper," says Howard. "They are writing about very personal problems. For many of these students, being able to get their feelings out carries them a long way toward solving problems that prevent achievement."

The Laptop Project is new, and MCHS admits they've barely scratched the surface. Still, the results are exciting and come with stunning individual success stories, like Leon, who confided to his teacher that he "couldn't write."

"Leon often said he could not write a science report," explains Howard. "When he was given a laptop, he retreated to a quiet part of the room and produced a comprehensive (350-word) well-written science report that generated an A from the teacher.

"The laptops are stimulating many students like Leon to WRITE, WRITE, WRITE! There is hardly a period when they are not in use by some class in the school."

Betty Lau, Humanities instructor at MCHS, now hears comments that most teachers only fantasize about.

'Can I have more work to do?'
'What else do I have to do to catch up?'
'I need more time for my paragraphs . . . can I check out a laptop to take home?'
'I'm going to write a real LONG letter!'

"Do you want to know one of the biggest problems we have? Students use the laptops so much that we're always running out of batteries!"

"The students at MCHS have discovered a new 'open sesame' to writing success," says Howard. "The laptop has created a positive attitude toward writing, and in so doing it has assisted us greatly in unlocking the educational potential of our students."

Are "reluctant writers" an endangered species in Seattle Public Schools? Given the enthusiasm of many teachers and administrators, and the power of Tandy laptops, it's easy to believe it may be only a matter of time.

Sharon Franklin, The Writing Notebook, Eugene, OR.

With gratitude to the many teachers and administrators who generously contributed their time and background material for this article.

Gold

You're telling me I'm selfish:
Well, yeah. I'm selfish
as a chip of gold,
competing with dull rocks
in the desperate prospector's
steel pan
for the sake of escaping
the grimy earthquake quarters
and rejoining with its own kind.

What makes you say I'm selfish?
Is it because on that sultry
day in June;
Rover's tongue rolled
to his chest
like red carpet,
and I sat sipping
a tall mug of ice water
under the arms of the shade tree?

If I'm selfish,
it must be the selfishness
of cruising
the 405 South
while the 405 North
has a bumper to bumper
traffic jam and saying,
"Better them than me."

If I'm selfish,
it's not like the vulture
that abandons
his egg unhatched
and flies
off into the thick, azure sky,
leaving the unborn to be adopted
by the wind.

Lalita Haynes

Lies

Words like claws
grasp for my face
striking,
          twisting,
                    ducking
as thick black smoke
escapes your forked tongue.

Glass eyes
strangle
my probing questions,
smothering
the spark of reality.

Icy tears
slither down slippery cheeks
and form
a little white puddle
of lies.

Angie Castro

Dreams Keep Me Snuggly-Warm

Dreams are blankets that keep me snuggly-warm.
They are the soft sweet voice that sounds so kind.
Dreams hold me tight like my mother's arms.

Reality is a magnet that attracts harm,
Pulling me in confusion, grabbing my mind.
Dreams are blankets that keep me snuggly-warm.

My mind is a bomb that only dreams can disarm
Because I could explode at any time.
Dreams hold me tight like my mother's arms.

When trouble sneaks near, my dreams sound the alarm
And throw away all the stress it can find.
Dreams are blankets that keep me snuggly-warm.

Reality is a giant forearm
Who hits me in the eye and makes me blind.
Dreams hold me tight like my mother's arms.

I have embraced Walter Mitty's charm
Because reality's contract I didn't sign.
Dreams are blankets that keep me snuggly-warm.
Dreams hold me tight like my mother's arms.

Jason Orbison

Carousel World

We immigrants are ivory stallions,
Imprisoned in imported carousels,
Nailed down by fusing poles of prejudice.
Discrimination rides our bruised, black backs.
Red-Russian czars rust our bloody hooves,
But passionate, purple hearts act like oil,
Sliding, guiding, greasing sapphire freedom
Into foreigners. Brown brains gnawed freedom.
Ruby eyes glared, stared and greeted freedom.
Rubber noses nibbled cherry-freedom pies,
Tongues pickled in the citrus of freedom.
Round-and-round, up-and-down, inch-by-inch we bleed.
We, the aliens, await our children.
Freed from green prejudice, offspring will bask
On iridescent merry-go-rounds.

Minh Hong

These poems are reprinted with permission from Jordan High School's literary art magazine, **Stylus**, Volume 17, 1991. Special thanks to Marie Tollstrup and to these wonderful poets from her creative writing classes. **Stylus** is produced on the Jordan campus using the Mac plus and Mac IIci computers and PageMaker software. Jordan High School, 6500 Atlantic Ave., Long Beach, CA 90805.

CHAPTER 4
TELECOMMUNICATIONS

This has been a most wonderful evening.
Gertrude has said things tonight it'll take her ten years to understand.
—Alice B. Toklas

The Electronic Field Trip

Linda R. Gorton

In Bainbridge, New York, a village about 175 miles northwest of New York City, Brenda Myers used a telephone call to put new life into her third grade students' writing.

After hearing the kids complaining that they had "nothing to write about" she suggested, "Why don't you ask an author if he or she ever feels that way?"

To give her students the opportunity to ask that and other questions, Ms. Myers took her class on an "Electronic Field Trip." Via a telephone conference call, she and her students paid a visit to children's book author James Howe, the author of *Bunnicula*, *Howliday Inn*, and *Celery Stalks at Midnight*. This "live" exchange convinced the students that even people who get their books published can have difficulty thinking of ideas and getting their thoughts down on paper.

A telephone conference call in this context is quite different than your touch tone phone with a speaker button. A Teleconferencing Systems International "Conferencer" was used to ensure that all students would be able to hear and talk. The TSI system includes multi-directional table-top microphones, stereo system type speakers, and a control unit that prevents voices on one end of the call from clipping off voices at the other end. Unlike more complicated telecommunications systems, the equipment works off a standard electrical outlet and modular telephone jack.

Preparation for the field trip was very important. Ms. Myers had each student write three questions he or she wanted to ask. The children were encouraged in particular to think about what they as writers might have in common with Mr. Howe. How does he get an idea? How does he make his writing better? What does he do when he gets stuck? In the class discussion that followed, duplicate questions were eliminated and each child was assured a question to ask during the conference call.

The children also read Mr. Howe's books before the call and wrote their own sequels to *Bunnicula*, which were mailed to him for his reactions. During the telephone conversation he and the children discussed the effort and perseverance involved in the process of writing and rewriting. The students' experiences with peer group editing found sympathy and support from Howe, who goes through the same thing when sending a manuscript off to an editor. The children were amazed.

"You mean you have to send your story to someone who just tears it apart and sends it back to you?"

The Electronic Field Trip gave the students opportunities for many other discoveries. They learned that authors must set aside part of each day to write. Nothing interferes with their writing time! They also learned that an author is as likely to use a computer as a typewriter or pen to write a story.

Brenda Myers believes that some of her students will remember that call to James Howe as long as they live. Certainly the connection was made between the process and rewards of writing. As young writers they found they have more in common than they thought with the famous author whose books they eagerly check out from the library!

Prewriting Activities for the Electronic Field Trip

- Write letters inviting the author to talk to the class by telephone.
- Write letters to parents inviting them to visit the class during the call.
- Write a sequel to one of the author's books.
- Write a portrait of what you think the author looks like or where he or she lives.
- List questions you want to ask the author about one of his or her books.
- List questions you want to ask the author about his or her writing process.

Writing Activities After the Electronic Field Trip

- Write thank you notes to the author.
- Write a description of what you and the author have in common.
- Write a story for the school newspaper about the telephone call.

Linda R. Gorton, Telelearning Coordinator, Delaware Chenango BOCES, Norwich, NY.

Tutoring via Computer:
A Writing Program Linking High School and College Students

Judy Dobler

Ed. note: In this column, Judy Dobler, Assistant Professor of Writing at Loyola College in Maryland, describes an exciting tutoring project via computer that she and education professor Bill Amoriell developed to strengthen the writing skills of underprepared students at Patterson Park High School in Baltimore. Here is Judy's account of the program and the results.

During the fall semester of 1985, officials from Baltimore City Public Schools were shocked to learn that 80% of the district's students had failed the Maryland Functional Writing Test (MFWT), scheduled to become a graduation requirement by May 1986. To help, Bill Amoriell and I devised a program to tutor 30 high school students while training our education majors to teach writing at the same time.

We used students in a 15-member reading methods class as tutors. Each Loyola student was assigned two Patterson students and given academic credit for tutoring. The credit, we hoped, would ensure the tutors' con-

tinued involvement in the project and compensate for the additional out-of-class work. In addition, we felt that limiting the project to a relatively small number of tutors and students would allow us to closely monitor the project.

Patterson administrators selected 60 eleventh grade students who had failed the MFWT twice but whose most recent scores (4.5 or 5.0) fell just short

---

In a project like this we trade efficiency for motivation. One of the Patterson students said it best when he wrote, "I wish we had more time to write to each other but that is what happens when you are just getting to do something you really like."

---

of the 5.5 needed for passing. Of these 60 students, 30 were randomly selected to participate in the project and the others formed a control group. All the students received additional help, as state law requires, but only the experimental group was tutored via computer.

Modems and the Kermit communications protocol linked Loyola's VAX

mainframe computer with the IBM-PC lab at Patterson. The computer link facilitated communication between tutors and students by shortening the time needed to send and receive a response. During the project, Patterson students uploaded their responses to the Loyola VAX where they were accessed, read, and commented on by the Loyola tutors. Files were then downloaded to the PC lab, beginning another cycle.

The tutors, mostly junior elementary education majors, were unfamiliar with the format of the MFWT and did not have previous instruction in writing and writing pedagogy. We used in-class time to remedy these problems. A test expert/high school English teacher provided information on the MFWT. She explained the prompt-response format, taught the tutors to rate actual responses holistically, the way professionals would, and gave all of us time to practice. After the session, the tutors generally knew what to expect and how to judge responses more accurately.

During another class session, I taught the tutors how to comment. Tutors practiced commenting on actual MFWT responses and learned how to (a) focus their comments so that students solved one problem at a time, (b) suggest ways to improve rather than merely judging or evaluating, (c) list the strengths of a response before commenting on its weaknesses, and (d) establish rapport by becoming "helpful friends" rather than teachers.

To reinforce the role of "helpful friend" and to overcome the impersonality of computerized responses, we went to Patterson to introduce the tutors to their students. They spent half an hour exchanging information about their interests, jobs, families, and future plans. From then on, all communication occurred via computer.

Both groups had to be taught to use their respective computer systems, so the first two writing activities were short exercises. Learning to use the computer turned out to be more difficult than we or the students anticipated. Patterson students had trouble mastering the computer and typing skills at the same time. Loyola tutors had trouble getting access to the computers. Both groups often began with "I just typed you this message and when I finished I erased it completely."

We found that having the tutors write their responses during their free time rather than class time tended to exaggerate problems. We also learned quickly that it was better for the lab teacher at Patterson to upload the responses, rather than the students, since the students had all they could do to write their exercises in the time available. Next time, a whole class will be tutored at once, rather than having individuals work during their free time.

We quickly learned to be flexible. Initially we had an "ideal" timetable worked out. Student responses would be uploaded on Tuesday and Friday afternoons and tutor comments on Tuesday and Thursday mornings. We had forgotten the human beings involved. Students and their tutors became ill; they had schedules which conflicted with our timetable, problems with the computer, and varying levels of interest. Eventually we

learned to take advantage of the system's ability to accommodate individual differences and came to expect only one complete interchange per week.

Throughout the project, we monitored the student exchanges, using both computer screens and printouts. We immediately noticed that the tutors were sloppy about spelling and grammar. Although we had said that a tutor's "authority" as a writing teacher often depends on meticulous spelling and grammar, the tutors' mechanics improved more quickly after one student wrote to his tutor, "I want to tell you I have found some spelling

---

Although we had said that a tutor's "authority" as a writing teacher often depends on meticulous spelling and grammar, the tutors' mechanics improved more quickly after one student wrote to his tutor, "I want to tell you I have found some spelling error in your paragraph . . . . Please don't take hard but I was just proof reading over it to make sure I am not the only making mistakes."

---

error in your paragraph. . . . Please don't take hard but I was just proof reading over it to make sure I am not the only making mistakes."

Our success was clear. The tutored group, averaging scores of 6.0, performed significantly better than the control group, which averaged 5.64. Furthermore, although both groups showed overall improvement, the experimental group scores increased an average of 1.25 points, while the control group scores increased .83 points.

More important improvements were perceived as well. We found a general increase in the length, specificity, and clarity of the student responses.

Students also learned to write faster and to say more in a shorter period of time.

The project clearly motivated the students to succeed, some for the first time. Doug's comment was typical: "I never thought I was that good a writer. I just wish the proficiency test was on computers like this, maby I would pass." (He did, raising his 1985 score of 5.0 to a score of 6.0.)

The greatest indication that the students cared, however, came from their stated determination to pass the MFWT—even though they knew by the time they wrote their last letters that the State Board of Education had postponed making the MFWT a graduation requirement. Several students, like Rose, said, "I know that we don't have to pass this test after all, but I am going to still try my best." (Her score went from 4.5 to 7.0.)

What have we learned? To maximize turn-around time at the beginning so that the students don't lose interest. To speed up mastery of the computer so that the students' attention is focused on the tutoring rather than on the computer. To limit revisions to one per prompt so that no one gets bored. To grade tutors' comments for quality, rather than quantity, so the tutors' grades don't depend on the quality of their students' work.

Finally, we, the instructors, have learned to be humble. We have learned that students can teach each other to write, even though they may not be as efficient or as thorough as we are. In a project like this we trade efficiency for motivation. One of the Patterson students said it best when he wrote, "I wish we had more time to write to each other but that is what happens when you are just getting to do something you really like."

Linda Stine, Associate Professor, Master of Human Services Program, Lincoln University, PA 19352.

Judy Dobler, Assistant Professor of Writing, Loyola College, Baltimore, MD.

kids.2.kids

Expanding the Writing Audience via Telecommunications

Steven Pinney

kids.2.kids *uses telecommunications to enhance the writing process. Teachers involved in this writing network meet regularly to design writing projects, evaluate previous projects, discuss technical problems, and enjoy each other's company. Many of us already have managed years of successful writing programs without the technical support of telecommunications, but are finding that by expanding the writing audience to classrooms in different geographic areas, students are not only more interested in writing but are motivated to improve their writing skills.*

The 1988-89 school year began with a general meeting at which time teachers planned the first of two major writing projects. "The Great Pumpkin Letter Writing Campaign" supported the network teachers as they presented the friendly letter format with a Halloween theme. Students were introduced to telecommunications via the "pen pal" concept; in this case the sending class was paired with a responding class of a different age group. The teachers' ability to get to know each other added to their commitment to the project and helped work out the details that would make the project run smoothly.

Each class was given one week to complete the writing and exercise the option to have read-around groups participate in peer editing. Because teachers recognized the value of clear writing directions, prompts were designed for the senders, and writing directions were embedded in the sender letter to assist the responders. Once sender letters were created on the word processor, the files were sent via E-Mail on the Newport-Mesa FrEdMail electronic bulletin board.

Responder classrooms downloaded the letters (my class had over 68 to answer) and proceeded to create letters of response to each individual student. Read-around groups met and gave the writers their comments regarding content, sentence structure, grammar, and spelling. After editing on the word processor (which helped students understand its value as an editing tool), the files were sent back to the sender class.

This first effort was a resounding success! Over 350 friendly letters, representing the writing talents of over 500 students of varying ages and skills, traversed the electronic lines. Not only were we enjoying the process, but telecommunications was linking students in a way previous classroom writing projects had not done. My own students were overwhelmed by the fact that their letters were real letters written for real people. You know telecommunications is making a difference when a student says, "My gosh, this kid can really write! I'm going to have to work hard on my response letter!"

Evolution of a Process

At the conclusion of the Great Pumpkin Project, we held another network meeting where we discussed the positive and negative aspects of this first effort. Our process of meeting, planning, executing the plan, and evaluating face to face provided us with a remarkable opportunity to build both the writing skills of our students and the **kids.2.kids** project itself. The project grew into a definable model that includes a beginning meeting where interested teachers get together to learn about the program and meet other interested colleagues. Besides evaluating the last project, consensus is reached at this time regarding writing directions, writing prompts, prewriting activity suggestions, and timelines for the next project. Flyers and writing directions

---

The Great Pumpkin Letter-Writing Campaign

Writing Situation

Halloween is a time when people dress in funny costumes to scare away ghosts. It is a time when people can be scared. The Great Pumpkin knows all about the true history of Halloween. He knows about how we came to practice trick or treating and all about the rituals of ghosts and goblins. He knows how scary things really are. The Great Pumpkin loves to receive mail.

The Great Pumpkin: Directions for Students:

Write a friendly letter to the Great Pumpkin asking him to please explain how Halloween came to be such a scary time. Share with him one of your greatest memories of fear and where it happened. Be sure to use all of your senses as you describe where you were when this occurred. Ask the Great Pumpkin to share one of his scariest moments with you.

Prewriting

Discuss Halloween mythology. (All Hollows Eve—actually a celebration of coven witches to honor the released souls of All Souls Day). Discuss the success of the Halloween horror shows and how grotesque costumes are thought to keep evil spirits away from you.

Discuss fear and how it heightens your awareness of the world around you. Cluster fear and the memory of a place where fear occurred.

---

also are created and shared with others, and the teachers in attendance make classroom partner commitments.

With the remarkable experiences of this first project behind us, we eagerly moved on to the next one—a project requiring a business letter to be sent to a responder school requesting a company's products or services. Over 500 business letters representing over 600 student writers were posted via electronic mail.

Spring 1989

In order to offer teachers and their students in the network a variety of writing and publishing formats, three new projects have been initiated. Each offers something unique.

The Electronic Express is the student newsletter for **kids.2.kids**. Each network school sends a news item about an interesting event on campus for all the network schools to read and enjoy. This project requires no matching of schools and provides a vehicle for network schools to learn about each other. The second project encourages students' use of different writing forms, including poems, essays, tall tales, short stories, and mysteries. Students whose work is posted on the bulletin board receive Certificates of Merit and may have their piece included in the printed *Writers'*

Anthology. This collection, representing the best posted writing of the year, will be available for the first time in June 1989. Each student author will receive a copy for his or her school library.

The third project, The Round Robin, exemplifies how technology can be applied to a familiar writing project. The project will link three schools in a cooperative writing activity. Teams from School 1 will design the characters, the first settings, and hint at the conflict. Teams from School 2 will develop the characters and expand on the conflict in a variety of settings, and School 3 teams will bring the conflict to a close.

The success of **kids.2.kids** has made telecommunications an indispensable tool in our classroom writing programs. This student writing network provides students with a purpose for writing, a real-world use for word processing, and a real audience to read their short stories, letters, and news items. With an audience beyond the classroom, students become authors who care about the quality and effectiveness of their writing.

Steven Pinney, KidNet, Newport-Mesa Schools, The Writing Center, Rm. 24, 3224 California St., Costa Mesa, CA 92626.

October 11, 1988

Dear Great Pumpkin,

We hate to bother you during your busiest month, but we just wanted to tell you about the scariest night of our lives. It was a horrible, horrifying Halloween night. We ambled down the sidewalk with loads of luscious candy. Then we approached an old, abandoned, aged mansion. We wanted to investigate the old mansion, hoping that we would discover a fortune in gold.

We opened the old, creaky gate and sauntered into the yard. We saw some tombstones with bones all around them. We got so scared we bolted into the mansion. Every time we took a step, the floor would creak. There were cobwebs in every nook and cranny. The bannister was broken as if hurricane Gilbert had just hit it. The steps were demolished and the windows were shattered and boarded up. We walked up the demolished stairs. When we got upstairs, we saw something lurking in the shadows.

Then suddenly the shadow disappeared. Something down there was stomping in the room. We cautiously walked to the end of the hallway, we turned the corner and suddenly the something jumped at us. It had long fingernails, black hair, green skin, red eyes, big nose, black shirt, black pants, black boots, big ears and a machetti in one hand. We got so scared we ran and pounced on it. Then someone noticed that the machetti was Toys R Us. We ripped the face off the monster and it was one of our friends! We collected all the candy that we dropped around the house. Then we left the mansion laughing with our friend.

If you're not too busy we would like to hear from you. We'd like to hear about the time when you were scared.

Sincerely,
Brian Ruduold, Ryan Crogan,
David Marcus, and
Chad Bollenbach

October 26, 1988

Dear Brian, Ryan, David, and Chad,

I really enjoyed reading your letter, especially the part about the loads of luscious candy. I am going to tell you about something that happened to me one night.

I was all alone in my pumpkin patch when I saw the owner of the lot walking towards me with a huge knife in his right hand. He was humming a tune about pumpkin pie, and how he really wanted to sink his fangs into one. I suddenly realized that he meant me!

I hurriedly tried to bury myself in the soft soil in order to hide myself. As he walked closer towards me, I noticed that he was wiping the long blade of his knife with a shredded piece of cloth. A large shiver began to run down my side as he edged closer to me. When he was right over head he started to bend over towards me. I was really starting to sweat seeds then. His large bulky hands picked me up into the air. Then his shifty eyes scanned my shell to look for cracks. Not finding any he set me on an old, wooden bench, and began looking for others.

When he had gathered a couple other pumpkins, he set us in a single file line. Then he looked us all over again to pick the best one. I quickly began messing myself up so that he would not pick me. He eliminated all of the other pumpkins except for the one beside me and myself. I was really scared because I was too young to pie!

He reached down and got ready to pick up his selection. I was really tense. Luckily, he picked up the one beside me and put me back down in the patch with the other pumpkins.

So this Halloween or Thanksgiving, think of the greatest pumpkin on Earth, the Great Pumpkin.

Your friend,
The Great Pumpkin
aka Jason Tomasovic and
Jeff Martel

Closing the Gap with a Home-Loan Program

Paul Reese

Over the last few years, P.S. 125 (Ralph Bunche School) has developed an extensive, integrated computer program which has generated great enthusiasm among students, families, and staff. As an inner city school located in Community School District Five in Central Harlem, issues of computer equity greatly impact these students. Most of them live in city public housing, and very few have access to computers outside of school.

Increased open access time in the lab became the first goal. The lab now opens at 8:00 a.m., when 25 students eagerly show up for one specific purpose: to use *MicroType Paws* (South-Western) to practice their keyboarding skills. During the lunch period the lab is available for students to work on extra projects, to use *Logo-Writer* (LSCI), to play simulation games such as *Where in the World is Carmen Sandiego?* (Broderbund),

The Pond (Sunburst), or *The Factory* (Sunburst). So many fifth graders signed up for an after-school club that the group had to be split in half and a second afternoon added.

At this point we began to look at how we might increase students' access even more. We were delighted to be asked to pilot a student-home computer loan program provided by the New York City Board of Education Division of Computers and Informa-

tion Science. Under this program we received 13 Apple //c computers and modems for students to use at home for a period of 6 to 12 weeks. With modems, the students would be able to call a local bulletin board and exchange messages from their homes, access the local news, and search an electronic encyclopedia. All in all a grand proposal, jammed with potential and excitement for the students, yet filled with unexpected challenges and discoveries.

The fifth and sixth grade students were chosen by their classroom teachers based only on their good work habits and responsible homework record. The students also knew that they would have to sign a contract, which involved accepting extra computer-related projects. In addition, both a parent and the student had to agree to attend a 4-hour training session and to take responsible care of the computer. The training workshop was to be held on Saturday so that parents would have the greatest possible opportunity to attend.

It should be noted that the students in the loan program, like their classmates, are no novices to computers. They prepare reports on the school-networked Apple //e and //GS computers. They use a special version of *Bank Street Writer III* (Scholastic) and *Bank Street Filer* (Scholastic) to create their own databases and use them to analyze data and prepare reports. They are equally comfortable using the network's mail system to send a report to their teacher or send a note to friends in other classes or via modem to students across the city or country.

Saturday Training

On the designated Saturday, a full 45 minutes before the 10 a.m. scheduled time, the first student and her mother entered the empty school building and made their way to the computer lab. Within 30 minutes, all 13 students had appeared, along with at least one parent per student.

The parents and students filled out name tags; several parents hesitantly shared that they had no computer knowledge and were very nervous about the project. However, the children first had to deal with their own nervousness as they were asked to introduce themselves and their parents (a task seemingly unfamiliar to them, but one which they managed fairly well with a little coaxing!).

The four hours flew by! We discussed with parents how the loaned computer supports and extends their child's learning environment in school. Students and parents opened boxes and began to set up their computers. Bewildered parents tried to take in new terms such as "boot," "format," "save files" etc. and were relieved to see that their children seemed quite familiar with the terminology and the programs, including a quick understanding of the slight differences between the stand-alone version of *Bank Street Writer III* and the network version they use in school. The fifth graders' competence showed as they directed the turtle during a demonstration of *LogoWriter*. I encouraged parents to supervise the programs their children used, since the computers came with a game disk which could dominate their time, and were also told how they could help their children develop good keyboarding habits.

Now it was time for students to sign the contract. When asked what a contract was, most of them said it was a paper to be signed. It was only after some thought that one student suggested that when you sign a contract you agree to do something. Thus, students were advised to read the contract carefully before they signed it. The contract stipulates that the student would:

1. Keep a daily log of computer activities.

2. Submit a weekly written project.

3. Select a major, independent computer project for the duration of the loan period.

4. Agree to meet with me once a week during lunch to discuss problems and review their progress.

After a short break for bag lunches, students showed their parents work in progress on the school's computer network. Then students chose additional software titles to take home, including *Bank Street Writer III*, *MicroType Paws*, and one edition of *Microzine* (Scholastic). The sixth graders also took *Bank Street Filer*. Other programs selected were *The Pond*, *The Factory*, *Geometric Supposer: Presupposer* (Sunburst) and some drill and practice math programs. Students with younger siblings were offered a selection of *Stickybear* (Weekly Reader) titles appropriate for the age of their brother or sister.

After the paperwork was finished, students and parents headed home, using shopping carts to transport their computers.

Students were required to write at home using *Bank Street Writer III*, with disks provided to transport data between home and school. Soon students started arriving early in the morning to print out assignments and other writing projects. The first writing centered on the computer with topics such as "My First Computer At Home" or "What I Did With My First Computer," followed by reviews of loaned software packages.

Students were encouraged to share the computer with their parents and siblings; in fact, they were given the responsibility of being the teacher for their families. I was surprised and pleased one morning to find myself helping a fifth grader correct word processing format errors in an 8-page paper his father had written for a course he was taking.

Adding Modems

The modems came a week after the original training and parents and students were called back on Friday for additional training. Now parents and children together would be able to explore the world of telecommunications. The parents seemed almost incredulous at that possibility.

We needed a computer program to operate the modem. *FredSender* was chosen because it can be freely copied and loaned to the students and is very simple. Bank Street College provided the use of its computer mail system as a base for the students' first electronic correspondence from their homes. The students practiced with their parents in the computer lab, using *FredSender* to dial the modem and connect to the Bank Street Exchange (BSE) and leave messages for each other. The modem and its connection to a local bulletin board would offer a means of supporting students and parents as they explored the many programs that would be used at home.

Their first assignment was to leave a message for everyone that weekend. By Sunday evening it was quite clear that something wasn't working. Only one student had been able to leave a message and it was missing lines. A week later the number had grown to three. Student after student reported to me that their modem was "broken."

Hundreds of times a day I lean over a student and troubleshoot problems, explaining why he or she might be having a problem. "You need a carriage return at the end of your title." "Wouldn't Bank Street Filer be a better program to help you keep track of your book list?" "Yes, that program has crashed, but you can re-boot it very easily." However, it is much harder to give quick advice when the problems are happening at home. Even though telecommunication is becoming more user-friendly, the fact is that it must communicate with computers of many kinds over phone lines with different standards and using different software packages—all of which leaves lots of room for special problems.

Home Visits

I decided that if this part of the program was to get off the ground, I would have to visit homes. I have taught in P.S. 125 for almost 20 years and this would be by no means my first visit to students' homes. Although past visits often found me the bearer of less-than-good news, this was not so on any of my ventures to "repair" modems. Parents and students were pleased and proud to welcome me into their homes. Although I felt a little awkward as I crawled behind couches and investigated telephone connections in all sorts of odd places, I was always made to feel welcome.

The "broken" modems were all fixed by minor adjustments such as correcting wires or altering the software to allow for pulse or touch-tone. In some homes additional wiring was needed where modular jacks were unavailable. One student lived in housing provided by nearby Columbia University, requiring a "9" to be dialed before reaching an outside line.

The home visits revealed a side of students and families that teachers seldom see. One living room proudly displayed a wall of framed elementary school awards and certificates. I recalled how often I had rushed to complete just such forms for award assemblies at school. It made me re-think their importance.

In one home the TV had been ousted from the table in the center of the living room, placed unplugged in the corner behind a chair, and the computer installed in its place of honor. Always short of space in New York City's small apartments, another girl had placed the computer on a tall dresser top. She had to sit on pillows on the end of her bed to reach the keyboard.

I asked one girl if she had been practicing her keyboarding, but to my dismay when I asked her to show her mother and me what she could do, she reverted to the hunt-and-poke method. I reviewed the correct method and showed her mother how to help. The mother explained that she got home from work at 11 p.m.—too late to supervise, but that she would help on weekends.

An unexpected dividend has been the level of parental involvement. Parents have discovered that they can learn about their child's school activities by observing their child's enthusiastic computer activities. Several parents now use the modem to send messages to teachers.

Once the modems were working, students began checking and leaving messages daily on the local Bank Street electronic mail board (BSE). Their initial messages were short and full of keyboarding errors. Many were composed while the modem was connected to the remote computer by phone line. However, they quickly learned to compose "off line" and upload their messages to the bulletin board. A few students have become quite proficient, expanding to some of the many free bulletin boards available in the New York area. Most students concentrate on correspondence with classmates, teachers, and adult mentors who use the Bank Street board. Exchanges are informal, although many students respond at considerable length to suggested topics from teachers and/or

mentors. Students absent for a day or more check with classmates about the day's activities and homework assignments.

This experience confirms my belief that it is very important for children who have limited or no access to computers to have the same opportunities available in more affluent homes and communities. Although a computer/modem loan program is not the easiest program to get up and running, the outcome is well worth it. A home computer program can be successful if it has the following key components:

- Parents must be involved in the training.
- The students' responsibilities and obligations must be clearly defined and regularly monitored.
- Technical support must be available.

Paul Reese, School Computer Coordinator, P.S. 125, Community School District Five, 433 West 123 St., New York, NY 10027.

From vanessa Tue Jun 14 21:31:38 1988
To: seth
Subject: Lost mail
Date: Tue Jun 14 21:31:36 1988

Hello Seth,
   I'm not one of the players who can hit the ball out of the park but I can hit the ball so I can reach 2nd base.Unfortunately we are not going to play against other schools if we become the champs.If we become champions I'm not sure what happens.My position is shortstopand we play the game in our school yard.Personally I don't like playing softball but its fun. Today my class played a game and it was a slaughter.The score was 7-1 the other teams favor.But the people who played did their best.They were overconfident and we did keep on striking them out but I could of made two points but this girl named Teja hit a good ball but the other team caught it.But still she improved from the practice we had.
   My favorite game is basketball .Right now the championships are taking place and I have not missed one yet. It's between the Detroit Pistons and the L.A.Lakers.The Lakers are leading by 1 game. One more thing can you give me the answer to your riddle that said how many balls of string does it take to reach the moon? I'm glad you like getting mail from me!Some people I've written to have'nt wrote back in years (or at least it seems like that!)
       Your computer pal,

Building a New Foundation for Global Communities

Margaret Riel

"I am a reporter and editor for an international newspaper and I'm only 13!"

"When we found out that people from other schools in other countries were going to read our ideas and information, we wanted it to be good writing, and we became interested in our subjects. After all, we were ambassadors for the 8th grade."

"Using the Long Distance Learning Network, we all worked together editing and choosing the best stories to feature in a booklet. It felt good to see our booklet displayed in school and to see how interested other students and teachers were in our projects."

These are the words of students who have participated in an electronic community of learners. When writing became a way to share their ideas across time and distance, teachers reported a surprising enthusiasm among students for writing and revision. Students worried about the accuracy of their information as well as the form of their writing. But it was not only the students who benefited when classrooms were electronically stretched into global Learning Circles. Teachers also reported professional and personal growth.

"There is a certain pride and dignity when you know that your work is being read by a great number of highly skilled educators," wrote Lorraine Sherwood, an elementary school teacher in Hilton, New York. Teachers and students located throughout the world were joined together in educational communities that redefined cooperative learning as *among* rather than *within* classrooms.

Although telecomputing is an exciting new tool for facilitating distant learning, new tools alone do not create educational change. Placing this tool in the hands of isolated teachers neither provides the vision of what can be accomplished with its power nor the plan for carrying out such a vision. The power is not in the tool but in the community that can be brought together and the collective vision that they share for redefining classroom learning.

Building an electronic community is a complex task best accomplished by careful planning, artistic designing, and skillful construction. These are the activities that characterize the AT&T Long Distance Learning Network as it begins its third year of helping teachers and students design new educational environments called Learning Circles. This article is about the process of building electronic communities of teachers and learners.

> **Although telecomputing is an exciting new tool for facilitating distant learning, new tools alone do not create educational change. The power is not in the tool but in the community that can be brought together and the collective vision that they share for redefining classroom learning.**

Surveying the Landscape

The AT&T Long Distance Learning Network began with a survey of the electronic landscape by education and technology experts. They found many electronic conferences, bulletin boards, and electronic mail systems designed to be used by teachers. But all of them invited individual teachers to log on and explore the new terrain alone. Teachers searched for projects that matched their own visions of electronic learning and tried to locate people with whom to carry them out. Some found ongoing projects to which they were able to contribute. However, many teachers were disappointed at the amount of time spent on line searching without success. In cases where a project was found, there was often too little control over the design, timing, and direction of the project to have it fit well into their classroom lessons.

Teachers who took the initiative to organize projects were faced with the difficult tasks of locating and organizing the group, designing the timeline, and directing the project. Many well-designed projects failed because others were not at the right place at the right time. Electronic novices internalize these failures privately and are discouraged at their inability to fulfill the promise that echoes in professional conferences and journals.

A pervasive feature of the electronic landscape was the waste of valuable teacher and learning time spent looking for a way to use this new tool. The educational engineers' recommendation to AT&T was to create a service that would enable groups of teachers and students to work collabora-

---

Learning Circles allow students from different cultures, regions, religions, ages, perspectives, and with a range of physical and mental strengths or disabilities to work together in a medium that treats diversity as a resource.

---

tively in a global context on topics that were part of their curriculum. This is the goal of the Long Distance Learning Network.

Designing Learning Circles

If telecomputing is a powerful tool for cooperative work among people separated by distances, why not begin your experience as a member of a group? The basic idea of an AT&T Learning Circle is to match teachers and students into small, geographically diverse, working groups to accomplish shared educational goals. To facilitate the group formation, teachers select a particular type of Learning Circle (Computer Chronicles, Mind Works, Places and Perspectives, Society's Problems, Global Issues, or Energy Works) defined by a curricular focus (journalism, creative writing, geography and history, social science, and science) at a grade level grouping (elementary, middle school, and high school).

The participants in a Learning Circle share a task, the publication of a collective journal or newspaper (e.g., the *Journal of Places and Perspectives, Mind Works: The*

Creative Writing Journal, or the *Energy Works Newsletter*). Participants agree to a specified time frame that defines the phases from the beginning to the closing of the Learning Circle. They each receive a shared curriculum guide with many ideas drawn from the experiences of past teachers. But the teachers and students in each Learning Circle work together to create the activities. Each class is invited to design a group project drawn from their curriculum. Learning Circles allow students from different cultures, regions, religions, ages, perspectives, and with a range of physical and mental strengths or disabilities to work together in a medium that treats diversity as a resource.

Curriculum Guides: Blueprints for Learning Circles

The Long Distance Learning Network provides a curriculum guide for each type of Learning Circle. Curriculum guides are frameworks that help teachers and students work together to build unique Learning Circles. The guides, like blueprints, communicate a general concept for an educational structure. Educators, both teachers and students, use these plans to give form and shape to the learning environment.

Developing Projects

Research on peer tutoring finds that the tutor rather than the tutee draws the highest benefit from the relationship. The truth is that one of the best ways to learn something is to teach it to someone else. The Learning Circle activities capitalize on this educational principle. The participants in the Learning Circle are teachers and they are learners. As teachers, each class organizes an educational activity for the rest of the learners on the network. As learners, they participate in the activities organized by other classes. No one person knows exactly what will take place over the semester, yet the activities are well planned and organized by skilled educators. Here are some examples of activities that have taken place over the network:

- Students have become local historians sharing information about the founding of their communities. Students in New York described how the early trading center at the junction of two railroad lines developed into a thriving business center and finally into a suburb of a larger city. Students in Australia shared stories of the discovery of opal mines, which led to the settling of Coober Pedy, where people live underground to escape the severe weather of the desert. From Canada came stories of native people trading sea otter furs with the British for blankets and tools, as well as stories about settlements established by the Loyalists fleeing from the New America.

- Students at all levels write at length about themselves, their feelings, their school, and their world. They write newspaper articles as well as more expressive pieces. Recipes for success, want ads for teenagers, telephone dramas, and peace messages have all been shared in Learning Circles. Stories that are started in one school are sent to other schools to be continued and concluded by students drawing on very different perspectives and life experiences.

- Elementary school students have taken over their local bureau of tourism by producing travel brochures for their area. "Welcome to Denmark . . . the land of the Vikings" or "Come to Israel" begin the guides. Another set of guides created by a circle of secondary students are called "Travel Brochures for Teens" and provide a look at an environment from their perspective. A teacher used this idea to make different time periods more vivid by having students create travel brochures from their area in a different historical period. One brochure invited tourists to the land of the Aztecs and began with the words "Journey to the secret places, enjoy the sunny days and cool evenings."

Teachers and students located throughout the world were joined together in educational communities that redefined cooperative learning as *among* rather than *within* classrooms.

- High school students begin to appreciate the complexity of society's problems when they work to design studies of the homeless, illiteracy, substance abuse, or explore differences in family patterns or causes of suicide across cultures. For example, students discovered that terms like "dependent" and "independent" have very different meanings in different cultural settings when they responded to a survey designed by Japanese students. Traditional Japanese mothers wanted children to be dependent on them for all of their daily needs so that the children would devote maximum time to studies. American parents encouraged early independence of students, feeling that taking responsibility for oneself is part of the education process. Students in Japan related dependence to the cultural value of group conformity in Japan, while independence seemed related to the value Americans place on individuality.

- Community comparison projects have been common on the Long Distance Learning Network; yet what students learn is anything but common. Students in the desert terrain of Coober Pedy, Australia, build their homes underground to escape the heat of the sun.

Students in Alaska report on the setting of the sun and schooling in the everyday of night. Skateboards take California students to school while snow shoes and skis are more common means of travel reported by students in Canada. All these contrasts help to challenge the unexamined assumptions that we unconsciously hold about the world.

The philosophy of Learning Circles on the Long Distance Learning Network is to provide teachers with the necessary direction and support to explore creative ways of integrating communication technology with their curriculum. The project approach to exploring and solving real problems that characterizes Learning Circle activities encourages the integration of different subjects and helps to place knowledge and skill in the context of their use in the adult community. Knowledge is constructed and owned as a consequence of interaction with the computer, teacher, and classmates.

Completing the Structure

Teachers and students from six to eight unique locations use telecommunications to put their minds together. They use the plans, tools, and equipment to build Learning Circles. When they are finished they have created new knowledge—mental structures that exist in the minds of all of the participants.

Each class contributes to the formation of a Learning Circle publication with reports of projects and collections of articles that were shared. But this tangible form is only a glimpse of the mental territory that is formed when people from around the world put their minds together in Learning Circles.

Teachers who participate in the construction of Learning Circles find a high return on invested time, not only in terms of student learning but in their own learning as well. Students, who witness teacher excitement over learning with others, are much more likely to realize the power and value of education. Through telecomputing, the foundation for the global community is growing, reaching out to draw information from many distant parts of the world into the electronically open classroom walls.

Margaret Riel, AT&T Long Distance Learning Network, 943 San Dieguito, Encinitas, CA 92093.

For more information about the Long Distance Learning Network, or for applications to join the next session, call (toll-free in the U.S.): 1-800-367-7225, ext. 4158, or write to: AT&T Long Distance Learning Network, P.O. Box 716, Basking Ridge, NJ 07920-0716.

Writing Across the College Curriculum: A Computer Assisted Model

Robert H. Weiss

Ed. note: The writing across the curriculum movement has benefited greatly from increased computer availability in campus classrooms and dorms. In this month's column Robert Weiss, Director of the Writing Program at West Chester University, describes an exciting new program West Chester is piloting this year in hopes of improving its writing emphasis courses through the use of computers, modems, and electronic mail.

Under a recent grant from the Pennsylvania State System of Higher Education, West Chester University offers special support to 17 faculty who teach in the writing across the curriculum program and who want to use word processing and computer networking to manage their students' writing. Limited access computer networking (LANs) are used to provide a model for improving teaching and learning in writing-intensive courses. Disciplines represented in this volunteer project include Childhood Studies/Reading, Communicative Disorders, Counselor/Secondary Education, Criminal Justice, English, Foreign Languages, Geography and Planning, Nursing, Political Science, and Psychology.

This project represents the university's first attempt to establish LANs between faculty and students. Each faculty participant was given the necessary hardware to communicate with the LAN from home or office and was trained in how to use that hardware effectively in a writing-emphasis course. The goal: to support classes specifically designated for computer assisted instruction (CAI) by providing instant communication among the IBM PCs in classrooms, the open lab, professors' offices, and the lab stations in student dormitories.

Writing Across the Curriculum at West Chester University

WCU has one of the oldest large-scale writing across the curriculum programs in the U.S. with a general academic requirement for writing-intensive courses beyond English Composition. Program goals include (a) using writing as a means of engaging students in their subject matter, (b) providing writing tasks intended to produce learning, and (c) improving writing skills through practice and feedback.

The Writing Program, which began in 1977, provides for approximately 140 writing-emphasis courses each semester. These are regular subject-matter courses that call for a significant amount of writing and for instructor attention to improving student writing. As a general university requirement, each undergraduate student must take three writing-emphasis courses in any discipline. A committee approves courses for the "W" (i.e., "writing-emphasis") designation based on a set of criteria that includes the quality, quantity, and variety of writing required. In-house lectures, seminars, and workshops provide opportunities for faculty interested in participating in this voluntary program to learn about assignment design and management, and a program newsletter is published three or four times a year.

West Chester's WAC Program is well regarded by students for accomplishing its objectives. A fall 1988 survey showed that 70 to 75% of the students (N=520) (a) wrote more in "W" courses than in other courses, (b) completed a variety of writing tasks, (C) understood course concepts through their writing, and (d) gained practice and acquired stronger skills as writers. However, only 32% of the students indicated that they had received help from their instructors in improving their writing *before* completing a final version of their papers.

Increasing Faculty/Student Interaction

The Writing Program committee, seeing the need to increase faculty attention to students' writing before completion of their final drafts, turned to word processing and computer networking. They believed that the task of working with student drafts is greatly simplified when the drafts are done on a word processor, when students receive a peer review of their work, and when the transmission of drafts is swift and convenient. With these needs and goals in mind, the committee developed a training project to help faculty (a) design and manage word-processed writing assignments and sequences of assignments, (b) comment profitably on early drafts of student writing through the use of West Chester's LAN, and (c) guide students to comment on each other's work through the same LAN.

This training was accomplished in one week of summer afternoons (15 hours), guided by the directors and/or staff of the Writing Program and Academic Computing Services. Faculty participants learned how to send networked messages to other faculty and students, how to use PC-Write (the freeware word processor readily available to WCU students), how to design assignments to incorporate word processing and drafts, and how to manage the paper flow.

Faculty participants initially expressed uncertainty about the success of the project. Several faculty, despite interest, felt the project was too ambitious. One faculty member did not want "to make this part of the course [writing and responding] larger than the course itself," and many others were concerned about the time that would be needed to work out a writing plan for the course. After going through the training, fewer participants expressed concern about using the network, commenting on student papers, and other potential obstacles; the range of concerns was limited to issues of time management.

Research and theory in the field strongly suggest that writing and learning improve when writing is assigned regularly in all disciplines; when assignments are varied in their purpose, audience, and mode; and when feedback is provided during the composing process rather than after the final product has been generated.

This fall and spring, participants will teach writing-emphasis courses using the network for peer and instructor feedback on writing. They will complete additional surveys to evaluate the project, explain their project activities to other faculty in a series of "free lunch" seminars, keep a weekly journal or log on their participation in the project, and complete a final written report summarizing and evaluating the outcomes.

Their students will take pre- and post-tests on their attitudes about writing, computers, and networking. We don't know what students' initial comments will be—we expect significant apprehension—but we hope that the chance to use PC-Write and to receive peer and instructor feedback on early drafts will be appreciated.

Anticipated Results

Expected outcomes at the end of the project year include 17 revised and upgraded writing-emphasis course syllabi in various academic disciplines, reflecting higher standards of student achievement and deeper student involvement in writing tasks that help them learn the course content. These syllabi also will reflect new teaching methods such as collaborative learning using the LAN. We also expect significant changes in faculty attitudes toward writing and CAI, as well as in student perceptions of writing and CAI.

Research and theory in the field strongly suggest that writing and learning improve when writing is assigned regularly in all disciplines; when assignments are varied in their purpose, audience, and mode; and when feedback is provided during the composing process rather than after the final product has been generated (NCTE, 1979). We hope that the project will support these findings and provide a model for improving teaching and learning in any academic discipline so that it can be extended to all of the university's 275 writing-emphasis courses and beyond.

Robert H. Weiss, Director, Writing Program and Director, Pennsylvania Writing Project, West Chester University, West Chester, PA 19383.

Linda Stine, Associate Professor, Lincoln University, PA 19352.

References

National Council of Teachers of English. (1979, March). *Standards for effective basic skills programs in writing.* U.S. Department of Education: Author.

. . . They started yelling at the sandfrog to give them back their water, but he went on sleeping. All of the other animals began throwing spears at him until one of the kangaroo's spears punctured him and water began streaming down the mountain, filling the rivers, creeks, billabongs, waterholes and lakes that had dried up . . . .

Aboriginal legend as retold by Laura, Tanya, Clayton, and Kevin from the Millcheile State School, Queensland, Australia

PALS Across the World:

Writing for Inter-Cultural Understanding

Jim Erwin

No one argues about the need for inter-cultural communication and understanding. Most of us, however (and certainly most school-age children), limit the scope of our communications to the friends and relatives we know. It has been easy to avoid the special challenges and opportunities of communicating with people from different cultures in favor of our own neighborhoods until recently. With the introduction of telecommunications into the classroom, geographic distances and the boundaries separating cultures have become transparent. The PALS Around the World Project has proven that sending a communication to a friend thousands of miles away is as possible as writing a letter to a friend around the corner. Certainly, it has proven that inter-cultural sharing can enliven the writing process and give it a vital context and purpose.

PALS is a six-year-old international writing project that includes over 400 schools in more than 15 countries. Students use telecommunications technology (put simply, a word processor and modem) to share their questions, answers, research, and creative writing with a "sister school" across the world. Through writing in an international context, children share information and ideas that help them shape global perspectives and understanding.

Teachers in the PALS Project find the presence of a "same age" audience to have a tremendous impact on their students' writing (certainly one that goes far beyond the motivation associated with a teacher and a red pen). Students want very much to be understood, something that they find takes careful planning when they cannot assume that everyone on the other end understands what they are writing about (just ask the American kids who wrote a long description to their PALS in Australia about something that happened at K-Mart!). Therefore, each

---

PALS Writing Activities

Over the past six years PALS Across the World has generated hundreds of fantastic classroom ideas. Here are just a few of these ideas:

- Have students brainstorm a list of "one-liners" that express important aspects of their school and community.

- Have your students write the beginning of a story (one page or so in length), and have students at their sister school complete the story. For an exciting extension of this activity, imagine three or four sister schools adding to the story and returning it to the original school to write the ending.

- Have students research and write legends or "tall tales" from their region.

- Have students create a monthly newsletter about events in their school, community, state, or country.

- Have students write about their favorite meals, including instructions for preparation. Coordinate a day at your school when these foods are prepared and everyone gets to try something new to eat.

stage of the writing process becomes very important. Students work cooperatively, brainstorming ideas for a first draft, rewriting, and sending a final copy only after much discussion about the cultural connotations of the words chosen.

There are specific levels of writing activities associated with the PALS Project that provide a progressive structure to the language arts curriculum:

- Letter Writing: Getting acquainted
- Report Writing: Formalized reports on different topics
- Poetry Writing: Sharing thoughts, feelings, and images of their world
- Electronic Journalism: Headlines from the ''Australian Gazette''
- Dialogue on Social Issues: Controversial Issues (i.e., apartheid)
- Script Writing: Plays and dialogue

Although many teachers and students stick to this pattern, others skip around to fit their specific needs and curriculum. In fact, if a teacher is willing to respond to the students' inspired ideas, PALS writing projects can cross curriculum lines with interesting results. An example of this occurred when students from a school in Alaska and a school in Australia began a correspondence about somehow running to each other's school!

To prepare for the run, students at both ends independently researched the geography between the two schools and made mileage calculations. After sending numerous reports back and forth, they established a halfway point in the middle of the Pacific Ocean and the route and mileage necessary to get them to their final destinations. To simulate the run, each physical education class kept track of how far they ran during PE (every activity had a running-related value). Students worked with their math teacher to convert these statistics into miles and kilometers and with their geography teacher to chart the course on a master map. The actual telecommunicated messages—written reports to the ''sister school'' about progress made during the week—were sent in language arts class. The school at the other end would receive the report and then calculate the new position. Celebrations erupted at both schools when they met halfway on an island in the Pacific and again when they ran the entire distance to each other's school.

The PALS Project has enjoyed such successes at most grade levels from kindergarten through college. Students gain new confidence in their ability to use language to communicate ideas and a new respect for the challenges and benefits of sharing with writing PALS from another culture. The experience reinforces the idea of a truly global community, one in which people are more similar than different, and one in which the effort to communicate is rewarded by an open door to a larger world of ideas.

Jim Erwin, Computer Education Coordinator, Lake Oswego School District, Lake Oswego, OR. For more information on the PALS Project, contact Jim Erwin, USA Director/Founder, 4974 S.W. Galen, Lake Oswego, OR 97035; ph. 503/697-0338; AppleLink: K0591; Dialcom ID 42:WEW001.

. . . THE OUTBACK
The Outback is like a large desert of saffron trees.
With trees like thorns sticking out of the side of mother nature,
Her yell in pain is the scream of a whistling kite,
flying high to search her face,
Her tear stained face.
The sun is a jewel in her Forehand,
Radiating its life across the land.
The animals are her life blood,
Her very precious life blood,
Mother nature feels the pain,
From the barren,
Dust laden, OUTBACK.

Shaun O'Connor, Year 8
Alice Springs, Northern Territory, Australia

. . . Two captains caught a whale a couple of days ago. Now we can have the feast in June. My dad is a whaling Captain. I have to babysit for my mom so she can go to the ice and cook for the crew. Does anyone in Australia do any hunting?

Hild Attungana
Tikigaq School, Pt. Hope, Alaska

CHAPTER 5
MULTIMEDIA

I used to be a design, but now I'm a tree.
—8-year-old

Lights, Camera, . . . MAG9C!

Pat Kolakowski and Jean E. Dean

Sometimes it takes a jumpstart from technology to get unmotivated students to produce the kind of writing of which they are capable. At least that's what Pat Kolakowski, writing advisor, found as a result of this project.

Michelle Sahady's fourth grade students at Hector L. Belisle Elementary School in Fall River, Massachusetts, were exposed to lots of wonderful literature, but they were reluctant to pick up and read a book on their own. Three times a week these 27 reluctant learners were invited into a Writers Workshop environment, but the writing wasn't happening.

Last year Michelle's students celebrated Book Character Day. They dressed, talked, and acted as their character for the whole day. They were so involved with their characters that one student, Tracy, said that she "felt like she really was Pippi Longstocking" when the day was over. Michelle explained to this year's class

---

Move over, Roger Rabbit, and see what teachers and students can achieve when this technology is made available to them!

---

the idea of Book Character Day, but two weeks after the announcement only two students had chosen characters. No one else was interested. The secret to motivating these children remained a mystery.

During this time I began a four-session workshop called Lights, Camera, Action, taught by training specialist Jean Dean at the Computer Technology Center. I wondered . . . could a video overlay card, computer, and camcorder be the key to motivating this class? In my role as writing advisor, I proposed the idea of videotaping Michelle's students in costume while they read a message in letter form to the class

Technical Information To Help You Get Started

The Apple video overlay card can be installed in either the Apple IIGS or an enhanced IIe. The IIGS is preferred because of the access to the control panel and the port for an earphone jack, which can be used with an adaptor to send computer audio directly to the target VCR. The card must be purchased directly from Apple and sells for around $390 with the educational discount. With graphics programs such as *Slide Shop*, *Dazzle Draw*, *Superprint II*, *VCR Companion*, and *PaintWorks Gold*, the user can make title screens, templates, and story illustrations with overlays. Students as young as second grade may want to take over these tasks themselves.

Cables are run from a source camcorder to the port attached to the overlay card, and from there to a target VCR. Using the software that comes with the overlay card, the teacher sets the key color, which tells the computer the one color that will be treated as transparent and allow the video to show.

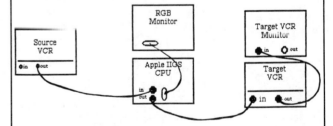

Note: For Pat's project, this cabling diagram shows both the source and target VCRs. If Pat's school had an overlay card on site, she could have put the camcorder as the source, cabled the

210

from the book character they represented. Written copies of these letters might also be put together in booklet form for other children to read. Although we knew this project would involve more time and energy on our part, we decided it was worth a try.

The Prologue

I told the class that I needed guinea pigs for a course that I was taking. I described the final product and the process we'd use. The students were mesmerized by the names of all the equipment that would be involved, but the fact that they would be stars made their eyes sparkle. Their energy grew; they listened carefully and even offered suggestions!

Along with choosing a character, they each wrote their letter, made cue cards for the taping, practiced

---

same way, and finished the project in one pass by running an audio cable from the camcorder directly to the target VCR to get the children's voices.

For the book character production described in this article, the slide was designed with an open book from clip art. On the left Pat typed the information about the student and the book. On the right she used a drawing tool to make that entire page a hot pink color, which she then designated as the key color. When the raw footage was run from the camcorder and had the proper computer graphic on the screen, a combination of the computer image and the camera image was sent to the target VCR tape. The right side of each book ''page'' holds the key color and shows the student in costume reading the letter. The rest of the screen holds the title information.

---

their parts, and decided on a costume. My job, with the help of Scholastic's *Slide Shop*, was to create the introductory script, a template containing the key color, and a list of credits for the end.

Here is one student's letter in her role as Violet, a character in *The Boxcar Children* by Gertrude Chandler Warner:

> Dear Class,
> I have brown hair and brown eyes. My name is Violet. I went on a fishing trip with my grandpa and we had a ball. I caught 2 fish and grandpa caught 5 fish. One day my three friends and I, Henry, Jessie, and Benny, were trying to find a mystery. One day we found an old man who lived by himself. In a yellow old beat up house that looked spooky. When he was in the house he vanished. We don't know how. But that's what we are trying to find out the mystery of the old man that lived by himself. Maybe you can help us.
>
> Your friend,
> Violet

Take One!

When filming day finally arrived, I entered the classroom holding my breath. Would more than six children be in costume? To my amazement, every single child was dressed, cue cards were made, and they were busy working together rehearsing their letters.

We marked the X for subject placement, went over the directions once, and began with Michelle, dressed as Caddie Woodlawn. There wasn't another sound. One by one, each child came up, spoke clearly, left the filming area, and was replaced by the next character.

Take Two!

We were finished!—or were we? We put the tape into the video player to see our finished product. NOTHING! We discovered that we had pushed the wrong buttons on the camcorder. Dare we try again? The kids made up our minds for us. The second take was as focused as the first. They were perhaps even a little better the second time, because their initial nervousness was behind them.

Edit and Print!

Was it perfect? Not entirely, but perfection wasn't our goal. When I brought in the raw tape to overlay with my graphics, there were a couple of instances where the student was off on the edge of the key color area for a second or two. It was also more time consuming to do in two stages what could have been done in one step with the overlay card in place during filming.

Was it worth it? Ask any student, any teacher, or any parent who saw it. The fact was, these students were no longer "reluctant learners"—they had tasted the joy of artistic creation. The quality of their writing and their understanding of their characters were apparent in the tape. It was an unbelievably great first project.

Epilogue

Move over, Roger Rabbit, and see what teachers and students can achieve when this technology is made available to them! This kind of project can be done in any grade level or subject area. Students can write stories, illustrate them with computer graphics, and with the help of overlay, these young writers can become live characters in their stories, reacting to the computer images they have drawn.

The concept is easy to learn and easy to teach. The cabling is simple, and most schools already own graphics programs. After the overlay card is purchased and installed, the only limit is the imagination of students and teachers—and the results are tremendous. As a consultant, I have worked in many classrooms with a wide variety of ages and abilities. The magic continues to work!

Pat Kolakowski, Writing Advisor, Fall River Public Schools, Fall River, MA 02720, and Jean Dean, Technology Consultant, Computer Technology Center, PO Box 7001, Somerset, MA 02726, with thanks to Michelle Sahady.

Opening Up Books

"Text: The Next Frontier"
—slogan on Voyager Company T-shirt

Linda Polin

At a preconference event at the National Educational Computing Conference in Phoenix last June, I experienced t-shirt envy. I saw Bob Stein, President of The Voyager Company, in a serious black t-shirt emblazoned with the slogan "Text: The Next Frontier." Intrigued by what seemed to be a return to an "old" medium by the man whose software most of us are using to create computer-based multimedia materials, I asked Bob for an interview to chat about the implications of the slogan.

There are two text projects underway at Voyager, each exploring a different aspect of the relationship between text and reader in a computer-based format. One project focuses on issues inherent in the inevitable transition from bound books to CD ROM books. The other exploits the opportunities implicit in the massive storage capacity of CD ROM to surround a central work with related material presented in a variety of formats.

The Next Text: Don't Panic

The first project, and the one we'll likely see on the market first, is the "machine readable" books project. Voyager is developing a series of four books for release in conjunction with the new Macintosh notebook computer, which Bob says is "quite book-like to me; it has the feeling of looking at a book." The titles are being selected to range from the popular to the traditional; Douglas Adams' *Hitchhiker's Guide to the Galaxy* will definitely be one title.

There is no special gimmick to this, and in our discussion we really couldn't propose any strong advantages to reading a novel off a computer screen. Indeed, Stein pointed out the "tremendous tradeoffs" and obstacles inherent in the computer and its screen-page. So—why? The answer is pure Stein: "We're basically taking the position that, like it or not, we're going to be reading on these things. There's probably some good to come of it, so let's get started. Our contribution is to put it into machine-readable form to try to develop as good a first pass electronic spine as we can while we improve the navigation."

Not the Same Place; Not the Same Thing

The problems inherent in this seemingly simple idea are a combination of the obvious and the fantastic. Consider, for example, the density of print we can display on a computer screen. It's not nearly as much as we can take in on the left and right pages of an opened book. Actually though, the effect, of this diminished "page" creates a very intriguing problem. According to Stein, "Paragraphs disconnected from pages don't make much sense as paragraphs anymore." Pointing to a single paragraph in the book he was holding he added, "If each card of the computer had this on it, suddenly you'd feel like you're reading pithy saying It's a dramatically bad difference, unfortunately."

The less obvious issues evolve from the package. "The major objection to reading on computer is it's not a friendly device for reading in terms of the aesthetics. That will change dramatically over the next five years. You will be able to lie under a tree or read on the toilet. All the physical objections will go away. But," he added, "it will never be for our generation as sensual to read a computer as it is to read a book."

There is, however, the potential to create a powerful effect from reading on computer that cannot be created in current book formats. In the "Hitchhiker's Guide," for example, Bob said the project group was toying around with the idea of adding a special multimedia ending (I won't say more in case you haven't read this highly amusing book). "I want to do that; I want to say to people, here is the text. Here—and you start to play with it."

Bob's remarks reminded me of post-modern, reader-response theories of the relationship between readers and writers. Electronic texts and the medium they are stored on allow the reader to tinker with the prose: to add, move, illustrate, delete. Imagine changing the font size and type to indicate dialogue, or to trace the author's use of a particular color. Imagine revising the ending of *The Great Gatsby*. It's not as easy as you think; it still has to fit with the rest of the book. Oh, unless you want to tinker with that too. On the subject of electronic text, Jay Bolter has argued that "the computer seems to negate those qualities of literature that the tradition regards most highly"—the 'authority' of the author, the 'fixity' of the text, the reader as 'eavesdropper.'" Something more is going on with electronic books than simply the transfer of words from paper to magnetic or optical storage.

Expanded Books: Value-Added Volumes

The second project, dubbed "expanded books," will produce CD ROM "books" with a rich set of linked and linkable multimedia materials related to the topic, context, and specific content of a central work. This project has a mission: to seduce readers back into text by offering them a richer text to enjoy. As Bob put it, "It's aimed at everybody who thought they'd never read another history book or Shakespeare play in their life. We're giving them another reason to go back."

Expanded books represent a much more ambitious undertaking requiring the selection, acquisition, and interweaving of a number of resources including video images, graphics, stills, other text material, and audio clips; and the development of other text tools such as glossaries, reference notes, timelines, and links. Currently, two titles are in production: Shakespeare's *MacBeth* and Volume 1 of Pantheon's U.S. history text, *Who Built America*. According to Stein, the release of expanded books products

is at least a year away.

The Shakespeare project takes as its central text the new Cambridge University Press edition of *MacBeth*. The CD ROM will contain the manuscript with a hypertext gloss of terms and notes. In addition, Voyager is considering providing an audio reading of the full play by a group of professional actors, including at least one well-known, classically trained actor. The main feature, besides the manuscript, will be audio notes provided by Dr. David Rhodes (UCLA), whose MacBeth lecture Stein wandered into one day and found so compelling that "I went right home and read the book." That's the kind of effect Bob is looking for from this project.

The navigational interface for the text will allow readers to skip along links that trace themes in the play. Stein cautions that the project will not do too much of this. More important, he argued, is a strong navigational system that will encourage and support the reader in making his or her own meaning through analysis, imagination, and insight. "We will do some 'pre-underlining,' but the real value is if you can start to read the text differently because the computer is willing to go out and do some housekeeping for you."

The history project is very similar but carries within it another element of Bob Stein's campaign to empower the thinking reader. The standard history text you and I have experienced, even in college, is really an extended essay about what's important and why it's important. Other than the opportunity to reflect on the analysis provided, most of the analytic and synthetic thinking has already been done. "What we can do here is supply the original sources, so the process of history is not so much 'here's the truth' but 'here's a filter, here's one author's reality.'"

The "spine" of the American history CD ROM series is the Pantheon text, but Voyager is augmenting it with photos, newspaper clippings, timelines, audio and video recordings of or about the events and people in the text. Bob showed me a bit of the work in progress. We looked at the Triangle Shirt Factory fire as an important event in labor history. From the essay on the event and its implications Bob pulled up newspaper accounts published in the Hebrew and English newspapers, copies of original photos, and even a film clip.

I think it's absolutely critical to recognize an important difference between typical interactive multimedia projects and the Voyager expanded books project. Many of the products I've seen strike me as instances of the tail wagging the dog. That is, the video footage is often the central element, and very little text is available at all, either online or in the manual. (Again, as I've mentioned in previous columns, Scholastic's *Point of View* series is a notable exception to the trend.) The Voyager products described here let the dog wag the tail. They place the text at the center and include augmenting material that illuminates meaning or provides the reader with the opportunity to do so. The mission does not seem to be to make the subject matter more entertaining, but rather to entice the reader into an active, thoughtful reading experience by doing a better job of presenting the subject matter. These products are about reading, not viewing.

The Politics of Reading

Okay, the expanded books project is marvelously rich, but is it sexy enough for the multimedia market? Will people want a multimedia history text, even if it is largely made up of primary source materials? I asked Bob if he worried that he was creating a product for six people. His quick reply was that those six might just be the ones who change the world. His more reasoned response was an appeal to developers and to the people who buy their products. He argued, ''What we're losing in giving up reading is that text—written words—are the most compact form of communication we have. You cannot deal with really complicated abstract issues with graphics or audio: Audio's too slow, and pictures are too expensive and . . . just try to explain to somebody the origins of the Persian Gulf War using just pictures and sound.'' The frightening thing is, there are developers who are doing exactly that: packaging sound bite images from network news as history.

In his controversial 1984 book, Neil Postman suggested that in the television age, thinking falls by the wayside because the dominant medium of communication is really only good for entertaining viewers; that in fact, in an age of television, news is defined as entertainment. Postman contrasted two dim visions of the future offered by Huxley in *Brave New World* and Orwell in *1984*. Orwell, he says, got it wrong. ''What Orwell feared were those who would ban books. What Huxley feared was that there would be no reason to ban a book, for there would be no one who would want to read one. . . . Orwell feared we would become a captive culture. Huxley feared we would become a trivial culture, preoccupied with some equivalent of the feelies, the orgy porgy, and the centrifugal bumblepuppy.'' Postman argued that Huxley's vision is much more likely to become reality than Orwell's. As the dominant medium of American culture, television and television-based multimedia products threaten to accomplish Huxley's brave new world by trivializing and decontextualizing topics of a serious nature. At least one company is re-exploring multimedia technology to amplify the power of the written word.

References

Bolter, Jay David. (1991). *Writing space: The computer, hypertext, and the history of writing.* Hillsdale, NJ: Lawrence Erlbaum.

Postman, Neil. (1984). *Amusing ourselves to death: Public discourse in the age of show business.* New York: Penguin.

To obtain information on Voyager Expanded Books and Machine-Readable Text projects and products, contact The Voyager Company, 1351 Pacific Coast Highway, Santa Monica, CA 90401; ph. 213/451-1383.

To obtain information about the Apple Macintosh notebook computer, see your local authorized Apple dealer. At this writing, the notebook computer is scheduled for rollout in October 1991.

POG-COG AND DROOM

Pog-cog is my friend.
He makes the sound of jin-gle jin-gle.
Sometimes he makes the sound of
Sna sna wa sna sna wa.
My other friend's name is Droom.
He makes the sound dom dom
Wom pa dp wom pa dom.
Sometimes he makes the sound of
ski ski ski.

Taneshia, grade 4

ZOT A TOT TOT

Very strange noises I hear all around.
Some go up and some go down
And some of the airplanes go "Zap, zoo, zoet."
And I hear children playing and they say
"Zot a tot-tot."
I hear my class banging on the tables.
The noise goes, "Knonk, knonk."
In the cafeteria, making noises
And they say, "Mantet, matt."
Some kids make chair noises
And they go, "Squirk, quirk."
And when people whisper, they go,
"Sp, sp, sp."

Yolanda, grade 4

The Shakespeare Project: Experiments in Multimedia

Larry Friedlander

Teaching lecture courses on drama and Shakespeare always left me feeling somewhat frustrated. Not with the students or with the works, but with the futility of talking about something not there—the performance itself. In class, all we have to guide our discussion is a printed text and no matter how rich and suggestive this text may be, it does not help us imagine the real experience of theater: communal, sensual, hallucinatory, fleeting as a dream.

In our tradition, learning has basically meant the study of texts. From its beginnings, the classroom has been a place to talk about the printed word. So, there is little resemblance between the classroom and the strange space in which a play occurs, or between a group of note-taking students and an audience immersed in the unfolding world of a play. And nothing in the background of these English (or sometimes indeed physics) majors helps them to imagine the mysteries of the performer's art: the impact of the actor's presence, the excitement of virtuoso playing, and the moment when the audience forgets itself and passes from being spectator to participant in the story as it unfolds before their eyes.

I decided there must be some way to break out of the box, some way to bring the theater—as process, change, spectacle, event—to the student. Not to transform the classroom into a theater (one might just as well buy them a season ticket to a good company), but rather to bring theater to them as a serious object of study.

This was the beginning of work on what eventually became the Shakespeare Project (SP)—a multimedia system on HyperCard with a two-screen workstation linking a Macintosh, videodisc player, and video monitor.

The Shakespeare Project

From the outset, I wanted to teach the full process of theater in an environment that would not reduce its richness nor force the ambiguous contours of this complex art form into a procrustean bed of rules, prescriptions, and rigid judgments. I wanted students to:

- See examples of the finest available work
- Study performances easily and flexibly
- Learn through partaking in the process of its creation
- Understand and experience the radical freedom of theater
- Uncover the range of choices concealed in the scripts, and
- Develop an eye for visual experience.

To begin, students choose from a menu called the Playbill. Six areas of exploration are available:

Performance. Students can watch selected scenes from major Shakespearean plays in two or more versions, as well as scenes from important contemporary, experimental European theater pieces. As the film unrolls on the video screen, the computer offers a wide choice of accompanying annotations and study aids, any two of which can be viewed simultaneously. For example, while watching a scene students can read about the actors' performance choices or the historical background of the production, or see other versions of the text. In addition, the instructor or students can write their own annotations. At any point the user can switch to another version of the same scene. The application will move to the same place in the new version as in the original version.

Study Area. Students can take multimedia tutorials on basic concepts and theatrical tasks. The tutorials introduce students to the full range of collaborative skills necessary to mount a production and are arranged according to the work done (e.g., by actors, directors, designers). I have tried to make the tutorials as interactive as possible and to exploit the interplay of film, text, and graphics. Concepts are explained and demonstrated visually; students then are given a fresh example and the freedom to do their own analysis.

Exploring. This area is a practice space containing a library of illustrative examples that are keyed to the tutorials. If students need to work on a difficult concept, they can spend time here working out problems or comparing their solutions to mine.

The TheaterGame. This animation program permits students to stage their own versions of a scene on a computer simulation program.

Browsing. This area includes a large collection of annotated images on theater with a dynamic index system. Students can organize and annotate their own series of images.

Notebook. Students can write multimedia essays, inserting visual quotes from film footage, images, and animations directly into the text. Special tools allow students to capture and record film images and footage.

Each area is designed to illuminate specific issues, provide students with conceptual and practical tools, or encourage hands-on experience. For example, viewing and comparing different productions of a scene in the Performance area vividly demonstrates how the performers' choices affect the final meaning of the work.

Consider the nunnery scene in *Hamlet*. From the text it is clear that Hamlet is angry with Ophelia, since he tells her he does not love her and accuses all women of treachery. At the same time, however, he expresses his longing and love for her and accuses himself of unworthiness. What is going on? Does he or does he not love her? Why is he so angry, and so self-abusive? The text presents a problem with which any production of the play must deal. As we watch different solutions, we are astonished by how radically free performers are to make their own meaning.

In one version Nichol Williamson plays Hamlet as rather seedy, lusting after an extremely lovely Ophelia. Here a good deal of the scene takes place on a bed. The performers solve the problems present in the script by imagining that Hamlet is not angry but is teasing Ophelia because he wants to seduce her.

In contrast, in a Russian version a tortured, noble-looking Hamlet is discovered in a dark hallway by a fragile Ophelia, whom he proceeds to humiliate and terrify. This Hamlet's illogical behavior is portrayed as stemming, not from sexual teasing, but from the repressed violence of a man who both loves Ophelia and suspects her of treachery.

Both versions present appropriate, indeed compelling, solutions to the same puzzle, yet they are utterly different. By moving back and forth between versions, students can see how the actors' choices create quite different scenes from the same text.

Theater is a complex visual event; many kinds of information and action occur at the same moment. Students often are sophisticated about the complex movement of a poem, but they have little training in dealing with similar complexity when it is visual and swiftly passing. Students need training to grasp the many layers of action and choice compressed in one moment of action. Because students can study in detail the way each moment is staged in the Performance area, they begin to discern and isolate the precise means used to generate these large differences in meaning. In one version a line is whispered insinuatingly; in another, the same line is accompanied with violent action (as Hamlet thrusts Ophelia out of his way).

By watching, comparing, pausing, reading, and taking notes (they can even program the film to stop and display notes at places of their own choosing), they can learn to see the intricate interconnections between sen-

---

Blocking sets the tone of the action, establishes the psychological relationships that govern the characters, and imparts mood, rhythm, and texture to the scene. The TheaterGame opens up the world of staging to students who have no access to practical theater.

---

sual detail (the design of costumes, lights) and psychological detail (the actors' motives, gestures, tones); to retain swiftly passing visual impressions; to connect the staging of an early scene with a later one; and generally to become as familiar with visual motifs as they are with literary image and metaphor.

Students can move in and out of areas instantaneously. For example, if they are puzzled by an unfamiliar term such as "actors' beats" or "interior monologue," they can ask for an explanation and be taken to the Study Area for a mini-tutorial on the subject. Further practice is available in the Ex-

ploring section, or they can browse through guided sequences of images on specific topics such as Elizabethan life or the stage history of *Hamlet*.

However, it is practical work with the concepts that brings them to life. After studying examples of staging and becoming familiar with the conceptual underpinnings of the subject, they can turn to The TheaterGame and make their own version of a scene.

The Theater Game

This animation program was designed as a stand-alone computer application to teach the importance of stage action or, to use the theatrical term, "blocking." Blocking is fundamental to performance because it determines the placement of the players vis-a vis each other and the audience and therefore controls how we view the unfolding action. To a large extent, the script leaves those vital decisions to the performers, and much rehearsal time is spent in working out the blocking, detail by detail, moment by moment. The importance of blocking to the final meaning of a scene cannot be overstated. Take, for example, a straightforward bit of dialogue:

He: How are you today?
She: I am glad you asked.

Simple enough. But as soon as we try to stage it, or "put it on its feet," as actors would say, we begin to see how our decisions determine what the words mean. As readers, we naturally begin by asking: Who are these speakers? Performers answer this question by asking concrete questions: Where are the characters and what are they doing? Are they looking at or away from each other? Do they move toward or away from each other? Are they sitting -at a table? -in bed? -in a public place?

Compare two possible scenarios. In the first, he moves forcefully toward her before speaking, touching her perhaps, and then utters his line. She stares at him, turns away, goes to and looks out of a window, and then answers with her face averted. In the second, he is sitting in a chair, opening a newspaper when he talks; she responds by walking across to him, taking the paper out of his hands. She then sits down next to him, lights a cigarette, puts her head on his arm, and finally says her line.

The stage actions create the illusion of narrative and psychological complexity. They create a little story for us about people we do not know. The blocking sets the tone of the action, establishes the psychological relationships that govern the characters, and imparts mood, rhythm, and texture to the scene.

The TheaterGame opens up the world of staging to students who have no access to practical theater. Users must choose a stage, props, and costumed characters from a series of menus. Then, having designed their set, they move the figures through a scene. Each movement is recorded and can be played back as a little film, either to be changed and edited or to be stored in a file. The program is not tied to any one scene or play; it works equally well with Shakespeare, Miller, or Ibsen.

Talking about staging leads into more general problems of interpretation. Here is an assignment I gave a class:

In *Hamlet* there is a long scene in which Polonius, the advisor to the King, tries to tell the King and Queen that he thinks the reason Hamlet is mad is that he is in love with Ophelia, his daughter, and that she has rejected Hamlet on Polonius's orders. Polonius takes an extraordinary long time to get to the point, dithering about madness and kings like a character out of *Alice in Wonderland*. The classic question is: What kind of man is Polonius? Is he simply a silly fool in love with the sound of his own voice? In fact, Polonius is often played this way, in pompous and comic contrast to Claudius. But if he is such a buffoon, how did he rise to be Prime Minister? The class was asked to find other ways

to conceive of him that would make the scene work.

Using The TheaterGame, students developed various alternatives. In one, the court is seen as a very dangerous place indeed, bristling with soldiers, with the King and Queen seated upstage and removed from the courtiers. In such a militaristic, totalitarian court, Polonius's speech is risky, indeed potentially subversive. To show this, the student had soldiers drift down and surround Polonius as he begins to broach forbidden topics. In this staging, Polonius's hesitancy and baroque flourishes stem from his fear as he gingerly approaches explosive subjects.

Through the Shakespeare Project, students can learn quite a lot about things not visible in a text—most of all, that the printed text in front of them with its fixed and seemingly authoritative structure is really just the starting point for the open-ended and playful exploration of possibilities.

Another student's solution is to place the focus on the Queen who, in this version, genuinely loves her son and is deeply distressed at his madness. Polonius is gentle and sympathetic to her, and so speaks haltingly and tactfully. She reacts by moving distractedly over the stage, unwilling to listen to the painful subject and dominating the action with her grief.

In the three versions, Polonius is successively a fool, a wary and vulnerable politician, and a gentle and considerate friend to the Queen. Students quickly see how they can control the effect of a moment by focusing attention on one character rather than another, or by reimagining the location or the emotional atmosphere.

Students also can use the materials

they see as the basis for their written work. We all know how frustrating it is to discuss a visual experience and have no way to illustrate your point. Film reviewers can quote characters' lines and describe the action and performance, but they cannot show the moment directly to their readers. Using the Notebook, students can do just that—write a multimedia essay, using not only text and graphics but bits of film, still images, and animation sequences.

Any time film is shown, users have access to a special "camera button." By clicking on the button and holding it down for as long as they wish, users capture and record footage, creating a kind of "visual quote" or footnote. They can write accompanying notes and store the footage and the notes in special archives to be retrieved when they wish. The information can be stored as an icon, which can be freely moved about from files to the writing area and inserted directly into the text. When readers come upon an icon, they click it to open the film, which then plays on the video screen, with or without accompanying notes. Students who have created scenes on The TheaterGame will be able to store the scene as an icon as well, which may be inserted into the essay.

Theater, of course, is not the only complex event that is difficult to teach in the classroom. I realized early on that my work with the SP could be applied to a broad spectrum of subjects. In the process, students can learn quite a lot about things not visible in a text —most of all, that the printed text in front of them with its fixed and seemingly authoritative structure is really just the starting point for the open-ended and playful exploration of possibilities.

Larry Friedlander, Professor, Department of English, Stanford University, Palo Alto, CA.

The Theatre Game is available through Intellimation, 130 Cremona, Santa Barbara, CA.

The Turnip

Nancy Scali

In the same way that a study of history is enriched through literature, examining the literature of other cultures helps even the youngest students to build a sensitivity to and respect for individual differences. Through discussion, comparison, and contrast, students discover the way other people see themselves. Fears, dreams, values, ideas, and similarities often are revealed.

In order to help my kindergarten students recognize and appreciate the ways in which children, families, and cultures are alike, we looked at *Tatterhood and Other Stories* by E. J. Phelps, *Crow Boy* by T. Yashima, *John Henry* by E.J. Keats, *The People Could Fly* by V. Hamilton, and a Russian folktale, *The Turnip*. Each story supported the ideas of caring, sharing, helping, and working together in positive ways.

The Turnip became a class favorite. During quiet reading, more and more students crowded around one another, looking at the book, paraphrasing the dialogue, making up several versions of the story, and even pretending to be the characters in the story. Clearly, a "movie" version of *The Turnip* would be an ideal project to integrate and reinforce the values students learned in this story.

Procedure: Students began by creating a storyboard. They drew pencil sketches of each necessary scene, which included:

- A title screen: **THE TURNIP**
- Grandfather planting a turnip seed
- Grandfather looking at his turnip plant
- Grandfather trying to pull his turnip out of the ground
- Grandfather asking Grandmother for help and the two of them trying to pull the turnip up
- Grandmother asking Granddaughter for help and the three of them trying to pull the turnip out of the ground
- Granddaughter asking the dog for help. . . .
- The dog asking the cat for help. . . .
- The cat asking the field mouse for help and the six of them trying to pull the turnip up
- The turnip coming out of the ground and all the helpers enjoying turnip soup for dinner
- An ending screen: THE END

Grandfather planting a seed.

Grandfather trying to pull up turnip.

Using an Apple II$_{GS}$ computer and the software *816Paint*, students converted the storyboard sketches into computer illustrations or movie scenes. These visuals were saved on disk for a later time.

A second group of students created dialogue for each scene. They practiced the dialogue until it was mastered and sounded natural to them.

Finally, movie day arrived!

Step 1: The dialogue was recorded on the classroom listening post tape recorder. Student helpers controlled the Play and Record buttons, while the dialogue team sequentially recorded their lines.

Step 2: A cable was attached to an Apple Video Overlay Card, which was installed in the computer and to the VCR Input junction. Using Apple *VideoMix* software and *816Paint* simultaneously, each movie scene was recorded onto videotape using student assistants to control the VCR Pause and Record controls.* After each scene was viewed for a few seconds, the next scene was loaded into the computer and readied for recording.

Step 3: The video was played several times in order for students to develop the timing for the soundtrack.

Step 4: Students selected a musical soundtrack for the background of their movie that was played on a record player. Other monitors controlled the VCR and the dialogue tape recording. As each scene appeared on the television monitor, students would control the dialogue tape, pushing the Play/Record buttons on a second tape recorder. This second recorder recorded the final soundtrack, which in-cluded background music and the best possible synchronization of the dialogue to their movie scenes.

Step 5: The movie video and the soundtrack were viewed several times until the counting tracks for the VCR and the tape recorder could begin together, keeping audio and visual imagery synchronized.

Step 6: A cable was attached to the video output of one VCR and to the video input of a second VCR. Another cable was attached to the earphone jack of the tape recorder (using an adapter) and to the audio input of the second VCR. Student assistants controlled the Play button on the first VCR and the tape recorder. Another assistant controlled the Record button on the second VCR.

Voila! The students had created a fantastic movie! *The Turnip* was a great success! Each and every student had a tremendous sense of accomplishment. Through the integration of language arts, visual art, and technology, this history lesson filled students with a sense of the positive things that can happen when everyone works together.

Nancy Scali, Arroyo School, 1700 East 7th St., Ontario, CA 91764.

*Using a Video Overlay Card and VideoMix software prevented the distortion, jumping, and horizontal interference that occurs when a cable is hooked directly into the video output junction of the computer. They also help keep the color of the artwork true to the original color palette. Without the VideoMix software, color can sometimes blur or become a totally different color.

Grandfather, grandmother, granddaughter trying to pull up turnip.

The mouse, cat, dog, granddaughter, grandmother, and grandfather pulling up turnip.

Enhancing Writing Through Integrated Media

Ted S. Hasselbring & Laura I. Goin

Mental models, constructed over time by learners, are necessary requisites to creating mental images.

Recent developments in computer technology now make it possible to link text, video, audio, and interactive computer programs in ways that were not possible previously. We refer to these multiple forms of linked media as *multimedia* or *integrated media*. We prefer the term integrated media because it reminds us that our goal is to integrate media in ways that facilitate learning, which is different from the goal of simply multiplying the number of media available to learners. Although the availability of additional media does not guarantee more effective learning, we believe that under appropriate circumstances integrated media can offer an enormous potential for learning. Unfortunately, the emergence of integrated media has far outstripped our knowledge of how they might effectively be used for learning. If we are to use integrated media effectively, then we must begin to develop an understanding of integrated media learning. The purpose of this article is to begin this process, especially as it relates to writing and students at-risk of school failure.

The Reading and Writing Connection

Most educators agree that there is a strong relationship between reading and writing. Anderson-Inman (1990) describes the similarities between reading and writing and concludes that both reading and writing involve the active process of creating meaning. For example, to comprehend what has been written, the reader must construct meaning from the writer's words by looking for relationships among the different parts of the text. This is not a passive endeavor, but rather one in which the reader works to combine his or her own background knowledge with ideas presented by the writer. Likewise, the process of writing requires that the writer be able to use his or her background knowledge to create a mental image, and then convert this image to words so that others can share it.

It can be argued that both reading and writing require that the learner be able to create rich mental images in order to be successful. For children with rich experiential backgrounds this is a task that is relatively straightforward. These children are able to use their background knowledge to form mental images from textual descriptions and thereby draw meaning from the text. Likewise, they are able to call upon their background knowledge to create rich

mental images of events and stories that can be converted into written text. Mental models, constructed over time by learners, are necessary requisites to creating mental images.

Unfortunately, there are many children who lack the necessary background knowledge to create rich mental images to help them understand written text or, for that matter, produce their own text. For example, a child who has no experience with oceans, waves, and storms likely will have difficulty creating a mental image of the passage from *Swiss Family Robinson* that describes their ship being smashed upon the rocks by the huge waves created by the storm. The inability to create such images is often the case with children who have impoverished experiential backgrounds.

The role of mental model-building on learning has been reviewed extensively (Glenberg, Meyer, & Lindem, 1987; Johnson-Laird, 1983; McNamara, Miller, & Bransford, 1991). Although different theorists have constructed somewhat different theoretical perspectives, the important point for our purposes is that an emphasis on mental model construction provides a framework for designing integrated media applications that provide support for writing.

Promoting Mental Model Building

Historically, authors and publishers have attempted to enhance mental model building in children's reading books through the use of pictures. However, research has shown that pictures may or may not enhance mental model building; it depends on the picture. For example, decorative pictures that do not provide information about the actual situations in the story do not help children remember or understand stories better. However, pictures that illustrate actual scenes from a story do improve children's memory and understanding for the story, especially if the pictures help organize complex scenes or parts of scenes that may be difficult to imagine (Levie & Lentz, 1982; Levin, Anglin, & Carney, 1987). Because mental models are in many ways like mental images (Sharp & McNamara, 1990), pictures that help children imagine scenes in a story should also help children construct good mental models.

The research discussed above was based on the use of static pictures such as those seen in texts. It seems clear that, in many instances, the ability to design integrated media systems that show dynamic illustrations of a story could provide much more support for mental model building than is possible through the use of static pictures alone. This hypothesis was supported in a study that incorporated the use of video technology with young children who had been identified as being at-risk of school failure (Johnson, 1987).

Johnson worked with 4- and 5-year-old inner-city children who were part of a special program designed to give them a head start in school. Johnson's study was designed to ask whether story comprehension could be improved if students had the opportunity to experience the story in a rich, video-based context. He divided the at-risk students into two groups. He read a simplified version of the first part of the *Swiss Family Robinson* story to one group and showed the other group a video of the same part of the story.

Johnson found that both the all-verbal group and the video group learned a great deal from the instruction; however, the video group learned far more. The addition of a video context gave them a great advantage. Apparently they were able to use the video images to fill in gaps in their experiential knowledge, which allowed them to gain a deeper understanding of the story.

Integrated Media Writing Tools

The research of Johnson and others has helped to shape our thinking about an integrated writing tool that can be used with at-risk students. This experimental tool, called *MediaWriter*, incorporates both reading and writing, the use of full-motion video, an animated tutor, and a concept called *dynamic support*.

MediaWriter is a Level 3 interactive video program that runs on the Macintosh family of computers.[1] *MediaWriter* brings video to the writing process by accessing video segments from a videodisc player attached to the Macintosh. A wide variety of videodiscs can be used with *MediaWriter*. For example, classic videodiscs like *Charlotte's Web* and *Swiss Family Robinson* can be purchased at many record and video stores for less than $40 and used with *MediaWriter*.

Dynamic support refers to the process of systematically decreasing the amount of assistance provided to novices as they progress in expertise and gradually assume parts of the task initially accomplished only by an expert (Riel, Levin, & Miller-Souviney, 1987). This notion of dynamic support is derived from the learning principle referred to as the ''zone of proximal development'' (Vygotsky, 1978). In a properly arranged teacher-student-computer environment there is the potential for creating the dynamic support necessary to improve students' learning dramatically. Software which provides dynamic support encourages the progressive development of skill by the learner. Initially, *MediaWriter* provides considerable support, but as students become more skilled, the support diminishes, turning control of the task over to them.

When using *MediaWriter*, the student interacts with an animated tutor that speaks and provides the student with dynamic support (see Figure 1). As the student first begins using *MediaWriter*, if needed, the tutor provides a great

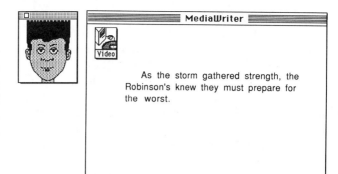

Figure 1. The third level of dynamic support offered by *MediaWriter* involves a description of a video clip. The tutor provides topic sentences for each paragraph.

deal of support. For example, at the first level of support, the tutor instructs the student to view a short video clip. After viewing the video clip, the tutor prompts the student to help write a story about the video the student just viewed. The dialogue might look something like this:

Ben was on his way to a _____.
    football game
    bike race
    picnic
    friend's house
(The tutor tells the student to click on the best choice)
But when he went outside to get on his bike
_____.
    his tire was flat
    the wheel was gone
    his bike was in a tree
    he fell down the steps
(The tutor tells the student to click on the best choice)

This type of structured prompting continues until the student and tutor write an entire story about the video. If the student cannot read the screen, the student can ask the tutor to read any word or passage. Also, if the student selects a wrong descriptor, the tutor goes back to that part of the video and shows the student what happened. This first level of dynamic support is designed to get the student to draw a relationship between the video image and the story that he or she writes with the tutor.

The next level of dynamic support provided by *MediaWriter* is similar to the first, but instead of selecting a response, the student must write an appropriate description. When all of the prompts are completed, the student should have a description of the video segment that he or she has partially written. Again, the idea is to get students to make the transformation from the visual image to text.

As students increase their ability to write from open-ended prompts, they take over more and more of the writing task. The third level of dynamic support offered by *MediaWriter* involves writing a description of a sequence of video clips where the tutor only provides the topic sentence for each paragraph. When asked, the tutor reminds students what should be contained in each paragraph. At this level of support students do most of the writing.

At the highest level, *MediaWriter* makes students responsible for producing complete texts on their own. The student can use the full power of the Macintosh for word processing plus much more. For example, the student can enhance a writing project with video, sound, and graphics, making the project a true integrated media production.

Students can enhance their writing projects using both still and moving video images from videodisc. Using the pop-up video controller built into *MediaWriter*, the student can select still or moving video segments to illustrate a project (see Figure 2). Using the controller, the students can control a videodisc player from the *MediaWriter* as if they were using a typical hand control device. Thus, students can scan forward and backward, pause, step, or play right from *MediaWriter* by pointing and clicking on the controller using the mouse. Once they have found a video segment that they want to use in their writing project, students can create a video button using the controller and insert that into the project. When readers encounter this button in a project, simply pointing and clicking on it lets them see the illustrative video segment.

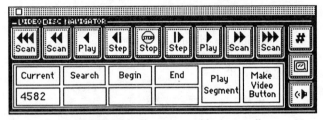

Figure 2. The *MediaWriter*'s pop-up video controller.

In addition to video, *MediaWriter* also allows sounds to be recorded digitally through the Macintosh and then attached easily to any writing project by the student. Once attached, sounds can be activated in the written text by pointing and clicking on a sound icon using the mouse. For example, if a student writes about steamboats, he or she could import the sound of a steamboat whistle so that the reader could experience the sound of a steamboat as well as read about it.

Finally, graphics can be imported or drawn in the writing projects. Students can select graphic images from art sources or they can create their own graphic illustrations using the drawing tools available to them in *MediaWriter*. Images can be cut and pasted or drawn onto the pages of a writing project as they would in a more traditional composition notebook. For example, in the steamboat project mentioned above, a student could select images of the *Clermont* or *Natchez*, two famous steamboats, to serve as illustrations for the project. In addition to hearing the sound of a steamboat, the reader now could see what one of these boats actually looked like.

Summary

The development of mental models is an important part of the reading and writing process. Unfortunately, children considered at-risk of school failure often lack the background knowledge and experience necessary for developing such models. We believe that the careful use of video can assist students to develop mental models necessary for reading and writing. We briefly discussed an experimental writing tool designed to help students use visual images for writing support. Although *MediaWriter* is an experimental tool, it is based on sound theory and empirical research. In the end, we believe that linking video and dynamic support to the writing process will assist students in developing mental models and thus enable them to become better readers and writers.

[1]For a complete description of the various levels of interactive videodisc programs, the reader is referred to the *Journal of Special Education Technology*, *X*(2), 1989.

References

Anderson-Inman, L. (1990). Enhancing the reading-writing connection: Classroom applications. *The Writing Notebook*, 7(3), 12-15.

Glenberg, A. M., Meyer, M., & Lindem, K. (1987). Mental models contribute to foregrounding during text comprehension. *Journal of Memory and Language*, 26, 69-83.

Johnson, R. (1987). Uses of video technology to facilitate children's learning (Doctoral dissertation, Vanderbilt University: Nashville, TN).

Johnson-Laird, P. N. (1983). *Mental models*. Cambridge, MA: Harvard University Press.

Levie, W. H., & Lentz, R. (1982). Effects of text illustrations: A review of research. *Educational Communications and Technology Journal*, 30, 195-232.

Levin, J. R., Anglin, G. J., & Carney, R. N. (1987). On empirically validating functions of riches in prose. In D. M. Willows & H. A. Houghton (Eds.), *The psychology of illustration: Basic research* (pp. 51-85). New York: Springer-Verlag.

McNamara, T. P., Miller, D. L., & Bransford, J. D. (1991). Mental models and reading comprehension. In R. Barr, M. Kamil, P. Mosenthal, & T. D. Pearson (Eds.), *Handbook of reading research* (pp. 490-511). New York: Longman.

Riel, M. M., Levin, J. A., & Miller-Souviney, B. (1987). Learning With Interactive Media: Dynamic Support for Students and Teachers. In R. W. Lawler & M. Yazdani (Eds.), *Artificial intelligence and education* (pp. 117-134). Norwood, NJ: Ablex.

Sharp, D. L., & McNamara, T. P. (1990). *Mental models in narrative comprehension: Now you see them; now you don't*. Paper presented at the meeting of the Psychonomic Society, New Orleans, LA.

Vygotsky, L. S. (1978). *Mind in society*. Cambridge, MA: Harvard University Press.

Ted S. Hasselbring & Laura I. Goin, Department of Special Education and Learning Technology Center, Peabody College, Vanderbilt University, Nashville, TN.

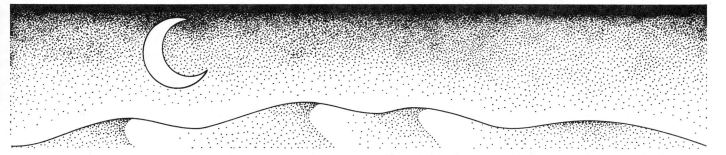

In Media Res: Sifting Through the Sands of Critical Thinking and Multimedia

Rose Reissman

Have you ever shared a video with your class that perfectly fit your curriculum, only to find that when you turned off the VHS, the key connections and sequential flow of the piece were lost on the students? Would you like to improve your students' critical viewing, peer interaction, and collaborative skills?

If so, consider this computer-centered critical thinking strategy using video.

First, select a video that relates to a subject theme —a history or science topic, for example—or a media version of a literary or nonfiction work. Next, reserve the computer lab and make certain that the word processing and drawing software students use is available. Divide students into teams of two to three, with a computer station for each team.

Explain to students that they will be viewing a video, but instead of starting at the beginning, the video will begin in the middle. Focus students' viewing toward anticipating *what came before* that point in the video—in other words, to anticipate the beginning of the story. Give them the opportunity to view the segment twice. Allow them sufficient time after the viewing to enter their ideas on the beginning of the video in note, paragraph, or visual form. Encourage students to focus on the events, actions, images, and/or narratives that might have preceded the segment.

After watching the 3- to 4-minute video segment, have students use the computer as an electronic notepad (or graphics pad) to jot down their ideas about what came before. Some students will want to use the drawing software available to sketch the images that they imagine preceded the segment. When students finish developing their verbal predictions and/or visual previews, encourage them to switch terminals in order to review and comment on the predictions of other teams. If desired, the "reviewer" teams may enter their responses on the monitor after the hypotheses.

Once students have returned to their own stations, explain that they have been involved in a media technology investigation called *In Media Res*, which means "in the midst of things." Tell students that writing or drawing what happened before a story or media piece begins is called a *prequel.* Allow them sufficient time (the rest of the period and another period if desired) to "flesh out" their prequel note/graphics files.

As a climax, allow students to see the video from the beginning. Have them compare and contrast the beginning with the one they created.

Out of the Sandbox and Into the Classroom

I used this strategy in two classrooms: a 5th/6th elementary class and a 10th grade English class. For the elementary students I chose *The Last Unicorn* by Peter Beagle; secondary students worked with Golding's *Lord of the Flies.* In both cases I was delighted with the way students approached this activity. After their initial viewing (they needed the additional review the first time around), they eagerly stood around each other's stations to comment on the prequel predictions.

> **In writing prequels, students are using technology and multimedia to promote critical thinking, predictive viewing, reading, and writing skills.**

During the actual screening, both groups of students smiled when their graphics "matched" the original story. Many elementary students felt that their graphics and narratives were "superior" to the original creation.

Tenth grade students compared and contrasted their prequel text with the actual beginning of *Lord of the Flies.* They then anticipated the sequel [or ending] of the book visually and verbally and compared their versions with the ending of the book. They also developed their own *In Media Res* projects to share with other high school English classes. The elementary group made an interactive "choose-your-own-ending" VHS slide show.

There are several benefits to this activity:

- It can be used in any grade 3-12 curriculum area.
- Students are using technology and multimedia to promote critical thinking, predictive viewing, reading, and writing skills.
- Including drawing software offers visual learners a visual literacy bridge to sequencing and writing skills.
- Through working in teams and critiquing each other's work, students have the opportunity to articulate their talents and gain recognition for their own unique learning styles.

Follow-Up Activities

- Have students add their personal reactions about the complete video to their In Media Res data disks.
- If graphics software is used, students may opt to storyboard the sequels to the screened excerpt. Or, they could develop a slide show and video transfer of their In Media Res slides. Video transfer increases the audience for students' projects, since copies of their tapes may be made for parent night, gallery shows, or to take home to share proudly with parents.
- Have students bring in and present excerpts from their favorite subject-related videos. Their classmates will be asked to develop various prequels to it.
- Encourage students to create a publication of student prequels/sequels using desktop publishing.

Off Computer Activities

- Have students write, illustrate, and storyboard prequels to a given media excerpt.
- Create a schoolwide In Media Res interactive multimedia exhibit of student projects.

Rose Reissman, Director, Writing Institute, Bay Terrace School of Business and Finance, PS 169Q, 18-25 212th St., Bayside, NY 11360.

The Other Half of Whole Language

Linda Polin

Suddenly the professor leapt forward toward the front row of students, grabbed a woman by the wrist, and pulled her to her feet. Then, pulling her backward and down, he laid her across his bent knee, stared out at each and all of us and began to howl. "Howl, howl, howl, howl! Oh, you are men of stones. Had I your tongues and eyes, I'd use them so that heaven's vault should crack." Frightened and transfixed, we stared back for the duration of the small moment of silence before he began to speak again, looking down at his dead Cordelia, "She's gone forever!"

Thus did Dr. Homer Swander teach us a valuable lesson: Shakespeare wrote plays, not novels. For the rest of that semester and in his modern theatre course, Dr. Swander reminded us of the difference between the stage and the page. In fact, midterm and final exams revolved around the planning and staging of a scene from the works under study. Productions were complete with costumes, props, blocking, and most important, a rationale for the decisions the student-troupe had made.

What's this got to do with whole language?

We tend to think of "whole language" in terms of its implications for reading and writing: a strong emphasis on the need for students to experience writing and reading in a variety of contexts and forms that are complete and meaningful. But "whole language" educators contend that speaking, listening, and observing (literacy models) are equally important to the development of literacy skills. And, rather than taking a sequential, developmental view, the "whole language" movement recognizes the developmental interdependence of reading, writing, speaking, and listening (Goodman, 1986). Language activities must also include speaking and hearing, performing and experiencing performance.

To have a strong opinion about the enactment of a literary work, a student must come to a deeper understanding of the meaning of the literature. The move from individual opinions to group consensus on those decisions should be accompanied by a rich discussion of that meaning and the support for particular interpretations. It is, in short, the kind of intellectual activity many English teachers seek for their students: small cooperative group work toward some final product—an activity that is at once emotional and intellectual, and certainly fun. It provides an alternative to essay writing and an opportunity for sustained oral language. It involves students in generating meaning.

Great stuff. But most students in high school or college literature classes do not bring with them recollections of live theatre or poetry readings. Although it is possible to organize a field trip to a local theatre for a matinee performance, most schools and school districts cannot afford the luxury of field trip transportation, compounded by the cost of theatre tickets. A few lucky districts or schools may find the means to provide a "poet-in-residence" program for their campuses. But what about the rest of us?

Fortunately, interactive multimedia technology can provide opportunities for our students to experience theatre and poetry as audio-visual productions. Perhaps with inspiration and our encouragement, they may be further motivated to generate their own productions of scenes or oral readings.

Interactive Multimedia Field Trips

Interactive multimedia is the buzzword used to describe any computer-based program for navigating a laser videodisc or CD ROM disc (CD ROM discs look like common audio compact discs but contain images as well as sounds). Not every laser videodisc program is an interactive multimedia package. There are two critical elements that determine whether a program can be called "interactive multimedia." First, a program must take advantage of multimedia. Multimedia means what it has always meant. It refers to the variety of presentation formats for information: film, stills, graphics, text, sound, animation, symbols. However, new technologies such as compact disc and laser videodisc make it possible to contain a variety of media in a single source. Thus a videodisc may contain any one or all of the formats listed above. Second, and most important, the "users" of the program must be able to interact with the multimedia through the choices they make in the program. This movement by choice through multimedia material is often described as "navigating." The computer software provides the navigation system or "interface" between the user and the multimedia storage device.

An excellent example of interactive multimedia is the Shakespeare Project, directed by Dr. Larry Friedlander of Stanford University (Friedlander, 1988; Miley, 1989). Using this program's tools, students can access videodisc players containing a variety of filmed versions of Hamlet, Lear, and MacBeth. For example, students may compare interpretations of Hamlet's interaction with Ophelia by contrasting a dark and moody Russian Hamlet with the seductive yet conflicted Hamlet of Nicol Williamson. Through the program students can quickly jump between identical scenes played by different actors. Students also have access to stage notes, diagrams, costuming information and choices, blocking, scripts, and something Friedlander calls *subtext*:

> Actors create an inner life for their characters by imagining the characters' basic assumptions, their goals and intentions, their feelings about the situation they are in and the people they are with. These decisions about the characters' inner life form the subtext of the interpretation, the level of feeling and motive operating beneath the text.

Students may add notes of their own and even "select" video clips that can be "attached" to an essay a student will write later. In short, the Shakespeare Project allows expert or novice students to study, design, and enjoy theater. The project familiarizes students with the entire process of theatrical creation—from finding an interpretation and a guiding concept to choosing appropriate designs to actually envisioning and executing the details of performance. Using the Shakespeare Project, students go beyond a mere reading of the text: They see a performance, study it in detail, interact with it, isolate and analyze its components, trace its processes, and make the play's world their own (Friedlander, 1988, p. 119).

Good News, Bad News
Okay, let's face it. The Shakespeare Project is an expensive one that required a lot of time, money, and people to complete. And, when projects such as these finally come to market they are very likely to be "big ticket" items that could gobble up too much of an always inadequate department or school budget. That's the bad news.

The good news is that it is possible for you and your students to do this at minimal cost, especially on the Macintosh computer, which includes much of the necessary software for creating your programs (i.e., free HyperCard). Increasingly, local music and video rental stores carry a number these videodiscs for sale, and there are often a few stores that are particularly well stocked in a variety of laserdisc titles. In addition, several education vendors offer videodiscs for educators. Bob Stein, president of The Voyager Company and a true film fanatic, has acquired the rights to move many classic films to videodisc for resale. The Voyager Company also sells a very affordable software package that works with HyperCard to select and organize the laserdisc images or scenes you wish to show.

Even without creating a program of your own, laserdisc player technology offers clear advantages over the VCR. For one thing, you can very quickly jump to exactly the spot in the film you wish to show. I know I wasted a lot of class time trying to find the segment I wanted on the VCR. Laserdiscs hold up much better than videotape to the wear and tear of repeated use and student handling. And, laserdisc players are affordable.

Authoring an interactive videodisc stack is harder for teachers than it is for students, mostly because students have less anxiety and more time. But, virtually no "programming" is required (with HyperCard or SuperCard) to generate a powerful stack. I have worked with small cooperative groups of high school English students (West High School, Torrance, CA) who polished off stacks on *The Grapes of Wrath* in a semester. This included voluntary appearances on Saturday mornings to get extra time with the scanner. Enroute and at completion, groups presented their stackware to the class, clearly proud of their work, deeply involved with their subject matter, and keenly aware of its relationship to the themes of the novel.

The Other Half of Whole Language
Obviously this is not a call to abandon books in favor of a "television" viewing of adulterated versions of stories, novels, plays, and poems. It is simply a reminder that an important element of language is the enjoyment of expressed meaning, speaking and listening, performing and experiencing performance. And, interactive multimedia technologies can provide manageable opportunities for students to experience this *other* half of whole language.

Linda G. Polin, Associate Professor of Education, Pepperdine University, Graduate School of Education and Psychology, 400 Corporate Pointe, Culver City, CA 90230-7627.

References
Friedlander, L. (1988). The Shakespeare project. In Ambron & Hooper (Eds.), *Interactive multimedia* (pp. 115-142). Redmond, WA: Microsoft Press.

Goodman, K. (1986). *What's whole in whole language?* Portsmouth, NH: Heinemann.

Miley, M. (1989). Multimedia: The inter-plays the thing. *MacUser, 5*(3), 111-113.

The Voyager Company, 1351 Pacific Coast Highway, Santa Monica, CA 90401.

Are You Ready for Interactive Videodisc?

Bernajean Porter

What's the difference between videotapes and videodiscs?

While both videotapes and laser videodiscs put images on the screen, there are three significant differences. First, information is coded on the surface of videotapes and must actually be touched by mechanical devices to decode its magnetic message; in the laser videodisc player, only a low-intensity laser beam ever comes into physical contact with the microscopic pits. Information is embedded inside the videodisc's plastic-coated platter. The physical contact of VCRs means that videotapes wear out after dozens of playings, while videodiscs can be played via laser beams indefinitely without a loss of quality of image or sound.

A second and more useful distinction is the difference in the way information is accessed. A VCR player can only decode information in a straight linear fashion, whereas the laserdisc player can access—at random and in seconds—any of tens of thousands of images. Using a remote control, users can search videodiscs by frame numbers, chapters, or time to find specific images in a matter of seconds.

Finally, videodiscs have two sound tracks. Although usually used for stereo, educational designers are finding creative uses for these sound tracks. For example, one audio channel might carry an English sound track while the other carries Spanish, Russian, or Japanese. One channel might contain the natural sounds of the video, while the other channel narrates the picture. One channel might contain audio instructions for adults with the other delivering simpler instructions on the same subject for a younger audience. Or imagine the creative use of these two channels to deliver the actual words of a Shakespeare play on one audio track with the actor's interior self-monologue on the other audio track. This inside peek at an actor's craft is something a printed play or videotape could not do.

How does the hand-held remote work on a laserdisc player?

A remote control can be purchased with most videodisc players on the market. It has some familiar features such as scanning forward and reverse, pausing, and stopping. The remote control also lets a user "still" or

---

Software is available for teachers and students to make their own barcode labels to customize textbooks, presentations, and reports, and to publish their own multimedia books.

"freeze" the video frame (generally only the CAV formatted discs). With the "step" control, a user can move forward or backward, one frame at a time through either still photographs or "frozen" film frames. The two audio channels can be controlled by using both in stereo or choosing a single channel while using the videodisc. The audio and video tracks can be controlled by turning them on/off while playing the videodisc. Finally, the remote control has a keypad to search for specific video "addresses" either by frame number, chapter number, or time. For example, using a hand-held remote control, System Impact's *Fractions* videodisc lets a teacher use one disc, laserdisc player, and monitor to deliver whole class instruction on fractions.

What is the barcode system for laserdisc players?

Barcodes are familiar to anyone who goes grocery shopping. Those familiar black and white stripes, used to support cost-inventory management systems, appear on everything from chicken pot pies to Bigg Mixx. The barcode magic wand now is available with laserdisc players as a new tool in the classroom. When a reader, learner, or teacher encounters a laser barcode within the text of a book, a wand-like barcode reader is passed over it to call up a corresponding sound, still, or moving picture to the color monitor.

Silver-Burdett just released a new Science Videodisc series with barcoding in their textbooks that helps learners gather information beyond the printed word. Software also is available for teachers and students to make their own barcode labels to customize textbooks, presentations, and reports, and to publish their own multimedia books.

What is the difference between the CLV and CAV videodisc formats?

Audio and visual data can be etched onto a laser videodisc in one of two formats: CLV or CAV. Both formats are useful, but only the second format presently unlocks the videodisc's extraordinary potential as an instructional tool.

Constant Linear Velocity (CLV). This format stores the information in a linear straight-line mode also called "extended play." On most videodisc players, CLV discs are watched straight through like a videotape. CLV discs are organized by time; minutes and seconds mark the "address" of the information. Sometimes CLV discs are organized into chapters, like a book. The user can search a disc by time or chapter. CLV does not have the ability to "step" (move through images one frame at a time) or "freeze frame" (stop the image like a snapshot). Note: Some very expensive videodisc players will allow you to still a CLV frame. However, schools generally are not using this high-end industrial player. CLV discs are typically less expensive, ranging from $19.95 to $49 per disc.

Constant Angular Velocity (CAV). This format stores each image of information by frame numbers. There are 54,000 frames of images on one side of a disc. Each image has an "address" number that allows the laser beam in the videodisc player to zip directly from one information storage area to another, skipping as need be over thousands of tracks in less than three seconds. Not only can the user find pictures on videodiscs quickly, but they can string together different video clips and have them appear in rapid succession no matter how far apart they are recorded on the videodisc. CAV discs typically are more expensive, ranging from $99 to $1200, depending on the amount of programming, instructional design, and curriculum support.

Although it is possible with high-end laserdisc players and special commercial authoring software to use CLV videodiscs for interactive lessons, CAV videodiscs dominate the marketplace and our classrooms.

What are the "levels" of videodisc use?

Levels 0 through 5 are used to describe the level of user interactivity and control of the videodisc. The higher the level, the more interactivity that is possible for the user.

Simply having a videodisc and laser disc player does not necessarily imply interactivity. Home entertainment laserdiscs (generally CLV) and players,

for example, talk of "Level 0" —you just turn on the machine and it plays a disc from start to finish.

Level 1 generally applies to instruction created with a laserdisc player connected to a color monitor while using a hand-held remote or barcode reader to access specific videoclips. Both CLV and CAV discs may be accessed by searching for frames, chapters, or time. *Fractions* (System Impact), *Windows on Science* (Optical Data), and *English Express* (Davidson & Associates) are examples of Level 1 use.

Level 2 uses laserdisc players with a microchip inside to specifically read programmed "stops" and "branched" choices on the videodiscs. This level is quite common in many commercial training applications.

Level 3 generally refers to a laserdisc player connected to a separate microcomputer and screen. This is the level for which many publishers are now developing products. *Animal Pathfinders* (Scholastic), *The Holy Land* (ABC News), and *Race to Save the Planet* (Scholastic) exemplify this level.

Levels 4 and 5 refer to the integration of artificial intelligence into the coding of the program. Few Level 4 and 5 applications are used in public education. They are used primarily in military and industrial training settings—for example, in a flight simulation for training pilots.

With the advent of barcode readers and new developments in laser optics, the distinction among levels is becoming less defined. The key questions to ask are: How interactive is the videodisc software? and What equipment do you need to use the instructional material you want to include?

What about "repurposing" and authoring?

Repurposing occurs when teachers or students use archival or generic topic discs to create their own lessons, presentations, or projects. Authoring software tools such as Hypercard,

Hyperstudio, Tutor Techware, and others allow users to customize and package their own knowledge with appropriate video clips from CAV videodiscs found in the marketplace.

A few recent videodisc programs like *The Holy War* contain built-in software tools for students to resequence their video and audio data into personalized documentaries or presentations.

Although some energetic teachers may find creating their own visual lessons worthwhile, it is a time-consuming task. More promising is a new role for teachers in creating the environment and the opportunity for students to use interactive videodisc as a creative tool as they work cooperatively to construct their own understandings using primary-source video, text, and sound. The project can culminate in a multimedia research presentation or video documentary.

Are there further resources you would recommend?

1. **1990 Guidelines for Computer-Interactive Videodisc.** The California Department of Education published an evaluation form for reviewing and purchasing computer-interactive videodiscs, including a section on consumer awareness issues and purchasing considerations.

2. **The Videodisc Monitor.** (P.O. Box 26, Falls Church, VA 22046-9990; 703/241-1799). This publication will keep you up to date with this industry.

3. **Catalogues listing educational videodiscs:**
   - Laser Learning Technologies (800/722-3505).
   - Emerging Technologies (612/639-3973).
   - Z-Tek (800/247-1603).

Bernajean Porter, Senior Partner, The Confluence International Group.

The Multimedia Essay *or* Designing is Thinking

Linda Polin

Let's call him Tom; it doesn't matter what his name is. You know him. He sits at the back of the room in sixth period, slouching, clothed in black, in one of two moods: truculent or vacant. Often he isn't there, and you don't miss him.

One semester last year I watched Tom find personal value in studying English literature. His class was almost through reading Steinbeck's *Grapes of Wrath* when the teacher asked students to work in groups of three or four to create an interactive multimedia presentation on the book. The groups were free to make their own meaning and purpose for the task. Tom's group got very involved with two ideas: parallels in society today and deeper exploration of the times in which the story took place. The students divided up the task by choosing things they were personally interested in researching. Tom volunteered to "get some art."

The second week of the project Tom came to class carrying a stack of art volumes up to his chin, each volume aflutter with torn paper bookmarkers. He cornered the teacher and with great exuberance narrated an impromptu display of the work of a number of Depression era artists. He flipped to pictures of murals depicting workers and described in considerable detail the nature and purpose of public art works commissioned under the WPA. Over the next several days he also composed his own artwork for the project, loyal to the style he had found in the artwork he studied. It turns out Tom is a very talented artist; he loves to draw and paint.

As the group moved toward compilation of their work into a single presentation, Tom encountered limitations of space and the need to "connect" with the work and purposes of his partners. I saw him suffer the decision of what to leave in and what to exclude. His teacher helped by encouraging him to base his decisions on a set of criteria and on the power of the selections to represent his ideas. Tom returned to the text and to discussions of the text with his peers, finding meaning in one medium through meaning he could understand in another. Through his interest in art,

---

I have seen students labeled "reluctant," or worse, bombard their teachers with demands for time and access to equipment to work on their projects after school, before school, and on Saturdays. It is not simply a matter of wanting to play with cool toys; these students are hooked by the power of their own production of knowledge.

Tom made a connection to literature and began to experience literature as an expressive art form in another medium.

Over the last three years I have sat in numerous high school English classrooms sharing teachers' excitement at the duration and depth of their students' interest in composing interactive multimedia essays and the quality of the analysis and discussion overheard among student partners. I have seen students labeled "reluctant," or worse, bombard their teachers with demands for time and access to equipment to work on their projects after school, before school, and on Saturdays. It is not simply a matter of wanting to play with cool toys; these students are hooked by the power of their own production of knowledge.

What is an Interactive Multimedia Essay?

Interactive multimedia is a hybrid concept born of two parents: hypertext and multimedia (in fact, some people use the expression hypermedia). The term "hypertext" refers to an environment and format for writing that allows for non-linear as well as linear organizations of text. Connections can be made hierarchically (from abstractions to details) or laterally (from detail to detail or abstraction to abstraction). Non-linear organization of text is accomplished by providing active links or "buttons" that take the reader from one section of text to another that the author has decided is related in some fashion and which may or may not be contained in the same document. So, for example, it might be possible to jump from a line in T.S. Eliot's *The Hollow Men* to a section of prose in Conrad's *Heart of Darkness*, or from a section of a student's essay remarking on the relationship between these two works to sections of the works themselves. The description of hypertext-like environments has been around since 1945; however, only recently has it been possible for people like us to create and experience hypertext using computer "authoring" software or pre-programmed packages.

Computers paired with computer-based technologies such as CD-ROM, video laserdisc, and sound and image digitizers make it possible to expand the variety of media among which links are made. Instead of forging links only between sections of text, we can now link text with sounds, images, or graphics. For example, it is possible to link the line from the Eliot poem and the prose selection from Conrad to a particular scene from Coppola's classic film, available on videodisc, *Apocalypse Now*. And, we can import our own drawings, sounds, animations, and graphics into the hypertext environment, much like Tom imported his own drawings into his group's *Grapes of Wrath* essay.

There is one more element to add to this concept of multiple linkages among a variety of media: interactivity. This refers to the deliberate inclusion of choices for the "reader" in the multimedia essay. Choices can be as subtle as whether or not to view an available link, or as substantial as deciding which pathway of connections in an essay to follow. For example, we can skip over Coppola if we want to. Alternatively, we can follow a conceptually "lateral" pathway away from the common themes represented in these works by Conrad and Eliot to examine other works by T.S. Eliot—a view of *The Love Song of J. Alfred Prufrock*, for example. Our choices are only limited by the choices built in to the interactive multimedia program we are viewing, and by our own interests. Perhaps because of the freedom of choice accorded the multimedia audience, "readers" are often referred to as "browsers" and their interaction is described as "browsing."

Designing is Thinking

Designing and constructing interactive multimedia presentations is as much a matter of composing as is the construction of a piece of writing. And, like writing, designing is thinking. Many educators have suggested that knowledge, as distinguished from information, can be more usefully thought of as design (Dunn & Larson, 1990; Perkins, 1986), the distinction being that when knowledge is connected to purpose, it transforms from static information to active application of understanding.

When deeply engaged in the composing process, students encounter "problems" that actually serve as opportunities to deepen and extend their understanding of the topic about which they are writing. In interactive multimedia compositions, these problems are at once more engaging for students and more complex. Consider, for example, decisions about media itself. What is the best representational format for an idea? Should the "reader" view a scene from *Apocalypse Now* and see the text of the parallel scene from *Heart of Darkness*, or should both be presented in text format with a hypertext link to commentary on the thematic and symbolic parallels? I have not yet seen a student who is not drawn into a deeper interaction with the subject matter by the opportunity to work in a variety of media, literally creating meaning by building connections among ideas and sharing that thinking with peers

---

The Nine Official Guidelines for HyperCard Stack Design*

1. Decide who your users are.
2. Decide what the subject is and what it is not.
3. Decide how to present the subject matter to your users.
4. Make your stack easy to navigate.
5. Introduce people to your stack.
6. Integrate text, graphic design, and audio design.
7. Plan on changing your stack several times.
8. Test early, test often, and listen to your reviewers.
9. When you're finished, check the stack one last time.

*(Apple Computer Inc., 1989)

Figure 1

---

through a multimedia essay.

Composition in multimedia shares many characteristics with composition of more traditional writing. The author must have ideas, represent them in some form, and organize and make connections among those ideas to accomplish some communicative purpose. Consider these guidelines for stack design. Substitute the word "audience" for "users" and "essay" for "stack" and the guidelines read like advice to student writers (see Fig. 1).

All That Glitters is Not Gold

Since Apple Computer introduced HyperCard in 1987, there has been increasing excitement about the educational potential of interactive multimedia. Products of two sorts have appeared in the marketplace: tools and educational products. The difference between them parallels a difference in beliefs about pedagogy and the nature of learning, and the educational role of interactive multimedia.

"Tools" are consonant with the view that knowledge is actively constructed by the learner. The Voyager Company's audio and video programs, for example, facilitate this experience by allowing the user to examine and build links between ideas and information represented in a variety of formats. Tools are content-free and structure-free; the user supplies the ideas and makes the connections.

On the other hand, most interactive multimedia "educational products" are "closed systems" of subject matter information in a variety of formats (often with an accompanying videodisc) with a fixed set of pathways to explore, representing strands or themes in the topic. Although the better of the "canned" packages include a toolkit for constructing additional pathways or reorganizing material, you are still limited to manipulating the material included in the package. You cannot, for example, access other video material or incorporate your own sounds, images, or text. (Scholastic's history package, *Point of View*, is a notable exception.)

"Canned" products make interesting teacher presentation materials and resources for student research, but often are the functional equivalent of textbooks. These packages present you with the completed construction of someone else's understanding of a particular topic. In contrast, open interactive hypertext environments with multimedia tools are the functional equivalent of blank pages. They carry no content but encourage users to construct representations of their own understandings. I believe interactive multimedia is most interesting as a sort of student workspace, not as a teacher presentation tool.

A Gentle Introduction with MediaText

Elliot Soloway, from the University of Michigan, has created an elegant, illustrated text processor called "MediaText." Short-sighted people who encounter MediaText will bemoan its lack of full hypertext multimedia features. Clever people will realize that its ease of use and multimedia functions make MediaText a perfect transitional experience for writers to explore multimedia expression of ideas. It is not a hypertext program in that it does not allow you to construct a variety of interconnected pathways among material. It does allow you one-step links between sections of text in a single document and files containing other documents or media formats.

MediaText allows the writer to do three things: write a text document, create "buttons" that activate a variety of media displays, and conceptually link those buttons to a section of the text by strategically placing them in a column that runs alongside the text. MediaText has simple menus for creating buttons that will do any of the following actions: bring up graphics or animations, find and run a section of video from a laserdisc player, find and display images or play sounds from a CD ROM player, play digitized sound recorded by the writer, display images or drawings scanned in by the writer, or open other documents. MediaText menus make it easy for the writer to create buttons that perform these kinds of tasks; the writer is limited only by equipment hooked up to the computer.

MediaText is an important package because it bridges the move between "word-processed" text as readers and writers have experienced it and interactive multimedia essays as described in this column. We still see on the screen the familiar flow of text: top to bottom, left to right. Familiar writing structures, like paragraphs and titles, still exist. However, the writer's palette now includes not just colorful written language but visual and auditory colors gathered from other sources or crafted by the writer. With MediaText the writer creates active, illustrated text.

The software is mercifully simple to learn and use. I spent 20 minutes with it at a recent conference and had no trouble, despite having neither a manual nor Elliot nearby. Dr. Soloway will be giving away a version of Media-Text at the NECC conference in Phoenix this June, and hopefully soon an affordable upgraded version will be available at a later date from a company to be announced. [Note: Media-Text is available for Macintosh and MS DOS systems.]

Linda G. Polin, Associate Professor of Education, Pepperdine University, Graduate School of Education and Psychology, 400 Corporate Pointe, Culver City, CA 90230-7627.

References

Apple Computer, Inc. (1989). *Hyper-Card stack design guidelines*. Palo Alto, CA: Addison-Wesley.

Dunn, S., & Larson, R. (1990). *Design technology: Children's engineering*. New York: Falmer Press.

Perkins, D. (1986). *Knowledge as design*. Hillsdale, NJ: Lawrence Erlbaum.

Soloway, E. (1991). *MediaText* [Computer program]. Ann Arbor, MI: Department of Electrical Engineering and Computer Science, University of Michigan.

The Voyager Company. 1351 Pacific Coast Hwy., Santa Monica, CA 90401.

MEASLES ARE A PAIN

Measles here, measles there.
Look at my measles everywhere!
Up my nose, inside my feet.
There's measle in my meat!
They spread quickly, they spread fast.
I think these measles are gonna last!
Maybe I got them from a squid.

Look! I found a measle kid!
How did I get them? Where? And why?
I bet they fell right from the sky.
So take my advice, show you care...
"Ouch, ouch, eeck!"
I just scratched a measle in my hair.

Swi, grade 3, Ponderosa Elementary

MindMapping Whole Media

John Boeschen

> **From clustered brainstorms to finely tuned classroom presentations, words remain the basic unit of expression. Whole media presentations are only as good as the words students use to give meaning to their thoughts and ideas.**

Yalcin had been in this country less than five months. His passive English was strong, but his active verbal skills were weak. Writing was a chore for him. Watching the thirteen-year-old try to put a few sentences on paper flashed me back to a frustrating and all too frequent situation I had experienced in my college days. On cold, wet mornings, the only hope of starting up my battered MG was to hand-crank it into life. CPR for a car. Sometimes it worked, but most of the time I had to hitch a ride into campus from a roommate.

More than once, I had observed Yalcin sputter into life like my old MG. He would push two disjointed sentences in the neighborhood of each other, then sit back at his desk and hitch a ride with a daydream to places far removed from his paper and pencil.

Adding Sights and Sounds to Words

On this particular Wednesday morning, Yalcin's sputter caught and transformed itself into a fine little purr. He was running on all four cylinders and the words were flowing. Two novel events had cleared the path for Yalcin's words:

1. He had just learned how to make his own video production with Apple Computer's videodisc *The Visual Almanac,* and,

2. He was recording his reactions to the movie he had just created in clustered form. A Macintosh computer helped him both to control the video production and to cluster his thoughts.

Yalcin was one of several non-English speaking eighth graders in a San Rafael, California, ACOT (Apple Classroom of Tomorrow) test site. One objective of the test site was to observe the impact of hi tech on a cross section of students from diverse ethnic and sociological backgrounds. I was in Yalcin's classroom as an independent developer beta testing a new Macintosh software product called **MindMap**. Yalcin was using **MindMap** to cluster his thoughts.

What's in a Word

As I watched Yalcin, I had a rare (for me) insight: With a computer mated to a videodisc and a CD-ROM player, kids could just as easily cluster sights and sounds to express their thoughts as they could cluster words alone. Mix together the three media—sights, sounds, words—in the same cluster or map, and that map becomes the foundation for a multimedia event.

Two converging roots make up the word multimedia: multiple and media. Multiple media. Whatever hi tech definition you care to associate with the term, at its heart, multimedia is simply two or more media working in concert to enrich an idea or concept. For example, blaring trumpets set the mood for a sophomore's history report on Charlemagne. Video images of Martin Luther King in Selma, Alabama, enhance a presentation on civil rights. A medley of sounds from wind instruments (spliced together from a CD of Herb Albert tunes) sparks a class discussion on the physics of making music. Sounds and images can rivet attention to our words and add both clarity and texture.

Teamwork

The very nature of multimedia—a collection of resources weighted toward different learning styles—makes it a rich environment for collaborative teamwork. When organizing students into teams, try to match individual student learning styles with the media in which they will be working. Imagine a writing project that links together video, sound, and graphics. Assign to the team at least one member who has strong verbal skills. This individual can be put in charge of gathering information from the library and other resources. A student who is spatially oriented becomes the group's graphic artist and computer screen designer. Kids with an auditory bent become managers of sound selection and use. Technically adept students oversee the proper use of the hardware, capturing video images and sounds with the computer keyboard and mouse.

Whole Media

Cognitive styles aren't as cut and dried as I've portrayed them in the previous paragraph. Nor are the tasks involved in multimedia writing projects so clear cut. Yet, with a balance of learning styles matched to media events, team members do become actively involved in group work. Sharing their insights and findings with each other sets the stage for group problem solving, too. Learning to identify problems and to seek solutions for those problems, then to analyze the possible solutions and to fine tune them into a finished report are higher order thinking skills that can flourish in a group environment.

The importance of sharing-response groups to whole language arts is well documented in journals and conference papers. The sharing and critiquing of information among members of multimedia writing projects is equally important. Keeping in mind the centrality of writing to multimedia, it's not a great stretch of the imagination to view whole media writing as a subset of a whole language arts program.

Whole Media Across the Curriculum

Whole media follows writing across the curriculum. The use of animation, sound, and video is appropriate to all subjects, from producing a report on twentieth century Canadian artists to a presentation on nineteeth century British politics to a scientific critique on the effects of industrial pollution in the upper atmosphere.

The most eclectic of educational videodiscs is *The Visual Almanac*, designed and produced by Apple's Multimedia Lab and distributed by Optical Data, Inc. The images and sounds on the disc are appropriate for grades K-12 and most subject areas (doubt my word only after you've experienced the disc). Each side of the videodisc holds 54,000 individual images with two separate sound tracks. An amazing collection of information.

When Yalcin got the media bug, he was playing with images on *The Visual Almanac*. At the time, *MindMap*, the software clustering tool he was using to record his experiences, did not have the tools necessary to link videodisc images to his thoughts. Now, *MindMap* with CD and video support does exist, enabling students to associate sounds and images directly to an idea or to individual words or phrases in that idea.

Repurposing with a Purpose

The process of linking images and sounds from videodiscs into presentations is called "repurposing." The videodisc a student uses as a source of images for a report on the circulatory system, for example, may have been designed for student nurses. Its original purpose was as a training tool, not as a repository

of images for a high school student. But, with the proper technology, that high school student can use the videodisc for a purpose not intended or foreseen by its original designers. (During repurposing, no physical changes occur on the disc itself).

Just as videodisc images can be repurposed, so can the sounds on CDs. The video tools in *MindMap* allow students to edit video clips to single frame accuracy (for a still image or for the exact beginning and ending points of a motion clip). CD sounds can be edited down to a single block, the smallest unit on a CD (75 blocks make up one second of CD sound). Such precision empowers kids to repurpose visual and auditory media with professional accuracy.

Videodiscs and CDs are available commercially for whole media presentations. The most comprehensive guide to educational videodiscs is the *Videodisc Compendium* published by Emerging Technology Consultants, Inc. (P.O. Box 12444, St. Paul, MN 55112; ph. 612-639-3973). The current compendium lists over 800 titles. Although videodiscs are just now finding their way into catalogs and publisher lists, the number of CDs on the market is expansive. The sounds on any CD you pull off a record store shelf can be repurposed by students into reports and presentations. For a listing of educational CDs, check out the *CD-ROM Shoppers Guide*, a quarterly publication from DDRI, Inc. (510 N. Washington St., Suite 401, Falls Church, VA 22046-3537; ph. 703-237-0682).

One Word More

Computers, videodisc, CD-ROM players . . . regardless of the hardware your students work with, at the heart of whole media creations is the writing process. From clustered brainstorms to finely tuned classroom presentations, words remain the basic unit of expression.

Before computers could orchestrate the sights and sounds on CDs and videodiscs, students were generally content to embellish the words of their reports with line drawings, photocopies, and photographs. Now they have multiple media. But if words don't reflect their thoughts, it's unlikely that any other media will add the needed clarity. Whole media presentations are only as good as the words students use to give meaning to their thoughts and ideas.

By the way, since discovering whole media and clustering, Yalcin and his classmates have graduated to high school. In their new school, they have been given a unique role in curriculum development—they are working with seniors to develop a multimedia science curriculum for incoming freshman. Yalcin's classmates supply computer and whole media expertise while the upperclass students provide the appropriate content. Writing, whole media, and collaborative learning cut across both curricula and age boundaries. And, as Yalcin and his cohorts could tell you, it's nice to be a freshman with friends in the senior class.

John Boeschen, 25 Valley View Drive, San Rafael, CA 94901.

*For more information on **MindMap** and **MindMap** with CD and video support, contact William K. Bradford Publishing Company, 310 School St., Acton, MA 01720; ph. 1-800-421-2009.*

The *MindMap* Process

Figure 1. The start of a map for a twentieth century timeline. Students brainstorm ideas on a blank map to create their clusters. Any number of ideas can be created, linked, and moved to different locations on the screen using the tools provided by **MindMap**. Students can copy and paste ideas into other maps as well.

Figure 2. Each idea a student creates has an insides similar to this screen. Clicking on an idea in a map opens up that idea to its insides. Once inside an idea, students add text to support that idea. From the text, they can create key words to highlight important concepts. They also can link the idea and individual words and phrases within the idea to sounds, images, and other maps and applications.

Figure 3. The map in Figure 1 has been refined into a timeline using **MindMap**'s built-in graphic tools. Clicking on each idea plays the sounds and displays the images students have linked to the idea. If the idea has been linked to another map or application, **MindMap** goes to that map or application. This type of whole media report (words, sounds, images) lends itself to presentations given before a classroom.

Figure 4. **MindMap**'s Report maker screen. Ideas from maps are listed automatically in the left window. Clicking on an idea places it in the right hand window, where it forms part of the printed report. Ideas can be selected in any order from the left window to create a report. Reports can be printed in outline format or with full text. Printing can be done directly from **MindMap** or reports can be exported to programs such as MacWrite II or PageMaker for further enhancements.

Figure 5. **MindMap**'s Key word and phrase index. As students create ideas, those ideas are added automatically in alphabetical order to the index. Any key words and phrases created within ideas also are added to the index. Clicking on an index listing takes the user to the idea in which the key word or phrase appears. Students also may do straight text searches from this screen for words that are not in the index.

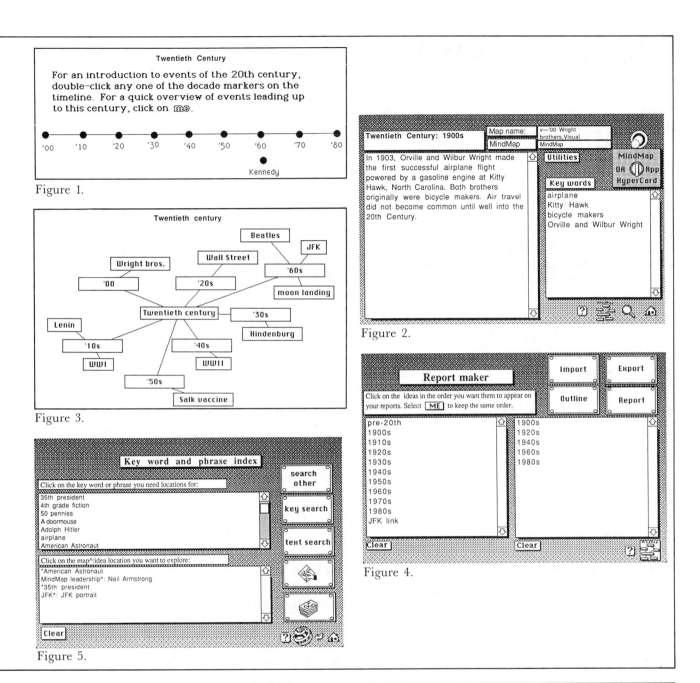

Figure 1.

Figure 2.

Figure 3.

Figure 4.

Figure 5.

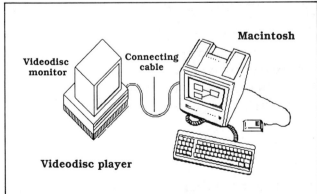

Figure 6. A basic whole media system showing all the components except the CD-ROM player.

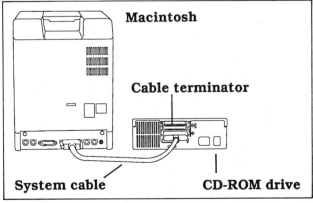

Figure 7. Connecting a CD-ROM player to a Macintosh.

Student Poetry

Lies

She doesn't know me.

Her eyes still see a child,
safely kept, protected by
her silent values. Yet, I know she
feels the undercurrents.

She doesn't understand me.
But when could she have learned?
I've left her always in the dark.
Conversations tell her life is "fine,"
while phone calls with friends fill
hours with crisis. Even drunken
strangers see a truer picture.

She loves me.
I long for the courage to shatter
her painted dreams, but I fear
only our friendship and her
wishing heart will break.
I'm torn between my
painful lies and
life's painful
truths.

by Lorie Feldenberg

For Two Men and a Lake

This lake is as small as a step across
unless I'm off the dock. Then it stretches
deep and wide, full of swimmers,
souls; fish ready to kiss my ankles.

When I was four, my father flung me
water-ward,
crying swim! for him,
I beat against the aqua tiles and lived.

For you, I dive down,
loving this lake as I do my father,
wrap seaweed in my hands, and rip the
bottom up.
All it holds, I give you:
plants, possible pearls, mud,
and the toys children let drown.

by Juliet Feibel

the basics of loving

you call on me
hours into my dreams
and i
loving you
spread darkness
on your eyelids,
and numbness
on your bones
i am the giver
of smoothness
hunting the ripples
that break the night
i am the safe clean lines
of daylight
that stay solid
when blackness fills your room

by Karen Sherman

US 1

If you'll come with me
now, while the sun is still
low behind the trees
like a prisoner behind steel
bars, and the air still chilled
and sharp,

to where the trees end
in a line, corralled and held out
by a fence that pulls forever,
and the brown grass covers
the dusty bluff
over the interstate

you can see for yourself
and fear for your own.
Or stand with me,
at the road's shoulder
and read the answers
in a broken carcass

and bones. Lost men
on twisted odysseys
clot traffic on the highway.
You can watch them creep past,
the shells of insects smeared
on tempered glass,

and choke in their exhaust.

by Andrew Haber

Reprinted with permission from *Crescendo*, a student publication of Horton Watkins High School, Ladue, Missouri.

236

CHAPTER 6
RESEARCH AND WRITING

There are a number of very important irreversibles to be discovered in our universe. One of them is that every time you make an experiment you learn more: Quite literally, you cannot learn less.

—Buckminster Fuller

The Absence of Research in Writing and Technology: What Questions Should We Be Asking?

William J. Hunter

In previous columns I have reviewed some of the available literature dealing with the use of different technologies in the teaching of writing and have commented on some studies in depth. As part of the work I do in preparing these columns, I have an online ERIC search conducted each month so that I can be aware of as much research as possible. I am always amazed at how little these searches find. Part of the problem is that I am always looking at a very short time span and only for publications indexed by ERIC. Still, I always find myself disappointed. This time I've decided to focus my attention on the absence of research.

The use of technological aids to writing is relatively new. With that newness there has been a sense of excitement and adventure, high expectations for marvelous improvements in writing quality, and a thirst for information about successful innovations. In the early 1980s, many classroom teachers shared their successes and their visions. Later in that decade, reviewers of empirical studies, myself included, found little hard evidence that the quality of children's writing improved when they used word processors. My students and I (Hunter, Jardine, Rilstone, & Weisberger, 1990) speculated about ways in which the body of research was deficient. In the first of these columns, I suggested reasons why the lack of results ought not be discouraging, but I think the enthusiasm has diminished and the expectations have begun to drop for, as a respected colleague recently said in an e-mail note to me, "I've stopped paying attention to computers in writing; after all, they are only tools." Yes, they are only tools. But does this mean that we should cease to be excited about what these tools can help us to accomplish? The Hubble telescope, after all, is only a tool.

I fear that what I see happening is one more iteration in the cycle of educational innovation. Characteristically, educators become excited about the potential of new methods and tools, small numbers of enthusiasts become committed change agents, and persuasive speakers and writers arouse the curiosity of large numbers of teachers. As an innovation spreads and gains acceptance, it is found to be less effective for the general population of teachers than it was for the committed pioneers. Research studies may show modest results overall; often the former innovation is understood to be part of the way some teachers like to teach, but not something that warrants widespread support or enthusiasm. I fear that technography is approaching such a downturn in interest.

While this dismays me, it does not depress me. I have recently had reason to reflect on all of the arguments I used to hear about how educational computing would be another flash in the pan like educational television. It seems to be taken for granted that educational television was a major flop. I am not convinced. The increasing availability of inexpensive yet powerful camcorders makes it much more likely that video can be used in schools as a form of creative expression. The growth of multimedia presentations has reinvigorated both educational computing and educational television. Far from being dead, educational television may be just entering its prime; perhaps technography also may be in the lull before the storm.

Let's take that as a working hypothesis. People will use word processing whether schools teach it or not. Word processors and their companion aids have made it big in the real world as productivity tools. In 10 or 15 years, input devices will have changed markedly and processing features may be refined, expanded, and improved, but in any case computing technologies will play a major role in much of what is committed to paper (or diskette or memory chip). Like television, technography may re-emerge with new educational potential in a world in which it is taken for granted. Here's the kind of research that we will need when that time comes.

Descriptive Research

For starters, we need some good *descriptive research*. How many teachers use word processors for their own writing? How many use them to prepare teaching materials? How many use them in the classroom? How do they use them in the classroom? What reasons do they give for this use? How many teachers allow/encourage/expect/require students to submit word processed documents? Do teachers give advice or assistance to students regarding ways in which they can use the text-handling features of a word processor to make both cosmetic and substantive changes in word choice, sentence ordering, paragraphing, sentence structure, and so on? Does any of the preceding differ according to grade level or subject taught? If so, do teachers have explanations for these differences? What benefits or problems do teachers attribute to the use of word processors? What stumbling blocks do teachers believe prevent them from using them in their teaching? What word processing features do teachers/students find most useful and why? Do students think they write more or better when they use word processors? Do teachers think students write more or better when they use word processors? What use is made of outliners, spelling checkers, style checkers, or other writing aids? Do students value such aids? Do teachers? What benefits do they expect/find when they use such aids? How frequently is telecommunication explicitly used as part of writing instruction? How much administrative support is there for innovative uses of writing technologies? How much parental interest and/or support? The list could go on.

Correlational Research

We need good *correlational research*. What variables predict teachers' attitudes toward technological aids to writing? What variables correlate with the amount of use teachers make of word processors or other writing software? What gender differences exist among teachers and students with respect to attitudes toward technological aids to writing, use of writing aids, or success in using them? What student groups will benefit most from the use of writing aids? What word processor characteristics correlate most closely with successful use by teachers

and students? Is the use of word processors associated with better achievement in writing or in other academic skills? Does students' enthusiasm for word processing correlate with the quality of their writing? Does the amount of time spent teaching the use of word processors predict either students' level of use or improvements in the length or quality of their written work? To what degree is students' enjoyment of reading (their own work or others') related to their success in writing (with or without technological aids)? And so on.

Qualitative Research

We need *qualitative research*. Exactly what does a student *do* when using a word processor? How does this differ (if at all) from what they do when they compose using pen and paper? What do student writers think about their document while they're producing it? What kinds of changes do students actually make at various points as they write and what prompts them to make those changes? To what extent, if any, are limitations in typing skill an impediment to successful use of word processors? Do students use the ''guess'' feature in spelling checkers and if so, how? How much editing (and what kind) gets done on screen and how much on hard copy? What difference does that make? Does the use of technological aids support or undermine attempts to use cooperative learning techniques? How important is a printed copy to different ages and types of writers? What effect does word processing have on the ways students talk about writing? What meaning and/or value do students or teachers

assign to the use of technological aids to writing?

Experimental Questions

And, of course, there are *experimental questions* like ''Do students who regularly use spelling checkers perform better on tests of spelling than students who do not?'' or ''Does explicit instruction in the use of large scale editing features (like moving a block of text) result in significantly more such changes appearing in students' writing?'' Traditionally, researchers have strongly favored questions of this type because they could lead to relatively strong statements about causal relationships, but I believe many experimental studies have been carried out prematurely in fields in which the state of the art is not well known, which is certainly the case for technography.

I always tell my graduate students that coming up with the questions is the hard part of research. Now that I've given you a head start, I expect to see your name on a future ERIC search.

———————————

William J. Hunter, Director, Education Technology Unit, 836 Education Tower, The University of Calgary, Calgary, Alberta T2N 1N4, Canada.

Reference

Hunter, W. J., Jardine, G., Rilstone, P., & Weisgerber, R. (1990). The effects of using word processors: A hard look at the research. *The Writing Notebook, 8*(1), 42-46.

The Effects of Using Word Processors: A Hard Look at the Research

William J. Hunter, Gail Jardine, Peter Rilstone, & Roslyn Weisgerber

One need only glance at an issue of *The Writing Notebook* to see that there is tremendous interest in and enthusiasm for the use of word processors in the teaching of writing. In our geographic area, this trend has been endorsed by the provincial department of education, which has made word processing a mandatory part of the junior high language arts curriculum and has prepared an inservice leaders' handbook to provide support for professional development activities (Alberta Education, 1988). Under these circumstances, it is highly appropriate to ask whether such changes in curriculum and instructional methods are supported by research findings. In attempting to answer this question, we and our colleagues (Hunter et al., 1988) found ourselves overwhelmed by the amount of information available and by the subsidiary questions that arose as we started our investigation. We found it necessary first of all to develop a working model of the writing process (Hunter & Begoray, 1990) and to address what many teachers and administrators see as a prior question—the role of keyboarding (Hunter, Benedict, & Bilan, 1989). Still, when we turned our attention to our original question: Does the use of word processors improve children's writing?, we found that we must still address other questions. What role do students' attitudes play in determining the impact of word processing? How can improvements in writing be measured? This article attempts to provide an answer to the original question after responding briefly to the other two issues.

The Role of Students' Attitudes

Systematic studies of people's attitudes toward the use of word processors are still rather rare (e.g., see Johnson, 1987), but teaching magazines and computing magazines are full of testimonials about the perceived benefits for individual writers and for groups of students. We find these testimonies persuasive and consistent with our own ex-

periences, but we also realize that there are many people who are unwilling to try to use a computer for any purpose or who resist learning to use a keyboard. Few of these people write articles about their feelings.

Still, some studies exist. Kurth (1987) and Coombs (1985) reported increases in self concept associated with the use of word processors. Several writers report increases in motivation and enthusiasm for writing (Coombs, 1985; Feldman, 1984; Hawisher, 1986; Johnson, 1987). Others have indicated that students using word processors desire to write more often (Daiute, 1983; Newman, 1984) or that they show more willingness to make changes in their writing (Kurth, 1987; Schwartz, 1982). Decreases in writing anxiety have been associated with the use of word processors (Branan, 1984; Feldman, 1984; Teichman & Poris, 1985). In contrast to this growing evidence of support for students' positive attitudes toward word processing, Fitch (in Hooper, 1987) reported no significant change in attitudes when students wrote with word processors. On the whole, though, it seems reasonable for us to believe that we can proceed to use word processors in the teaching of writing, confident that many students will enjoy the experience. Future research will undoubtedly help us to identify exceptions and how best to deal with their concerns.

Measuring Achievement in Writing

There seems to be a growing consensus among language arts educators that holistic methods of evaluating writing are best suited to measurement in the classroom. These methods involve global judgments by trained readers who have been provided with a focus for the evaluation, usually related to the writer's purpose. The Educational Testing Service, owners of a near monopoly on multiple-choice testing, have elevated holistic scoring to a high art in their 30 years of experience with marking essays on the English

Composition portion of the Scholastic Aptitude Tests (ETS, 1989-1990). Moore and Kennedy (1971) point out two disadvantages of using standardized tests to assess writing ability: They fail to reflect changes in English curricula after 1960, and they are built primarily around ease of scoring. Consequently, each item tests one and only one skill or concept. Moore and Kennedy argue that ". . . such fragmentation is highly artificial. In writing, . . . the pupil must put everything together. . . [and] cannot afford the luxury of being concerned solely with isolated skills" (p. 441). This concern is also reflected in White's (1985) claim that "inappropriate testing has been destructive to the teaching of writing for the last two generations" (p. 9). Although we recognize the virtues of holistic scoring for pedagogic purposes and for large scale assessment, we wonder whether a more atomistic approach might not be better suited to research on the effects of different kinds of writing instruction.

Standardized tests and holistic marking of essays are not the only alternatives available to us. In Britain, "analytical" marking has long been used on national exams, where particular writing skills are evaluated in the context of actual writing samples. However, Wilkinson, Barnsley, Hanna, and Swan (1980) believe this procedure overemphasizes vocabulary, grammar and punctuation, proper sentence structure, spelling, and handwriting, and fails to consider such important aspects of writing as purpose and sense of audience. They also cite previous research to make the case that analytical marking and holistic or impression marking do not differ in reliability. Wilkinson et al. also determined that using four independent holistic markers required no more time or effort than what is required for one analytical marking.

Developers of multiple-choice tests are now focusing on indirect tests of isolated abilities (e.g., Benton & Kiewra, 1986). They argue that holistic assessment is not to be trusted, and that students should take a variety of separate standardized tests, each designed to tap "discourse production strategies at various levels" indirectly. For example, they suggest that skill at solving five-letter anagrams corresponds to "the propositional strategies that are employed in word generation and clause formation" (p. 384). They validate their series of tests of information-processing abilities by correlating each test score with the subject's holistic score on two narrative paragraphs, each written in 10 minutes. Vast amounts of time, effort, and financial support would be required to develop standardized tests of every ability involved in writing well. It is not clear whether such an investment is warranted. In the end, such tests might leave writing assessment in the same place that Kendall, Mason, and Hunter (1980) found the measurement of reading comprehension: After gathering data with four different item types on four different "story types," they wondered ". . . which, if any, of the operational definitions used here is actually reading comprehension" (p. 235).

Future developments aside, it appears that the reliability of holistic scoring methods and their obvious face validity justify their being the preferred evaluation procedure for

research on the writing process. However, it seems likely that future researchers will be interested in identifying more precisely what aspects of student writing are responding to differences in teaching methods (e.g., Does regular use of grammar checkers result in greater use of the active voice?) and that some type of atomistic measurement will be developed to address these questions.

To a certain extent, these developments have already begun to take place in the form of procedures for evaluating students' efforts at revising their writing. Bridwell (1981) reviewed the efforts in this area and proposed a seven-level classification of revisions: surface, lexical, phrase, clause, sentence, multi-sentence, and text. In a similar vein, Faigley and Witte (1984) recommend assessing instances of revision such as additions and deletions to determine whether they affect the structure and meaning of a text at a micro or macro level. That is, are they *surface* changes or *meaning* changes? They emphasize the need to consider the situational variables of a writing task: the author's reason for composing, the format of the composition, the writer's

---

We shouldn't expect word processors to relieve us of the responsibility of teaching students how to write; rather, we should be seeking ways in which the availability of word processors can help students to set higher personal goals and then concentrate on helping them develop the competencies necessary to achieve those goals.

---

knowledge of the subject area and his or her audience, the degree of formality required for the writing, and the length and complexity of the task. The same writer may demonstrate different revision behaviors and skills in different writing situations.

The Effects of Word Processing on the Quality of Writing

Strong opinions about the effects of word processing are easy to find. For example, Herrmann (1987) reported that learning to handle the keyboard interferes with the writing process. Yet Branan (1984), Willer (1984), and Ho Chung Qui (1986) cite increased amounts of creative writing by children with learning disabilities when they were taught word processing.

- **Studies of composition length.** Although composition length is not meant to be a measure of the quality of writing, investigators have examined this variable with the expectation that students who write more will eventually learn to write better. Kurth (1987) found no significant difference between control and treatment groups in length of compositions produced. Her subjects were high school students who were participating in an experimental writing course as a voluntary extracurricular activity. Some of these highly motivated subjects took their writing home to work on. It seems likely that these subjects would continue to rethink and revise their work until they were satisfied—regardless of the amount of extra time it would take to write by hand. With writing time controlled, however, Etchison (1985) found that students using word processors made greater increases in the length of their compositions from pre to post instruction. His students had two days to plan their compositions, one hour to write, and then were given a one-hour revising session two days later.

Willinsky (1990) found that education students whose normal course assignments were prepared on word processors wrote approximately 20% longer papers than those using typewriters or pen and paper.

- **Studies of holistic quality.** Hawisher (1986) and Cross and Curey (1984) found that overall quality ratings for essays produced with word processing were similar to those for essays produced with pen or typewriter. Willinsky (1990), using grades obtained on assignments for a variety of education courses, found no significant difference in marks earned by students who word processed their assignments, those who typed them, and those who wrote in long hand. Etchison (1985), on the other hand, found gains in holistic quality of essays written with a word processor were five times greater than those written with pen and paper. It is important to note that Etchison took pains to control many other factors that might affect the quality of the final product (e.g., time allotted to the writing task, writing environment). It is quite likely that with his timed writing sessions, Etchison provided an empirical indication of the relative speed with which students can compose and revise on a word processor after a semester of use.

- **Analytic studies.** Etchison (1985) also measured changes in syntactic variables such as free modification, number of clauses, average number of words per clause, and type of embedding, but found no significant differences in these areas between students who used word processing and those who did not.

- **Other variables.** Suggestions of other factors that influence the quality of writing when using a word processor include context of the assignment (Herrmann, 1987), conferencing (Etchison, 1985), time and the opportunity to develop new skills in areas where concepts are new (Coombs, 1985), and classroom demonstrations of the technology as a means to an end (Cross & Curey, 1984). Cross and Curey also stated that the overall effects of word processing on writing vary with the writer and with general factors related to the teacher and the class. Finally, there is some evidence that using word processors may lead to an improved sense of audience (Macarthur, 1988; Wheeler, 1985).

The research we have encountered, although limited, indicates that the quality of documents prepared with word processors is at least as high as that obtained with other writing tools and that other variables are more important determinants of writing quality. Macarthur (1988) cautions that improvement should be credited to instruction and skill development rather than to the writing tool. Other authors (Hooper, 1987; Hult, 1986; Kurth, 1987; Opack, 1986) suggest that writing instruction must be given concurrently with the teaching of word processing skills if better quality writing is expected to result.

The Effects of Word Processing on Revision

Several studies examined differences in the ways writers approach revision when using a word processor as compared to other writing tools. Some have focused on the number of revisions made (e.g., Cross & Curey, 1984; Hawisher, 1986), while others focused on the kinds of revisions made (Hawisher, 1986; Kurth, 1987; Willinsky, 1990). Macarthur (1988) and Hult (1986) compared word processing revisions between experienced and inexperienced writers.

In a critical review of the literature, Hooper (1987) concluded that word processors ease the revision process (Nash, 1985), that most revisions are purely cosmetic (Womble, 1984), and that fewer substantial revisions are made by students using word processors (Harris, 1985). Students in Willinsky's (1990) study also indicated that their most frequent revising activities were minor changes—spelling and grammar corrections or the addition, deletion, replacement, or reordering of words. In this study, students using word processors reported more revisions in all these categories than did students using typewriters or pens. They also reported more additions of sentences and of paragraphs— more significant changes than those found in most earlier studies.

Hawisher (1986) examined the effects of word processing on the revision strategies of college students and observed that the amount of revision was not positively correlated with quality ratings and that students make the same kinds of revisions (i.e., surface versus meaning changes) regardless of the writing tool used. These observations were based on between-draft revisions and may not apply to revisions made in the process of composing. In a later study, Hawisher (1987) found no qualitative difference in the revisions made by those who used a computer compared with those who wrote with pen. She suggested that the initial draft, "the point of utterance," has a greater effect on the ultimate quality of the product than do the revisions students make. However, it may well be that this is simply a reflection of the minimal amount and quality of revision that other researchers found to be the norm.

Hult (1986) found that inexperienced writers focus their revision efforts at the level of word changes, resulting in surface revisions. Experienced writers tend to see composition as a complete activity; therefore, they make more changes in style and content. Macarthur (1988) found that experienced writers make more revisions than inexperienced writers when both groups are using word processors. He also cautioned that easing the physical requirements of revision will not result in better compositions unless students know how to evaluate and correct their writing.

In a study of professional writers, Lutz (1987) observed that they made different kinds of revision when they used word processors than they made using pen and paper. The computer's small window on a document seemed to encourage local editing but may have limited the writer's perspective on the document as a whole, thereby discouraging deep revision of the text. Revision was more effective when done with pencil and paper or when done on hard copy.

Of course, it is unreasonable for us to expect that simply changing writing tools will change the kinds of revisions writers make. As Hult (1986) has argued, the development of effective revision strategies requires that we teach the *value* of functions such as moving and deleting blocks of text. It should also be clear that students will need instruction and support in knowing what to revise—they will need to learn how to evaluate and improve their own writing in order to know how to use the word processor.

Related Issues

One way to increase the utility of computers and word processors for the teaching of writing may be to use software that will guide the processes of generating, organizing, composing, and revising text. For example, to reduce the cognitive demands that writing makes on children, Woodruff, Bereiter, and Scardamalia (1981-82) gave elementary students word processors that could provide on-line support to assist with composing via a hierarchy of writing aid menus. Although the students frequently summoned this assistance and believed that it improved their writing, the researchers found that it made no significant difference in either the quantity or the quality of the students' compositions. Daiute (1986) also reported that the availability of on-screen writing aids did not help eighth grade students to improve the quality of their writing.

Although Kurth (1987) also reported that the use of a computer did not improve the quality or quantity of junior high school students' writing, the students she worked with had fewer spelling errors when they used a word processor with a spell checker than they had when using pencil and paper. The high visibility of text on a screen also seemed to foster more conversation about writing. Kurth concluded that the quality of students' writing is affected more by good instruction than by the writing tool.

Postscript

If we take this research at face value, we can conclude that many students enjoy using word processors and that there is little strong evidence to support the current enthusiasm for using word processors in the teaching of writing. But should we take this research at face value? Our answer would have to be a clear and unambiguous ''no.'' Much of the research was based on samples of university students, nearly all of it relied on comparisons of students who chose to use word processors (as opposed to using random assignment), few of the studies made any effort either to teach students the use of word processors or to ascertain their levels of word processing expertise, and none of the studies made any reference to systematic instruction in the writing process or in revision strategies. It is as if we were to study the impact of calculators by studying the ways they are used by students who do not know how to multiply or divide or what a square root is. We are only beginning to learn how to structure research on this question and we should avoid overreacting to the early results.

Etchison's (1985) study provides some directions for future research by involving serious efforts to control some of the more obvious extraneous variables. The finding that using word processors does make marked differences in the quality of compositions when rigid time limits are imposed may help to explain why so many other studies found little or no difference. The usual pattern, both in research and in classroom practice, is to allow students generous time limits for writing assignments (e.g., to give several weeks notice of due dates). We suspect that under these circumstances, students compose and revise until they achieve some personal quality standard and then stop. It does not matter what writing tool they are working with, they continue to work until they satisfy their personal ''level of acceptable performance'' or LAP point, and then quit. Researchers will not see a difference in quality, but it is entirely possible that students using word processors achieved their LAP point much more quickly and in a less onerous way than those using other writing tools. Students would certainly find this to be reason enough to use word processors, but teachers would likely be disappointed with the interpretation that no improvements in writing quality can be expected no matter how refined technological aids to writing may become.

However, we need not accept that conclusion. We need only to turn our attention to the question: How do we get students to elevate their LAP point? How do we get them to expect more of themselves? We think the answers lie in more active instruction; for example, by teaching the elements of the writing process in conjunction with teaching the capabilities of word processors, by helping students to understand the demands of style and audience, by teaching strategies for evaluating compositions and making revisions, and by encouraging students to seek and use feedback on drafts. In short, we shouldn't expect word processors to relieve us of the responsibility of teaching students how to write; rather, we should be seeking ways in which the availability of word processors can help students to set higher personal goals and then concentrate on helping them develop the competencies necessary to achieve those goals.

William J. Hunter, Education Technology Unit, 836 Education Tower, The University of Calgary, Calgary, Alberta, Canada T2N 1N4.

Gail Jardine and Roslyn Weisgerber, graduate students, Educational Psychology Department, The University of Calgary.

Peter Rilstone, Calgary Board of Education.

243

References

Alberta Education. (1988). The writing process using the word processor: Inservice leader's reference manual. Curriculum Support Branch, Edmonton, Alberta, Canada.

Benton, S. L., & Kiewra, K. A. (1986). Measuring the organizational aspects of writing ability. *Journal of Educational Measurement, 23*(4), 377-386.

Branan, K. (1984). Moving the writing process along. *Learning, 13*, 221.

Bridwell, L. (1981). Revising strategies in twelfth grade students' transactional writing. *Research in the Teaching of English, 14*, 197-222.

Coombs, M. (1985, September). *Exploring the composing process with microcomputers.* Annual meeting of the National Reading and Language Arts Educators' Conference, Kansas City, MO. (ED 267424).

Cross, J., & Curey, B. (1984). *The effect of word processing on writing.* Bloomington, IN. (ED 247921).

Daiute, C. (1983). The computer as stylus and audience. *College Communication, 34*(2), 134-135.

Daiute, C. (1986). Physical and cognitive factors in revision: Insights from studies with computers. *Research in the Teaching of English, 120*(2), 141-159.

Etchison, C. (1985). *A comparative study of the quality of syntax of compositions by first year college students using handwriting and word processing.* (ED 282215).

Educational Testing Service. (1989-1990, Fall/Winter). Grading essays for ETS: 30 years experience in holistic scoring. *ETS Developments*, pp. 7-9.

Faigley, L., & Witte, S. (1984). Measuring the effects of revision on text structure. In R. Beach & L.S. Bridwell (Eds.), *New directions in composition research* (pp. 95-108). New York: Guilford.

Feldman, P. (1984, February). *Using microcomputers for college writing: What students say.* Paper presented at the spring conference of the Delaware Valley Writing Council and Villanova University's Department of English, Villanova, PA.

Harris, J. (1985). Student writers and word processing: A preliminary evaluation. *College Composition and Communication, 36*, 323-330.

Hawisher, G. (1986, April). *The effects of word processing on the revision strategies of college students.* Annual meeting of the American Educational Research Association, San Francisco. (ED 268546).

Hawisher, G. E. (1987). The effects of word processing on the revision strategies of college freshmen. *Research in the Teaching of English, 21*(2), 145-159.

Herrmann, A. (1987, December). *Research into writing and computers: Viewing the gestalt.* Paper presented at the annual meeting of the Modern Language Association, San Francisco. (ED 292094).

Ho Chung Qui, J. (1986). *Word processing and learning disabled children.* Unpublished report, Jennie Elliott School, Calgary, Alberta, Canada.

Hooper, S. (1987). Using word processing in high school and college writing instruction: A critical review of the literature. (ED 286203).

Hult, C. (1986, March). *The computer and the inexperienced writer.* Annual meeting of the Conference on College Composition and Communication, New Orleans, LA. (ED 271772).

Hunter, W., & Begoray, J. (1990). A framework for writing process activities. *The Writing Notebook, 7*(3), 40-42.

Hunter, W., Begoray, J., Benedict, G., Bilan, B., Jardine, G., Rilstone, P., & Weisgerber, R. (1988). *Writing and word processing: A critical synthesis.* Calgary, Alberta: The University of Calgary, Education Technology Unit.

Hunter, W., Benedict, G., & Bilan, B. (1989). On a need-to-know basis: Keyboarding instruction for elementary students. *The Writing Notebook, 7*(2), 23-25.

Johnson, V. M. (1987). Attitudes toward microcomputers in learning. *Education Technology, 29*, 47-55.

Kendall, J., Mason, J., & Hunter, W. (1980). Which comprehension? Artifacts in the measurement of reading comprehension? *Journal of Educational Research, 73*(4), 233-236.

Kurth, R. (1987). Using word processing to enhance revision strategies during student writing activities. *Educational Technology, 27*(1), 13-19.

Lutz, J. A. (1987). A study of professional and experienced writers revising and editing at the computer with pen and paper. *Research in the Teaching of English, 21*(4), 398-421.

Macarthur, C. (1988). The impact of computers on the writing process. *Exceptional Children, 54*(6), 536-542.

Moore, W. J., & Kennedy, L. D. (1971). Evaluation of learning in the language arts. In B. Bloom, J. T. Hastings, & G. F. Madaus (Eds.), *Handbook on formative and summative evaluation of student learning* (pp. 399-445). New York: McGraw-Hill.

Nash, J. (1985). Making computers work in writing class. *Educational Technology, 25*, 19-26.

Newman, J. (1984). Online: Reading, writing and computers. *Language Arts, 61*, 758-763.

Opack, M. M. (1986). Effective instruction in word processing: Maximizing minimal competence. *Educational Technology, 26*, 33-36.

Schwartz, M. (1982). Computers and the teaching of writing. *Educational Technology, 22*, 27-29.

Teichman, M., & Poris, M. (1985). *Word processing in the classroom: Its effects on freshman writers.* Poughkeepsie, NY: Marist College.

Wheeler, F. (1985). Can word processing help the writing process? *Learning, 13*, 54.

White, E. M. (1985). *Teaching and assessing writing.* San Francisco: Jossey-Bass.

Wilkinson, A., Barnsley, G., Hanna, P., & Swan, M. (1980). *Assessing language development.* Oxford: Oxford University Press.

Willer, A. (1984). Creative writing with computers: What do elementary students have to say? *Computers, Reading and Language Arts 2*(1), 39-42.

Willinsky, J. (1990). When university students word process their assignments. *Computers in the Schools, 6*, 83-96.

Womble, G. G. (1984). Do word processors work in the English classroom? *The Education Digest, 50*, 40-42.

Woodruff, E., Bereiter, C., & Scardamalia, M. (1981-82). On the road to computer assisted compositions. *Journal of Educational Technology Systems, 10*, 133-148.

Research on Writing Technologies in Grades K-12

William J. Hunter

Although readers of *The Writing Notebook* are likely to be enthusiastic about the use of word processors and other writing software, research on the effects of using these aids in teaching writing to elementary and secondary students has been limited and not terribly positive. Research on older students is of limited value, not only because of differences in the age of the learners and the dynamics of teaching, but also because of weaknesses in the research itself. This column will attempt to keep readers informed about current research developments that may have implications for the teaching of writing in grades K-12. Readers are invited to submit information about their own action research projects as well as questions they would like to see addressed in future columns.

In the last issue of *The Writing Notebook* ("Effects of using word processors: A hard look at the research," Sept./Oct. 1990, pp. 42-46), my colleagues and I reviewed some of the research on the effects of using word processors as part of the instructional process in writing. In addition to the heavy concentration on university and college students, the research suffers from several problems.

- There is considerable disagreement about how to measure quality of writing. Most studies have involved relatively brief interventions.

- Experimenters generally have not ensured that students were familiar with the writing process.

- Few studies involve systematic instruction in the use of word processors.

- Available studies have not attempted to teach students word processing skills in the context of a process approach to writing instruction.

- Only one study examined writing under controlled timing conditions (so it is possible that students using word processors write with the same quality as other students, but with less investment of time).

Our review looked only at quantitative studies. There is an ample supply of anecdotal reports by individual teachers who have used word processors to good benefit, but we did not find any rigorous qualitative examinations of the use of word processors (although I expect that I will be better informed once this column hits the streets). This is particularly unfortunate, since questions about the use and the effects of word processors lend themselves to the kind of intense observation and analysis that characterizes qualitative research.

One recent study that has overcome some of the difficulties of previous research was carried out by Jane Steel-man of North Carolina State University, who presented her results at the National Educational Computing Conference in Nashville last June. The study used a newspaper writing program as a vehicle for testing the effects of teaching writing with a word processor. Two groups participated in the writing project, only one of which used word processors. The other group constructed a newspaper manually, and a third group was taught using the same methods and materials that had been used in the school in prior years (i.e., no newspaper project, no word processors, and no deliberate emphasis on process writing). The participants were 75 sixth grade students in a middle school located in a low socio-economic community. Her subjects were randomly assigned to one of three classrooms using a procedure that assured appropriate representation by sex and race.

Steelman measured the students' writing apprehension, writing "ability," and writing quantity. Writing ability was assessed using an eight-point scale developed by the researcher. At the start of the study, there were no differences among the groups on any of these measures. At the end of the study, the students in the control group were writing less and writing less well than students in the newspaper groups. In fact, the control group students wrote shorter papers, on average, at the end of the study than they had at the beginning. There were no significant differences in writing apprehension.

Although a case could be made that the study should have employed more powerful statistical techniques, the results are interesting for a number of reasons. The program served middle school students, included training in both word processing and the writing process, and lasted for a reasonable amount of time. While the reported differences do not show that word processors enhance the quality of writing (the experimental groups differed significantly from the control group, but not from each other), the students who used word processors did obtain higher averages on both the quality and quantity measures than did the students in the other experimental group. These differences did not reach statistical significance, but they lend support to the author's belief that "an environment in which more computers are used could certainly produce greater gains in writing achievement." It is worth noting that the students accomplished what they did in a lab in which the 21 students shared seven computers, hardly an ideal set-up for word processing.

Steelman's research is far from giving an unqualified endorsement to the use of word processors in the teaching of writing. However, it does indicate that the time spent in teaching word processing and the process approach to writing are not wasted. Steelman notes that "the preliminary activities of teaching the word processor, keyboarding, and presenting revision strategies took as much time as the total time devoted to many previous studies." Yet this time was apparently well spent—at the end of the study the students who used a word processor wrote at least as well as the other students who learned the writing process, and both of these groups outperformed students in a more traditional classroom. At worst, then, the students in the word processing group got the advantage of learning the additional skill of using a word processor without any loss in their writing achievement. Some may think that may not be enough to justify the additional time and trouble, but it does represent a considerable achievement. Given the limited computer resources and the somewhat higher scores of the word processing students, this study at least gives us reason to be hopeful.

Another hopeful presentation at the Nashville conference was Ihor Charischak's "Dynamic Writing: A Glimpse into the Future." Extrapolating from the features of *LogoWriter*, Charischak imagines a future student, Billy, who works with (not yet existent) software called *Dynamic Writer* to tell the story of the voyage of Lewis and Clark. Billy's story is filled with maps, images of the office of Thomas Jefferson, and scenes of Lewis and Clark's voyage. Billy's report includes an attractive cover "page" and the whole thing is presented on the computer screen. Charischak demonstrated a *LogoWriter* version of the future Billy's story and captured a lot of interest and imagination in the audience. Of course, it is possible to do such dynamic writing now, and one might well expand this notion to include the incorporation of student-scripted and/or student-produced video sequences or stills borrowed from a laserdisc. The story of Billy reminded me of one of the more interesting projects I have received from a teacher-in-training—a *LogoWriter* "play" about an arachnid love triangle. The student told a good story enriched by images, animation, and sound effects. She had no previous programming experience and disliked computers, but she managed to produce a fine piece of work with just a three-week unit on Logo. So, we can be hopeful not only about the impact of word processors on writing, but also about the more general utility of microcomputers as devices for creative communication.

Still, after a decade or so, is it enough to be hopeful? Perhaps. Long-time computer advocate Betty Collis also spoke of her hopes at the NECC Conference in Nashville. She hoped for a new wave of "young lovers" who will be passionately involved in using computers to unlock human potential in students. She spoke of her own long familiarity with computers and of eventually "falling in love" with the idea of "the potential of computers in education." This fits nicely with my own conviction that education is all about love: love for children, love for learning, love for a specific subject area, for ideas, for playfulness, for problem solving, for helping, for self as helper, for the world and all its inhabitants—the love the ancient Greeks called *agape*. So I share Betty Collis's hope. I also hope that in this column I will be able to look dispassionately at the developing research while remaining passionate about the ideas and practices examined in that research. It should be fun. Tune in next time.

William J. Hunter, Director, Education Technology Unit, 036 Education Tower, The University of Calgary, Calgary, Alberta T2N 1N4, Canada.

Technography Place

William J. Hunter

By calling the column Technography Place, I meant to create a sense that this is sort of a Sesame Street for ideas about writing technologies. I will be attempting in this column to focus on research that has implications for the choices K-12 teachers make in using different writing tools and different methods of working with these tools. I would be pleased to receive questions or suggestions from teachers regarding topics, articles, or controversies they would like to see addressed in future columns. I want Technography Place to serve as a location for the meeting of minds.

One last note before addressing this issue's research report. I feel obliged to comment on "what counts as research?" While I confess to a fascination with multivariate analyses and large N's, I also find that I am not often impressed with the way in which such studies [fail to] impact classroom teaching. On the other hand, I enjoy the reports of individual teachers regarding their success [or not] with an innovation in their classrooms, but I worry about how well such experiences transfer to other teachers, other classes, other places. So, I'll do no wholesale censorship of methods of research. Rather, I will use this space to share my understandings of whatever catches my fancy and will gladly include opinions expressed by anyone who cares to comment on prior columns. And now, let's take a look at something new.

A Junior High Project

Slowly but surely we are beginning to accumulate research that can guide us toward more constructive uses of word processors in conjunction with process-oriented language arts instruction. A study by Canadian researchers Dudley-Marling and Oppenheimer (1990) is one of the latest editions to this body of research. Methodologically, it employs anthropological field methods: extensive observation accompanied by detailed notes, which are later subjected to careful summary and analysis. A research assistant spent six months observing the integration of word processing into grade 7 and 8 language arts classes in a middle school near Toronto, Canada. The teachers had had relatively little experience with instructional use of computers. After a brief period of general observation, the researcher began to focus on students who, for various reasons, proved to be particularly interesting as case studies. In addition to field notes, the intensive data collection included audio and video tapes, interviews with various participants, samples of students' writing, and relevant school board documents.

Some studies have found that experienced writers do considerably more revision than inexperienced writers, an explanation that has clear implications for a study of junior high school writers. However, I think the more important consideration is that students must learn *what* and *how* to revise, regardless of the writing tool they employ.

Description of Program

Students were involved in a variety of writing assignments during the course of the study. Teachers were strongly oriented to "explicitly teaching basic writing skills." For the most part, teachers were the primary audience for the students' writing, but some works were shared and/or posted. The researchers indicate that two of the teachers tended to focus on "specific editorial suggestions" with all drafts, while another said he could not respond to drafts and considered the work handed in by students to be "final drafts." These observations are consistent with two of the problems I attributed to technographic research in the last issue (Hunter, 1990): (a) The experimenters have not assured that students were familiar with the writing process; and (b) students have not been taught word processing skills in the context of a process approach to the teaching of writing. Until we begin to address these problems, we will not have genuine tests of the effects of using word processors.

Dudley-Marling and Oppenheimer (1990) discuss their results in terms of four themes that emerged in the analysis. I will focus on the ways in which their observations tend to conform to what has been shown in the research.

Theme 1: Writing First Drafts

Dudley-Marling and Oppenheimer (1990) observed that many students persisted in preparing first drafts in longhand throughout the period of observation. Limited access to computers explained some of this, but the researchers also expressed concern that the limited keyboarding skills of the students was a deterrent to composing at the computer.

The teachers were uncomfortable with a typing tutor program because of its heavy reliance on drills. In a review of the literature on keyboarding, my colleagues and I (Hunter, Benedict, & Bilan, 1989) tried to make the point that keyboarding is a psychomotor skill and may therefore be responsive to drill and practice in the same way shooting baskets or swinging a baseball bat improves with practice. Language arts teachers who have become accustomed to condemning the role of drill in language teaching may be inclined to overgeneralize their distaste for the technique. If so, we may be unwittingly placing a block in our students' progress in writing with word processors. Indeed, one way of dealing with a shortage of hardware may be to ensure that students accomplish more in the little time they do have on the machines. However, we would do well to remember Wetzel's (1985) advice that if access to hardware is severely limited, "... there is no time—or need—to teach keyboarding" (p. 17).

Theme 2: Revision and Editing

The conclusions of Dudley-Marling and Oppenheimer on the subject of revision and editing are neatly summarized in their statement that "Both teachers and students stressed the important role of revision in writing in our interviews with them, but revisions that were observed during this study tended to be mostly minor and editorial in nature" (p. 34). Although they observed some significant deletions as students started assignments, they interpreted these not as revisions but as new starts, since the students appeared to write on new topics. Movement of blocks of text was so noticeably absent that the investigator asked if students had been taught the commands. They hadn't. The "computer coach" reasoned that moving blocks of text was "a revision strategy that could not be expected of grade 7 and 8 students." In one poetry unit, students did make use of deletions after the procedure had been modeled by the teacher. Ironically, this unit was conducted in longhand.

There has been a fair amount of research on the effects of word processing on revision, mostly with post-secondary students (see review in Hunter, Jardine, Rilstone, & Weisgerber, 1990), and it is consistent with the findings of Dudley-Marling and Oppenheimer. Some studies (e.g., Hult, 1986; Macarthur, 1988) have found that experienced writers do considerably more revision than inex-

perienced writers, an explanation that has clear implications for a study of junior high school writers. However, I think the more important consideration is that students must learn **what** and **how** to revise, regardless of the writing tool they employ.

Dudley-Marling and Oppenheimer put it this way: "It is unlikely students will revise their work unless they have been deliberately taught to do so (e.g., Cantano, 1985; Solomon, 1985)" (p. 36). I am certain that most writing teachers believe that they do just that. It is odd, to say the least, that technographic research persistently finds that students are not being deliberately taught strategies for revision. A recent article that takes some initial steps toward defining how we might begin to see what is required in the way of teachable strategies can be found in Sudol (1990).

Theme 3: Ownership

Dudley-Marling and Oppenheimer also consider the possibility that students' enthusiasm for revision is diminished when they perceive revisions as changes made to satisfy the teacher. For example:

> Teacher: "Why did you say this?"
> Student: "I saw that it didn't make sense.
> Teacher: "I wanted you to move this up here where it goes with this. We talked about this last week. . . go and fix it." (p. 37)

There are several other examples, but they are too depressing to discuss. The feeling of ownership is not necessarily a technography issue. However, a fundamental precept in the teaching of writing ought to be that children can be expected to learn to enjoy writing and take pride in their self-expression only if they are not made to feel that their role is to transcribe the teacher's words. I can't help but add that I think this is also a moral issue: Isn't depriving someone of ownership akin to theft?

Theme 4: Social Interaction and Collaboration

Although Dudley-Marling and Oppenheimer report a high level of writing-oriented student discussion (including phone calls after school), they observed this discussion in both word processing and longhand writing classes, so it does not reflect any particular advantage for word processing. Such interaction was encouraged by the teachers as part of the writing process. Students' peer criticism tended to focus on the kinds of issues raised by the teacher (e.g., word choice, spelling, punctuation). Students found this valuable, since it tended to lead them to higher marks. We can only speculate that they would also have modeled teacher feedback dealing with substantive questions regarding content and/or clarity had teacher models for this behaviour been more apparent.

Afterthought

So, that's one more study. Are we getting anywhere? You must be able to guess my answer just as I can guess yours. I wouldn't be writing this and you wouldn't be reading it were it not true that we believe that research on writing and word processing would yield productive results. Dudley-Marling and Oppenheimer have extended our understanding by confirming some of what we already know. To a considerable extent, they have shown us once again that weak teaching does not become strong merely by the addition of technology.

William J. Hunter, Education Technology Unit, 836 Education Tower, The University of Calgary, Alberta, Canada T2N 1N4.

References

Cantano, J.V. (1985). Computer-based writing: Navigating the fluid text. *College Composition and Communication, 36*, 309-316.

Dudley-Marling, C., & Oppenheimer, J. (1990). The introduction of word processing into a grade 7/8 writing program. *Journal of Research on Computing in Education, 23*(1), 28-44.

Hult, C. (1986, March). *The computer and the inexperienced writer.* Annual meeting of the Conference on College Composition and Communication, New Orleans, LA. (ED 271772).

Hunter, W. J. (1990). Technography Place: Research on writing technologies in grades K-12. *The Writing Notebook, 8*(2), 36-37.

Hunter, W. J. Benedict, G., & Bilan, B. (1989). On a need-to-know basis: Keyboarding instruction for elementary students. *The Writing Notebook, 7*(2), 23-25.

Hunter, W. J., Jardine, G., Rilstone, P., & Weisgerber, R. (1990). The effects of using word processors: A hard look at the research. *The Writing Notebook, 8*(1), 42-45.

Solomon, G. (1985). Writing with computers. *Electronic Learning, 5,* 39-43.

Sudol, R. (1990). Principles of generic word processing for students with independent access to computers. *College Composition and Communication, 41,* 325-332.

Wetzel, K. (1985). Keyboarding skills: Elementary, my dear teacher? *The Computing Teacher, 13*(9), 15-19.

Grandma
Christine Vasquez

I sit at the kitchen table,
Watching your wrinked, shaking hands
Caress candy tasting spices
While crimson, hot chili
Boils
     Gurgles.

I can't wait to drench
Sesame, crunchy crackers
Into the moat of pebbles and mud.

Smiling at my sunshine face,
Hands as soft as down,
Embrace my cheeks to lavish
Chick-a-dee
        Peck
           Peck
              Pecks.

from the Stylus, Volume 17, Jordan High School, Long Beach, California

Students with Learning Disabilities: Research Results on the Use of Technology

William J. Hunter

I wager that this fall brought some unusual responses to the tired old essay question: "How did you spend your summer vacation?" I'd also guess that some of the most interesting answers were written in Russian. We witnessed unbelievable political and social changes in the Soviet Union this summer, changes so dramatic that they call attention to the very idea of change. In three days the Soviets displaced a government and established new leadership only to have the old President return and announce impressive new initiatives. Yet the average Soviet citizen has waited years to see reasonable supplies of basic foodstuffs on store shelves. Clearly some changes happen more quickly than others.

Comparing these two extremes to the speed with which schools and teachers have adopted word processing as part of their writing program, we also get very different impressions of our progress. On one hand this relatively minor change in the technology of writing seems to be taking place incredibly slowly (it's no coup!). On the other hand, although microcomputers have had a place in schools for about 12 years, they are often seen as rivals to technologies that are hundreds of years old. In this column I want to take a brief look at the way thinking has changed regarding one specific application: using word processors to teach writing to students with learning disabilities.

In 1984, Klieman and Humphrey reported that they often heard the following arguments against the use of computers by special education students:

1. Computers are too complex for special education students and will only frustrate them;
2. Special education children will wreck the computers;
3. The use of computers will serve to limit social skills development in special education students; and
4. Special education teachers do not have the time to learn a new technology.

Following a 10-week experience with using computers for spelling drill and practice in two special education classrooms, Klieman and Humphrey concluded that all of the above arguments were invalid and that, in fact, quite positive effects were found. At about the same time, Messinger (1983) reported that students with learning disabilities at Lakewood Elementary School in Sunnyvale, California, not

---

Consider revising documentation . . . if we expect children to learn to write well, we should provide them with good models.

---

only learned to master the use of computers for learning in mathematics, spelling, and language, but their achievements were so impressive that within a year they served as tutors for 100 other children!

Messinger quotes one teacher as saying: "First the kids saw the computers as smart. Then they saw they were controlling the computers, and the feeling of being smart transferred to themselves. Then they taught others! Their self-confidence just took off!"

At that point in time, it seems that we were capable of being surprised to learn that kids with learning problems could use computers profitably. The suggestion that they could benefit from the use of word processors was just

beginning to emerge (e.g., Rude-Parkins, 1983).

How far have we come in the past eight years? David Majsterek seeks to provide some answers in his recent article in *Intervention in School and Clinic* (Majsterek, 1990). Majsterek reviewed the research on the use of word processors to teach writing to students with learning disabilities. Although he found the body of research inconclusive, he was able to draw a number of lessons from the literature. He presents these lessons in the form of four guidelines:

1. **Use a process approach.** In fact, he advocates teaching process writing *first*.

2. **Consider revising documentation.** Majsterek provides specific suggestions (taken from Collins & Price, 1986) for writing clearer manuals for student use. The essence of these suggestions is that if we expect children to learn to write well, we should provide them with good models.

3. **Consider machine skills instruction.** Majsterek provides suggestions for selecting a word processor that will be easy for students with learning disabilities to use. However, he believes that part of the solution lies in separating instruction in *writing* from instruction in *using a specific word processor* from instruction in *using a keyboard*. He recommends that each of these be the focus of direct instruction.

4. **Teach keyboarding.** This topic receives attention in *The Writing Notebook*. Majsterek points out that there is no research specifically based on students with learning disabilities. Nevertheless, he provides a series of suggestions derived from research on

the general population (e.g., keyboarding can start at grade 4 and can be taught by any teacher who can type).

How far have we come in eight years? No one seems to be surprised that children with learning disabilities can learn to use word processors. Although Majsterek found the literature limited and the results "mixed," his assumption seems to be that we will continue to use this technology and he takes the responsibility of providing guidance to help us do it better. He also mentions, along the way, research by Outhred (1989) that suggests that word processors may have greater impact on the length of compositions and the spelling accuracy of students who are initially weak in these areas.

Okay, it isn't the fall of the Berlin Wall, but we have made gains. We are no longer surprised to find that microcomputers can be useful to any group of kids. We are no longer as fearful for the safety of equipment used in special education classes. We have learned to see how computers can support students who learn differently or more slowly. It's not the revolution some enthusiasts predicted, but I have to see these changes as a sort of pedagogic coup; I guess we could call it a coup d'ecole.

William J. Hunter, Director, Education Technology Unit, 836 Education Tower, The University of Calgary, Calgary, Alberta T2N 1N4, Canada.

References
Collins, T. G., & Price, L. (1986). Micros for LD college writers: Rewriting documentation for word processing programs. *Learning Disabilities Focus, 2*(1), 49-54.

Klieman, G.M., & Humphrey, M.M. (1984). Computers make special education more effective and fun. *Creative Computing, 10*(10), 95-101.

Majsterek, D.J. (1990). Writing disabilities: Is word processing the answer? *Intervention in School and Clinic, 26*(2), 93-97.

Messinger, M. (1983, August/September). Computer literate LD students shine at Lakewood elementary school in Silicon Valley, CA. *Journal of Learning Disabilities*, 426-427.

Outhred, L. (1989). Word processing: Its impact on children's writing. *Journal of Learning Disabilities, 22*, 262-264.

Rude-Parkins, C. (1983). Microcomputers and learning disabled adolescents. *The Pointer, 27*(4), 14-19.

A Brief Report on Three Recent Summaries

William J. Hunter

Not long ago, research on the use of word processors in the teaching of writing was almost nonexistent. One could even say that not long ago word processors were nonexistent. Things have changed. Any personal computer owner now has a rich variety of word processors from which to choose and any writing teacher can now consult more research than there is time to absorb. Fortunately, reviews of this research have begun to emerge. Indeed, this column has its origins in a summary and review of the research on keyboarding, word processing, and the writing process that my students and I did three years ago.

In this issue, I will report briefly on three recent summaries. The first two are not reviews, but bibliographies compiled by the ERIC (Education Resources Information Center) Clearinghouse on Reading and Communication Skills. ERIC calls these annotated bibliographies "Focused Access to Selected Topics" (FAST). I will be reporting on FAST 10 and FAST 11. The third piece is both a synthesis and a review conducted by Anna Liechty as a masters degree "exit project" at Indiana University.

FAST 10: Word Processing and Writing Instruction

Fast 10, prepared by Michael Shermis, is intended to present sources that contain "creative ideas and new computer strategies for teaching revision and using word processors in the classroom." The bibliography is divided into three sections:

Strategies, Techniques, and Exercises. This section includes 13 articles and one book dating from 1983 to 1989. Most are concerned with strategies for using computers to increase the quantity and quality of students' revisions. Several describe existing projects; one describes ways to use two specific writing programs (*Bank Street Writer* and *Story Tree*). One article refers to *The Writing Notebook* as offering "a wealth of creative ideas for using word processors in the classroom."

Effects, Benefits of Word Processor Use. Eleven articles dating from 1983 to 1988 are reported. Although several of the articles seem to concentrate on how or why the use of word processors ought to improve writing, at least four reported some specific benefits of word processor use. Two points appear repeatedly in this collection: (a) Students have insufficient time to use word processors, thus limiting the gains possible, and (b) students tend to be more motivated and happier about writing when they do it on a word processor.

Selected Word Processors. This section reports on four articles (1984 to 1987) that suggest variables to be considered in evaluating writing software.

FAST 11: Word Processing and Writing Instruction for Students with Special Needs

FAST 11, also prepared by Shermis, is more focused. Again, he has grouped the studies into three categories:

Learning Disabled. The 13 articles in this section (1986 to 1988) are concerned primarily with the appropriateness of using word processors to teach writing to students with learning disabilities, the difficulties that can occur in doing so, and strategies for approaching the task. Two studies report on the results of projects in which word processors were used with students with learning disabilities, one indicating "great promise" for use of the technology. Two articles were annotated bibliographies of research in this area.

Basic Writing. Six of the nine articles in this section (1982 to 1988) report some positive benefit resulting from using word processors to teach writing in remedial classes. Most often, the benefit was an increase in the volume of writing done. Two articles report no benefit and indicate difficulties that occurred in attempting to use word processors. The last article is a position paper describing problems that computers can pose for students in a writing center.

English as a Second Language. All four of the articles in this section (1984 to 1987) discuss the opportunities that word processors present to teachers of English as a Second Language.

FAST bibliographies can be found in ERIC microfiche collections or by writing to ERIC Document Reproduction Service, 3900 Wheeler Ave., Alexandria, VA 22304. For information and price lists, call 1-800-227-3742.

Liechty's 'Exit Project'

Liechty's project contains an extensive annotated bibliography, but she also summarizes the findings and draws implications from them. Among her conclusions:

- There is strong evidence that children using word processors spend more time on writing

- Students write more when using word processors, especially if they are also given instruction in the writing process

- There is some evidence that students reread (or monitor) their writing more when they use word processors

- Students' attitudes toward computing and toward writing are generally more positive when they have had experience with word processors

- Studies of the process variables, planning and revision, yield mixed, sometimes conflicting results

- Students are more willing to work collaboratively when using word processors

- Measurable improvements in the quality of work written using word processors is found most often when students were also given instruction in the writing process.

Liechty's report is available as an ERIC document.

Patterns are beginning to emerge. One of them is that word processors may be part of a rare class of educational tools—those that have the potential to have greater benefit for the less able student. Another is that word processing makes most sense as a device for teaching process writing. But perhaps the most important pattern that I see is the consistency with which researchers report that students' attitudes toward writing improve when they use word processors. It reminds me of a truism that my old creative writing professor used to love spouting: A writer is the only artist who hates his work. We would all nod in recognition when he said that, but I always felt uneasy with my acceptance of that statement. If I didn't love to write, why did I do it?

My professor wrote because he got paid for it. He was a journeyman writer who analyzed pulp magazines and sent them what he knew they would publish (under a pseudonym he would never reveal). My lifetime income from writing would buy a reasonably good VCR, but here I am—writing. Clearly, I like doing this. I even write things I have no intention of publishing, let alone selling. Some of it is shared with a few close friends. Some sits in folders I may not open for years. Still, it made sense when my professor said writing was hard work. Perhaps his error was in thinking that music and art and dance are not hard work. Or perhaps it was in thinking that people engage in hard work only for money, not for love. In any case, it became easier for me to love writing when I started to use a word processor. It also made me much more enthusiastic about the place of computers in schools. Somehow, ease of revision makes it possible to pay less attention to the hard work and more attention to the satisfaction of self-expression. Perhaps this is what students are finding, that this technology has made the art of writing more available and the work less odious.

William J. Hunter, Director, Education Technology Unit, 836 Education Tower, The University of Calgary, Calgary, Alberta T2N 1N4, Canada.

References

Liechty, A. (1989). *The efficacy of computer assisted instruction in teaching composition.* Unpublished manuscript, Indiana State University (ED 314 023).

Shermis, M. (1989). *Word processing and writing instruction.* Focused Access to Selected Topics (FAST) Bibliography, No. 10 (ED 307 606).

Shermis, M. (1989). *Word processing and writing instruction for students with special needs.* Focused Access to Selected Topics (FAST) Bibliography, No. 11 (ED 307 607).

CHAPTER 7
WRITING ACTIVITIES

If you ask me what I came to do in this world, I, an artist,
I will answer you: I am here to live out loud.

—Emile Zola

Classroom Writing Activities to Support the Curriculum

Judy Piper

This activity is designed to help teachers create word processing files in many different subject areas for students to complete throughout the school day. In this way a teacher can individualize learning in the classroom with students able to complete work at their own pace. The files provide easy make-up and review lessons for individual students and give all students many opportunites to practice using the word processor.

Wanted!

For an interesting social studies activity, have students write want ads for items or services from long ago. Sharon Shanahan, Co-director of the Great Valley Writing Project, shared this assignment in a workshop. To begin, have students brainstorm all the items needed by a rider for the Pony Express, for example. Then select one or more of the items and write the ad, specifically stating what qualifications are necessary.

Wanted!
One Pony Express rider with a soft behind. Must not weigh over 100 pounds or carry more than will fit in two saddlebags. Needs to wear boots that have already been broken in. Only the experienced traveler, those who can ride from dawn to dusk, need apply. Contact Ohio Tack & Saddle Company, Columbus, Ohio.

E-X-P-A-N-D Those Sentences

Revision is an important part of the writing process and one which students must be taught. You can focus on adding more descriptive words to sentences with young students or new writers. Start with a very simple sentence and have students add a color word. Then have them put in a proper noun, which will reinforce capitalization skills. Use ⟨ ⟩ to show students where words should be added.

1. The ⟨ ⟩ house was built. (color)
2. The red house was built on ⟨ ⟩ Street. (Name)

Respond To It

Students need an opportunity to respond to examples of good writing by professional authors. These selections also can serve as models for their own writing. Have students underline the most descriptive words or the ones that stick in their mind after they've read the passage. The following paragraph comes from *Harriet the Spy* by Louise Fitzhugh.

Sport and Harriet stood staring, their mouths open. The fat lady stood like a mountain, her hands on her hips, in a flowered cotton print dress and enormous hanging coat sweater. Probably the biggest sweater in the world, thought Harriet; probably the biggest shoes too. And her shoes were a wonder. Long, long, black, bumpy things with high, laced sides up to the middle of the shin, bulging with the effort of holding in those ankles, their laces splitting them into grins against the white of the socks below.

Classroom Writing Activities to Support the Curriculum

Judy Piper

These activities are designed to link literature, writing, technology, and the history/social science curriculum.

Judy B. Piper, Coordinator, Educational Services Division, Stanislaus County Department of Education, 801 County Center Three Court, Modesto, CA 93355.

LANGUAGE ARTS

Young children love the picture book, *Rosie's Walk* by Pat Hutchins. In just a few pages with only 32 words, the story of Rosie the hen unfolds. After reading the book, make sure to have the children recall what happens to the fox who stalks the colorfully illustrated hen throughout her walk. Then write a new class book with your students following that pattern and reinforcing the concepts of over, under, around, and through. Print the story using any word processor with large print, one phrase per page, and have each child draw accompanying pictures for an individual copy to share with friends or family.

LIFE SCIENCE

National Geographic has produced an interactive CD ROM program for the IBM world called *Mammals*. It is an impressive resource of information that contains still pictures, text, movie clips, range maps, and mammal sounds. After students have had time to work with the program, introduce the book, *A Snake is Totally Tail* by Judi Barrett. It includes such gems as: "A toucan is basically beak" and "A seal is seemingly slippery." Have students research several of their favorite mammals and brainstorm "sentences" about them following this pattern. Each student can choose their favorite to word process and illustrate for a class book.

VISUAL ARTS

In *Look, Think & Write*, Leavitt and Sohn (National Textbook Co., 4255 W. Touly Ave., Lincolnwood, IL 60646-1975) take you through exercises that "help you become a better writer through learning to see clearly and accurately, and to transform what you see into writing that will communicate your thinking with clarity and style." One of these techniques, developing detail lists, can be used with the laserdisc program, *The National Gallery of Art*. Using the Hypercard stacks, simply choose a picture to reinforce a current topic or unit of study.

After a vacation break, you might want to use one of my favorite paintings, "Children Playing at the Beach" by Mary Cassatt (1884). Have students first work alone to develop a detail list and write simple sentences about the picture. Then have them work in pairs to combine these into rich, descriptive sentences and even paragraphs.

Classroom Writing Activities to Support the Curriculum

Judy Piper

These activities are designed to link literature, technology, and the visual and performing arts.

Judy B. Piper, Coordinator, Educational Services Division, Stanislaus County Department of Education, 801 County Center Three Court, Modesto, CA 95355.

LITERATURE

E. B. White described his classic story, *Charlotte's Web*, as a tale of ". . . friendship and salvation, a story of miracles—the miracle of birth, the miracle of friendship, the miracle of death." Children love to hear this story read to them even before they can read themselves.

Paramount Pictures offers a video of *Charlotte's Web* featuring Debbie Reynolds as Charlotte, Paul Lynde as Templeton the Rat, Agnes Moorehead as the Stuttering Goose, and Henry Gibson as Wilbur the Pig. This technology can be used in different parts of a unit for a variety of instructional outcomes. When a video clip is used in the middel of a lesson as part of a direct teaching activity, its purpose might be to provide additional information for better understanding. Stop reading on page 36 when Charlotte introduces herself to Wilbur, and turn on the video at this point. Watch your students' reactions as they see Charlotte wrap up the fly. Stop the tape before they see Wilbur's reaction and ask them for their own. (This is a great activity to practice listening and speaking.)

WRITING

One of the most interesting applications of the Hypercard program is a novel study by Kevin Lynch of the book, *Charlotte's Web*. (The stacks were designed by Kevin Vine.) Apple is currently using this young man's project as a demo in training. Your local educational Apple rep should have a copy of it.

Try showing the video *Spider* by Beacon as a prewriting activity during your *Charlotte's Web* unit. This little piece of life is accompanied by classical music as it tells the story of a spider building its web. A bird appears, but the story is left open-ended . . . a perfect opportunity for students to write the conclusion.

VISUAL/PERFORMING ARTS

A number of programs can be used by students to design their own spider webs. Logo can be used by students to use higher level thinking skills to program the turtle to create a web. *Dazzle Draw* or other paint programs also make creating webs an easy project for students. Some may even want to add their own spiders. Drag out that video camera that is stored somewhere in your school, and tape your own versions of Booktalks as seen on *Reading Rainbow*. Students can practice their speaking and drama skills as they present their favorite books to the class. *Charlotte's Web* is sure to be someone's favorite!

Classroom Writing Activities to Support the Curriculum

Judy Piper

The thinking, meaning-centered curriculum promotes instructional practices that relate the learning task to what students already know or have experienced. The themes in the following pieces of literature encourage children to share their personal experiences.

Judy B. Piper, Coordinator, Educational Services Division, Stanislaus County Department of Education, 801 County Center Three Court, Modesto, CA 93355.

COURAGE

Fairy tales have always been enjoyed by young and old alike. *The Paper Bag Princess* by Robert Munsch is a contemporary story where the princess rescues the prince from the dragon. Discis Books™ has a CD-ROM version of this story featuring a feisty heroine. Students can ask the computer to explain or pronounce unfamiliar words in English and Spanish, and they can have their favorite passages "read" to them. The accompanying teachers' guide suggests the following activities:

- Write a letter from Ronald to Elizabeth where he apologizes for being ungrateful when rescued.
- Rewrite the story from the dragon's point of view.
- Pick a partner and write and illustrate your own fairy tale.

FEAR

Children experience many fears on the road to adulthood. In *Harry and the Terrible Whatzit* by David Gachenbach, the hero is sure there is something terrible down in the cellar.* Use a video clip from the movie *Home Alone*, where Kevin descends into the basement of his house, to illustrate this common fear. Both Harry and Kevin eventually confront and conquer their fear. After reading the book and showing the video clip, have students brainstorm their own fears, past or present. Begin with "Fear is. . . ." Record students' responses on a word processor and publish a group poem to share in the school newspaper.

(*For younger students you might also use the book *There's a Nightmare in My Closet* by Mercer Mayer.)

POWER

In *The Magic Finger* by Roald Dahl, there are several surprises when an 8-year-old girl becomes irate with the people who live on a neighboring farm. She uses her "magic finger" on these avid hunters, who experience a role reversal and spend time as four enormous wild ducks. I've often used this book with students as a prewriting activity, followed by an opportunity for them to explain what they would do if they had a "magic finger." For a science activity, ask students to focus on the environment and write about how they could use this power to improve life on our planet.

Classroom Writing Activities to Support the Curriculum

Judy Piper

Judy B. Piper, Coordinator, Educational Services Division, Stanislaus County Department of Education, 801 County Center Three Court, Modesto, CA 93355.

THE HOLY LAND

Videodisc technology is not new, but several products now are available for the educational market. *The Holy Land,* developed by ABC News and distributed by Optical Data, contains two particularly thought-provoking clips that lend themselves to writing in a response log. Show "The Children of Palestine" to your students, and then have them respond to these questions, which you have entered into a file on any word processing program:

- What things do the children collect that reflect their war experiences?
- How do the children express their feelings about Palestine?

Next, show the chapter titled "The Children of Israel" and have students respond to these questions:

- How are the feelings of the children of Israel similar to those of the Palestinian children? How are they different?
- What did you see or hear the children say that makes you realize the tensions and fears experienced by these children?

GTV

Many creative forces collaborated to create *GTV: A Geographic Perspective on American History.* Some features included in this program are shows on the American Revolution, the Civil War, Map Rap, and chapters entitled "American Journals" and "Population Clocks." This interactive computer videodisc can be used by the teacher for instruction or as a visual database for student research. Fortunately, the shows can be shown with only a videodisc player, using the chapter numbers.

One show on Side 2, "Getting Up to Speed," talks about modes of transportation that helped our nation grow. After students view this clip, assign them the job of advertising executive for a new railroad company. Discuss how various ads persuade people to use a product. Their assignment is to write an ad that would make people want to try out this new method of travel. Encourage students to use graphics to draw attention to their ad. Use a program with graphics capabilities such as *The Children's Writing & Publishing Center,* available for Apple II and MS-DOS. For the Macintosh, both MS Word and MS Works allow graphics to be imported into a written document.

THE VIDEO EXCYCLOPEDIA OF THE TWENTIETH CENTURY

Video newscasts are becoming a popular assignment in history/social science programs. One source is *The Video Encyclopedia of the Twentieth Century.* The addition of Hypercard stacks for the Mac makes searches easy for students to perform. First, students select the desired stories from the videodiscs in this collection and transfer them onto a videotape. Then, they work in groups using a word processor to write scripts to accompany their newsworthy events. With more sophisticated equipment, students can produce a video overlay of their newscast right onto the videotape.

Classroom Writing Activities to Support the Curriculum

Judy Piper

These activities are designed to link literature, technology, and the visual and performing arts.

Judy B. Piper, Coordinator, Educational Services Division, Stanislaus County Department of Education, 801 County Center Three Court, Modesto, CA 95355.

LITERATURE

Judith Viorst has written many books, several of which are now considered classics for children. *The Tenth Good Thing About Barney* tells the story of a little boy whose cat dies and how he learns to deal with the loss of his friend. His mother suggests that he think of ten good things about Barney to say at the funeral in order to help him overcome his great sadness.

There are many units, from families to pets to even death, into which this book could be integrated. In this activity, the focus is on the attributes the boy selects to best describe Barney.

WRITING

Ten Clues (from Sunburst), a computer program designed for students in grades 4 to 6, also involves attributes, this time as students guess a word or phrase using a set of predetermined clues. As a group, have your students practice writing clues based on the critical and variable attributes of different objects, animals, or people until they are comfortable. Then they can use the program to write games about their own pets.

VISUAL/PERFORMING ARTS

Have students draw a picture of their pets (either real or fictional—or even a stuffed animal), making sure no one else in the class sees the picture. Divide the class into pairs and assign one student in each pair to be the "artist." Artists are given a blank piece of paper (or students may use the computer for drawing) and sit so that the other players are behind them. The players are to give the artists clear directions to help them draw a picture on the blank paper or computer that is as much like the original as possible. When players are unable to think of any more directions, have them compare the two pictures! They can be mounted together on a large sheet of construction paper to display in the classroom.

Classroom Writing Activities to Support the Curriculum

Judy Piper

These activities are designed to link literature, technology, and the visual and performing arts.

Judy B. Piper, Coordinator, Educational Services Division, Stanislaus County Department of Education, 801 County Center Three Court, Modesto, CA 95355.

LITERATURE

Tomie dePaola has written and illustrated more than 150 children's books, many of which are favorites with youngsters around the world. His latest book, *The Art Lesson*, is the story of a little boy who wants to be an artist, but his creative efforts are thwarted by his teacher. In an interview with *Sesame Street Magazine* (October 1989), dePaola is asked whether the book is autobiographical:

"It's very autobiographical. I can still hear Miss Gardner say, 'You're only getting one piece of paper, so don't ruin it!' and 'These crayons are school property, so you can't peel them, break them, or wear down the points!' "

WRITING

The Art Lesson is a wonderful example of an **autobiographical incident**, a type of writing The California Assessment Program (CAP) uses in its Grade 8 Writing Assessment. The CAP Writing Guide describes an autobiographical incident as "a well-told story about a specific occurrence in a writer's life. It uses sensory details to engage the reader in the event. It also includes some kind of self-disclosure, implied or stated, about the significance for the writer. The author's voice is natural and honest, allowing the reader to experience and share the feelings of the author during the event."

Use *The Art Lesson* as a springboard for students to write their own autobiographical incident using any word processing program. You may choose to help your students along by adding a series of prompts (or use the CAP Writing Assessment Handbook Student Revision Guides).

VISUAL/PERFORMING ARTS

"Scanning" offers a method for systematically looking at art with students. This approach to developing aesthetic skills is based on the work of Dr. Harry S. Broudy at the University of Illinois.

A painting such as Vincent Van Gogh's *The Bedroom at Arles* is an example of an autobiographical incident that is presented visually instead of verbally. When scanning a reproduction of this painting, have students look closely at the work. Ask them questions such as: Did the artist pay close attention to details? Does this painting look like a photograph? Was this work painted several years ago or hundreds of years ago? (Why do they think so?) Have them list some words to describe the feeling or mood captured in this work. They might also compare this painting to others by Van Gogh or other paintings from the same period. Can they find more examples of autobiographical incidents?

Classroom Writing Activities to Support the Curriculum

Judy Piper

These activities are designed to link literature, writing, technology, and the history/social science curriculum.

Judy B. Piper, Coordinator, Educational Services Division, Stanislaus County Department of Education, 801 County Center Three Court, Modesto, CA 93355.

LITERATURE

Cultures around the world have used fables over the centuries to teach young children the values that they hold. Arnold Lobel wrote *Fables*, a book of "twenty original fables about an array of animal characters from the crocodile to the ostrich." These are truly modern morals that readers won't find in the classic *Aesop's Fables*.

Use *Banner Mania* from Broderbund Software to print several of Lobel's morals. Put them on the bulletin board or hang them from the ceiling. Then, read a fable to your students and see if they can guess the correct moral from the ones displayed around the room.

After this exercise, have students work in pairs to write their own fables. Let them use *Banner Mania* to print their morals. After they hang them around the room, let them share their fables, read-around style. Your students will enjoy hearing each other's fables and matching up the morals . . . oh, be prepared for a few good laughs along the way.

VISUAL ART

When my second grade son, Ryan, came home last week with folded paper stars, I wondered how his teacher had managed to help him accomplish such a feat. Unfortunately, he tried to show me how to make them and he could no longer remember. Almost the same day, one of our technology leaders turned in her final project, a video on origami. It occurred to me that a good exercise for him (and his classmates) would be to write the directions for making his treasured stars. The teacher could show the video without sound and have students work in groups to write the directions. Or the video could be set up at a center or in a corner of the room for students to play and replay the tape to make the directions fit the video sequence. With this kind of writing exercise, I'm sure Ryan could continue to create stars to his heart's content.

ENGLISH/LANGUAGE ARTS

Illiteration is fun for everyone! Read (or sing, if you're brave!) the book *A My Name is ALICE* by Jane Bayer, with illustrations by Steven Kellogg. Here's a sample:

I my name is Ida and my husband's name is Ivan.
We come from Iceland and we sell ice cream.

Have students pick a letter and write a whole story about their character using this technique. Here's a story one sixth grader wrote about a leprechaun:

There once was a leprechaun named Shaun Shaunoley. He liked to do a lot of things like stamp collecting and playing sand ball. He also liked to eat snails, slugs, shortcakes, strawberries, and strange, strangled sea gulls. He lived in a place called Serpenstands, which was a small leprechaun city.

One day when Shaun got sick, he turned chartreuse and looked like he was shriveled and shrunk. In fact he was shrinking! He had shortitis. He got smaller and smaller, until one day he shriveled and shrunk all the way and "spoofed" and was gone forever.

Classroom Writing Activities to Support the Curriculum

Judy Piper

These activities are designed to link literature, writing, technology, and the history/social science curriculum.

Judy B. Piper, Coordinator, Educational Services Division, Stanislaus County Department of Education, 801 County Center Three Court, Modesto, CA 93355.

LITERATURE

Molly's Pilgrim is the story of a third grader who is teased by the other girls in her class because of her imperfect English and old country dress. Barbara Cohen, the author, said, "I think I'm a writer because I spent my childhood listening to my relatives tell stories about each other. All my writing is in some way inspired by my experience." Molly, whose character is based on a member of Cohen's family, doesn't think she'll ever belong until the day she brings Mama's Pilgrim doll to school and realizes "it takes all kinds of Pilgrims to make a Thanksgiving." You may also want to use the video version of *Molly's Pilgrim* to begin a discussion or writing assignment.

Related reading:
  Journey to America by Sonia Levitin
  The Statue in the Harbor by Jeffrey Eger
  Gooseberries to Oranges by Barbara Cohen
  Watch the Stars Come Out by Riki Levinson

WRITING

Barbara Cohen has the following suggestions for sharing this book with students: Using your friendly word processor, have students write a letter to parents, explaining the story and inviting them or other relatives (grandparents are a wonderful resource!) to talk with the class about their native land, to tell a folktale, or teach a few words in their native language.

Students might be asked to write a diary as if they were one of the characters in the book. Or divide the class into two groups: one for Sakkot and one for Thanksgiving. (You might easily include other harvest festivals and traditions.) Each group studies that holiday, writes a brief explanation, and prepares food to share with each other at the harvest feast. The recipes can be word processed as a great beginning for a class cookbook.

Related materials:
  First Thanksgiving Feast by Joan Anderson
  Jewish Kids Catalog by C. M. Burstein
  Holiday Treats by Deborah Hautzig

HISTORY/SOCIAL SCIENCE

Molly's Pilgrim is an exciting addition to a history/social science unit on immigration. Ask students which country their ancestors lived in before coming to America and when they came. Use a timeline-generating program such as *Timeliner* (Tom Snyder Productions) to design a class chart of this information.

Jan Beekman, principal of Caswell School in Ceres, CA, also suggests students plan a trip from the Soviet Union to New York to Winter Hill. They must decide where they think Winter Hill might be, in what decade the story occurred, and plan their trip accordingly. Or have them plan the trip with the itinerary of their own ancestors, starting with their country of origin at the time they first came to the United States.

TITLE INDEX BY CHAPTER

263

AUTHOR INDEX

PUBLICATIONS FROM THE WRITING NOTEBOOK

THE WRITING NOTEBOOK JOURNAL

Each issue of this quarterly journal contains a wealth of practical information, ideas, and strategies for teaching writing in all curriculum areas supported by technology, with a continuing focus on literature-based writing, cooperative learning, and process writing. A unique publication supported by many of the leaders in writing and technology. $32; bulk subscription rates are available. ISSN 0749-2537. Back issues are also available; limited to supply on hand; $7.

MAKING THE LITERATURE, WRITING, WORD PROCESSING CONNECTION
(The Best of *The Writing Notebook*, Vol. 1)

A collection of the best ideas, lesson plans, curriculum units and thought-provoking articles from *The Writing Notebook*. The potential for bringing together the teaching of literature and writing supported by technology has never been greater. This 200-page spiral-bound anthology, with 13 chapters and over 90 exciting and timely articles, will provide the inspiration. $21.

WRITING AND TECHNOLOGY: IDEAS THAT WORK!
(The Best of *The Writing Notebook*, Vol. 2)

This brand new anthology of the best articles, ideas, curriculum units and lesson plans from *The Writing Notebook* takes off where **Vol. 1, Making the Literature, Writing, Word Processing Connection**, left off. Includes some-never-before published material! $25.

REPRINT PACKETS FROM *THE WRITING NOTEBOOK*

By request from inservice workshop coordinators, teacher trainers, district-level supervisors, college and university course instructors, and computer coordinators! These 13 reprint packets, organized around specific topics, are ideal for workshops and class packets. Priced to fit your budget.

Whole Language - Finally! This packet combines all the journal articles on this important and timely topic from the two Whole Language issues (one of which is now unavailable as a back issue) plus an assortment of other lesson ideas on the topic (49 pages, $10).

Literature, Writing, and Art - Fans of Nancy Scali's regular column in *The Writing Notebook* will be glad to see all of her outstanding ideas available as a packet, plus several other writing and art ideas (18 pages, $7).

Hypercard - The 5-part series by Stephen Marcus is showcased in this packet, along with several other exciting Hypercard articles and activities (20 pages, $8).

Telecommunications - Writing via telecommunications adds a healthy dose of enthusiasm and real-world purpose to students' writing. Contains specific writing ideas, information on existing telecommunications writing programs, and student writing samples (28 pages, $10).

Staff Development - Tried and tested ideas for staff development in writing and word processing. Includes cooperative learning and staff development, and training for technology (30 pages, $10).

Publishing Student Writing - Includes a 3-part series on design issues in desktop publishing and great ideas for publishing projects in all curriculum areas (42 pages, $10).

Keyboarding - Includes both philosophy and activities (11 pages, $6).

Writing as a Process - Fourteen articles on this topic, including strategies, specific activities for all grade levels, and templates (59 pages, $10).

Writing Using Specific Software - Ideas and templates for writing using FrEdWriter, LogoWriter, and other language arts software (44 pages, $10).

Cooperative Learning - Ideas for making cooperative learning work in your classroom. Includes hints on structuring cooperative learning groups, templates for peer editing, and specific curriculum units (39 pages, $10).

Curriculum/Study Units - Seven specific units for classroom use at all levels, including a scope and sequence of story writing plus other writing activities. Some units include reproducible worksheets (22 pages, $7).

Poetry and Story Writing - Wonderful ideas and strategies for all levels. Includes samples of student writing at different grades (39 pages, $10).

Writing Across the Curriculum - A dazzling assortment of ideas and lesson plans for incorporating writing into many different curriculum areas (67 pages, $10).

—————————————————— *Coming Soon!* ——————————————————

WRITING FOR EXCELLENCE: Writing Ideas from the Model Writing Projects Contest 90-91

This book highlights the elementary, middle school, and secondary winners of the Model Writing Projects Contest sponsored by *The Writing Notebook*. It features many of the outstanding lesson plans and writing activities received at all levels. If you want to create a new writing program, or are looking for ways to improve your current one, this book is highly recommended. $26.

The Writing Notebook Order Form

The Writing Notebook Journal

Please specify quantity.
____ 1-10 subscriptions, $32 each
____ 11-25 subscriptions to one address, $27 each
____ 26 + subscriptions to one address, $25 each

Journal Subtotal $_____

Books

Please specify quantity.

Making the Literature, Writing, Word Processing Connection

(The Best of The Writing Notebook, Vol. 1)
200 pages, spiral bound.
____ 1-10 copies, $21 each
____ 11-25 copies, $19 each
____ 26-99 copies, $16 each
____ Over 100 copies, $14 each

Writing and Technology: *New!* Ideas That WORK!

(The Best of The Writing Notebook, Vol. 2)
Books will be shipped in May.
____ 1-10 copies, $25 each
____ 11-25 copies, $22 each
____ 26-99 copies, $18 each
____ Over 100 copies, $16 each

Book Subtotal $_____

> *Coming Soon:*
>
> **Writing for Excellence:**
> **Writing Ideas from the Model**
> **Writing Projects Contest 1990-91**

Back Issues of The Writing Notebook

Limited to supply on hand. Please specify quantity. $7 each.
___ Vol. 4(2) Nov/Dec 1986 (Keyboarding)
___ Vol. 5(1) Sept/Oct 1987 (Pen Pals)
___ Vol. 5(2) Nov/Dec 1987 (Global Awareness)
___ Vol. 6(1) Sept/Oct 1988 (Drama and Play Writing)
___ Vol. 6(2) Nov/Dec 1988 (Cultural Relevance)
___ Vol. 7(1) Sept/Oct 1989 (Writing Environments, Part 1)
___ Vol. 7(2) Nov/Dec 1989 (Writing Environments, Part 2)
___ Vol. 7(4) Apr/May 1990 (Writing Across the Curriculum)
___ Vol. 8(2) Nov/Dec 1990 (Whole Lang. & the Writing Process)
___ Vol. 8(3) Jan/Feb 1991 (Teacher Training Using Technology)
___ Vol. 9(1) Sept/Oct 1991 (Writing to Think Across the Curriculum)
___ Vol. 9(2) Nov/Dec 1991 (Teaching Revision)
___ Vol. 9(3) Jan/Feb 1992 (School Restructuring &Technology)
___ Vol. 9(4) Apr/May 1992 (Cooperative Learning and Writing)

Back Issue Subtotal $_____

Reprint Packets of Articles from The Writing Notebook

Created especially for workshops and inservice training on specific topics. New packets are in bold. All other packets (except *) have been expanded as of August '91. Please specify quantity.
____ **ESL/Bilingual Students and Writing** (42 pages, $10)
____ Whole Language (49 pages, $10)
____ Literature, Writing & Art (18 pages, $7)
____ Hypercard (20 pages, $8)
____ Cooperative Learning (39 pages, $10)
____ Keyboarding (11 pages, $6)
____ Writing as a Process (59 pages, $10)
*____ Writing Using Specific Software (44 pages, $10)
___ Curriculum/Study Units (22 pages, $7)
____ Staff Development (30 pages, $10)
____ Poetry and Story Writing (39 pages, $10)
____ Writing Across the Curriculum (67 pages, $10)
____ Publishing Student Writing (42 pages, $10)
____ Telecommunications and Writing (28 pages, $10)

Reprint Subtotal $_____

Total $_____

plus Shipping $_____

Grand Total (U.S. $)_____

SHIPPING

For destinations _inside_ the U.S.
If your order is $0 - $32, add $4.25
" " " $33 - $55, add $6.25
" " " $56 - $75, add $7.50
" " " $75 - $99, add $8.50
On orders of $100 or more, we will bill you.

For destinations _outside_ the U.S.
We will bill you for shipping. Use the boxes below to let us know if you desire surface or airmail shipping.

☐ Surface   ☐ Airmail

Please send me free The Writing Notebook brochures for dissemination.
Quantity needed:_____   Date Needed:_____

Name/Title_____ Date _____

Address_____

_____

City _____ State_____ Zip_____ Phone _____

Make checks payable to "Creative Word Processing"
CREATIVE WORD PROCESSING IN THE CLASSROOM
P. O. Box 1268 • Eugene, OR 97440-1268 • Phone 503/344-7125